Discovering *Dune*

CRITICAL EXPLORATIONS IN SCIENCE FICTION AND FANTASY
A series edited by Donald E. Palumbo and C.W. Sullivan III
Earlier Works: www.mcfarlandpub.com

Discovering *Dune*

Essays on Frank Herbert's Epic Saga

Edited by DOMINIC J. NARDI
and N. TREVOR BRIERLY

Foreword by Timothy O'Reilly

CRITICAL EXPLORATIONS
IN SCIENCE FICTION AND FANTASY, 81
Series Editors Donald E. Palumbo *and* C.W. Sullivan III

McFarland & Company, Inc., Publishers
Jefferson, North Carolina

This book has undergone peer review.

LIBRARY OF CONGRESS CATALOGUING-IN-PUBLICATION DATA

Names: Nardi, Dominic J., Jr editor. | Brierly, N. Trevor, 1970– editor.
| O'Reilly, Tim, author of foreword.
Title: Discovering Dune : essays on Frank Herbert's epic saga
/ edited by Dominic J. Nardi, and N. Trevor Brierly ;
foreword by Timothy O'Reilly.
Description: Jefferson, North Carolina :
McFarland & Company, Inc., Publishers, 2022. |
Series: Critical explorations in science fiction and fantasy; 81 |
Includes bibliographical references and index.
Identifiers: LCCN 2022029886 | ISBN 9781476682013 (paperback : acid free paper) ∞
ISBN 9781476646725 (ebook)
Subjects: LCSH: Herbert, Frank. Dune series. |
BISAC: LITERARY CRITICISM / Science Fiction & Fantasy
| LCGFT: Literary criticism.
Classification: LCC PS3558.E63 Z64 2022 | DDC 813/.54—dc23/eng/20220719
LC record available at https://lccn.loc.gov/2022029886

BRITISH LIBRARY CATALOGUING DATA ARE AVAILABLE

ISBN (print) 978-1-4766-8201-3
ISBN (ebook) 978-1-4766-4672-5

Front cover image Nataniil/Shutterstock

Printed in the United States of America

*McFarland & Company, Inc., Publishers
Box 611, Jefferson, North Carolina 28640
www.mcfarlandpub.com*

Dominic:
Kelly and Antoinette, for guiding me through the desert.

* * *

Trevor:
For Becky, my Chani.

Table of Contents

Acknowledgments

An edited academic volume such as *Discovering* Dune: *Essays on Frank Herbert's Epic Saga* is inevitably a collaborative effort. In addition to the authors listed in the Table of Contents, this book benefited from the help and encouragement of countless people during the past few years. As editors, this support proved invaluable to helping us see the book to completion. Here, we hope to express our gratitude to those who made a difference along the way (and apologize in advance if we forget to mention anyone).

We both owe a significant debt to Dr. Corey Olsen and the Mythgard Institute. The two of us met through a Mythgard conference, the annual Mythmoot. In fact, the idea for this book came out of a discussion after the June 2018 Mythmoot. As Dune fans, we were inspired by—and, to some extent, envious of—the academic community that had grown around J.R.R. Tolkien's works. Just as importantly, the Mythgard community helped introduce both of us to the scholarship on science fiction and fantasy literature. Neither of us works as a fulltime professional academic, but through Mythgard we found our voices as scholars and learned practical skills—such as how to circulate a call for papers—that would later prove invaluable to completing this book.

As we explain in the Introduction, we undertook this book project in order to help reinvigorate the scholarship on the Dune saga. However, in working on this book, we came across a copious scholarship that provided fresh insights into the saga and generated new ideas for research. Tim O'Reilly's biography of Frank Herbert is one of the first serious treatises on Herbert's philosophy and his works, and it is still a touchstone for serious scholarship on Dune. Tim indirectly helped inspire *Discovering* Dune and we are humbled that he agreed to write a foreword for this book. We are also indebted to the many other scholars who have published their research; in this book, we build upon—and hopefully honor—their work.

Several of the contributors to this volume presented early drafts of their essays at various conferences. We would like to thank conference participants at Mythmoot 2019 and 2021, and the Popular Culture Association's 2019 Annual Meeting, amongst others, for their helpful feedback.

We also want to recognize those individuals who had planned to participate in this project but, due to circumstances beyond their control, ultimately could not.

Because this book contains so many quotes from Frank Herbert's six Dune novels, we wanted to proceed with the cooperation and permission of the Herbert Estate. The Herbert Estate is incredibly busy with a variety of new Dune licensing projects, including the new film adaptations, so we appreciate the fact that Byron Merritt and John Silbersack were so prompt in responding to our queries. We would also like to thank Sherri Marmon and Beau Sullivan of Penguin Random House, Louise Henderson and Tom Costello of Orion Publishing Group, and Nora Rawn of Trident Media Group for helping us navigate any copyright issues. Their assistance made it possible for our essays to use extensive quotes from Frank Herbert's novels.

Of course, this book project—and the friendships forged through it—would not have happened without Frank Herbert himself and his vivid imagination. The fact that scholars are still interested in *Dune* more than 55 years after its publication is a testament to Frank Herbert's intellectual prowess. In many ways, our lives would have not been the same had Frank not shared his stories.

We chose McFarland as our publisher because of its experience publishing academic works about pop culture and enjoyed working with them. Our editor Gary Mitchem was extremely helpful in walking us through the publishing process and quickly responding to our many questions. We would also like to thank Donald Palumbo, editor of McFarland's "Critical Explorations in Science Fiction and Fantasy" series and a fellow Dune scholar, as well as the two anonymous scholars who reviewed this manuscript and generously provided extensive feedback.

Finally, as noted above, this book is a passion project that ended up consuming much of our free time for more than a year. We are both fortunate that our spouses not only tolerated our working late nights and weekends on a book about the Dune novels, but even encouraged us.

All of our work will have been worth it if you, our readers, gain a deeper appreciation for the Dune saga.

Foreword

TIMOTHY O'REILLY

"Whatever you do, don't 'dullify' it," Frank Herbert told me when I began work in 1978 on what was to be the first book length study of his work. (In the interest of scholarly accuracy, I should disclose that he attributed that sage advice to his granddaughter.) Regardless of the source, the sentiment landed like a seed in fertile soil.

I was not an English professor or professional critic but a fan, a 24-year-old who was eager to share my enthusiasm for the ideas I found in Frank's books and for the stories that had made them so alive in my mind. For me, writing about Frank and his books was not dry dissection, but a conversation with him about what is true in the world. And it really was a conversation. I interviewed Frank several times when he was on author tours, and several times by telephone. But I wasn't just pumping him for information. I was bringing to the conversation my own experience teaching non-verbal communication, General Semantics, and paranormal states at Esalen, the retreat center that was at the heart of the 1970s human potential movement. I had also been an avid reader of Stewart Brand's *Whole Earth Catalog* and follow-on journal, *The CoEvolution Quarterly*, so both ecology and evolutionary theory were meat and drink to me. And my formal training was in Classics, so I was well aware of the power of poetic myth, the idea of the hero, and the way that knowledge is passed down through time via a kind of mental DNA.

I certainly got more out of the conversations than Frank did. He read the draft of my book and gave me feedback about it. He became a mentor and father figure, who encouraged me to keep writing. I did just that, building a career as an author, educator, activist, entrepreneur, and investor at the frontiers of technology. In preparation for writing this foreword, I reread my nearly forty-year-old book and I was struck by how many of his ideas have become part of my mental toolbox. The advice that I give to technologists and aspiring entrepreneurs has been shaped by my

1

conversations by Frank as surely as the Fremen dream of the ecological transformation of Arrakis was shaped by Pardot Kynes, and their mythos about a coming savior was shaped by legends planted by the Bene Gesserit centuries before.

This is not to say that I eschewed the traditional tools of scholarship. I did a close reading of all of Frank's novels and stories and all of his essays, newspaper articles, and letters that I could find. Many of these had been collected by Professor Willis McNelly in the Cal State Fullerton Frank Herbert archive. Will gave me access to them and to his own one-on-one interviews with Frank in a true act of intellectual generosity. I also learned a lot from people whom Frank described as influences, like Santa Rosa psychotherapist Ralph Slattery and his former colleague Walt Blum at the *San Francisco Examiner*, and from Poul Anderson and Jack Vance, his colleagues and friends in the science fiction fraternity. I even spoke with legendary folklorist Albert Lord, whose ideas about oral-formulaic epic reminded me of the way the Bene Gesserit encoded information so that it could be passed down through generations even in the absence of a written scripture.

That being said, I'm delighted to see scholars far better trained than I was taking Frank's work seriously, and am fascinated by the many directions explored in this volume. There is so much more to be learned from this man and the imaginative worlds he created. And I'm so happy that they haven't dullified it either.

But let me return to the question of "what is true" and why Frank's work seems even more important today than it did in the tumultuous '60s.

Frank wrote: "It is a mistake to talk about the future. I like to think of futurism as an art form. There are as many possible futures as we can create." That idea has been echoed since by computer pioneer Alan Kay, who once said "It is easier to create the future than it is to predict it." I work every day with people who are trying to do just that.

When I meet entrepreneurs working on tools for electronically mediated collective intelligence, I am reminded of Frank's belief that the human species as a whole is a kind of super-organism, an organism that is not done evolving. When I see demonstrations of brain-machine interfaces and debates about artificial intelligence I am reminded of his insistence that we must search deeply to understand what is truly human and work to preserve and extend it rather than handing over our future to machines.

Every day I see the blind hunger for certainty that is exploited by populist leaders. They may not wear the trappings of religious messiahs, but they tap the same vein in the human character. And every day, I am reminded that humans have untapped reserves of capability and courage to stand up to that impulse.

Frank believed that humans seek stability and control in a world that constantly surprises us, and that we must learn instead to get better at responding to uncertainty. That seems about as relevant as it comes in the age of COVID-19 and climate change. We cannot take for granted the world we live in, and we must step up to shape the one our children will inherit from us.

I know that we must meet an unknown future, surf the waves of crisis, and survive. And every day, I'm glad that I have had Frank Herbert as a guide.

Timothy O'Reilly is the founder, CEO, and Chairman of O'Reilly Media, which delivers online learning, publishes books, and runs conferences about cutting-edge technology. He is the author of many technical books and, in 1981, wrote a critical appraisal of *Dune* and other early novels of Frank Herbert that is still regularly cited as the definitive treatise on Herbert's works.

Introduction

"A beginning is a very delicate time..."

DOMINIC J. NARDI *and* N. TREVOR BRIERLY

As anyone who has picked up this book undoubtedly knows, Frank Herbert's *Dune* (1965) is one of the best-selling and most popular science fiction works in history. In 1966, *Dune* became the first novel to win both the Hugo Award and the Nebula Award. It is widely regarded as a masterpiece of speculative fiction on par with J.R.R. Tolkien's *The Lord of the Rings*. Herbert's sequels—*Dune Messiah* (1969), *Children of Dune* (1976), *God Emperor of Dune* (1981), *Heretics of Dune* (1984), and *Chapterhouse: Dune* (1985)—also became bestsellers and received literary praise, even if they never achieved the same popularity as the original novel. There have been several high-profile adaptations of *Dune*, including David Lynch's 1984 film, which has since become a cult classic, and the 2000 Sci-Fi Channel mini-series *Frank Herbert's Dune*, as well as a sequel, *Frank Herbert's Children of Dune*, which adapted the first two sequels. *Dune* is also widely credited with having influenced other works of science fiction, most notably George Lucas's *Star Wars*.[1]

However, despite the Dune saga's importance to the science fiction genre, there has been relatively limited scholarly engagement with Frank Herbert's fiction, especially compared to the sustained scholarly attention to J.R.R. Tolkien or Octavia Butler. As William Senior notes in a 2007 article in the *Journal of the Fantastic in the Arts*, there is "oddly enough, little literary criticism—and there's not that much on [Frank] Herbert to begin with...."[2] Tim O'Reilly's *Frank Herbert*, one of the first and most influential biographies of Frank Herbert, was published in 1981 and has long been out of print.[3] Two later edited volumes about the Dune saga—*Dune and Philosophy* (2011) and *The Science of Dune* (2008)—provide important insights into the Dune universe, but were published more for general audiences than for academic audiences. Throughout the years,

5

other scholars have published individual articles and books about the Dune saga, mostly on philosophy, political leadership, or ecological change.

After creating a comprehensive bibliography of the existing Dune scholarship—which we include as an appendix in this book—we believe that the primary deficiency is not quality or even quantity, but rather that the study of *Dune* and of Frank Herbert's works in general never coalesced into an academic subfield. Indeed, in preparing this book, we found more than 20 academic books and dozens of journal articles, as well as assorted Ph.D. dissertations, master's theses, and conference papers, about the Dune saga and Frank Herbert's other works. There *is* academic interest in Dune. However, we also found that relatively few of these works cite each other because discussions of the novel are often segregated into disciplinary silos. There is no equivalent of Tolkien scholars like Tom Shippey or Verlyn Flieger, no prominent scholar who has dedicated the majority of their academic career to the study of Frank Herbert's fiction and whose scholarship serves as a touchstone for the field. The two most cited works—O'Reilly's and Touponce's literary biographies—though still very useful, were published during the 1980s.[4] There is no equivalent of *Tolkien Studies* or even *The Heinlein Journal*. Moreover, the first Dune novel receives most of the scholarly attention; as Jennifer Simkins notes in *The Science Fiction Mythmakers*, "most studies treat *Dune* as a novel in isolation, without reference to its sequels."[5]

Discovering Dune: *Essays on Frank Herbert's Epic Saga* is our attempt to reinvigorate and refocus the scholarship on *Dune* and Frank Herbert generally. This book provides a collection of essays that offers critical insights into the Dune novels. It is one of the first English-language edited volumes of scholarship dedicated to the study of Frank Herbert's fiction.[6] Our primary goal in this book is to offer unique scholarship from a variety of disciplines and using new analytical approaches. As discussed below, the topics covered range from the influence of Byzantine history on the character of Princess Irulan to reinterpreting Paul Atreides as a disabled deviant. A secondary goal is for this book to serve as a reference point for future Dune scholarship. The essays in this book, as well as the comprehensive bibliography in the appendix, will hopefully make it easier for scholars and fans to access the existing scholarship on Dune and to eventually make contributions of their own. Throughout this book, we italicize "*Dune*" when referring to the 1965 novel by Frank Herbert or the film adaptations by that title, but do not italicize "Dune" when referring broadly to the franchise and story setting.

Scholars of Dune

Because of the central importance of politics to Frank Herbert's works, this volume starts with a group of four essays exploring how the Dune novels depict political leadership and power. In *"Dune* and the Meta-Narrative of Power," Edward John Royston examines the ways in which elites in *Dune* exploit political narratives and the power of such narratives. In "Political Prescience," Dominic J. Nardi demonstrates how political leaders can exploit prescience to amass political power while avoiding the paradox of foreknowledge. The essay uses a game theory model in order to conceptualize how prescience equips users to make strategic decisions. The next two essays focus on *God Emperor of Dune*, particularly Leto Atreides II, a critically important and understudied character.[7] In "'The greatest predator ever known': The Golden Path and Political Philosophy as Ecology," Michael Phillips argues that Leto's self-proclaimed role as "predator" in fact leads to a mutually symbiotic relationship between ruler and subject, presenting politics as a form of sociobiology. By contrast, Caroline Anne Womack in "He Who Controls Knowledge Controls the Universe: Leto II and the Golden Path" combines the literature on behavioral biology and classical philosophy to show how Leto took advantage of human proclivities toward violence.

Part II covers some of the historical and religious traditions that influenced Frank Herbert, as well as how those influences provide greater insight into the Dune story. In "Frank Herbert's Byzantium," Maximilian Lau compares Princess Irulan to Byzantine Princess Anna Komnene (1080–1150s), and then uses the comparison to show how traditional narratives overlook the ability of both female figures to control the historical record. Although other scholars have noted the presence of Islamic terminology in the Dune saga, R. Ali's essay "Beside the Sand Dunes: Arab Futurism, Faith, and the Fremen of Dune" takes a new approach by focusing on how the Dune saga fits within the Arab Futurism movement. He notes that *Dune* is one of the first major works of science fiction to depict a future in which Islam not only survives but thrives. N. Trevor Brierly's "'A critical moment'" considers religion within the novel, particularly the role of the Orange Catholic Bible in Paul's awakening.

Discovering Dune Part III then examines depictions of science and technology in the Dune saga. Leigha High McReynolds's "Locations of Deviance" offers a reading of the Bene Gesserit breeding program as a eugenics program, with the implication that Paul's deviance from the norm challenges the very idea of a standard genetic code for humans. In "From Taming Sand Dunes to Planetary Ecology," Paul Reef situates the first three Dune novels within the context of the environmental movement. He shows how the novels reflected changing societal norms about conservation of natural resources and environmental protection during the latter half of the twentieth century. Next, Willow Wilson DiPasquale's "Shifting Sands" ties together political and ecological themes in the saga by arguing that Herbert subverts heroic archetypes in order to warn readers against relying on a "savior" figure to address environmental challenges. Her essay also presents an argument for importance of the Dune sequels to Herbert's political message.

Finally, Part IV builds upon the existing literature about philosophy in the Dune saga with four essays about ethics, choice, and the nature of humanity. Nathaniel Goldberg's "The Sands of Time" leverages a distinction between the metaphysics of time versus the epistemology of time in order to explain how Paul Atreides is able to see the future while maintaining his free will. "The Choices of Muad'Dib" presents Jeffery L. Nicholas's argument that Herbert crafted *Dune*, particularly Fremen culture, as an implicit response to Nietzsche's praise of the "will to power." Curtis A. Weyant's "'I suggest you may be human'" examines how different groups within the Dune books define humanity, with particular attention given to how Paul combines elements of all of the competing definitions. Finally, in "Belief Is the Mind-Killer," Kevin Williams shows how the Bene Gesserit are key to understanding Herbert's skepticism of overarching belief systems. This essay is also important because it is one of the few pieces of scholarship to focus on *Heretics of Dune* and *Chapterhouse: Dune*.

As editors, we selected these essays as representative of the potential insights that serious critical analysis of the Dune saga could yield. We have attempted to put forth scholarship on a wide range of topics. However, *Discovering* Dune was never intended to provide a comprehensive survey of the scholarship on Dune. Indeed, there are several important topics that do not receive sustained attention from our contributors, including representations of race and sexual orientation; mythic structures and the hero's journey; and warfare, among others. After some deliberation, we also decided to focus exclusively on Frank Herbert's six Dune novels. By necessity, this means our book does not include any studies of the various TV or movie adaptations, or the prequels and sequels written by Brian Herbert and Kevin J. Anderson. It also does not cover the Dune fandom, merchandising, or fan-fiction. Because this book is an attempt to reinvigorate Dune scholarship, we thought it preferable to begin with Frank Herbert's original six novels.

As noted above, we were both heavily influenced by the field of Tolkien Studies, which often considers authorial intent—as expressed through Tolkien's letters, interviews, and drafts—when interpreting his works.[8] Likewise, most of the essays in this volume at least consider Frank Herbert's interviews and nonfiction publications. Even if we do not let Herbert dictate our conclusions, this interpretive move necessarily affects our analysis because Herbert made forceful claims about how readers should interpret his works. We believe considering authorial intent is justified because the Dune texts are inextricably intertwined with Herbert's philosophical interests (to the point where some readers accuse him of being overly didactic in the later books). However, we also recognize that ours is not the only approach to Herbert Studies. During the past few years, there has been some reexamination of Herbert's treatment of race and gender in response to growing concern about representation in popular culture. For example, Asher-Perrin and others have concluded that Paul's arc in the first book embodies elements of the "white savior" trope[9]—despite Herbert's insistence that his story critiqued that type of charismatic leadership.[10] We hope future academic studies can build upon our book from a reader receptivity approach, including "bad readings" or misinterpretations.

Revival of Dune

This book comes during a significant revival of the Dune franchise. In 2019, Ace books released new editions of all six of Frank Herbert's Dune novels, with new artwork on the covers. Legendary Entertainment, which currently holds the film and television motion picture rights to *Dune*, released a film adaptation of *Dune*—directed by Academy Award nominee Denis Villeneuve (*Arrival, Blade Runner 2049*) and featuring several A-list actors—in October 2021. In June 2019, Legendary TV announced an original television show *Dune: The Sisterhood* to air on HBO Max. In addition, Funcom announced plans to release multiple video games based on the Dune setting, one of which will be an open-world massively multiplayer online game. GaleForce Nine rereleased the classic Dune board game, which was originally released in 1979, and Dire Wolf released the deckbuilding game "Dune: Imperium" in 2020. Modiphius Entertainment released a new Dune role-playing game "Dune: Adventures in the Imperium" in early 2021. In addition, Dune fandom has grown and become more active online, including several new YouTube channels and podcasts focused on the franchise.

As noted above, *Discovering* Dune does not directly address any of these developments. This is partly due to timing—most of these projects were only recently announced at the time of this writing—but also because of our decision to focus exclusively on the novels. However, we expect this book to complement the ongoing Dune renaissance by reinvigorating academic as well as popular interest in Dune. Just as Peter Jackson's *Lord of the Rings* movies indirectly encouraged fans to seek out scholarship on Tolkien's works, so too we hope these new adaptations leads fans to seek a richer understanding of Herbert's original texts. If nothing else, *Discovering* Dune can serve as a gateway into the broader scholarship on the Dune saga.

NOTES

1. Kaminski, *The Secret History of Star Wars*, 57–58. See also Brennan, "Frank Herbert's *Dune*," for a catalogue of similarities between the two storyworlds.
2. Senior, "Frank Herbert's Prescience," 317.
3. Although it is available on O'Reilly's website at https://www.oreilly.com/tim/herbert/.
4. O'Reilly, *Frank Herbert* and Touponce, *Frank Herbert*.
5. Simkins, *The Science Fiction Mythmakers*, 171–172.
6. In late 2020, Le Bélial published *Dune—exploration scientifique et culturelle d'une planète-univers*, which contains 14 essays about subjects ranging from gender to geopolitics, edited by French astrophysicist Roland Lehoucq.
7. But see Fjellman, "Prescience and Power."
8. Although some recent scholarship, such as Fimi's *Tolkien, Race and Cultural History*, have focused on reader reception of the Middle-earth saga.
9. Asher-Perrin's "Why It's Important to Consider Whether Dune Is a White Savior Narrative." In addition, Carroll, "Race Consciousness" notes that some right-wing nationalists have interpreted *Dune* as an endorsement of authoritarianism.
10. Herbert, "Dune Genesis."

WORKS CITED

Asher-Perrin, Emmet. "Why It's Important to Consider Whether Dune Is a White Savior Narrative." *TOR.com*. March 6, 2019. https://www.tor.com/2019/03/06/why-its-important-to-consider-whether-dune-is-a-white-savior-narrative/.

Brennan, Kristen. "Frank Herbert's *Dune*." *Star Wars Origins*. Last modified August 28, 2007. http://www.moongadget.com/origins/dune.html

Carroll, Jordan S. "Race Consciousness: Fascism and Frank Herbert's *Dune*." *Los Angeles Review of Books*. November 19, 2020. https://lareviewofbooks.org/article/race-consciousness-fascism-and-frank-herberts-dune/.

Fimi, Dimitra. *Tolkien, Race and Cultural History: From Fairies to Hobbits*. Basingstoke, UK: Palgrave Macmillan, 2008.

Fjellman, Stephen M. "Prescience and Power: *God Emperor of Dune* and the Intellectuals." *Science Fiction Studies* 13, no. 1 (1986): 50–63.

Grazier, Kevin R. (editor). *The Science of Dune: An Unauthorized Exploration into the Real Science Behind Frank Herbert's Fictional Universe*, Science of Pop Culture. Dallas, TX: BenBella Books, 2008.

Herbert, Frank. "Dune Genesis." *OMNI* 2, no. 10 (July 1980): 72–76.

Kaminski, Michael. *The Secret History of Star Wars: The Art of Storytelling and the Making of a Modern Epic*. Ontario, Canada: Legacy Books Press, 2008.

Lehoucq, Roland. (editor). *Dune—exploration scientifique et culturelle d'une planète-univers*. Saint-Mammès France: Le Bélial, 2020.

Nicholas, Jeffery (editor). *Dune and Philosophy: The Weirding Way of the Mentat*, Popular Culture and Philosophy Book 56. Chicago: Open Court, 2011.

O'Reilly, Timothy. *Frank Herbert* ("Recognitions" Series). New York: Frederick Ungar, 1981. https://www.oreilly.com/tim/herbert/.

Senior, William A. "Frank Herbert's Prescience: Dune and the Modern World." *Journal of the Fantastic in the Arts* 17, no. 4(68) (Winter 2007): 317–320.

Simkins, Jennifer. *The Science Fiction Mythmakers: Religion, Science and Philosophy in Wells, Clarke, Dick and Herbert*, Critical Explorations in Science Fiction and Fantasy Book 54. Jefferson, NC: McFarland, 2016.

Touponce, William F. *Frank Herbert*. Boston: Twayne Publishers, 1988.

PART I

Politics and Power

Dune and the Metanarrative of Power

EDWARD JOHN ROYSTON

Political scheming, ecological transformation, ancient legends, super-powers, giant worms, and geriatric space drugs—*Dune* and its sequels have it all. They are imaginative and thoughtful science fiction novels that can be interpreted in many different ways. In "Dune Genesis" Frank Herbert points to the ecological concepts and the concerns about demagogues and despots that informed his writing and many of its interpretations. The parallels with the twentieth-century Middle East are undeniable, and it is difficult not to read the Fremen as Arabs, the spice as oil, and the whole thing as a science fantasy riff on *Lawrence of Arabia*.[1] The spice can also be interpreted in light of psychedelic drugs.[2] Paul's rise from desolation to power and his nominal connection to heroes of Greek myth invite epic interpretations.[3] The politics and scheming that form much of the novels' action invite Machiavellian ones.[4] The novels' philosophical concerns with power and superhumans invite Nietzschean readings.[5] The consequences of wielding that power even invite interpretations concerning neoliberal economic dynamics.[6] In this essay, I offer another way in which to interpret the Dune series, a way that can bridge these many avenues of interpretation, the stories and legends that underpin the series, and its connections to ecology, history, and politics. Here, I propose reading *Dune* and its sequels as metanarratives about the power of narratives. These novels are not just stories about ecology, politics, and all the rest; they are also stories about the stories that people create, coopt, and control about and around those subjects and the power they seek by doing so.

Birgit Neumann and Ansgar Nünning define metanarration and metafiction as "umbrella terms designating self-reflexive utterances, i.e., comments referring to the discourse rather than the story." More specifically, they explain that "metafiction describes the capacity for fiction to

13

reflect on its own status as fiction," while "metanarration is concerned with the act and/or process of narration."[7] These are specific narratological terms. Marie-Laure Ryan and Ernst van Alphen define narratology as "the set of general statements on narrative genres, on the systematics of narrating (telling a story) and on the structure of plot."[8] Or in other words, narratology is the systematic analysis of narrative structures and devices. Metanarrative and metafiction most commonly refer to "unnatural" narratives that undermine their own sense of fictional authenticity through events and actions that could only occur in a fictional narrative. A wonderful example of such undermining can be seen in Mel Brooks's *Spaceballs*, in which Brooks, as the character Yogurt, hawks *Spaceballs* merchandise, and the villains Dark Helmet and Colonel Sandurz fast forward the video cassette of the film to see what happens next. In these moments, the film drops its façade of faux authenticity and invites the audience to laugh along with the characters who appear to be fully aware that they are characters in a farce.

Dune is, of course, not this explicitly self-reflexive. Herbert's narrator never explicitly reflects upon its own narration, nor does the novel drop its façade of authenticity to make jokes about selling flamethrowers to children. But the novel's arrangement, narrative style, and plot structure all implicitly foreground its fictional and narrated nature. Its characters and events are focused upon controlling and manipulating narratives—ecological, mythic-religious, and political—as a means towards gaining and exercising power. The concept of narrative and a concern with its power tie together *Dune*'s discourse and story. Reading *Dune* as a metanarrative provides an interpretive frame that unites its many varied elements along a single line of ethical inquiry: what are the preconditions for and the consequences of manipulating the narratives that define human society?

This essay discusses how Frank Herbert's *Dune* and its sequels explore that question. It is divided into two parts. In the first, it describes the many ways in which *Dune* implicitly foregrounds its own fictional and narrated nature, inviting readers to consider narrative as they read. In the second, it discusses *Dune*'s story, the actions and schemes of its characters, and how these focus around narrative control. Both of these sections focus primarily upon *Dune*, but also draw from its sequels.

Foregrounding Narrative

The first and clearest way in which the Dune novels foreground narrative is that narratives are always of overarching concern for the characters. Emperor Shaddam Corrino IV plots with Baron Vladimir Harkonnen to create a cover story for his role in the destruction of House Atreides. Paul and Jessica Atreides rely on the Bene Gesserit's Missionaria Protectiva, which, centuries earlier, intentionally and wantonly seeded "infectious superstitions" and myths designed to be exploited by Bene Gesserit sisters in their times of need, to survive and rise to power among the Fremen.[9] At Paul's moment of victory, when he agrees to marry Irulan Corrino in order to secure the imperial throne, Jessica reassures his true love, Chani, that despite his political marriage, she will be remembered as his wife.[10] Paul then comes to fear the consequences of the legend he creates and spends two novels—*Dune Messiah* and *Children of Dune*—trying to destroy it. His son, Leto II, spends two novels—*Children of Dune* and *God Emperor of Dune*—and 3,500 years building upon that legend and guiding it towards the fulfillment of his Golden Path for humanity. Fifteen hundred years later, factions preserved and birthed by that legend fight over its legacy in *Heretics of Dune* and *Chapterhouse: Dune*.

Herbert's choices of what specifically to describe and narrate foreground these characters' concerns. *Dune* and its sequels, despite being high space opera, are often more focused on the deception and deliberation that precede and follow action than the action itself. This often results in an abandonment of any narrative suspense. The reader is told what will happen long before it happens. The Baron Harkonnen has Piter de Vries "outline … the salient features" of their plot to destroy the Atreides.[11] More than a hundred pages later, that attack finally happens, but much of its violence takes place in the background. After the attack, the Baron makes clear to his nephew Rabban that he must control the narrative of what happened on Arrakis: "That is the story. And any rumor that there were Sardaukar here, it must be laughed at."[12] Were the true story of what happened on Arrakis to get out, the Harkonnens' entire plot would fall apart. Later in the novel, Paul spends an entire chapter preparing to ride a worm, but his actual test does not take place until two chapters later.

Dune and its sequels are novels full of people talking and thinking, and those people are often talking and thinking in narrative terms. The Baron Harkonnen demonstrates his sense of drama by calling Arrakis a "superb setting for a unique victory."[13] Paul is worried about his "terrible purpose."[14] Jessica knows her actions convey "something symbolic."[15] The first ghola-Idaho, Hayt, feels that he "existed in a dream controlled by some other mind."[16] Here the novel almost crosses the line into being explicitly self-referential. These characters become aware that they are playing roles and the symbolic meanings of the actions they perform. For example, when Jessica meets the Shadout Mapes, she soon comes to understand that she is acting out the "*The Coming of the Reverend Mother to free you*," an incantation from the Bene Gesserit's constructed Missionaria

Protective myth.[17] Speaking like the author of humanity's destiny that he is later in the saga, Leto II explains, "All of history is a malleable instrument in my hands."[18] In the excerpts from his Stolen Journals, he asserts he took from humanity "their right to participate in history."[19] He will be the sole author of humanity's history during his reign.

God Emperor of Dune also implicitly reminds readers of the constructed narrative nature of that history in its references to the competing Oral and Formal Histories. The latter are the official history promulgated by Leto II's government and religion; the former are the alleged spoken words of Leto II's ancestors and contemporaries drawn from his own ancestral and personal memories. These two contradictory narratives are both the products of Leto II's manipulation, demonstrating his power to control narratives. His rebellious descendent, Siona, and her followers debate the truths of these narratives.[20] They resist the power of narrative as they succumb to it. Siona believes herself to be fighting against Leto II's tyrannical rule, but she is really the end product of that rule, the person he has spent thousands of years breeding. She will come to destroy him but becoming the instrument of that destruction is his ultimate intention for her.

Frank Herbert alludes to this contention with narrative power in "Dune Genesis," where he writes, "my superhero concept filled me with a concern that ecology might be the next banner for demagogues and would-be-heroes."[21] Herbert's superhero concept is his belief that humanity is periodically overtaken by "messianic convulsions" when people succumb to a messianic superhero figure "who can wrap himself in the myth fabric of the society."[22] These superhero figures cast themselves in a mythic role, a narrative role, as a means to achieving and exercising power. Herbert's great concern with such figures is that people are prone to forgetting that these superhero figures are still just humans with human faults, and thus hand over too much systemic power to them. People fall prey to the stories they tell, seeing them as the characters in those stories, and not the complex humans they really are. Characters like Paul, Alia, and Leto II are examples of superhero figures. Paul wields the role of Lisan al-Gaib to control the Fremen and take the empire. Alia wields the role of Saint-Alia-of-the-Knife to hold onto her regency as she descends into abomination. Leto II wields his roles as heir to Paul's throne and the inhuman God Emperor to enforce his peace and force humanity to follow his Golden Path.

Herbert's concerns here mirror those of many scholars, including Kenneth Burke and Walter Fisher. In his "Definition of Man," Kenneth Burke expands his definition of humanity as the "symbol-using animal" to include also the "symbol-misusing animal" in part because of "our many susceptibilities to the ways of demagogic spellbinders."[23] Burke's concern here is that our ability to use symbols to communicate meaning has the potential to be abused by demagogues. Language can be abused to leave people "filled with fantastic hatreds for alien populations ... or with all sorts of unsettling new expectations."[24] History, especially the twentieth century's, provides ample examples of this sort of abuse. Building upon Burke, Walter Fisher suggests recognizing narrative as a paradigm to identify "the meaning and significance of life in all its social dimensions" because "humans are essentially storytellers."[25]

As mentioned, these novels primarily depict people speaking and thinking. They are telling their stories to each other and themselves. This focus on speech and thought over action serves to highlight characters' values and motives, providing them ample opportunities to explain themselves. Values are defined: "she said a good ruler has to learn his world's language, that it's different for every world."[26] Plots are described: "Piter, outline for my nephew the salient features of our campaign against the Atreides."[27] Motives are divulged: "I made a shaitan's bargain with the Baron."[28] There is an emphasis on causality here, an emphasis on the narrative's *plot* in E.M. Forster's terms. Forster distinguishes the *story* from the *plot* by the former being just a sequence of events and the latter being a sequence of events with causal relationships. In his examples, "the king died then the queen died" is a story, while "the king died then the queen died because the king died" is a plot, because the latter includes a causal relationship between the events.[29] Characters in *Dune* and its sequels explain the motives and purpose for their actions, in dialog or thought. Perhaps the one trait that defines all of Herbert's characters is their general need to justify their actions if at least only to themselves. Even the despicable Baron Harkonnen justifies the cause for his actions by invoking ancient grudges and the Harkonnen efforts to "tame" Arrakis.[30]

Narrative causality is further emphasized by the two most significant of *Dune*'s superhuman powers: ancestral memories and prescient visions. Leto II makes use of "safaris" into his ancestral memories to recall human history at a personal level and see causal patterns emerge.[31] Paul's concern with his "terrible purpose" and Leto II's commitment to his Golden Path are both predicated on their ability to use prescient visions to observe the results of their and others' actions. Paul knows his path leads to jihad with or without him. His legions need "only the legend he had already become."[32] That jihad happens in the twelve-year narrative gap between *Dune* and *Dune Messiah*. Leto II knows his Golden Path has already saved humanity. He declares, "[w]ithout me there would have been by now no people anywhere, none whatsoever."[33] And the ultimate effects of the Golden Path, Siona's gene and the rebirth of the spice cycle, will ensure humanity's continued survival. "He knew he had succeeded. He could not see me in the future," Siona explains to Duncan after they have killed Leto II.[34] Ancestral memories and prescient visions allow Paul and Leto II to see and manipulate the causal patterns of history. They possess an Orwellian control of history. And Herbert's focus on his characters' interiority allows the audience to read the motives behind their interpretation and manipulation—their authorship—of history.

The extent to which characters like Paul and Leto II are prescient about the effects of the mythic roles they occupy gives them a reflexive quality. They are characters aware of their roles in a grand narrative. That is not to say that they are aware of being characters in a novel, but that they are aware of themselves as the heroes, or superheroes, of myths that they are coopting or creating. There is an implicit sort of reflexivity here, a hinting towards metafiction. Paul consciously takes on the role of a messianic character for the Fremen. "*I cannot do the simplest thing without its becoming a legend,*" he thinks as he prepares for his test as a sandrider.[35] Paul knows all his actions have come to carry narrative weight. People will tell stories about these moments in his life. After his Fremen defeat a band of Sardaukar disguised as smugglers, Paul thinks, "*I didn't even draw my knife, but it'll be said of this day that I slew twenty Sardaukar by my own hand.*"[36] As the God Emperor, Leto II also knows the symbolic weight of his actions, which is why he has the Tleilaxu ambassador flogged despite not allowing any word of their attempted assassination to get out.[37] Doing so will instill fear, specific fear into the Tleilaxu who will know the extent of their failure, and a general fear of his capacity for unexplained violence into the rest of his subjects.

Even characters without prescience know they perform narrative roles. "My propaganda corps is one of the finest," Duke Leto admits to his son Paul.[38] Like his son and grandson, the Duke knows that stories will spread about him, and he tries to exercise control over those stories. His successful propaganda corps is mirrored by the successful religions Paul and Leto II establish in their own names. Through Irulan's writings, Paul's priesthood and Leto II's Fish Speaker army, the legends and myths about them are codified into religious narratives. Emperor Shaddam IV uses the Harkonnens as cover and cutouts to avoid having a role in the story of House Atreides's destruction. Feyd Rautha manipulates many people to secure his role as heir apparent to his uncle, the Baron Harkonnen. Paul's success at coopting the Fremen messiah narrative and Liet-Kynes's ecological transformation narrative thwarts these efforts by Shaddam IV and Feyd.

The narratives the Atreides coopt and create fall into recognizable patterns and serve to further foreground the importance of narrative. As scholars like Robert Cirasa, Donald Palumbo, and Emily Ravenwood have all noted, *Dune* is recognizably a hero's journey. The novel reflects upon this directly: "They've a legend here…. It follows the familiar messiah pattern."[39] Paul is a young man who must overcome travels and trials and gain secret knowledge and powers to bring salvation to his adopted people. But it is a hero's journey where the hero is conscious of the symbolic power of his steps along that journey because he knows that the journey is, in part, a creation by the Bene Gesserit and its Missionaria Protectiva myth. Paul knows he must test himself with the Water of Life, and he also knows that in doing so, he will confirm to the Fremen that he is their Lisan al-Gaib.[40] His personal journey to avenge his family requires that he also become the messianic superhero, with all of its symbolic implications, of his Fremen allies. Donald Palumbo explains how this hero's journey narrative repeats itself throughout the series. Leto II, the prominent ghola-Idahos, and ghola-Miles Teg all follow Paul as monomythic heroes.[41] The Dune series repeats this monomythic narrative structure, rendering it a major motif.

In addition to focusing on their characters' narrative concerns and following an easily recognized narrative structure, the Dune novels foreground narrative in their very discourse and presentation of that narrative. Each chapter begins with a fictional epigraph taken from a text that exists in the fictional universe of *Dune*. These epigraphs serve to highlight the artifice and the constructed nature of the Dune series narrative in two ways. First, they comment upon and foreshadow the chapters they precede. But their nature as such clear narrative devices also serves to highlight that these epigraphs and the chapter breaks they occupy are narrative devices designed to curate dramatic tension. *Dune*'s opening epigraph begins: "*A beginning is the time for taking the most delicate care that the balances are correct.*"[42] This passage emphasizes that this scene has been selected as the opening of the narrative, that it is beginning *in media res* and events are already underway. Michael R. Collings notes that this opening "fulfills a[n] … epic demand—that the 'fable' begin 'in the middle of things.'"[43] In doing so, it indicates narrative structure and invites a set of expectations about how the narrative will unfold.

Second, by being presented as in-universe paratexts, these epigraphs imply that the narrative in the reader's hand is not the only narrative about these characters and their experiences. They point to other perspectives and purposes beyond those presented in the main text. Princess Irulan's "Introduction to a Child's History of Muad'Dib"[44] implies one perspective and purpose; "Stilgar's preface to 'Muad'Dib: The Man' by the Princess Irulan"[45] implies yet another perspective and purpose in conversation with the first. This second way of establishing the constructed narrative nature of the Dune novels is reinforced by their other elements of paratextual content. *Dune* contains four appendices presented as in-universe paratexts that further comment on the narrative's events. *Dune Messiah* opens with the transcript of the tortured interrogation of Bronso of Ix, whose histories contradict the official Atreides narrative. *God Emperor of Dune* contains excerpts from records and commentaries, some by Leto II's adversaries, some by Leto II himself, and some by historians long after his death who have discovered what appears to be his own personal journals. The main text of the novel is framed as the contents of these journals, and its epigraphs are drawn from the different text known as the "Stolen Journals," which are stolen by Siona in the first chapter of the main text. Not only are these epigraphs, transcripts, and reports presented as different texts by different authors with different perspectives and motives, they are also presented as being in conversation and conflict with each other, implying a complex interrelation of perspectives and purposes. Paradoxically and cleverly, these faux paratexts both reinforce the fictional facade of an authentic narrated universe while implicitly calling into question the authenticity of the narration. The fictional universe is drawn more fully, but readers are invited to question the truth of the story about it that they are reading.

All of these strategies push narrative itself into the foreground in Frank Herbert's Dune novels. Characters manipulate myth and history and show a reflexive concern for how their actions are interpreted. The novels' narratives focus on the characters' deceptions and deliberations while following a recognizable narrative structure. The main narrative text is framed with faux paratexts that suggest other perspectives, other ways to narrate these stories. Foregrounding narrative with these strategies invites reading *Dune* and its sequels as, among other things, an examination of narrative power. What results from such a reading is subject for the next section.

The Metanarrative of Power

Dune and its sequels explore many ways in which characters contend with narrative power. By narrative power, I mean both the power narratives grant to people, such as the safety and claim to leadership that the Lisan al-Gaib myth affords Paul, and the power narratives exert over people, such as the awe and loyalty that myth compels the Fremen to feel towards Paul. To discuss this exploration of narrative power in closer detail, this section focuses on *Dune* alone and how Paul Atreides coopts and enacts the Fremen messiah myth, as well as the terrible consequences he foresees resulting from his actions.

Paul Atreides is not born a messiah. He is an exceptional individual, trained to the highest standards in many disciplines, and he possesses latent powers and great potential due to being a product of the Bene Gesserit breeding program. But he is not the product of divine or supernatural providence as the Fremen and much of the universe would later come to believe. He comes to believe that he possesses a "terrible purpose," but this is the result of his encounter with The Reverend Mother Gaius Helen Mohiam.[46] While Paul will eventually come to identify himself as the Kwisatz Haderach, readers will also learn of Count Fenring, "one of the might-have-beens, an almost Kwisatz Haderach," indicating that there are others who possess similar potential to Paul's.[47] Like Paul, Count Fenring is invisible to the prescient vision of others. The Count may only be incapable of becoming the Kwisatz Haderach because he is a "genetic-eunuch" and incapable of being bred to disseminate his power as part of the Bene Gesserit's breeding program.[48] Significantly, Paul is not the child that was planned by that program. Jessica was to have a girl who would have been destined to breed with Feyd-Rautha, whom Paul will instead slay. And, just as importantly, the destiny he comes to fulfill as the Fremen's messianic Lisan al-Gaib is the product of the Bene Gesserit's Missionaria Protectiva, "protective legends implanted in [the Fremen] against the day of a Bene Gesserit's need."[49] Paul chooses to take on a mantle of destiny that is the product of human artifice. There is no cosmic, divine, or magic force underpinning it. Any power that role brings comes from a belief in the myth that underpins it.

This myth is something the Bene Gesserit manufactured for their own ends. It becomes something Paul coopts for his own ends. From the very outset, the major mythic arc that underpins the novel is revealed to be a human construct, something crafted by humans for human purposes. The Fremen, following the lead of Liet-Kynes, believe in it whole-heartedly to the point where they give themselves almost entirely over to it, allowing Paul to change their customs to suit his needs—he rejects the Fremen's succession custom to keep Stilgar as his right hand—but this does not change the fact that the myth was sown among them by the Bene Gesserit for their own needs.[50] In less charitable terms, no matter how real it feels to its Fremen adherents, it is just a fiction the Bene Gesserit wrote and Jessica and Paul acted out in pursuit of safety and power.

This is significant because it grounds the legendary and mythic aspects of *Dune*'s narrative in entirely human social terms. Paul exists not to fulfill some great destiny ordained by a supernatural power as the Fremen believe but because his mother chose her and Duke Leto's desires over those of her sisterhood. Paul fulfills a destiny that was invented by humans for entirely human reasons. It only exists so that its latent power may someday be exploited. Paul only fulfills it because exploiting that latent power will help him enact his vengeance against the Harkonnens.

Paul is an opportunist. He takes best advantage of what options he has to avenge his family. Paul needs something tangible to offer the Fremen besides the destruction of their shared enemies. To provide this something, Paul coopts a second narrative: Liet-Kynes' narrative of ecological transformation.[51] Kynes himself is already predisposed to believing in Paul's mythic role: "He prided himself on being a scientist.... Yet the boy fitted the ancient prophecy so precisely."[52] And through the ecological transformation project, Kynes has himself taken on a semi-mythical role among the Fremen. He is Liet, their leader who even gives orders to naibs like Stilgar.[53] He has "gone native," absorbing the Fremen culture, including its myths.[54] The mythic and ecological narratives coexist. Already they are ready to be intertwined. Paul takes advantage of this opportunity, but he is not the first to think of taking advantage of either narrative. His father specifically directs his attention to the Lisan al-Gaib myth and openly discusses a belief in using ecological means to transform Arrakis and the lives of its people.[55] Paul pays attention and learns. He is a good student.

The point here is to demystify Paul and the legend he becomes. Yes, Paul is exceptional, but he is the most exceptional among many exceptional figures in the novel. And he is exceptional because he has been trained to be so by his parents, not because of divine preordination as the Lisan-al-Gaib. As Juan A. Prieto-Pablos notes:

> [A]ll of [Paul's] skills are not qualitatively different than those of ordinary human beings; they are the result of painful and slow personal progress, rather than something acquired suddenly and accidentally, or just given.... [Paul] is the result of millennia of genetic manipulation and Bene Gesserit teaching, plus a series of unexpected circumstances, but much of what he becomes is the product of the hard learning of an extraordinary disciple who soon surpasses his masters.[56]

Paul is a mythic figure because he develops his abilities and works to wrap himself in a myth that is ready-made for his use.

But even as he successfully enacts his mythic role to avenge his family, Paul becomes wary of what he has done. As he spends time among the Fremen and his prescient powers grow in their spice-rich environment, Paul's "terrible purpose" comes into focus.[57] Paul sees the coming jihad, when the Fremen will conquer the galaxy in his name, whether or not he is alive to lead them: "Nothing less than the deaths of all the troop gathered here, and now—himself and his mother included—could stop the thing."[58] Only if everyone dies who knows and believes in Paul's narrative will that narrative lose its power. The myth that will sweep him into power will sweep past him and across the universe. At first, though, Paul is too caught up in the wonder of his experience, the narrative he can see unfolding before him through his prescience to step back and think of how to stop it.[59] And while Paul feels he must avoid the jihad "at any cost," he merely hesitates before stepping further into the role of the Lisan al-Gaib.[60] Paul himself becomes caught up in the very narrative he coopts: "The more he resisted his terrible purpose and fought against the coming of the jihad, the greater the turmoil that wove through his prescience."[61] Paul is made reflexive about his narrative role. He may know how the narrative he is a part of will end, but not how it will arrive at that ending.

Paul takes his final step into embodying the mythic roles of the Lisan al-Gaib and Kwisatz Haderach, drinking the Water of Life, to get a better view of the course of his narrative.[62] The effect of this is to put Paul in a coma for three weeks and allow the narrative climax to come. He has seen that the ships of the Guild are now in the space above Arrakis.[63] The narrative has taken hold, not just of the Fremen whom Paul recruited with it or of Paul himself, but of the entire universe: "Every Great House has its raiders above us … waiting."[64] All of the climax's pieces are now in place. Paul's enemies are conveniently arrayed before him. Now Paul must respond, and he does so by threatening the spice, the substance that underpins the very structure of the universe.[65] This will be a terrible sacrifice for the Fremen, but such is their belief in Paul as their messiah that they support him unconditionally.

This is the ultimate power of narrative in *Dune*. It takes on a course of its own, shaping people and events to it. The Fremen give themselves over almost entirely to their believed messiah. They are willing to sacrifice the spice cycle, the ecological system that underpins their entire way of life. Paul coopts, but never really controls this Fremen messiah narrative. He uses the narrative to achieve justice or vengeance for his family, but in doing so, he becomes a figure of the narrative. As Joshua Pearson notes, "Paul's victory over the Harkonnens and the Emperor thus comes at the cost of his capitulation to his true antagonist in the novel—jihad—his terrible purpose."[66] He sees the inevitability of the jihad, but not whether or not he will live. He will be the Fremen messiah figure either way.

The way Paul's narrative challenges the present order demands the attention of all the leaders and powerful figures of *Dune*'s universe. It draws them all into the conflict and renders them all into an audience for the final symbolic duel between Paul, the man who chose to become legend, and Feyd-Rautha, a proxy for the order Paul would overthrow.[67] The narrative is so powerful, so compelling to all involved, that the symbolic consequences of this duel are respected as real consequences. Ultimately, the power of narrative is something to respect and be wary of. Paul, an exceptional and just man—he has an *"instinct for rightness"*[68]—tries to wield its power, but he finds himself succumbing to a narrative design over which he has little power. In ending this way, *Dune* adds a cautionary note to Paul's victory. Paul must enter into a sham marriage to take on yet another narrative role as the new emperor, and he is wary of the coming jihad, but he avenges his family and brings new freedom to the Fremen, and the novel's main text ends with Jessica assuring Chani that future narratives about this time will recognize that she is Paul's real wife.[69] While *Dune* spends much of its length cautioning about narrative's power as a motivational force, it also ends on a note recognizing narrative's power to convey truth.

Ultimately, the later novels reveal that Paul is neither willing nor able to control the narratives he has coopted and created. After a struggle, his son Leto II will emerge as his heir in *Children of Dune*, but to control his father's narratives Leto II will have to embrace his role as an abomination and transform himself into an inhuman, immortal worm-god. To control the human narrative requires sacrificing one's humanity. The consequences of Leto II's rule are devastating. He completes the promised ecological transformation of Arrakis, destroying the spice ecology and the Fremen way of life. Their culture and countless others are obliterated. Humanity lives across thousands of worlds, but individual humans rarely travel far from their place of birth. To control the human narrative, Leto II must control nearly all aspects of human life. Freedoms, even basic choices such as what to wear and eat, are proscribed. Leto II sacrifices his own humanity and steals away the humanity of his people. Even he must eventually fall victim to the narrative he has created, his death freeing humanity from his terrible reign and allowing them to expand across space and ensure their survival. His actions serve to preserve humanity against the existential threat of the machine intelligence, but at a terrible cost.

Conclusion

The Dune novels demonstrate the terrible preconditions and consequences of controlling the human narrative. They serve as a warning: "Don't give over all your critical faculties to people in power, no matter how admirable those people may appear to be."[70] Paul Atreides wraps himself in a narrative specifically made to be exploited; the narrative takes control of his life and leads inevitably towards a jihad that "kill[s] sixty-one billion people, sterilize[s] ninety planets, completely demoralize[s] five hundred others [and] wipe[s] out the followers of forty religions."[71] While *Dune* itself ends before these terrible crimes take place and its ending is rendered as a moment of victory for Paul, it is not without its own tragic costs. Paul will dishonor Chani and enter into a sham marriage. Their firstborn child is slain in their conflict with the Harkonnen and the Emperor's Sardaukar. Paul's sister, Alia, is born an abomination possessing (and ready to be possessed by) ancestral memories. And the lives of many, many unnamed people are lost in the final battle. All this because a young man chose to take on a mythic role to achieve his ends. Paul is sympathetic, his motives respectable. His son Leto II is even more so. Leto II sacrifices his own humanity and generations of human freedom and progress to free humanity from attempts to control its collective narrative as part of his Golden Path. Despite his efforts, thousands of years later, the Bene Gesserit still manipulate religious, political, and ecological narratives in their war against the Honored Matres. As Herbert himself notes, "[e]ven if we find a real hero (whatever- or whoever- that may be), eventually fallible mortals take over the power structure that always comes into being around such a leader."[72] Paul and his son are "real heroes" in the most positive sense, but the consequences of them taking upon their heroic roles are still terrible for themselves and all of humanity.

Paul and Leto II are an embodiment of Frank Herbert's theory "that superheroes are disastrous for humankind."[73] This is expressed in the destruction of Paul's jihad and the despotism of Leto II's peace. Herbert asserts, "The mistakes of superheroes involve too many of us in disaster."[74] And while Paul's jihad and Leto II's peace lead ultimately to humanity's survival, they are disastrous for those who must endure them. From the perspectives of their victims, the jihad and enforced peace are calamitous mistakes. Paul and Leto II coopt and create narratives that trap and damage them and all those around them. Herbert writes:

> Systems originate with human creators, with people who employ them. Systems take over and grind on and on. They are like a flood tide that picks up everything in its path. How do they originate?[75]

The systems that come about in *Dune* and its sequels originate in narratives about politics, ecology, and myth that are intentionally created to be exploited. Paul builds a legend and then a religion and empire upon a seeded superstition and ecological promise. It "grinds" him and those who follow and all else in its path like one of the giant worms who serve as a central motif of the series. Read as metanarrative, *Dune* and its sequels are a mythic science-fiction cycle that cautions against the power of political, ecological, and mythic narratives. They form a grand narrative that condemns grand narratives. *Dune*'s power as a narrative is in its reflexive examination of narrative power, the metanarrative of power.

Notes

1. See, for examples, Asher-Perrin, "Why It's Important to Consider Whether *Dune* is a White Savior Narrative," and Kennedy, "Lawrence of Arabia, Paul Atreides, and the Roots of Frank Herbert's *Dune*."
2. See, for example, Higgins, "Psychic Decolonization in 1960s Science Fiction."
3. See, for examples, Cirasa, "An Epic Impression," and Collings, "The Epic of *Dune*: Epic Traditions in Modern Science Fiction."
4. See, for example, Mulcahy, "*The Prince* on Arrakis."
5. See, for example, Pearson, "Friedrich Nietzsche Goes to Space."
6. See Pearson, "Frank Herbert's *Dune* and the Financialization of Heroic Masculinity." It is perhaps a testament to Pearson's reading and my own that we arrive at many similar conclusions from very different perspectives.
7. Neumann and Nünning, "Metanarration and Metafiction."
8. Ryan and van Alphen, "Narratology," 110.
9. Herbert, *Dune*, 553.
10. *Ibid.*, 516.
11. *Ibid.*, 18.
12. *Ibid.*, 255.
13. *Ibid.*, 15.
14. *Ibid.*, 28.
15. *Ibid.*, 52.
16. Herbert, *Dune Messiah*, 267.
17. *Ibid.*, 59.
18. Herbert, *God Emperor of Dune*, 129.
19. *Ibid.*, 382.
20. *Ibid.*, 56.
21. Herbert, "Dune Genesis," 72.
22. *Ibid.*, 72.
23. Burke, "Definition of Man," 3, 5.
24. *Ibid.*, 13, 15.
25. Fisher, "Narration as a Human Communication Paradigm," 3, 7.
26. Herbert, *Dune*, 34.
27. *Ibid.*, 18.
28. *Ibid.*, 172.
29. Forster, *Aspects of the Novel*, 93.
30. Herbert, *Dune*, 15, 21
31. Herbert, *God Emperor of Dune*, 165.
32. Herbert, *Dune*, 509.
33. Herbert, *God Emperor of Dune*, 345.
34. *Ibid.*, 420.
35. Herbert, *Dune*, 411.
36. *Ibid.*, 448.
37. Herbert, *God Emperor of Dune*, 140.
38. Herbert, *Dune*, 110.
39. Ravenwood, "Rightwise Born Kings," 108.
40. *Ibid.*, 471.
41. Palumbo, "The Monomyth as Fractal Pattern in Frank Herbert's *Dune* Novels," 435.
42. *Ibid.*, 3.
43. Collings, "The Epic of *Dune*: Epic Traditions in Modern Science Fiction," 136.
44. Herbert, *Dune*, 187.
45. *Ibid.*, 361.
46. *Ibid.*, 28.
47. *Ibid.*, 514.
48. *Ibid.*
49. *Ibid.*, 59.

50. *Ibid.*, 451–2.
51. *Ibid.*, 149–50.
52. *Ibid.*, 114.
53. *Ibid.*, 115.
54. *Ibid.*, 117.
55. *Ibid.*, 113, 140.
56. Prieto-Pablos, "The Ambivalent Hero of Contemporary Science Fiction," 67.
57. *Ibid.*, 337.
58. *Ibid.*, 338.
59. *Ibid.*, 340.
60. *Ibid.*, 368.
61. *Ibid.*, 410.
62. *Ibid.*, 462.
63. *Ibid.*, 471.
64. *Ibid.*, 471.
65. *Ibid.*, 472.
66. Pearson, "Frank Herbert's *Dune* and the Financialization of Heroic Masculinity," 173.
67. Hebert, *Dune*, 509.
68. *Ibid.*, 12.
69. *Ibid.*, 516.
70. Herbert, "Dune Genesis," 72.
71. Herbert, *Dune Messiah*, 135–6.
72. Herbert, "Dune Genesis," 72.
73. *Ibid.*, 72.
74. *Ibid.*, 74.
75. *Ibid.*, 74.

Works Cited

Asher-Perrin, Emmet. "Why It's Important to Consider Whether *Dune* is a White Savior Narrative." Tor.com, March 6, 2019. https://www.tor.com/2019/03/06/why-its-important-to-consider-whether-dune-is-a-white-savior-narrative/.
Brooks, Mel, dir. *Spaceballs*. 1987; Beverly Hills, CA: MGM Home Entertainment, 1990.
Burke, Kenneth. "Definition of Man." *Language as Symbolic Action: Essays on Life, Literature, and Method*, Berkeley: University of California Press, 1966: 3–24.
Cirasa, Robert. "An Epic Impression: Suspense and Prophetic Conventions in the Classical Epics and Frank Herbert's *Dune*." *Classical and Modern Literature* 4, no 4. (1984): 195–213.
Collings, Michael R. "The Epic of *Dune*: Epic Traditions in Modern Science Fiction." In *Aspects of Fantasy: Selected Essays from the Second International Conference on the Fantastic in Literature and Film*, edited by William Coyle, 131–39. Westport, CT: Greenwood Press, 1986.
Fisher, Walter R. "Narration as a Human Communication Paradigm: The Case of Moral Public Argument." *Communication Monographs* 51 (1984): 1–22.
Forster, E.M. *Aspects of the Novel*. New York: Penguin, 1963.
Herbert, Frank. *Chapterhouse: Dune*. 1985 New York: Ace Books, 1987.
Herbert, Frank. *Children of Dune*. 1976 New York: Ace Books, 1987.
Herbert, Frank. *Dune*. 1965 New York: Ace Books, 2005.
Herbert, Frank. "Dune Genesis." *OMNI* 2, no. 10 (July 1980): 72–76.
Herbert, Frank. *Dune Messiah*. 1969 New York: Ace Books, 1987.
Herbert, Frank. *God Emperor of Dune*. 1981 New York: Ace Books, 1987.
Herbert, Frank. *Heretics of Dune*. 1984 New York: Ace Books, 1987.
Higgins, David. "Psychic Decolonization in 1960s Science Fiction." *Science Fiction Studies* 40 no. 2 (2013): 228–245.

Kennedy, Kara. "Lawrence of Arabia, Paul Atreides, and the Roots of Frank Herbert's *Dune*." *TOR.com*, June 2, 2021. https://www.tor.com/2021/06/02/lawrence-of-arabia-paul-atreides-and-the-roots-of-frank-herberts-dune/.

Mulcahy, Kevin. "*The Prince* on Arrakis: Frank Herbert's dialogue with Machiavelli." *Extrapolation* 37, no. 1 (1996): 22–36.

Neumann, Birgit, and Ansgar Nünning. "Metanarration and Metafiction." *The Living Handbook of Narratology*, 2014. http://www.lhn.uni-hamburg.de/node/50.html

Palumbo, Donald E. "The Monomyth as Fractal Pattern in Frank Herbert's *Dune* Novels." *Science-Fiction Studies* 25, no. 3 (1998): 433–58.

Pearson, Brook W.R. "Friedrich Nietzsche Goes to Space." *Dune and Philosophy: The Weirding Way of the Mentat*, Popular Culture and Philosophy Book 56, edited by Jeffery Nicholas, 189–206. Chicago: Open Court, 2011.

Pearson, Joshua. "Frank Herbert's Dune and the Financialization of Heroic Masculinity." *CR: The New Centennial Review* 19, no. 1 (Spring 2019): 155–180.

Prieto-Pablos, Juan A. "The Ambivalent Hero of Contemporary Fantasy and Science Fiction." *Extrapolation* 32, no. 1 (1991): 64–80.

Ravenwood, Emily. "Rightwise Born Kings: Feudalism and Republicanism in Science Fiction." *Extrapolation* 46, no. 3 (Winter 2005): 500–18.

Ryan, Marie-Laure and Ernst van Alphen. "Narratology." *Encyclopedia of Contemporary Literary Theory: Approaches, Scholars, Terms*, edited by I.R. Makaryk, Toronto: University of Toronto Press, 2003, 110–116.

Political Prescience

How Game Theory Solves the Paradox of Foreknowledge

DOMINIC J. NARDI

Near the beginning of *Dune*, Paul Atreides reflects that he "always remembered the dreams that were predictions."[1] This sentence alerts the reader that some characters in the story have prophetic powers. Indeed, throughout Frank Herbert's Dune saga, Paul, the God Emperor Leto II, and other characters regularly use the mélange spice in order to access prescience and peer into the future. However, this ability presents a paradox: if a character possesses knowledge of the future, can he or she also possess free will? On the one hand, the Dune novels describe prescience as the ability to view all possible futures, not merely *the* future. This suggests a certain amount of ambiguity as to the accuracy of prescient visions. On the other hand, those with prescience generally treat their visions as reliable and act upon them. In fact, in many cases, the events depicted in prescient visions eventually do come to pass.

In this essay, I argue that prescience can be reinterpreted as a way to solve complex game theoretic problems. Doing so helps resolve the paradox of foreknowledge. Like prescience, game theoretic models show possible futures based on possible decisions an individual could make. Individuals have the freedom to choose the path—or paths—that they expect will yield the greatest benefit. With enough information, it should be possible to determine which branch of a game is most likely to occur. In such a situation, none of the players would make a different decision because the mix of opportunities and threats from other players will compel them down a certain path. From the outside, it might appear as if determinism had prevailed as players follow a predictable path. However, players retain the agency to choose differently; the outcome is only predictable because players can see the lone pathway that will maximize their

29

expected benefits and no rational player would choose otherwise. Seen this way, characters in the Dune saga can use prescience to view the expected outcomes in possible futures and act accordingly, without losing free will.

Prescience also plays an underappreciated role in shaping the politics of the Dune universe. In earthly politics, limits on a government's ability to gather information help to constrain state power and can create opportunities for opponents of the regime to operate. For example, dissidents can mobilize antigovernment protests if the police cannot adequately predict their next move. By contrast, rulers like Paul and Leto II who have prescience have an insurmountable advantage over their subjects. They can anticipate and plan for almost any challenges to their rule. Dissent becomes impossible when an authoritarian government can predict the actions of its subjects. Uncertainty preserves freedom, while prescience begets tyranny.

I begin this essay by discussing the nature of prescience in the novels and explain how other scholars have attempted to reconcile free will and prescient powers. Next, I present a game theoretic model of prescience, with illustrative examples from the novels, and explain how game theory helps to resolve the paradox of foreknowledge. I then pivot to use the insights derived from the model to explain why prescience proved so politically advantageous to the Atreides family. I conclude with thoughts on how focusing on the link between prescience and power in the Dune saga yields new insights about the applicability of Herbert's magnum opus for the twenty-first century.

The Paradox of Prescience

From the Oracle of Delphi to the crystal balls in the Harry Potter franchise, prophecy has been a part of speculative fiction for millennia. In theory, prophecy precludes the possibility of free will; if an individual can accurately know the future, then how could they make any meaningful decisions affecting that future? Different stories have handled this paradox of foreknowledge in different ways. Some stories are content to conclude that humans lack free will. In the Greek tragedy *Oedipus Rex*, after an oracle tells Laius and Jocasta that their son Oedipus will murder his father and marry his mother, they order a soldier to kill the boy; however, in doing so they inadvertently set in motion events that will fulfill the prophecy.[2] In such stories, prophets possess absolute knowledge of the future and, once the prophecy is conveyed, humans lose any possibility of agency. At the opposite extreme, in Isaac Asimov's Foundation series, free will can prevent prophecies from coming to fruition. Hari Seldon, a psychohistorian who uses statistical data analysis to predict future events, hides his predictions because "by knowledge, your freedom of action would be expanded" and potentially introduce variables not accounted for in his calculations.[3]

More frequently, however, stories leave the relationship between free will and prophecy ambiguous by obscuring information about the future from the characters. This is partly why so many prophets speak in cryptic riddles and vague metaphors. For example, the three witches in William Shakespeare's *Macbeth* tell the Thane that "no man that's born of woman" can harm him and that he will not be overthrown until the Great Birnam woods move.[4] Macbeth initially believes these conditions are impossible to fulfill, and thus does not know how to appropriately prevent the prophecy from manifesting. Alternatively, the narrative might raise doubts about the accuracy of prophecies. As *Game of Thrones* showrunner David Benioff noted in an interview, prophecies in George R.R. Martin's story "don't always come true,"[5] while prophecy as a whole is depicted as untrustworthy.[6] If prophets can err or misinterpret their visions, then a character's free will is only constrained by the extent to which he or she believes the prophecy. Ultimately, such stories leave unresolved the question of whether or not characters would have had the agency to avoid any prophesized outcomes.

The Dune saga takes a unique approach to prophecy and free will. Prescience is both limited and comprehensive, both accurate and inaccurate. In one of the "Arrakis Awakening" epigraphs in *Dune*, Princess Irulan notes that Paul Muad'Dib's prescient powers, his power to see the Future was limited. Just as we cannot see without light, and cannot see out of a valley, there were things hidden from him. The future was not set in stone, it could change with nothing more than choosing one word instead of another.[7] Like the human senses, the extent to which prescience allows users to accurately view the future depends in part upon the quality and quantity of information received. Unlike a Delphic Oracle, prescient prophecies in Dune are not presented as cryptic messages that need to be interpreted, but rather as clear visions of what might or might not come to pass.

At times, it appears that prescient characters can accurately predict the future in minute detail. For example, even after a stone burner attack blinds Paul in *Dune Messiah*, he could still "see" the physical world around him by relying on his prescient visions, "fitting himself into the vision so tightly that it could not escape."[8] His prescience proves at least as reliable as his sense of vision. On the other hand, some prescient visions clearly do not come to pass. While fighting Jamis in the Cave of Ridges, Paul sees "his own dead body with blood flowing from a gaping knife wound," despite the fact he ultimately kills Jamis.[9] Prescience is also revealed to have blind spots that can affect the accuracy of any prescient visions. In the last chapter of *Dune*, Paul feels "a pang of foreboding" when he realizes that Count Hasimir Fenring never appeared in his visions and wonders if the failed Kwisatz Haderach "*is the one who kills me?*"[10] In *Dune Messiah*, the conspirators against the Atreides regime take advantage of the fact that Spacing Guild Navigator Edric is invisible to prescience in order to hide their plot.

The Dune texts also vary between depicting prescience as the ability to see *the* future versus merely seeing *one* future out of many. In describing his newfound powers in Book One of *Dune*, Paul tells Jessica that "there are branchings" in his sense of the future.[11] Indeed, as noted above, when fighting Jamis, Paul saw possible outcomes that never occurred. *Dune Messiah* describes Paul as remembering not only probable futures, but also "countless projections, things never fated to be" as well as "false pasts."[12] However, characters with prescience often rely upon their visions of the future and seem resigned to their fates, which strongly implies that prescience does not just present all possible futures equally, but also provides information about which future is most likely to occur. Near the end of *Dune*, Paul concludes that trying to avoid the jihad is futile; even if he dies, Paul realizes that his Fremen followers would "rage out from Arrakis" inspired by "the legend he already had become."[13] In *Children of Dune*, Leto II even bemoans the fact that prescience robbed him of the joy of "surprise," suggesting that he had accurately seen most of the events of his life up to that point.[14]

Scholars of the Dune novels have tried to reconcile these potentially paradoxical—if not contradictory—depictions of prescience. Lawrence Luton analogizes the use of prescience to the observer effect in physics, which states that the mere observation of a phenomenon inevitably changes that phenomenon; accordingly, "There is no such thing as THE FUTURE" because the act of using prescience changes the extent to which prescient users can know the future, and therefore changes the future itself.[15] He rejects the argument that prescience is a form of "absolutely accurate knowing" and concludes that it is instead "interdependent with the person or persons in which it is found and with the contexts in which it is exercised."[16] The narration in *Dune* does suggest a kind of observer effect, noting that a "Heisenberg indeterminacy intervened" when Paul tried to use prescience during his fight with Jamis.[17] However, Luton's argument understates the extent to which prescience in the Dune saga is depicted as accurate and reliable. To the extent that there is an observer effect, it does not render prescience useless or the future unknowable. Even if epistemologically the characters do not possess an "absolutely accurate knowing," functionally they often behave as if they do.

In *Dune and Philosophy*, Sam Gates-Scovelle attempts to understand prescience by making an epistemological distinction between prediction and knowledge.[18] Knowledge requires a person to know with absolute certainty about the existence of a phenomenon. Because free will depends upon the belief that one's choice could alter future events, Gates-Scovelle concludes that if prescience provided absolute knowledge of the future, then it would threaten free will. Instead, he concludes that prescience is more like a prediction of the future. As the seventeenth-century French physicist Pierre-Simon de Laplace noted, absolute prediction can also threaten free will because of the necessary relationship between past causes and future effects; if one knows with absolute certainty all that has happened in the past and present, then there is only one possible outcome in the future.[19] Gates-Scovelle believes the Dune novels preserve free will because prescience is only "a computation of the most probable futures," not an absolute prediction.[20] Some futures viewed through prescience might appear inevitable (with a probability of 1 or 100 percent), other futures might appear impossible (with a probability of 0 or 0 percent), while others still might appear much less certain (with probabilities ranging anywhere between 0–1). Thus, Paul, Leto, and other prescient characters have the free will to make choices, and in doing so affect which of those probable futures will in fact occur.

The analogy of prescience to computation is not merely a convenient way to escape the paradox of foreknowledge; the Dune novels themselves often describe prescience as a form of computation. Paul's awakening at the end of Book One of *Dune* is described as an "inflow of data or the cold precision with which each new item was added to his knowledge … adding sense impressions, extrapolating, computing."[21] At least in the beginning of his awakening, Paul himself views his prescient awareness as "a computation of most probable futures."[22] In one of the epigraphs in *Children of Dune*, Palimbasha even claims, "Only in the realm of mathematics can you understand Muad'Dib's precise view of the future."[23] However, the Dune novels never attempt to describe the precise contours of prescient computation, potentially making it difficult for readers to visualize how a prescient user navigates probable futures and avoids the paradox of foreknowledge. Gates-Scovelle begins to unpack this aspect of prescience through his analogy to probabilities, but the explanation does not adequately explain how, given probabilistic futures, some future events—such as the jihad—still appear inevitable. Paul's ability in *Dune Messiah* to navigate while blind seems to require more precision than possible from even precise computation of probable futures.

Games Within Games

In this section, I present a game theoretic approach to prescience that builds upon Gates-Scovelle's analogy of prescience to computation, but also clarifies how prescience alters a user's strategic decision-making behavior. Game theory is the use of mathematical models to study strategic interactions between rational decision-makers. A key insight of game theory is that individuals are constrained by how they expect other individuals to respond to their actions. Game theory is useful because it helps to simplify complex decision-making and because the most consequential decisions in politics often happen behind closed doors. Even when interviewed, some political elites have incentives to misrepresent their actions in order to hide potential wrongdoing or unpopular actions. Game theory allows researchers to overcome this information asymmetry to make conclusions about how political actors would behave given a clear set of assumptions about each individual's preferences.

A common critique of game theory is that human beings do not always behave rationally and most cannot perform the complex mental calculations required to solve game theoretic models.[24] The concept of "bounded rationality" acknowledges that a player's decision-making ability is limited by his or her cognitive functions, as well as practical concerns such as time and resources. Scholars have usually responded to such criticisms by pointing out that game theory is a model, which by necessity requires simplification.[25] Moreover, rationality as defined by game theorists merely means that players know their preferences and act to maximize their payoffs given the choices in a game.[26] It does not require players to be either devoid of emotion or good at math.

Nevertheless, this critique of game theory is particularly inapplicable when applied to the Dune saga. The primary characters in Frank Herbert's novels are all part of the political, economic, or religious elites, exactly the types of individuals who would be more likely to approach decisions rationally and strategically. Herbert's characters are infamous for their "plans within plans within plans."[27] They regularly try to anticipate the plans of other characters and adjust their own plans accordingly. For example, when discussing the Harkonnen trap for the Atreides on Arrakis, Piter de Vries states, "Loveliest of all is that the Duke will know, too. He knows now. He can already feel the trap."[28] The Harkonnen trap works not because Duke Leto is entirely ignorant of the risk, but rather because the Harkonnens knew he would not suspect his Suk doctor, Wellington Yueh.

In fact, after the Butlerian Jihad, the Mentat school trained humans to perform the types of mathematical calculations required to solve complex games. Herbert never uses the term "game theory" in the novels, but the way Mentats calculate an optimal strategy for their political patrons comes across very much like solving game theoretic problems.[29] A deleted chapter from *Dune*—and later included in Brian Herbert and Kevin J. Anderson's *The Road to Dune*—would have made the comparison between

Mentat political analysis and computations even more explicit by listing the types of problems Mentats could solve: "Mathematical questions. Military questions. Social questions. Probability questions. They could swallow all sorts of information and spew out answers when the answers were needed."[30] However, even Mentats are subject to bounded rationality and limited by the data available to them. As the Baron Harkonnen observes, "The way to control and direct a Mentat ... is through his information. False information—false results."[31] Unlike those with prescience, Mentats can only predict the future based on past and present data; they cannot actually view probable futures. Notably, at the beginning of *Dune*, Paul is being trained as a Mentat, but his prescience combined with Bene Gesserit training affords him greater abilities than a regular Mentat.

As an example of how prescience can solve complex game theoretic models, Figure 1 presents a stylized version of the confrontation between Paul Atreides and Padishah Emperor Shaddam Corrino IV at the end of Book Three of *Dune*. Both characters face decisions. Paul can choose either to hide in the desert or to confront the emperor. If Paul confronts the emperor, Shaddam must then decide if he will abdicate or call Paul's bluff. In the latter scenario, Paul can then either surrender or go through with his threat to release the Water of Life above a pre-spice mass, destroying all spice production. The game ends at any of the terminal nodes, when there are no decisions left to be made.

For each possible outcome, Paul Atreides receives the first payoff, while Emperor Shaddam receives the second. If Paul hides, he receives no payoff (0) while Shaddam receives some positive payoff represented by β (i.e., $\beta > 0$). If the emperor abdicates, Paul receives a payoff represented by α such that $\alpha > 0$. If the emperor calls Paul's bluff, Paul would ultimately prefer to destroy the spice than surrender; as such, the loss Paul suffers from destroying the spice ($-\alpha$) is marginally less than that of surrendering ($-\alpha-\varepsilon$), even if it means his followers would suffer from spice withdrawal. By contrast, the Emperor would clearly suffer if Paul destroys the spice, not only because he and other elites are addicted to mélange, but

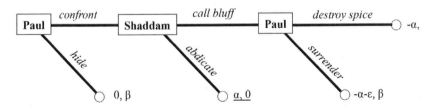

Figure 1: Paul vs. Shaddam Game. Note: $\alpha > \varepsilon > 0$ and $\beta > 0$. **Equilibrium outcomes are underlined.**

also because the Imperium's economy depends on it; this outcome is represented by a payoff of -β. Ultimately, Paul's payoff would be maximized if he confronts Shaddam and the emperor abdicates (α), while Shaddam's payoff would be maximized if Paul chooses to hide and avoid the confrontation altogether (β).

This type of game can be solved through backwards induction, a process of comparing the relative payoffs of each player for each possible decision at the terminal node to determine how other players would act. In this case, because -α > -α-ε, Paul would choose to destroy the spice rather than surrender. Knowing this, Shaddam would abdicate because 0 > -β. Therefore, knowing this, Paul would choose to confront the emperor at the initial decision node because α > 0. However, solving this type of game correctly is only possible if both Paul and Emperor Shaddam know the potential payoffs and moves of the other player, a situation known as complete information. Paul must know that Shaddam's payoff structure would lead him to abdicate instead of letting the spice be destroyed; if he mistakenly believes that Shaddam would call his bluff, Paul would instead choose to hide, risking a suboptimal outcome.

In the real world, games of complete information are relatively rare; we cannot know with certainty the preferences of other strategic actors. However, prescience could help users solve such games by providing data about future possibilities, including information about potential payoffs and moves of any other players. Prescience also implicitly addresses concerns about bounded rationality in game theoretic models because the mélange spice induces an awakening and expands the powers of the user's mind, giving him or her higher cognitive skills. With prescience, Paul can view the outcomes at each decision node and know that—given his preference structure in the game—Shaddam would abdicate rather than call his bluff. Although Paul retains free will and could still choose to hide, he has no incentive to—and would never—choose to do so. Thus, in this scenario, prescience would reveal a future that appears to be certain because the outcome is in equilibrium; neither player would ever choose differently because the strategies of "confront" and "abdicate" maximize their respective payoffs.

Figure 2 depicts a situation in which prescience shows probable futures with multiple possible equilibrium outcomes instead of a single predetermined outcome. The game is similar to Figure 1 except that there exists uncertainty about Emperor Shaddam's intentions. With a probability of p between 0 and 1, Shaddam is not reckless and would always abdicate instead of letting Paul destroy the spice (just as in Figure 1). However, with a probability of $1-p$, Shaddam is reckless and would prefer to call Paul's bluff, even if doing so risks the destruction of the galactic economy. If he calls Paul's bluff, Shaddam would suffer -β, but this would still be smaller than the cost to his pride were he to abdicate (-β-ε). Knowing this, Paul would choose to hide instead of confronting the emperor, resulting in no net gain (0) for him but a victory (β) for the emperor. In other words, the equilibrium outcome in the possible futures depicted on the lower branch of the game differs from the outcome in futures depicted by the upper branch.

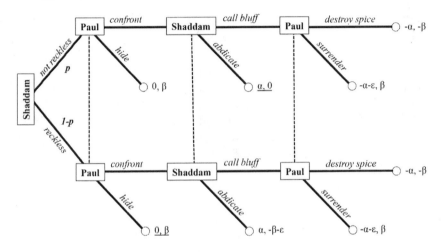

Figure 2: Paul vs. Shaddam Game with Incomplete Information. Note: $\alpha > \varepsilon > 0$ **and** $\beta > 0$. p **is the probability that Shaddam is not reckless. Equilibrium outcomes are underlined.**

If prescience allows users to view all possible branching futures, then Paul would see the equilibrium outcomes in both branches of Figure 2. Without knowing the value of p, it would be impossible for Paul to know how to make that initial decision between hiding and confrontation in a way that maximizes his payoff. Fortunately, prescience appears to provide users with information about which futures are *probable*. Even if prescience does not assign a precise numerical value to p, knowing the *relative* value of p can help Paul find an optimal strategy. If, for example, Paul uses prescience and observes that Shaddam behaves recklessly in most visible futures, that would imply p is relatively low ($p < 1-p$), and so hiding becomes a relatively more attractive strategy.[32]

Ultimately, prescience can transform games of incomplete information into games of complete information—at least for players with prescience. This gives prescient users a significant advantage in that they can anticipate the strategies of other players and thereby maximize their payoffs. Moreover, if—as is the case with Shaddam by the end of *Dune*—other players know that prescience gives prescient users this advantage, then they will view any threats that prescient users make as inherently credible.[33] Shaddam has little incentive to call Paul's bluff because he knows that Paul knows what would happen after the bluff is called, but Shaddam himself does not. Importantly, this game theoretic approach shows how prescience can provide users with accurate and reliable information about the future—or possible futures—without obviating free will. The equilibrium outcomes in Figures 1 and 2 are based on Paul's understanding of his strategic interests after having viewed branching futures. He retains the capacity to choose a suboptimal strategy, but has no incentive to do so.

Of Prophets and Politicians

For decades, scholars have examined the political themes in the Dune saga, particularly Herbert's deconstruction of charismatic leadership.[34] In an afterword to *Dune*, Frank's son Brian claims the novel serves as a warning against placing too much faith in political leaders.[35] In "Dune Genesis," Frank Herbert himself notes, "Beneath the hero's facade you will find a human being who makes human mistakes."[36] Several scholars note that this critique applies not only to the Harkonnens, the villains of the story, but also to the Atreides, the nominal heroes.[37] *Dune* chronicles Paul's ascent to power, so readers initially sympathize with him; yet, in *Dune Messiah*, we learn that Paul has become a despot responsible for the deaths of billions. Stephen Fjellman notes that telling much of *God Emperor of Dune* from Leto II's point of view forces readers to confront any fantasies they might have about benevolent dictatorship.[38] Scholars have compared the strong, centralized reigns of Paul and Leto II to Thomas Hobbes's Leviathan.[39] Kevin Mulcahy even interprets the Dune saga as a refutation of Niccolò Machiavelli's *The Prince* in its skepticism of conniving political leaders.[40]

Prescience plays a critical yet underappreciated role in enabling Paul and Leto to consolidate their Leviathan-like political control. As explained in the previous section, prescience provides the data and computational power necessary to solve complex games, enabling users to choose the optimal strategy in any given political situation. Prescient rulers can counter the moves of political rivals and distribute just the right amount of patronage—or proverbial "bread and circuses"—to appease the masses. *God Emperor of Dune* explicitly acknowledges the relationship between political power and prescience. An in-universe text known as *The Welbeck Abridgment* notes that Leto's "ability to predict future events, an oracular ability much more powerful than that of any ancestor, is still the mainstay of his political control."[41] As Gates-Scovelle explains, the "terrific power of oracles in the Duniverse is that they are tyrants with dominion over time, over the events they see and the people in them."[42] Knowledge is power, and absolute knowledge is absolute power.

By contrast, uncertainty can constrain and undermine political leaders, especially in political crises like regime transitions. Figure 3 depicts a model of a top-down transition from authoritarianism to democracy.[43] A dictator faced with political opposition can either maintain the status quo or liberalize the regime by enacting a constitution that protects basic rights. Paul Atreides faced a similar decision in *Dune Messiah*. During a meeting of the Imperial Council, Stilgar reports of agitation from Sector Ixian for a constitution. Paul rejects the proposition out of hand, claiming that a constitution is "social power mobilized and it has no conscience. It can crush the highest and the lowest...."[44]

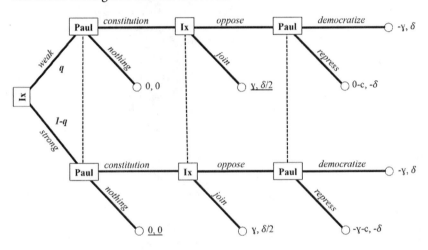

Figure 3: Top-Down Political Transitions Game. Note: $y > c > 0$ and $\delta > 0$. q is the probability that the Ixian opposition is weak. Equilibrium outcomes are underlined.

However, following Figure 3, if Paul decided instead to liberalize, the Ixian opposition would then have a choice of either endorsing his government or continuing to oppose it. If the Ixians join the government, they would receive a constitution (with a payoff of $\delta/2 > 0$), while Paul's regime would emerge with a broader support coalition (with a payoff of $y > 0$). By contrast, if the Ixian opposition continues to oppose the regime, then the regime could decide either to repress the opposition or to continue liberalization. It would cost Paul's regime c in resources ($c > 0$) to launch a military campaign to repress the Ixians, who would suffer δ in losses ($-\delta < 0$). By contrast, if the regime undergoes a transition to democracy, then Paul and his Fremen supporters would lose ɣ portion of their power (-ɣ < 0)—especially if they are voted out of office—while the Ixian opposition would win δ share of the legislative seats in any election ($\delta > 0$).

Paul's optimal strategy depends on the strength of the Ixian opposition. With probability q, as depicted in the upper branch of Figure 3, the Ixians are weak and Paul's regime could easily defeat any insurgency. In this scenario, Paul would prefer to repress the Ixians instead of democratizing because repression is less costly than democratization (-c > -ɣ). Knowing this, the Ixians would welcome a constitution ($\delta/2 > -\delta$), even if it falls short of their broader goals for democratization. This would broaden Paul's support (and gain him ɣ), so he would agree to a constitution. However, if the Ixians have stronger support—which is the case with probability $1-q$, as depicted in the lower branch in Figure 3—Paul would find it too costly to repress them (-ɣ-c < -ɣ). As such, the Ixians would be empowered to force Paul to choose to democratize if the game reaches the third decision node. Knowing this, Paul would refuse to offer any hint of compromise and instead maintain the status quo. Through prescience and knowledge of probable futures, Paul could determine the probable strength of Ixian opposition (q) and choose the optimal strategy.

In a game of complete information, there is in theory no equilibrium under which an authoritarian regime would willingly democratize; dictators want to keep power and will only offer concessions if the opposition is too weak to push for full democracy. That said, top-down democratic transitions do occur in the real world because dictators exist in a state of incomplete information. They often lack critical information about dissidents, which can lead them to miscalculate. For example, during the late 1980s, protests led by the Solidarity trade union threatened the stability of the communist regime in Poland. In 1989, the government tried to coopt Solidarity and agreed to hold legislative elections. The regime's party, the United Workers' Party, expected to win the election; instead, Solidarity and its allies won a large majority. A year later, Solidarity leader Lech Walesa was elected president. Poland's leadership had liberalized in the expectation that doing so would coopt a threat to the communist regime, but it made a strategic miscalculation because it lacked critical information about popular support for Solidarity.[45] Had Poland's communists anticipated that outcome, they might have opted to crack down violently on their political opponents, just as China's Communist Party had at Tiananmen Square on June 4, 1989.

As noted in the previous section, in the Dune universe, prescience transforms the game into one of complete information—but only for the dictator. Through prescience, Paul—or Leto—can view each branch of the game and how any potential opposition would respond to liberalization. This in turn would reveal the true strength of opponents such as the Ixian Confederacy, helping the rulers of Arrakis avoid making the same mistake as Poland's communists. Given this, Figure 3 raises an interesting interpretation of the Ixian opposition in *Dune Messiah*. Although Paul seems categorically opposed to a constitution, or any legal codification of government power,[46] his decision could also be rooted in prescient visions revealing that the Ixians were stronger than the book suggests at face value. Indeed, in *God Emperor of Dune*, Leto II tells Siona that because of his rule the Ixians no longer create machines capable of "*arafel*," or apocalypse.[47] As mentioned in *Heretics of Dune*, the Ixians became a major power after the collapse of Leto's empire. Thus, perhaps Paul also refused a constitution in order to prevent Ix from gaining strength before the Golden Path could reach fruition.

Tellingly, Paul and Leto's regimes only falter when they encounter blind spots in their prescience. In *Dune Messiah*, the Guild Navigator Edric hid the Tleilaxu conspiracy that nearly compels Paul to abdicate in return for a ghola of the recently deceased Chani. In *God Emperor of Dune*, Siona Atreides manages to assassinate Leto II because she is invisible to prescience. As Gates-Scovelle notes, "Freedom, Herbert is trying to say, is predicated, not on knowledge, but on a mixture of knowledge and ignorance."[48]

Ironically, Paul and Leto II themselves eventually conclude that prescience would lead to absolute despotism. Both have visions of humanity's destruction by an unknown power that could use prescience; victory would be impossible if the enemy knew humanity's every move. Fjellman argues that, as Paul sees the plots around him intensify, he realizes that each "successive plot requires an escalation of his control if it is to be thwarted," and so he ultimately decides to go into the desert and "give chance back to the world."[49] Leto had modified the Bene Gesserit's secret breeding program in order to develop prescience-cloaking genes and Siona, one of the first carriers of those genes. Indeed, one of the goals of Leto's Golden Path and the subsequent Scattering is to free humanity from prescience. Thousands of years later, in *Heretics of Dune* and *Chapterhouse: Dune*, humanity has developed no-globes and no-ships, technology that can evade prescience. In short, for humanity to thrive, humans need freedom from prescience.[50]

Conclusion

By reinterpreting prescience as the ability to solve complex game theoretic problems—the ability to view branching decisions and payoffs in all possible futures—this essay helps reconcile the prophetic powers of prescience with the free will Herbert's characters seem to possess. Game theory shows how prescient users could view multiple futures while at the same time concluding that some futures are nearly certain to occur. Because prescient users will then make decisions based on their interests, they can act in ways consistent with their future visions without losing free will; in equilibrium, prescient users might never deviate from a strategy that maximizes their utility, even if they retain the agency to do so. That said, the game theoretic approach presented in this essay is a simplified model of the prophetic abilities obtained through prescience; it admittedly does not capture the entirety of prescience. Prescient users can sense much more than decisions they might face in the future; they can also sense the sights, sounds, and smells of that future. Prescience is more than a single—or even infinite—game, and ultimately remains beyond normal human comprehension.[51]

In the early twenty-first century, human beings do not have access to spice-fueled prescience—and likely never will. However, recent advances in data analytics and artificial intelligence have made it easier to identify patterns and make reasonably informed predictions about human behavior. During the past decade, governments around the world have started to use predictive algorithms on massive datasets about their own citizens, sometimes to solve legitimate public policy challenges, but often to increase the power of political elites. In the United States, elected politicians in some states use extremely refined information about constituents to redraw congressional districts in order to advantage their party; in effect, representatives choose their voters.[52] During the past decade, the Chinese government has created a massive surveillance network of cameras, online censorship, and data-collection systems designed to identify and stifle dissidents.[53] Just as scholars in the twentieth century interpreted *Dune* as providing a warning about charismatic leaders and environmental destruction, the use of prescience to maintain Atreides rule should serve as a warning against the exploitation of big data and the erosion of privacy in the twenty-first century.

NOTES

1. Herbert, *Dune*, 6.
2. Sophocles, *Oedipus Rex*.
3. Asimov, *Foundation*, 80.
4. Shakespeare, *Macbeth*, V.iii.6.
5. See Hibberd, "'Game of Thrones': George R.R. Martin on That Creepy Flashback Scene." For example, Maester Aemon becomes convinced that Melisandre had misread the signs that had convinced her Stannis Baratheon is Azor Ahai reborn. Martin, *A Feast*

for Crows, 648. Although Martin has not concluded the series, Stannis's defeat by Ramsay Bolton strongly implies that he will not fulfill this prophecy.

    6. One maester even remarks that:

> prophecy is like a treacherous woman. She takes your member in her mouth, and you moan with the pleasure of it and think, how sweet, how fine, how good this is… and then her teeth snap shut and your moans turn to screams. That is the nature of prophecy… Prophecy will bite your prick off every time (Martin, *A Feast for Crows*, 850).

    7. Herbert, *Dune*, 352.
    8. Herbert, *Dune Messiah*, 240.
    9. Herbert, *Dune*, 479.
    10. *Ibid.*, 769.
    11. *Ibid.*, 320.
    12. Herbert, *Dune Messiah*, 250.
    13. Herbert, *Dune*, 783. Earlier in the novel, Paul does seem less certain about the inevitability of the jihad. After the fight with Jamis, he tells himself that he "*cannot*" let the jihad occur. Presumably, if Jamis had killed Paul, he would never have become "the legend" to inspire the Fremen. However, by the time he confronts Emperor Shaddam, he had passed any branching pathways that did not involve jihad. Herbert, *Dune*, 500.
    14. Herbert, *Children of Dune*, 73.
    15. Luton, "The Political Philosophy of Dune," 46.
    16. *Ibid.*, 93.
    17. Herbert, *Dune*, 478.
    18. Gates-Scovelle, "Curse of the Golden Path," 42.
    19. Laplace, *A Philosophical Essay on Probabilities*, 4.
    20. Gates-Scovelle, "Curse of the Golden Path," 48.
    21. Herbert, *Dune*, 305–306.
    22. *Ibid.*, 314. See also Brierly, "A critical moment," in this volume on Paul's awakening.
    23. Herbert, *Children of Dune*, 234. Elsewhere in the novel, Ghanima calls Palimbasha a "mathematical boor" and decries his focus on math to explain prescience. Herbert, *Children of Dune*, 198. However, this does not necessarily mean that math is an inappropriate tool for "modeling" certain aspects of prescient abilities, even if it does not capture the entirety of prescience.
    24. See, e.g., Simon, "A Behavioral Model of Rational Choice."
    25. Clark, Golder, and Golder, *Principles of Comparative Politics*, 19–21.
    26. *Ibid.*, 56.
    27. Herbert, *Dune*, 29.
    28. *Ibid.*, 33.
    29. Political scientists had begun to use game theory extensively by the 1950s, especially in the context of international relations. However, there is no evidence—either from letters or notes contained in *The Road to Dune* or in published interviews—that Frank Herbert was versed in game theory.
    30. Herbert, Herbert, and Anderson, *The Road to Dune*, 237.
    31. Herbert, *Dune*, 375.
    32. Technically, the optimal strategy depends on the probability *and* size of relative payoffs. In this case, the positive and negative payoffs are nearly symmetrical (i.e., Paul is comparing α and $-\alpha$, while Shaddam is comparing β and $-\beta$), which average out to 0. Thus, to simplify the analysis, I only focus on how the value of p affects strategic decisions.
    33. Initially, the Emperor's Guildsmen doubt that Paul has prescient abilities, noting, "We cannot know how it will go… But this Muad'Dib cannot know, either." However, shortly afterward, they determine through their limited powers of prescience that Paul is indeed prescient and capable of carrying out his threat. Herbert, *Dune*, 755.
    34. See, for example, Rudd, "Paul's Empire," 52–55; O'Reilly, *Frank Herbert*; Mulcahy, "The Prince on Arrakis," 36.
    35. Herbert, Afterword to *Dune*, 871.

36. Herbert, "Dune Genesis."
37. See, for example, O'Reilly, *Frank Herbert*; DiTommaso, "History and Historical Effect in Frank Herbert's *Dune*," 321; Minowitz, "Prince versus Prophet," 136; and Erman and Möller, "What's Wrong with Politics in the Duniverse?" 64.
38. Fjellman, "Prescience and Power," 54.
39. Butkus, "A Universe of Bastards," 75. See also Phillips, "The greatest predator ever known," in this volume.
40. Mulcahy, "The Prince on Arrakis," 22.
41. Herbert, *God Emperor of Dune*, 77.
42. Gates-Scovelle, "Son of the Curse of the Golden Path," 212.
43. Game adapted from Clark, Golder, and Golder, *Principles of Comparative Politics*, 292–308.
44. Herbert, *Dune Messiah*, 76.
45. See Clark, Golder, and Golder, *Principles of Comparative Politics*, 308–10.
46. There are other passages in the Dune novels that express skepticism about codified law. For example, in *Chapterhouse: Dune*, the Bene Gesserit Mother Superior Darwi Odrade argues, "Give me the judgement of balanced minds in preference to laws every time. Codes and manuals create patterned behavior. All patterned behavior tends to go unquestioned, gathering destructive momentum." Herbert, *Chapterhouse: Dune*, 253.
47. Herbert, *God Emperor of Dune*, 420.
48. Gates-Scovelle, "Son of the Curse of the Golden Path," 212.
49. Fjellman, "Prescience and Power," 52.
50. Frank Herbert passed away in 1986, before he could write a sequel to *Chapterhouse: Dune* (1985). Brian Herbert and Kevin J. Anderson's *Hunters of Dune* (2006) and *Sandworms of Dune* (2007) later reveal this threat to be thinking machines.
51. As famously noted by statistician George Box, "all models are wrong" but some are useful. Box, "Science and Statistics," 792.
52. McCune and Tunstall, "Calculated Democracy."
53. Qiang, "The Road to Digital Unfreedom."

Works Cited

Asimov, Isaac. *Foundation*. 1951. New York: Bantam Books, 2004.
Box, George E.P. "Science and Statistics." *Journal of the American Statistical Association* 71, no. 356 (December 1976): 791–799.
Butkus, Matthew A. "A Universe of Bastards." In *Dune and Philosophy: The Weirding Way of the Mentat*, Popular Culture and Philosophy Book 56. edited by Jeffery Nicholas, 75–88. Chicago: Open Court, 2011.
DiTommaso, Lorenzo. "History and Historical Effect in Frank Herbert's *Dune*." *Science Fiction Studies* 19, no. 3 (1992): 311–25.
Erman, Eva, and Niklas Möller. "What's Wrong with Politics in the Duniverse?" In *Dune and Philosophy: The Weirding Way of the Mentat*, Popular Culture and Philosophy Book 56, edited by Jeffery Nicholas, 61–74. Chicago: Open Court, 2011.
Fjellman, Stephen M. "Prescience and Power: *God Emperor of Dune* and the Intellectuals." *Science Fiction Studies* 13, no. 1 (1986): 50–63.
Gates-Scovelle, Sam. "Curse of the Golden Path." In *Dune and Philosophy: The Weirding Way of the Mentat*, Popular Culture and Philosophy Book 56, edited by Jeffery Nicholas, 37–50. Chicago: Open Court, 2011.
Gates-Scovelle, Sam. "Son of the Curse of the Golden Path." In *Dune and Philosophy: The Weirding Way of the Mentat*, Popular Culture and Philosophy Book 56, edited by Jeffery Nicholas, 207–18. Chicago: Open Court, 2011.
Herbert, Brian. Afterword to *Dune*, by Frank Herbert, 868–83. 1965. New York: Ace Books, 2007.
Herbert, Frank. *Chapterhouse: Dune*. 1985. New York: Ace Books, 2007.

Herbert, Frank. *Children of Dune*. 1976. New York: Ace Books, 2007.
Herbert, Frank. *Dune*. 1965. New York: Ace Books, 2007.
Herbert, Frank. "Dune Genesis." *OMNI* 2, no. 10 (July 1980): 72–76.
Herbert, Frank. *Dune Messiah*. 1969. New York: Ace Books, 2007.
Herbert, Frank. *God Emperor of Dune*. 1981. New York: Ace Books, 2007.
Hibberd, James. "'Game of Thrones': George R.R. Martin on That Creepy Flashback Scene." *Entertainment Weekly*, April 12, 2015. https://ew.com/article/2015/04/12/game-thrones-cersei-flashback/.
Hobbes, Thomas. *Leviathan*. 1651, edited by C.B. MacPherson. London: Penguin, 1968.
de Laplace, Pierre-Simon. *A Philosophical Essay on Probabilities*. 1814. Translated by Frederick Wilson Truscott and Frederick Lincoln Emory. New York: John Wiley & Sons, 1902.
Luton, Lawrence S. *The Political Philosophy of Dune*. Doctoral dissertation, Claremont Graduate University, 1979.
Martin, George R.R. *A Feast for Crows*. New York: Bantam Books, 2005.
McCune, David, and Samuel Luke Tunstall. "Calculated Democracy—Explorations in Gerrymandering." *Teaching statistics* 41, no. 2 (2018): 47–53.
Minowitz, Peter. "Prince versus Prophet: Machiavellianism in Frank Herbert's *Dune* Epic." In *Political Science Fiction*, edited by Donald M. Hassler and Clyde Wilcox, 124–47. Columbia, SC: University of South Carolina Press, 1996.
Mulcahy, Kevin. "*The Prince* on Arrakis: Frank Herbert's Dialogue with Machiavelli." *Extrapolation* 37, no. 1 (1996): 22–36.
O'Reilly, Timothy. *Frank Herbert* ("Recognitions" Series). New York: Frederick Ungar, 1981. https://www.oreilly.com/tim/herbert/index.html.
Rudd, Amanda. "Paul's Empire: Imperialism and Assemblage Theory in Frank Herbert's *Dune*." *MOSF Journal of Science Fiction* 1, no. 1 (2016): 45–57.
Shakespeare, William. *The Tragedy of Macbeth*, edited by Sandra Clark and Pamela Mason. Arden Shakespeare, 3rd ser. London: Bloomsbury, 2015.
Simon, Herbert. "A Behavioral Model of Rational Choice." In *Models of Man, Social and Rational: Mathematical Essays on Rational Human Behavior in a Social Setting*. New York: Wiley, 1957.
Sophocles. *The Theban Plays: Oedipus Rex, Oedipus at Colonus and Antigone*, edited by George Young. Dover Thrift Editions. Mineola, NY: Dover Publications, 2006.
Xiao Qiang. "The Road to Digital Unfreedom: President Xi's Surveillance State." *Journal of Democracy* 30, no. 1 (January 2019): 53–67.

"The greatest predator ever known"

The Golden Path and Political Philosophy as Ecology

MICHAEL PHILLIPS

At the climax of *God Emperor of Dune*, the tyrannical God Emperor Leto II gives the rebel Siona Atreides a vision of a possible future should humanity not follow his Golden Path:

> The seeking machines would be there, the smell of blood and entrails, the cowering humans in their burrows aware only that they could not escape ... while all the time the mechanical movement approached, nearer and nearer and nearer ... louder ... louder![1]

In this future, humanity—pointedly described here in animalistic terms—has fallen prey to its own technology. In order to avoid this annihilation, however, Leto uses his powers of political organization and combines political philosophy and ecological principles to create conditions under which humanity can evolve to become less susceptible to such threats to the species.

Beginning 3,500 years after the original Dune trilogy, *God Emperor of Dune* presents the universe under the rule of Leto II, the son of Paul Atreides. The previous novel in the series, *Children of Dune*, concludes with the nine-year-old Leto and his twin sister Ghanima escaping an assassination plot. Leto covers himself with sandtrout—the larval form of the great sandworms that produce the mélange spice—and begins his metamorphosis into a sandworm. By *God Emperor of Dune*, Arrakis has been terraformed into a lush green planet, the sandworms are gone, and the spice cycle has ended. In the intervening millennia, Leto instituted the Golden Path, a grand, long-term strategy by which humanity may avoid

46

the foreseen extermination by thinking machines. In response to Leto's oppressive rule, a group of radicals led by Siona—the product of Leto's breeding program—plots his assassination, while the latest in a series of Duncan Idaho gholas begins to rebel against his God Emperor. Leto's death at the novel's climax enables the Scattering in which, free of Leto's tight control, humanity spreads out across a now open universe and is able to evolve into new modes of being. Unlike the utopian schemes of previous political philosophies, Leto's Golden Path is not concerned with creating a perfect political structure. Its goal is merely survival.

This essay analyzes Leto's reign to show how he uses the principles of sociobiology to inform his political philosophy. Undoing the binary of natural and artificial, sociobiology sees culture—and therefore politics—as a phenotypic adaptation to manage the conflict that results from the competition for resources.[2] Communities are formed so that humans can survive amidst a hostile environment and protect themselves against other groups. As R.D. Alexander states about early humans: "predators became chiefly responsible for forcing men to live in groups, and that those predators were not other species but larger, stronger groups of men."[3] Human culture emerges then from the struggle between predator and prey, each of which conditions the other into further adaptations.

In *God Emperor of Dune*, Leto appropriates this language of sociobiology. When Leto describes himself as "the greatest predator ever known,"[4] his prey is humanity, and the goal of his predation is the "improvement of the human stock."[5] He presents a beneficial view of the predator-prey relationship, which produces new syntheses from otherwise opposing forces. The Reverend Mother Tertius Eileen Anteac of the Bene Gesserit considers oppositional conflict to be the defining principle of life, while ecology is the management of such conflicts. She observes, "that there is a principle of conflict which originated with the single cell and has never deteriorated."[6] Leto counters that life is not founded upon a struggle in which one life form must annihilate the other. Rather, a dialectic emerges through which conflict does not resolve in some final, triumphant outcome, but instead is a continual process in which organisms improve themselves and their chances for survival. Leto extends this ecological viewpoint to his political philosophy. Just as mutual conditioning improves both the prey and the predator, Leto fights his rebels not to stamp out rebellion, but to improve the character of the rebels. In doing so, he improves his ability to combat rebellion. As he tells Siona, "I sharpen my claws on the likes of you."[7] This principle is reformulated in military terms in order to emphasize the benefits of conflict: "Enemies strengthen you. Allies weaken."[8] This strengthening comes in the survival adaptations the predator produces in its prey, which in turn influence the predator.

The Leviathan and Docility: Hobbes, Foucault, and Freud

Describing the art of government as "the mastery of chaos,"[9] Leto posits the role of the sovereign to be the mediation of competing desires of its subjects. In this sense, Leto implicitly follows the writings of Thomas Hobbes by setting himself up as a (quite literal) Leviathan. In *Leviathan*, Hobbes conceives the human animal as a machine, likening it to clock-work,[10] and the Common-wealth is intended as an analog of the human machine. As C.B. MacPherson notes in his introduction, Hobbes's political philosophy was influenced by geometry and the physics of Galileo, which posit a universe structured by abstract, constant laws. When applied to human society, these laws require the reduction of human beings to machines:

> Hobbes's bold hypothesis was that the motion of individual human beings could be reduced to the effects of a mechanical apparatus consisting of sense organs, nerves, muscles, imagination, memory and reason, which apparatus moved in response to the impact (or imagined impact) of external bodies on it.... All human actions could be resolved into elementary motions of body and mind which the scientist could recombine in a way that would explain everything.[11]

Thus, the complexity of human behavior is reduced to responses to outside stimuli based on the desire for security and comfort, as well as the fear of pain and death. This same mechanistic scientific approach is then applied to society as a whole, in which the various individuals within the multitude are like parts within a watch moving according to predictable laws and postulates.

For Hobbes, the goal of human life is happiness, or "Felicity," defined as the satisfaction of material appetites.[12] In the proverbial State of Nature, all humans are engaged in the constant contest for ends with which they satisfy their desires. They will therefore accept some restraint of their powers for the sake "of their own preservation" and to get themselves "out from that miserable condition of Warre, which is naturally consequent (as hath been shewn) to the naturall Passions of men, when there is no visible Power to keep them in awe."[13] Since laws necessarily act as constraints upon desires, they are "contrary to our naturall Passions" and so require a sovereign for enforcement.[14] A social contract is thus instituted whereby individual wills are transferred to a collective unity: "that Mortall God," the Leviathan, in which "the Multitude is united in one person."[15]

The multitude-in-one is explicitly illustrated in Leto, who with regards to the memories of all his ancestors that he possesses declares,

"Those billions are my one."[16] He therefore stands as gestalt of human society and history. Leto's physical form also recalls the Leviathan in a biblical sense. More importantly, however, Leto is the central power that controls a state coincident with the whole universe. His political position is reflected in the myriad of sandtrout that cover his metamorphosing body serving as his skin while Leto himself is "the force that moves the whole."[17] In Hobbes, the Leviathan is an analogy in which the state is envisioned as an organism, with various groups paralleling different body parts beneath the sovereign as the ruling head. Competing factions are brought to heel into a forced harmony as cooperating components under the aegis of the sovereign.

Although Leto expresses a distrust of centralized power, his Imperium follows that pattern. While witnessing the Siaynoq ritual, Duncan Idaho observes that the "lines of power extended directly from Leto out into the populace, but the lines did not often cross."[18] His government has a hierarchical structure with Leto as the controlling head. The aim of the Golden Path, however, is to undo such structures in favor of a rhizomatic decentralization. Because humans cannot survive individually, they must form communities in order to exist, and cooperation between subjects creates a network of interdependency. As Leto muses in his journals, "I watch the sharing of food. This is a form of communication, an inescapable sign of mutual aid which also contains a deadly signal of dependency."[19] While such altruism is necessary, it is the first chain of dependency between subjects that can lead to reified power structure. Leto explains to Duncan, "humankind is like a single-celled creature, bound together by a dangerous glue."[20] There is a paradox to community: it is required for survival, but the unity it produces is dangerous. The Scattering's ability to avoid extinction depends upon a decentralization of humanity foreshadowed in Leto himself. In an assassination attempt, Duncan aims at Leto's brain, but fails since "it was not even a brain of human dimensions anymore, but had spread in nodal congeries throughout his body."[21] This decentralization is finalized at Leto's death when he dissolves into his constituent others: sandtrout that will grow into sandworms, each with a pearl of his awareness.[22] Aside from restarting the spice cycle, this dissolution also symbolizes what will occur as a result of the Scattering when humanity is no longer unified under a centralized power.

In order to maintain order amongst its constituent parts, the state as envisioned by Hobbes must necessarily constrain the desires and energies of its subjects. In *Leviathan*, this constraint is accomplished by the brute force of the "publique sword," but later developments in the technology of sociopolitical organization saw the appearance of subtler, and arguably more effective, methods of attenuating the human tendency to disorder.

In *Discipline and Punish*, Michel Foucault traces the history of punishment as it shifted from bodily punishment to the conditioning of subjects in the modern penitentiary system that produces docile bodies and purports to prevent criminality before it can happen. Such docile bodies represent the Hobbesian dream of individuals as components of a machine working together under the drive of the Leviathan:

> Thus a new demand appears to which discipline must respond: to construct a machine whose effect will be maximised by the concerted articulation of the elementary parts of which it is composed. Discipline is no longer simply an art of distributing bodies, of extracting time from them and accumulating it, but of composing forces in order to obtain an efficient machine.[23]

Through a process of observation and examination that produces a standardized norm against which the individual is measured for deviation, individual bodies are homogenized, serialized, and articulated. In the early penitentiaries that established this system, activity was controlled by the timetable "to establish rhythms, impose particular occupations, regulate the cycles of repetition."[24] In other words, behavior is channeled into set patterns such that bodies behave like machine components. This machined docility encapsulates precisely what Leto warns against: the reduction of human activity to repeating patterns that through their predictability render the species vulnerable.

Just as the disciplinary regime attenuates deviations from the norm, Leto observes that "the secret of community lies in the suppression of the incompatible."[25] Here he appears to describe what Julia Kristeva terms the Abject—that which must be cast out due to its threatening the social order: "It is what escapes that social rationality, that logical order on which a social aggregate is based."[26] Moreover, "it is thus not lack of cleanliness or health that causes abjection but what disturbs identity, system, order. What does not respect borders, positions, rules. The in-between, the ambiguous, the composite."[27] However, casting out this source of instability does not assuage the conflict; it merely represses the conflict such that it remains and will inevitably rechannel itself into other means of expression.

Whereas Hobbes constructs society around a centralized sovereign and Foucault observes how modern society uses discipline in order to produce docile bodies, Sigmund Freud argues in *Civilization and Its Discontents* that the constraint of individual desires—as required by civilization—will create instability by generating neuroses. Like Hobbes, Freud believes that humans are motivated by the satisfaction of desires and the avoidance of suffering. He also cites the competition between individuals as a major source of human suffering. The Leviathan of social regulations is therefore instituted to maximize happiness. And yet suffering persists, which leads Freud to suspect "a piece of unconquerable nature may lie behind" and that civilization itself produces unhappiness precisely because of the constraints it places on individual desires.[28] As such, a return to a more natural mode of existence could alleviate suffering.

According to Freud, in contrast to nature, civilization requires beauty, cleanliness, and order. This drive to order is derived from astronomy and inculcates the same mechanistic repetition of regulated patterns upon human subjects.[29] Human beings do not follow the same organization of astronomical bodies, but "on the contrary, human beings exhibit an inborn tendency to carelessness, irregularity and unreliability in their work, and that a laborious training is needed before they learn to follow the example of their celestial models."[30] Civilization produces order through the restriction of individuals' possibilities of satisfaction, but such restrictions produce a desire for freedom. Civilization is not "the road to perfect pre-ordained men," such as the docile bodies produced by Foucault's discipline. Rather, it "is built upon a renunciation of instinct" that leads to "cultural frustration" as desires necessarily overflow their restrictions.[31] Similarly, Leto asserts that civilization is based on cowardice and taming: "You restrain the will. You regulate the appetites. You fence in the horizons."[32] With the concern for the fencing in of horizons, Leto's critique has metaphysical implications that will be explored later, but he follows Freud's view that the restrictions necessary for the project of civilization produce a dialectic between the will and its appetites, as well as that which regulates them.

Freud identifies two impulses within the human psyche. On the one hand, Eros is "the instinct to preserve living substance and to join it into ever larger units."[33] This impulse is countered by Thanatos, "another, contrary instinct seeking to dissolve those units and to bring them back to their primaeval inorganic state."[34] Whereas civilization is "a process in the service of Eros" as it seeks to combine individuals into "one great unity," Thanatos, that is "the inclination to aggression ... constitutes the greatest impediment to civilization."[35] Given that in a Hobbesian state of nature, any neighbor is a potential prey or predator, this aggression is natural to human beings and must be attenuated by social regulations.[36] This attenuation is achieved by guilt, namely the redirection of aggression against the ego through the formation of a superego that "is ready to put into action against the ego the same harsh aggressiveness that the ego would have liked to satisfy upon other, extraneous individuals."[37] This redirection might produce social stability, but the resulting frustration leads to neurosis so "the price we pay for our advance in civilization is a loss of happiness through the heightening of the sense of guilt."[38] To Leto, it is a much higher price: the ever-increasing imposition of order will render people susceptible to being supplanted by thinking machines—either through the literal extermination as foreseen by Leto or through an erosion of human animality due to "the machine way of thinking."

Leto offers tyranny in exchange for peace, but such control inevitably invites its own overthrow. He describes his "peace" as "enforced tranquility" and observes that "humans have a long history of reacting against tranquility."[39] The pastoral community of Goygoa illustrates the bland, unrewarding life of such tranquility. Goygoa was built on the site of the legendary Sietch Jacurutu, which was originally founded by renegade Fremen who preyed on other Fremen for the water in their bodies. This group—the Iduali—represent an Abject cast out as a result of their threatening the social order (or, rather, the political ecology) of Dune. Indeed, after the Fremen banded together to wipe out the Iduali, the Jacurutu became a taboo subject and was scrubbed permanently from memory.[40] The taming of Jacurutu into Goygoa does not constitute a reintegration of the Abject, but rather its further repression. When Duncan visits Goygoa, he finds the wife and child of one of his previous selves. Just as the desert had been turned to green hills, and Jacurutu to Goygoa, Duncan also had the possibility of enjoying tranquil peace and easy domesticity. As Leto later muses on the previous Duncan, "I would have preferred him to live out his days there in peace, but you well know, Duncan, that you are not a seeker after peace."[41] Duncan's rebellion illustrates precisely why he has value to Leto's breeding program as a wild atavism that can return to humanity the ability to resist the temptations of security and tranquility (even though the ghola is a product of Tleilaxu artifice).

Though the Bene Gesserit believe that, for example, the restrictions on transport have made human beings more sessile,[42] Leto's aim is precisely the opposite. Desires are pent up for explosive release as "holding people planet-bound ... fills them with a longing for travel."[43] When Duncan expresses his disgust at the institutionalized homosexuality in Leto's Fish Speakers, Moneo tells him, "if you try to suppress it, you only increase its power."[44] To suppress desire is to condition humans into being docile subjects, which is ultimately a futile endeavor; these desires can never be fully controlled and can instead reemerge in harmful ways. During a reverie in his ancestral memories, Leto thinks of a nomad horde and asks "where has all of that vigor gone?"[45] Human life in this ordered society has become denaturalized. Human beings, due to a surfeit of tranquility and security, have become overly constrained. Not only does this present the problem of rendering the species susceptible to predators (specifically, machines), but it also raises the larger, philosophical problem of constraining the experience of reality by reducing it to mere mechanism. The disciplinary solution to Hobbes's problem of rebellious wills requires a renunciation of desires and energies. This renunciation truncates human experience.

Nature exceeds artificial, technologically imposed limitations. The satellites that control the weather on Arrakis fail to live up to the machine ideal of perfection for "such perfection was machine-fantasy which faltered under human management."[46] At the very beginning of the novel, Siona and her group of rebels must cross the fittingly named Idaho River in order to escape the predatory D-wolves. Though the product of Ixian artifice, the river also demonstrates the failure of human organization to completely contain and constrain nature as "the water refused to stay in the straight lines Leto's engineers had designed."[47] The river overflows the patterns imposed on it, analogous to Leto's desire for his subjects.

Patterns of History and Machine(d) Minds

History follows a series of patterns, and, as a large-scale polity, Leto's empire is an aggregate of various patterns. One particularly dominant pattern is the pharaonic model, "a disease of government" that Leto defines as the imposition of a strong central power along the lines of Hobbes's proposed Leviathan.[48] It also corresponds to the conception of the State outlined by Gilles Deleuze and Félix Guattari in which the state "is defined by the perpetuation or conservation of organs of power."[49] This perpetuation and conservation of power is part of the pattern of government.[50] Leto observes there is an inherent tendency towards tyranny in all governments, and while it does present the advantage of easier decision-making, the desire for hierarchy leads to frustration along the lines suggested by Freud.[51] Rebellion—ostensibly a means of casting off such imposed patterns—serves instead to reify them. Leto declares that "all rebellions are ordinary and an ultimate bore" because they simply perpetuate old patterns in that "all rebels are closet aristocrats."[52] Just as the repression of desires does not control them but rather rechannels them to emerge elsewhere, suppressed radicals create more problems and produce a cycle of revolution as they ultimately reconstitute the very power structures they seek to overthrow.

Indeed, although Siona represents the *new*—she "lives on the surface of enormous energies" and "was like a clean slate upon which great things might yet be written"[53]—she is still susceptible to the trap of patterns. Though she thinks the Fremen ceremony is stupid, "she dared not break the pattern of it."[54] Her father Moneo is even more bound by patterns. Described as machine-like—dependable but limited—he is upbraided by Leto for raising "reason above all else,"[55] to the extent that Leto exclaims,

"Moneo! Sometimes I think you were made by the Ixians."[56] Consequently, Moneo sees people as machines. When he bests Duncan in combat, he sneers at the ghola, "You're just an older model."[57] While Moneo is technically correct in that Leto's breeding program has improved human capabilities, his statement belies his limited view. First, he thinks in linear, mechanistic terms that insist upon a straight line of material progress. Second, Idaho's obsolescence, or rather "vintage," is part of his strength; his "wilder" nature means that he is able to break out of the patterns that constrain Moneo. Indeed, in this very instance, Idaho shocks himself as his attack on Moneo violated his programming to always defend any Atreides. Though the attack was a failure, it shows nonetheless an ability to adapt behavior in the face of new contingencies and, as such, represents a means by which the ossification of patterns can be attenuated.

For Leto, the random—that which escapes patterns—is essential. He tells an earlier Duncan Idaho ghola, "Chance is the nature of the universe."[58] The prescient Leto tires of the utter predictability of a patterned universe. Absolute knowledge of the future brings boredom, and this "holy boredom" is "good and sufficient reason for the invention of free will."[59] In Christian mythology, the emergence of free will is bound up with the story of the Fall in which free will first asserts itself as disobedience of divine law. Whereas the story of the Fall is traditionally intended as a condemnation of human fallibility, here that very fallibility justifies human existence despite—or rather because of—its detrimental possibilities. Hwi Noree comments "that the Lord Leto is always seeking after newness and originality, but that he is wary of the destructive potential in such things."[60] Indeed, "Leto loved surprises, even nasty ones,"[61] for even in their negative aspect, they reintroduce contingency and thus revitalize a universe which would otherwise degrade into the sterility of frozen patterns. Leto even equates "absolute prediction" to "death."[62] To behave in completely predictable patterns relegates human beings to the status of machines, and thus the Golden Path aims to break people out of such patterns.

Much like human contingency, technology is a double-edged sword. Insisting on the infinite possibilities of material progress, the Ixian technocrat Malky declares, "Man can invent everything."[63] Leto counters that such creativity carries destructive potentiality as people can also "invent catastrophe."[64] These possibilities work in a dialectic such that "history is the constant race between inventions and catastrophe. Education helps but it's never enough. You must also run."[65] Leto links technology with "arafel," a Hebrew word meaning "fog, mist, darkness," but also associated with the Apocalypse. The Golden Path is intended to break the link between technology and death, as indicated in Leto's last words: "Do not fear the Ixians.... They can make the machines, but they can no longer make *arafel*."[66] Indeed, Ixian machinery—specifically the technology of the no-room that renders objects invisible to prescient vision and the navigational computers that can replace the Spice-dependent Guild Navigators—is a part of the Golden Path as it serves to obscure the totalizing vision of the prescient panopticon, as well as to break the pattern of hydraulic despotism from the dependence on spice.

Considering the Ixian mechanical brain, Leto and Anteac discuss the distinction between machine intelligence and human intelligence. When Leto asks whether automation can approach conscious intelligence, Anteac responds "no" because a "machine cannot anticipate every problem of importance to humans. It is the difference between serial bits and an unbroken continuum. We have the one; machines are confined to the other."[67] The mechanized mind fractures reality into serialized segments like components of a machine. Machines are confined within their preprogrammed, established patterns that entail an atomized view of reality as discrete points rather than a holistic continuity. The appeal of the reliability and predictability of machines, however, also points to their danger. By privileging order and predictability, machines—and, more importantly, the reliance on machines—make human beings more machine-like. Leto reminds the Bene Gesserit Truthsayer Marcus Claire Luyseyal of this danger: "The devices themselves condition the users to employ each other the way they employ machines."[68] Individuals then become mere components within the larger social machine, fulfilling Hobbes's vision of society as clockwork. Human intelligence, on the other hand, enables thought beyond set patterns and is therefore more suited to adaptation. As Leto states, "Intelligence creates…. That means you must deal with responses never before imagined. You must confront the new."[69] The Golden Path conditions humanity so that it may survive in the face of new, unknown environmental stimuli; it essentially opens the horizon of existence.

In "Can Thought Go on Without a Body?" Jean-François Lyotard considered the possibility of future machines carrying on the human experience after the extinction of the species. Lyotard conceives people as technical devices that filter and process information, but whereas machines "think in a binary mode," human thought "doesn't work with units of information (bytes), but with intuitive, hypothetical configurations. It accepts imprecise, ambiguous data that don't seem to be selected according to preestablished codes or readability."[70] This mode of thinking is a manifestation of the human biological body, just as binary logic is a manifestation of the computer's digital "body." In order to reproduce human thought, the machine must be structured along the same lines as the human body. This structure is dependent on the difference of gender that Lyotard holds as the embodiment of desire, particularly erotic, for "sexual difference is a paradigm of an incompleteness of not just bodies, but minds too."[71] The motivation for human thought, says Lyotard, is desire: the desire to engender thought where before was unthought. Lyotard's formulation draws a link between the sort of machine thought described by Anteac and the preclusion of desire. In Freudian terms, then, what machines—and machine-thinking—lack is a capacity for Eros.

Machines represent death, the extinction of organic life. The Ixian hunter-seeker machine ("self-propelled death with a machine mind") is designed to "seek out life and reduce that life to its inorganic matter."[72] The result is a state beyond death, outside of the life-death binary, an "ultimate sterility" with no possibility for further life. While this sterility comes in the literal extinction at the hands of a technological singularity, it also connotes the over-reliance on technology. Reliance on machines causes not just an atrophy of human powers, but also a reduction of the human condition. As Leto warns, "The Ixians do not recognize that machine-makers always run the risk of becoming totally machine."[73] Whereas the hunter-seeker and such technology see death as the negation or annihilation of life, Leto presents another view, one that does not rely on the confrontation of two opposing forces, but rather sees them as complementary, cooperative forces. Although the exact manner of his death is, by design, outside of his prescient vision, Leto describes how he "will die four deaths" and "all of these deaths contain the seed of resurrection. ... Each cycle is a reaction to the preceding cycle."[74] He undoes the binary of life and death by making death a part of life. It is "the most profound experience for any creature" as it contains the seeds for further life cycles.[75] If death is seen as a frontier of existence, Leto then points to a means of transcending this frontier: the death of the individual—in this case the divinely mortal God Emperor—opens the possibility of the immortality of the species.

Transcending the Frontier: The Next Step in Evolution

The ossification of patterns, however, negates this transcendence and threatens the survival of the species by producing a bounded horizon with no frontier. Seeking respite from the intrigue at court, Duncan asks to be allowed to escape to some frontier. Leto warns him, however, that in this Imperium, controlled by patterns and predictability, "There is now no place to go where others of us cannot follow and find you."[76] The frontier is a liminal space, a threshold for further development. It can therefore be a threat to organized power structures. Leto describes the nature of aristocratic barriers against frontiers that:

not only enclose planets and land on those planets, they enclose ideas. They repress change…. The surest sign that an aristocracy exists is the discovery of barriers against change, curtains of iron or steel or stone or of any substance which excludes the new, the different.[77]

To the aristocratic mind, such as Moneo's, the new is something abject to be cast out. The conservative aristocrat seeks instead "a return to an idealized past, a past which never in fact existed."[78] Indeed, Leto wants to eliminate "the bourgeois infatuation with peaceful conservation of the past" as it represents repetition of cyclical patterns.[79]

The frontier represents the possibility of escaping the past.[80] Leto's Gift is the removal of history from cycles and convergences. In his dying words, he tells Duncan and Siona:

> I give you a new kind of time without parallels…. It will always diverge. There will be no concurrent points in its curves. I give you the Golden Path. That is my gift. Never again will you have the kinds of concurrence that once you had.[81]

The contrast of curves and parallels here recalls Deleuze and Guattari's distinction between "royal" and "nomad" science.[82] The royal science of the state searches for universal laws that can be reproduced homogeneously according to the logic of the segmented line in "which everything seems calculable and foreseen."[83] As such, it constitutes a closed horizon that limits thought to repeatable, serial, and linear patterns. Whereas royal science extracts constants from variables, nomad science places "variables themselves in a state of continuous variance."[84] It is concerned with particulars rather than universals. The difference between the two forms of "science" can be seen with a comparison of chemistry and alchemy. Chemistry, on the one hand, follows the royal model in that it produces universal categories based on fixed, intrinsic properties that determine the behavior of any given, defined substance. Alchemy, on the other hand, posits material as being continually in flux, always in a state of becoming, flowing from one state to another; this particular piece of lead can be turned to this particular piece of gold.[85] Another example of the distinction would be between the "ideal, fixed essence" of the circle (as conceived by royal science) and the "vague and fluent essence" of roundness (as conceived by nomad science).[86]

Deleuze and Guattari associate royal science with regular, parallel, and segmented lines whereas nomad science is based on curves, spirals, and vortices and "operates in an open space throughout which things-flows are distributed, rather than plotting out a closed space for linear and solid things."[87] Recalling Lucretius's concept of the clinamen,[88] the curve represents deviation from the straight line, that which escapes the universal, much how the individual in the disciplinary society is mea-sured by their deviation from the standardized norm. With its focus on multiplicities, heterogeneity, and becoming, nomad science operates within an open horizon: "it does not ground itself in an all-encompassing totality but is on the contrary deployed in a horizonless milieu that is a smooth space, steppe, desert, or sea."[89] This horizonless milieu is the goal of the Golden Path, as opposed to the closing of horizons and minds that results from a mechanistic worldview.

The closing of minds is symbolized in the cluttered, urbanized land-scape of terraformed Arrakis in which "there is no spiritual freedom" and "everything is closures."[90] Leto seeks to restore the "outward view" found in open landscapes such as the desert. When Leto takes Siona into the Sareer, the last remnant of the planet-wide desert that gave Dune its name, the desert is presented as an endless horizon in which Siona feels "the loss of all familiar reference points."[91] This openness of horizon is a character-istic of smooth spaces that, for Deleuze and Guattari, engender "nomad" rather than "royal" thought. In the desert or the steppe, they write, "There is no line separating earth and sky; there is no intermediate distance, no perspective or contour.... The variability, the polyvocality of directions, is an essential feature of smooth spaces of the rhizome type."[92] Or, as Leto tells Siona: "You are in the unmistakable midst of infinity."[93]

In the smooth space of the desert, the patterns and traces produced by human existence—their operation and inscription upon the land—are erased by the implacable forces of nature as the wind covers Leto and Sio-na's tracks.[94] With this human-imposed order shorn away, the desert can offer an experience of the infinite and eternal. Traditionally a source of enlightenment, the desert provokes "thoughts of religion" as it incites a desire to impose order on otherwise inchoate formlessness.[95] Although the enclosed space of a cave may be the opposite of the open desert, the darkness inside has the same effect of removing all reference points. Thus, Joseph Campbell ascribes the same transcendent possibilities to the cave temples of prehistory as "when the sense of time and space was gone, the visionary journey of the seer began."[96] Siona undertakes a visionary jour-ney in the Sareer. The thirst brought about by the desert is called "*pati-yeh*, the thirst at the edge of death," and by bringing the human body to its biological limits, the very threshold of existence, it brings "clarity of thought" which enables the subject to attain a higher awareness through "*tedah ri-agrimi*, the agony which opens the mind."[97] This enlightenment is a microcosm of the Golden Path itself: an imposition of strictures that push the subject toward a breaking out of those constraints. In this case, bodily hardship leads to mental awakening and merger with the infinite.

Leto wants a direct experience of reality. He beholds the whole, not atomized segments or opposing forces. Moneo, on the other hand, cannot behold the totality of existence. Leto asks him, "Why do you insist on taking pieces out of the continuum? … When you see a spectrum, do you desire one color there above all the others?"[98] To desire one color is to perceive one color atomistically, distinct from all the others, rather than seeing the spectrum as a continuity in which all colors exist together with no distinct lines of differentiation. Moneo cannot exist in a world with an unbounded horizon. Leto exhorts him to "take charge of [his] own existence" and tells his majordomo, "there's no reassuring ceiling over you, Moneo. Only an open sky full of changes. Welcome it. Every sense you possess is an instrument for reacting to change."[99] For Moneo, the only transcendence can be death. As the bridge carrying Leto and Hwi to their wedding is destroyed and Moneo falls "freely … in the ecstasy of awareness. The universe opened for him like clear glass, everything flowing in a no-Time."[100] At the moment of his death, Moneo transcends his existence and extricates himself from history. His flow into an open universe of "no-Time" renders him into a state similar to Hwi, who, to Leto engaging in a temporal probe of his bride-to-be, "seemed timeless—outside of time in a deeply peaceful way."[101] However, whereas Hwi could exist in such a state of constant becoming, it is only through death that Moneo can transcend.

By attaining the visionary experience, Duncan is a foil to Moneo. His climbing the wall that separates Tuono village from the surrounding desert is a symbolic journey of transcendence. When Nayla—the Fish Speaker that Leto has placed as a mole within the rebellion—sees Duncan at the top of the wall, she beholds him as "a demiurge who stood *next* to God. But he could breed."[102] Duncan has reached the threshold of the eternal and thus becomes the "true visionary," which Leto defines as a "person who has stood in the presence of God with the full knowledge of where he stands."[103] The individual who has experienced the infinite and eternal is a threat to the political order: Leto describes such a person as "the most immediate danger to my stewardship" because "visionary ecstasy releases energies which are like the energies of sex—uncaring for anything except creation."[104] The release of these powerful erotic desires carries the potential for instability.

Nonetheless, the energies released through "visionary ecstasy" allow for the transcendence that Leto is trying to effect through the Golden Path. Duncan standing at the top of the wall symbolizes humanity standing at the threshold of the next step in its evolution. His joining with Siona—whose very name connotes the promised land of Zion—will enable not only the preservation of the human species, but along with other developments consequent to the Golden Path (such as Tleilaxu-manufactured spice, Ixian computers, and no-ships hidden from prescient vision) it will also prevent the formation of centralized, unitary power structures that undermine the human condition. More generally, the Scattering symbolizes an opening up of humanity's horizon—a reintroduction of an endless frontier that restores the outward view and offers new possibilities for the continual evolution of the species. The goal of Leto's predations has been achieved. As a result of his conditioning over the millennia, his prey has become less susceptible to potential threats whether they be predatory machines or even tyrannical Leviathans such as Leto himself.

NOTES

1. Herbert, *God Emperor of Dune*, 348.
2. Lorenz, *On Aggression*, 113.
3. Alexander, 116, quoted in Ruse, *Sociobiology*, 56.
4. Herbert, *God Emperor of Dune*, 12.
5. *Ibid.*, 54.
6. *Ibid.*, 144.
7. *Ibid.*, 249.
8. *Ibid.*, 40.
9. *Ibid.*, 21.
10. Hobbes, *Leviathan*, 81.
11. *Ibid.*, 28–29.
12. *Ibid.*, 160.
13. *Ibid.*, 223.
14. *Ibid.*, 223.
15. *Ibid.*, 227.
16. Herbert, *God Emperor of Dune*, 222.
17. *Ibid.*, 11.
18. *Ibid.*, 172.
19. *Ibid.*, 207.
20. *Ibid.*, 234.
21. *Ibid.*, 22.
22. *Ibid.*, 354; cf. 86.
23. Foucault, *Discipline and Punish*, 164.
24. *Ibid.*, 149.
25. Herbert, *God Emperor of Dune*, 145.
26. Kristeva, *Powers of Horror*, 65.
27. *Ibid.*, 4.
28. Freud, *Civilization and Its Discontents*, 38.
29. *Ibid.*, 46.
30. *Ibid.*, 47.
31. *Ibid.*, 50.
32. Herbert, *God Emperor of Dune*, 310.
33. Freud, *Civilization and Its Discontents*, 77.
34. *Ibid.*, 77.
35. *Ibid.*, 81.
36. *Ibid.*, 68.
37. *Ibid.*, 84.
38. *Ibid.*, 97.
39. Herbert, *God Emperor of Dune*, 77.

40. Herbert, *Children of Dune*, 213.
41. Herbert, *God Emperor of Dune*, 170.
42. *Ibid.*, 63.
43. *Ibid.*, 203.
44. *Ibid.*, 272.
45. *Ibid.*, 4.
46. *Ibid.*, 262.
47. *Ibid.*, 8.
48. *Ibid.*, 108.
49. Deleuze and Guattari, *A Thousand Plateaux*, 357.
50. cf. Rudd, "Paul's Empire: Imperialism and Assemblage Theory in Frank Herbert's *Dune*," for an analysis of Paul's empire at the end of *Dune* as an assemblage, that is a whole defined not by its constituent components so much as by the *interactions* between them. When these interactions are restructured, as Rudd argues that occurs when Paul restructures the Galactic Imperium of the Padishah Emperor Shaddam, a new assemblage is produced: "Paul's empire, composed of the elements of Shaddam's (re-arranged and placed in new relations to each other), along with elements from Fremen culture and militia power, is in fact an entirely new assemblage, both properly oriented to its linear historical processes and also a total paradigmatic shift from the previous empire" (47).
    However, it is not clear if and to what extent Paul's new assemblage is a break from history and its patterns. Though the lines of power may be rearranged, Paul remains the central, charismatic leader with the Fremen replacing the Sardaukar. As shown in *Dune Messiah*, Paul is ultimately unable to exercise complete control over the empire he has assembled, but his description in Rudd's concluding statement presages Leto's ability to break from history's cycles, progressions, and other patterns: "No single, all-seeing individual may orchestrate the concert of imperial forces; but occasionally, a charismatic and powerful individual such as Paul Muad'Dib Atreides has the ability to break through systems, shift paradigms, and change the paths of those forces" (56).
51. Herbert, *God Emperor of Dune*, 240.
52. *Ibid.*, 21.
53. *Ibid.*, 30.
54. *Ibid.*, 43.
55. *Ibid.*, 307.
56. *Ibid.*, 29.
57. *Ibid.*, 275.
58. *Ibid.*, 16.
59. *Ibid.*, 35.
60. *Ibid.*, 51.
61. *Ibid.*, 16.
62. *Ibid.*
63. *Ibid.*, 331.
64. *Ibid.*
65. *Ibid.*
66. *Ibid.*, 355.
67. *Ibid.*, 149.
68. *Ibid.*, 151.
69. *Ibid.*, 149.
70. Lyotard, "Can Thought Go on Without a Body?" 292.
71. *Ibid.*, 298.
72. Herbert, *God Emperor of Dune*, 200.
73. *Ibid.*, 200–201.
74. *Ibid.*, 202.
75. *Ibid.*, 204.
76. *Ibid.*, 233.
77. *Ibid.*, 234.
78. *Ibid.*, 330.

79. *Ibid.*, 340.

80. Higgins's "Psychic Decolonization in 1960s Science Fiction," examines *Dune*'s depiction of a marginalized, colonized frontier rising up against its imperial oppressors. The decolonization of the Fremen under Paul's leadership coincides with the internal decolonization that Paul undergoes when he ingests the Water of Life. The consequent near-death experience gives him "access to complete and perfect information" and so frees him "from the unpredictable terrors of contingency" (239). Higgins notes, however, that the decolonial project depicted in *Dune* is undermined as the marginalized Fremen are led by the imperial outsider Paul (preceded by the imperial agents Pardot and Liet-Kynes) such that "[r]ather than dismantling the Imperium, the novel posits the redemption of Empire through the enlightened guidance of a male superman who has successfully decolonized his own inner space" (236–7). Higgins' statement that Paul's knowledge frees him the "terrors of contingency" overlooks how Paul sees himself as bound by the history he foresees. Indeed, in *Dune Messiah*, Paul describes being "consumed by the raw power" of oracular vision: "Terrible purpose! In that moment, his whole life was a limb shaken by the departure of a bird... and that bird was *chance*. Free will. *I succumbed to the lure of the oracle*, he thought" (40). As such, just as the exterior decolonization is problematized by its resulting from imperial agents, the purported interior decolonization remains questionable or, at least, not fully demonstrated.

81. *Ibid.*, 353.

82. Deleuze and Guattari use the term "science" to describe both these forms of knowledge production, which might be a bit misleading. The commonly accepted definition of the scientific method would align with so-called "royal" science. It may be therefore more constructive to use the terms "thought" or "epistemology" instead.

83. Deleuze and Guattari, *A Thousand Plateaux*, 195, 369.

84. *Ibid.*, 369.

85. Alchemy is used as an example here by virtue of its easy apposition to chemistry. Deleuze and Guattari consider metallurgy to be the nomad science *par excellence* for much the same reasons ascribed here to alchemy (cf. *ibid.*, 410–411).

86. *Ibid.*, 367.

87. *Ibid.*, 361.

88. cf. Lucretius, *On the Nature Of Things,* 36.

89. Deleuze and Guattari, *A Thousand Plateaux*, 379.

90. Herbert, *God Emperor of Dune*, 59.

91. *Ibid.*, 264.

92. Deleuze and Guattari, *A Thousand Plateaux*, 382.

93. Herbert, *God Emperor of Dune*, 268.

94. *Ibid.*, 267.

95. *Ibid.*, 264.

96. Campbell, *The Masks of God*, 397.

97. Herbert, *God Emperor of Dune*, 291.

98. *Ibid.*, 307.

99. *Ibid.*, 342.

100. *Ibid.*, 350.

101. *Ibid.*, 130.

102. *Ibid.*, 347.

103. *Ibid.*, 315.

104. *Ibid.*

Works Cited

Alexander, R.D. "The Search for an Evolutionary Philosophy." *Proceedings of the Royal Society of Victoria* 84 (1971): 99–120.

Campbell, Joseph. *The Masks of God: Primitive Mythology.* 1959. London: Penguin, 1976.

Deleuze, Gilles, and Félix Guattari. *A Thousand Plateaux: Capitalism and Schizophrenia.* 1980. Translated by Brian Massumi. Minneapolis: University of Minnesota Press, 1987.

Foucault, Michel. *Discipline and Punish: The Birth of the Prison.* 1975. Translated by Alan Sheridan. New York: Vintage, 1995.

Freud, Sigmund. *Civilization and Its Discontents.* 1930. Translated and edited by James Strachey. New York: W.W. Norton, 1989.

Herbert, Frank. *Dune.* 1965. New York: Berkley, 1977.

Herbert, Frank. *Dune Messiah.* 1969. New York: Berkley, 1975.

Herbert, Frank. *Children of Dune.* 1976. New York: Berkley, 1977.

Herbert, Frank. *God Emperor of Dune.* 1981. New York: Berkley, 1982.

Higgins, David M. "Psychic Decolonization in 1960s Science Fiction." *Science Fiction Studies* 40, no. 2 (July 2013): 228–245.

Hobbes, Thomas. *Leviathan.* 1651, edited by C.B. MacPherson. London: Penguin, 1968.

Kristeva, Julia. *Powers of Horror: An Essay on Abjection.* 1980. Translated by Leon S. Roudiez. New York: Columbia University Press, 1982.

Lorenz, Konrad. *On Aggression.* New York: Harcourt Brace and World, 1966.

Lucretius. *On The Nature of Things.* Trans. Wendell Clausen. New York: Washington Square Press, 1965.

Lyotard, Jean-François. "Can Thought Go on Without A Body?" 1988. Translated by Bruce Boone and Lee Hildreth. In *Materialities of Communication,* edited by Hans Ulrich Gumbrecht and K. Ludwig Pfeiffer, 286–300. Stanford, CA: Stanford University Press, 1994.

Rudd, Amanda. "Paul's Empire: Imperialism and Assemblage Theory in Frank Herbert's *Dune.*" *MOSF Journal of Science Fiction* 1, no. 1 (January 2016): 45–57.

Ruse, Michael. *Sociobiology: Sense or Nonsense?* Dordrecht: Netherlands D. Reidel, 1979.

He Who Controls Knowledge Controls the Universe

Leto II and the Golden Path

Caroline Anne Womack

Frank Herbert's *God Emperor of Dune* is one of the most polarizing books in the Dune series.[1] Some fans dislike the fact that because the book is set thousands of years after *Children of Dune*, the only familiar characters are Leto II and a Duncan Idaho ghola. Another issue for some readers is that Leto II is not relatable due to his prescience, ancestral memories, and the fact that he is physically more sandworm than man. The novel is also divisive due to the abrupt change in narrative structure from the previous Dune novels. The first three novels deal primarily with the Atreides family, one of several Great Houses residing on planets throughout the Dune universe and part of the Landsraad. Taking a different approach from the broad, sweeping story that spanned several generations, *God Emperor of Dune* focuses on Paul Atreides's son Leto II at the very end of his reign on Arrakis. The novel is less about family drama or political intrigue and more about humanity as a whole, as shown through Leto's palaverous speeches to Moneo, Duncan, and Hwi Noree. Rather than covering all 3,500 years of his reign, the novel focuses only on the last few months. This compressed timeframe heightens the intensity of the almost Aristotelian drama. While Leto himself is almost entirely sandworm in appearance, the physical changes to Leto's body only serve to enhance his deep understanding of human nature as expressed by his decision to sacrifice himself in order to save humanity from itself.[2]

Leto II's plan to save humanity through the Golden Path using his ancestral memories and prescient vision is, like all humanity itself, flawed. He follows through with his intention to become both god and tyrant to his people in order to teach humanity a lesson, but, as is often the case, history is bound to repeat itself. The collective human memory is short and people easily forget the horrors of the past. Additionally, if only Leto's version of history is permitted to survive, without multiple perspectives, this decreases the chance that humans will remember everything. As all humans are flawed, so too is Leto, even if he is slowly metamorphosing into a sandworm. Ironically, the closer he evolves into a full sandworm, the more human his consciousness becomes.

This essay explores Leto's terrible purpose, his problematic Golden Path, and his ultimate tragic fall. Through the lens of Robert Sapolsky's approach to human behavior and Aristotle's view of the tragic hero, I take both a scientific and literary approach to examining Leto's character. I discuss the human proclivity toward violence in certain approved situations and explore the aspects of Leto II's character that portray him as a dangerously sympathetic tyrant. Leto II's metamorphosis and reign as God Emperor conveys how the death of a universally hated symbol of stability ultimately unites humanity in such a way that they realize their full potential to evolve and avoid destruction.

Leto the Tyrant

In his book *Behave*, Sapolsky deconstructs the reasons behind human behavior through both neurobiological and cultural perspectives. He argues that both the best and the worst of human behaviors, such as our empathy and our predisposition toward violence, are rooted in biology.[3] He concludes that the tribal "Us" versus "Them" mentality which is activated in the amygdala causes humans to be easily manipulated and what is considered "right" depends on cultural context. Oxytocin, a hormone which plays a role in social bonding, serves only to increase the effects of this and our inherent biases.[4] Sapolsky concludes that the studies conducted by Carsten de Dreu show that oxytocin mostly likely evolved to increase group cohesion in humans—our sense of "Us"—and subsequently causes people to view outsiders—"Them"—as a threat. De Dreu's second study reveals that people are more willing to sacrifice those classified as an outsider than a person identified as a member of their social group, meaning that this hormone makes humans ethnocentric and xenophobic.[5] In spite of this, there are universal morals that ought to unite us, such as the Golden Rule, as well as taboos against "at least some type of murder and of theft … and sexual practice."[6] Even without a human sense of morality, compassion, or empathy, G.E. Rice and P. Gainer's study shows that rats help free other rats from a trap, even if they are not biologically related or rewarded with socializing afterwards.[7] Inevitably, whether it is for a culturally acceptable act of "good" or "evil," we, like the rats, face choices and how we make those choices defines who we are. Although violent acts are a part of our biology, ultimately, all people are capable of making compassionate decisions.[8]

Leto would seem to agree with Sapolsky's conclusion that violence is an intrinsic part of human nature, something that is unavoidable and only to be despised under certain circumstances. Sapolsky claims that "[humans] build theologies around violence, elect leaders who excel at it."[9] Similarly, in order to create his peace, God Emperor Leto must use violence, which he believes is justified. During the very first year of his reign, he had at least nine historians executed. After they were "rendered unconscious" they were "then burned on pyres of their own published works" so that Leto alone would be in charge of preserving his own version of history.[10] From there, Leto's Fish Speakers—a fanatical religious group of warrior women solely devoted to their God Emperor—enforce the peace on other planets in the known universe. Violence goes hand-in-hand with religion, as divine blessing allows the perpetrators to feel morally justified in committing violent acts against those whom they deem as "outsiders."[11] In another act of Leto's cultural homogenization, as the desert on Arrakis dies out, the Fremen are relegated to museums, merely mimicking rituals of the past without knowing or understanding the meaning behind them.

The Fremen way is not the only culture Leto's reign represses. Everyone must worship the God Emperor and any attempt to challenge his rule is culled by the Fish Speakers.[12] Leto purposefully allows some rebellion to occur so people can vent their frustration, but he ultimately ends up co-opting the leaders. He does so in order to reassert his dominance and even goes as far as to declare that rebels inevitably become his most devoted followers; Moneo, Leto's majordomo in God Emperor of Dune, is a notable example of this.[13] For the people in Leto's empire to see an influential rebel leader turn into a loyal servant of the God Emperor only reinforces the public perception that Leto is truly a god.

The homogenization of family life, including the physical appearance of homes and cities, serves to unite the people within his empire. Dancing is prohibited except in the remnants of the spice orgy, which is now dubbed "Siaynoq," a religious festival held every ten years for the Fish Speakers to commune with the God Emperor. Having removed the families of the Great Houses, the local governments are ruled by proxy through Fish Speakers stationed on every planet. Although Leto permits the Bene Gesserit Sisterhood to survive, it is only authorized to do so under his direct control, down to the very allotment of spice he grants them. It is interesting that although the Bene Gesserit continue to educate women from the former Great Houses, Leto abolishes the male-dominated Mentat school. This begs the question of whether Leto fears educated men in particular or men generally, given that, as Sapolsky notes, male testosterone biologically leads to increased anxiety, which under the right circumstances also increases aggression.[14] In a conversation with Duncan about why he has a female army, Leto insists it is because men are "susceptible to class fixations" that in turn "create layered societies" which are the "ultimate invitation to violence," whereas women "make common cause … which transcends class and caste."[15] Leto, in this case, has his houris reeducate men to "wean the violent drives away from their adolescent fixations"[16] so that the men will mature. Due to Leto's belief that women are naturally less aggressive than men, he encourages the society to be female-dominated while limiting the men to serve as breeding stock.

Removing opportunities for the education of men and limiting free speech allows for greater control, but also contradicts Leto's goal of breeding smarter, more astute humans. The Duncan Idaho ghola who serves Leto acts as a mirror to the "barbaric" past, but also serves a reminder of what has been lost. Leto could have accurately preserved all of the diversity of human culture, including humanity's origin on Earth, because he can remember everything in perfect detail through the voices of his ancestors. Instead of being a teacher and educating the people under his rule, he keeps this knowledge of the past from them in order to maintain control, thinking that he knows what is best for humanity. It is later revealed in *Chapterhouse: Dune* that:

> The Order of Mentats, founded by Gilbertus Albans; [received] temporary sanctuary with Bene Tleilaxu who hoped to incorporate them into Tleilaxu hegemony; spread into uncounted "seed schools"; suppressed by Leto II because they formed a nucleus of independent opposition.[17]

Education, except schools entirely controlled by the dictator, leads to free thinking and that must be suppressed in order to control people.[18] This is perhaps why Leto appears to only breed through the Atreides line rather than through other noble lineages. Leto also keeps his subjects planet-bound in order to "keep them out of mischief."[19] Ultimately, his intention with this oppression is to increase their intrinsic desire to leave home and explore the universe.

Controversially, Sapolsky claims that the concept of free will itself is more an innate desire for human agency than a biological truth.[20] This begs the question of how much people in the Dune universe can trust prescience. One deviation from a perceived future could alter it entirely, but from the perspectives of both Paul and Leto, every possible outcome they could see results in the destruction of the human race.[21] The only way forward is the Golden Path. Nevertheless, by not allowing people to make their own mistakes and removing free will, it does not make their lives any happier or more fulfilled. How do we know that the Golden Path truly is the only way to save humanity? How truly reliable are Paul and Leto? How reliable is prescience? If prescience originates from a human entity, is it not also capable of human fallibility? When Leto refuses to let humans carve their own path, he is limiting their agency. Perhaps leaving humans to their own devices would have led to a brighter future without the machinations of the God Emperor. Because free will is taken away and humans cannot live as long as Leto, they have no choice but to go along with his decisions for the human race. With all of his knowledge of the past and the future, there may have been other ways to allow humans to evolve on their own without being so repressed, but those options are forbidden, with Leto even going so far as to decide, like the Bene Gesserit, who would breed with whom.

It is interesting to note that Leto only desires to use the Bene Gesserit breeding program to breed through the Atreides line a way for humans to hide from prescient vision, but there is no indication that he desires to attempt to remove the violent urges inherent in human DNA. In fact, Leto has been breeding the very best humans, as Moneo tells a humiliated Duncan: "[Leto] has been breeding us for a long time, Duncan, strengthening many things in us. He has bred us for speed, for intelligence, for self-restraint, for sensitivity. You're … you're just an older model."[22] Sapolsky notes that both the best and worst qualities of humans are part of our biology, which makes it all the more questionable as to why Leto would not attempt to get rid of negative traits.[23] Do humans need to have violent urges in order to survive what Leto cannot see coming in the future? Is violence a necessary evil for our species to evolve?

Leto's own evolution into a giant sandworm is ironic because worms or other snake-like animals are considered symbols of evil in many religions. Both Judaism and Christianity view the snake as representative of evil.[24] In European medieval literature, wyverns, dragons, serpents, and worms are used interchangeably as symbols for Satan.[25] In *God Emperor of Dune*, Leto's followers call him Shai-Hulud and, after his final transformation into the Divided God, he declares, "When I am gone, they must call me Shaitan."[26] More than 1,500 years later, *Heretics of Dune* confirms that the priests believe "The Tyrant begat Shaitan."[27] In Islamic theology, *shaitan* is a demon or devil,[28] while in Biblical Hebrew the word for snake, *nachash*, is also used interchangeably for sorcery or witchcraft. Biblical Hebrew also uses the word *tannin* or sea serpent for a symbol of evil.[29] This is explicitly echoed in *Chapterhouse: Dune* when the Rabbi, speaking to the Reverend Mother Rebecca, discusses the nature of God. He agrees that Leto II was a tyrant and "had Satan's own powers."[30] Disagreeing that

Leto was actually God, he adds, "I share [the Bene Gesserit] fear of that. He was not so much prescient as he was cement. He fixed the shape of what he saw."[31] Leto's metamorphosis is similarly reviled and feared by a portion of the populace who are not indoctrinated followers of his religion. With the monopoly on spice, Leto II has a tight hold on the Bene Gesserit, Ixians, and Tleilaxu. These three groups play a precarious game for thousands of years, trying to please him to obtain more spice allotments, but also to steer clear of his wrath. Similarly, at the novel's beginning, a group of Fremen rebels, led by Siona, steal Leto's journals in an effort to find a way to destroy "The Worm" Leto.

When characters such as Siona and others outside of the city of Arrakeen (now called the Festival City of Onn) refer to Leto as "The Worm," it deemphasizes the fact that Leto's brain is human and the decisions he makes are the product of several millennia of human ancestral memories. Dehumanization is a common response to individuals who commit unspeakable acts of violence. Society regularly refers to terrorists, murderers, and war criminals as something other than human. Dehumanizing Leto as the monstrous Worm allows the rebels to not only separate themselves from the possibility that they too could commit such atrocities, but also enables them to justify killing him. It would be unethical for the rebels to kill another human, but his almost entirely sandworm body removes the human connection to their crime. In an article from *The New Yorker*, Daniel Mendelsohn discusses the "great ethical wisdom" in allowing Boston Marathon bomber Tamerlan Tsarnaev to be buried on American soil:

> ...for in doing so, you are insisting that the criminal, however heinous, is precisely not a "monster." Whatever else is true of the terrible crime that Tamerlan Tsarnaev is accused of having perpetrated, it was, all too clearly, the product of an entirely human psyche, horribly motivated by beliefs and passions that are very human indeed—*deina* in the worst possible sense. To call him a monster is to treat this enemy's mind precisely the way some would treat his unburied body—which is to say, to put it beyond the reach of human consideration (and therefore, paradoxically, to refuse to confront his "monstrosity" at all).[32]

Refusing to confront the monstrosity of Leto's actions is to refuse to admit that all humans are capable of such atrocities. To ignore the fact that Leto is human at least in his consciousness—and, through Other Memory, is in touch with much of humanity's past—trivializes both his actions and his assassination. Duncan ultimately decides to turn on Leto because, in his opinion, The Worm is no longer an Atreides; he is an abomination. Sapolsky posits, "the tool of the propagandist is to effectively exploit symbols of revulsion in the service of hate."[33] In allowing Siona to escape his D-wolves at the novel's beginning, knowing she had his secret journals,

Leto's journals end up serving as a type of propaganda. Leto permits his enemies to find a weakness they can exploit. Their revulsion of The Worm is what drives the rebels to assassinate Leto and release humanity from his tyranny, paving the way for Leto's desire to die.

In stark contrast to Golden Ages of the past—such as the rule of Pericles in ancient Greece, Caesar Augustus in ancient Rome, or Elizabeth I in England—Leto's Peace is not a time of cultural advancement or exploration. His reign is 3,500 years of stagnation and cultural repression. Unlike the previous Golden Ages, in which people prospered during times of external war, Leto enforces peace at home and abroad in spite of the human need for rebellion. In reference to the Golden Path, Leto declares that he promises humanity "a lesson their bones would remember."[34] He claims that humans "say they seek security and quiet, the condition they call peace. Even as they speak, they create the seeds of turmoil and violence. If they find their quiet security, they squirm in it. How boring they find it."[35] In an effort to support the Jacobite Rebellion against King George I, Lord Bolingbroke astutely observes in his treatise *The Idea of a Patriot King* that:

> absolute stability is not to be expected in any thing[sic] human ... the best instituted governments, like the best constituted animal bodies, carry in them the seeds of their destruction: and, though they grow and improve for a time, they will soon tend visibly to their dissolution.[36]

This is, perhaps, why Leto emphasizes the religious aspects of his tyrannical reign: in separating himself as a god, he is not only omniscient and prescient, but can also claim immunity from human laws. In the eyes of the several generations of people living on Arrakis and other planets under his rule, he appears to be omnipotent and immortal. The repression of culture and any sort of rebellion is linked to his becoming a god to his people, unquestionable and inconceivable. Leto's views on this are expounded upon in epigraphs containing quotes from Leto's journals in *Heretics of Dune* and also in his didactic speech to Sister Chenoeh in *God Emperor of Dune*:

> I am not a leader nor even a guide. A god. Remember that. I am quite different from leaders and guides. Gods need take no responsibility for anything except genesis. Gods accept everything and thus accept nothing. Gods must be identifiable yet remain anonymous. Gods do not need a spirit world. My spirits dwell within me, answerable to my slightest summons.[37]

Just like the Mandate of Heaven in imperial China or the divine rule of ancient Egyptian pharaohs, the implication here is that a god cannot be wrong and therefore people cannot defy his decisions. Similar to Eastern mythological rulers, such as Emperor Jimmu of Japan who claimed to be a descendant of the Sun Goddess Amaterasu, Leto justifies his rule using the iconography of godhood and his religious following.

The age of "Leto's Peace" is hardly worth admiring. Its sole goal is preserving humans from what we can assume is the threat of the resurgence of thinking machines.[38] Like the mythical King Arthur's reign, the Golden Age of Leto's Peace cannot last. Inevitably, the violence that is so ingrained in the human psyche cannot be pacified. Leto knows this and even uses violence as a civilizing force. Nobert Elias's book *The Civilizing Process* dissects the concept of civility and shows that humans are not more or less "civilized" now than we were in the past; instead, there are just different, socially approved outlets for violence in modern societies.[39] It is therefore plausible that thousands of years into Leto's future humans will still have the natural propensity toward violence. Leto ultimately cannot know if his tyranny will succeed in preserving humanity after it is no longer visible to him. The peace would turn out to be temporary, as seen in the conflicts between the Bene Gesserit, Honored Matres, Ixians, Tleilaxu, and Face Dancers in *Heretics of Dune* and *Chapterhouse: Dune*. This is also seen in Brian Herbert and Kevin J. Anderson's continuation of the series in *Hunters of Dune* and *Sandworms of Dune* in which thinking machines return to wreak havoc on humanity.[40] However, in spite of this ongoing violence, humans have spread throughout the galaxy enough that they end up prevailing against the thinking machines.[41]

Leto the Tragic Hero

Although *God Emperor of Dune* can be read through a sociocultural and biological critique of humanity as a whole—for it is a warning about the destructive nature of blindly following any sort of ruler or religious leader—it is also important to take a more intimate look at what drives the character of Leto II. Leto is not just a symbolic tyrannical leader, but also a person who made certain choices that ended up carving the path for the future of the human race. Several aspects of *God Emperor of Dune* adhere closely to Aristotle's views on what makes a good tragedy. Aristotle's ideal plot should be in a compressed timeframe to increase the tension and immediacy of the tragedy.[42] Unlike other novels in the Dune series, *God Emperor* takes place within the span of a few months and primarily on the planet of Arrakis. Aristotle also believed that the protagonist should be a sympathetic hero who is from a Great House, like the Atreides.[43] Stephen Fjellman argues that academics or intellectuals in general find it easier to sympathize with Leto because of his desire to look at the past as an example of what humans are capable of in order to avoid making the same mistakes in the future.[44] Fjellman also states that intellectuals often dream of wielding such pervasive power so that they can effectuate change more quickly than would be possible through more democratic means. The ability to empathize with Leto paints him as a tragic hero. Herbert purposefully depicts this tyrant as sympathetic to prompt readers to reexamine their own morality as they judge Leto's decisions.

Another aspect of the Aristotelean tragic hero is the *hamartia*, or tragic flaw. Although some might argue that the Ixians are correct—that love is Leto's weakness—it is in fact Leto's hubris that inevitably causes his downfall.[45] Leto not only knows that he is more intelligent than others, but he also knows that he is undefeatable. This arrogance leads him to make several errors in judgment which incite the seed of rebellion within the universal society. At the end of *Children of Dune*, Leto displays his now impenetrable skin by walking through fire and having the naibs strike him with various weapons, such as knives and acids. He even "[ate] their poisons and laughed at them."[46] This public demonstration, and the way he mocks the Fremen attempts to destroy him, shows his arrogance. Not only does Leto flaunt his power, but he also intimidates the people so that they will both fear and be in awe of this self-imposed god. Afterwards, there is a ceremony in the Great Hall, announcing Leto as the new leader. The naibs from various Fremen tribes pay homage to him, giving him "gifts fitting for a god of terrifying powers, a god of vengeance who promised them peace."[47] They cannot understand Leto or his newfound powers, nor can they ignore him. The naibs openly decide it is in their best interest to bow in reverence to this paradoxical leader lest they incur his wrath.

For thousands of years afterward and throughout *God Emperor*, Leto continually amuses himself by manipulating certain factions and playing them against each other. He even openly brags that he can defeat the Ixians.[48] Leto also enjoys hearing himself talk, going on long diatribes about various topics with Moneo, Duncan, Siona, and Hwi in order to showcase his intellectual superiority. This arrogance inevitably causes him to make several tragic errors. Even though his choices are unlike the tragic errors in judgment made by Creon in *Antigone* and Oedipus in *Oedipus Rex*, the errors are equally as fatal because Leto is the conductor of his own fate.

Leto's first fatal error in judgment stems from the creation of Hwi Noree in the no-chamber on Ix. Although Leto indirectly arranges this and senses Hwi's origin, he can not anticipate that she will become the center of a love triangle between his favorite servant, Duncan, and himself. Leto also does not anticipate just how deeply he will fall in love with her. Because he trusts Hwi implicitly, he sends her on a mission to speak with the secret Mentat Reverend Mother Anteac on his behalf. During this interesting conversation, Anteac questions Hwi as to whether or not she is privy to the plot to destroy the God Emperor. Although Hwi informs her that she knows the Ixians bred her for the specific purpose of "beguiling" the God Emperor so that they might have some insight into his decision-making process, Anteac cannot determine if Hwi is trustworthy for "Hwi [speaks] in an odd flatness which even Anteac's truthsense and abilities as a Mentat [find] hard to decipher."[49] The fact that Anteac cannot read Hwi begs the question of Hwi's true nature. One could interpret this exchange as indicating that Hwi is knowingly part of the plot to destroy Leto. Perhaps she never did love him and was actually putting on a façade the entire time. Regardless of her true intentions, Leto aids in his own destruction by having Hwi tell Anteac about the no-chamber and informing Anteac of Hwi's creation.

Leto's *anagnorisis*, or recognition, comes in the form of regretting his actions. After having fallen hard for Hwi, he desperately wishes he could reverse the metamorphosis and have a human body again, thinking "To hell with the Golden Path!" and questioning, "When I made this choice, what were my expectations?"[50] Even though Leto was born with the memories of all of his ancestors, his body was still that of a child when he took on the burden of the sandtrout. At only nine years old, Leto was still physically new to the world while being simultaneously very old mentally. Even though he was born with prescient vision, the memories of all of his ancestors, and knew full well the consequences of this choice, he still was unable to live and experience adulthood as a human being. With only Other Memories as a comfort, he was unable to make new memories of his own. How fair is it for Leto to be unable to live a full human life? This, in itself, is a tragedy. Hwi observes that Leto pities himself because he is "the ultimate loner forced to look at what might have been," while she insists that his "original unselfish choice fills [him] now with selfishness."[51] After this exchange, Hwi leaves him alone and Leto silently weeps. Falling in love with Hwi causes him to realize too late that he could no longer fully enjoy the life of a human. This is when Leto experiences his *peripeteia*, or reversal of fortune.[52]

Later, when Hwi asks Leto if he might have been wrong about his Golden Path, he admits, "Anything and anyone can fail, but brave good friends help."[53] It is his good friend and servant Duncan who ends up betraying Leto, partially due to his jealousy over Hwi. Forbidding Hwi and Duncan from being together increases Duncan's feeling of being trapped. This also leads Duncan to realize that Leto's rule is corrupt, which motivates him to join Siona's cause, believing her to be the true Atreides in contrast to the abomination Leto. Jealousy, in turn, compels Leto to move up the timeframe of his wedding and to change its location, which is ultimately another grave mistake that unexpectedly leads to his death.

More than 3,500 years before, when Leto first merged with the sandtrout, he asks Ghanima to help him find a way to die.[54] Ghanima explains to Farad'n, "[Leto] gives more than anyone ever gave before. Our father walked into the desert trying to escape it. Alia became Abomination in fear of it.... But Leto! He's all alone."[55] We can only postulate that Ghanima might have been the one to come up with the idea to help the Ixians create a no-chamber invisible to prescience so that Leto could die and that the universe would not be tied to any one particular fate. In his final act of self-sacrifice, Leto falls from his cart into the water and faces his death with dignity:

> As he slipped from the cart, he saw the scimitar arc of the river, a sliveredged thing which shimmered in its mottled shadows, a vicious blade of a river honed through Eternity and ready now to receive him into its agony.[56]

The shape of the water being a scimitar is reminiscent of the scythe carried by the allegorical figure of Death. In his fall, Leto does not cry out or object to his final demise. Rather, he gives in to his fate, which is to live on forever in the sandworms, a type of living death where he will maintain his consciousness, but without the ability to speak.[57] Though his death is slow and his body painfully disintegrates, he continues to impart what wisdom he can to those who planned and executed his murder. He begs them to remember him and, in doing so, this will lead to his redemption: "Remember what I did! Remember me! I will be innocent again!"[58] This desire for innocence could be a childlike fear of him facing the consequences of his actions, fear of the agony he must endure. Or it could be his desire for people to eventually understand that he did all of this out of a deep love for humanity and his desire to protect us from complete annihilation in the coming apocalypse.

Additionally, we are also left with a fear for the unknown future of his society, the "universe of surprises" that he longed for.[59] For Leto, the worst fate is to know all possible futures because "to know the future absolutely is to be trapped into that future absolutely."[60] Like Tiresias in Sophocles' tragedies and the Soothsayer in Shakespeare's *Julius Caesar*, no one ever listens to the prophets until it is too late. Prophets suffer in knowing the future and being unable to stop it. Like the mythological Cassandra, they are filled with frustration because no one believes them or people question their sanity. In her article, "The 'Moi-peau' of Leto II in Herbert's Atreides Saga," Marie-Noelle Zeender claims that once Leto merged with the sandtrout and allowed Haram to be the gatekeeper to his ancestral memories, he was no longer sane, but rather psychotic. She also argues that "in [Leto's] delirium, he even goes as far as to say that he is an integral part of the planet, thus granting himself not only a universal dimension but also a cosmic one."[61] However, this depiction oversimplifies the plot of *God Emperor of Dune*. If Leto had been insane, he would not have been able to stay in power for nearly three millennia. Leto is not depicted as delirious in any part of the novel; the decisions he makes are deliberate and calculating, not the whims of a madman. He is focused solely on the amelioration of the human race through his sacrifice. Even as he falls to his death, he does so in the full knowledge that his death will bring new life to Arrakis. Everything he says comes to fruition just as he foretold. The universality of his actions is epic in nature not only for the continuation of spice, but also for humans to survive in the Scattering.[62]

Although not planned or seen in prescience by Leto, his goal was to eventually die after teaching humanity a lesson about tyrants, and he does achieve this goal. He tells Duncan and Siona that the Golden Path is his gift to humanity, saying, "I give you a new kind of time without parallels.... It will always diverge. There will be no concurrent points on its curves."[63] This is precisely what Ghanima believed. In *Children of Dune*, she predicted that:

> [Leto will] lead humans through the cult of death into the free air of exuberant life! ... When his Empire falls.... Oh, yes, it'll fall. You think this is Kralizec now, but Kralizec is yet to come. And when it comes, humans will have renewed their memory of what it's like to be alive. The memory will persist as long as there's a single human living. We'll go through the crucible once more, Stil. And we'll come out of it. We always arise from our own ashes. Always.[64]

What Ghanima refers to here as "Kralizec" is the "war at the end of the universe" which is actually in reference to the Famine Times and the Scattering after Leto II's death. Ghanima could see the dangers of what was to come and it does not have to do with Ixian machines.

Similarly, just before his death, Leto's final words are "Do not fear the Ixians.... They can make machines, but they can no longer create *arafel*."[65] The Hebrew word *arafel* means the Apocalypse, which indicates that machines will not cause the destruction of the human race. In other words, although the Ixians have the ability to create machines and artificial intelligence, Siona's descendants will be humans who are invisible to prescience and will not be hunted by thinking machines. Through the Scattering, the Ixians themselves will no longer be a threat. John Grigsby views Leto's pronouncement as claiming that through his oppression he has saved humanity from "both determinism and the religious-like faith in machines that had taken possession of them over the course of time."[66] At the end of *God Emperor of Dune*, Leto bequeaths Siona with just the essence of the Golden Path to light humanity's way into the future, and she knows what needs to be done.[67] Although Leto cannot foresee what will happen during or after the Scattering, because he cannot anticipate what humans will do, he hopes humanity will spread widely enough that the impending threat will not destroy all of humankind.

Conclusion

Just as there are paradoxes inherent in human nature, which are evident through analyzing human motivations through both sociological and biological approaches, so too are there paradoxes evident in the novel *God Emperor of Dune*. This is why it is important to examine the novel's overarching themes and symbols, as well as the inner drive of the protagonist as a tragic hero. Sapolsky's analysis of humanity through moral philosophy and biology, both genetic and social reasons behind human behavior, give an overall picture of why Leto's rule succeeds in both indoctrinating a vast majority of the human population and also increasing the human desire to expand beyond the known reaches of the galaxy during the Scattering after Leto's death. Similarly, through Herbert's use of a compressed timeframe, his empathetic presentation of Leto, and the universality of the plot, *God Emperor of Dune* aligns closely to Aristotle's view of what makes a good tragedy. Universality of plot signifies that what happens in the story and how characters behave is probable or likely in that situation. Leto's actions and reactions are what any person would do, if they had prescience and his knowledge of the future. Although Alia succumbs to abomination in fear of the Golden Path and Paul outright refuses to take up the burden, it is likely that Ghanima would have made similar choices.[68]

Leto, as the paradoxical ruler of the known universe, has much to lose and the conclusion of *God Emperor of Dune* leaves the reader feeling both pity and fear. We pity Leto's destruction, having gotten to know the inner workings of his mind, his plan for the human race, and his terrible, awesome sacrifice. Although the downfall of Leto's empire concludes with a greater understanding of Leto's sacrifice and arouses pity over Leto's death, the primary message we are left with is one of fear: urging us to prevent any single entity from taking control of all of humanity ever again. Leto succeeds in creating the desire for space travel. He permits the creation of no-globes and no-ships, and breeds the gene in Siona that makes humans invisible to prescience, freeing them from his own agony. Inevitably, Leto gives humanity what he promised: a universe of the unknown. He reinvigorates human curiosity in exploring the universe. Humanity will no longer be static; everyone will be free, but they will also be united in their fear and hatred of Leto II, The Tyrant, and their once God Emperor.[69]

NOTES

1. For further commentary on fan objections, see Jim Arrowood's *Dune Saga Podcast* episode "Listener Feedback #13."

2. In an epigraph from *Heretics of Dune*, written 10,000 years since Leto began his metamorphosis into a sandworm, Gaus Andaud ponders several questions as to Leto's motivation. "Was he driven by the desire for long life?… Was it the lure of power?… Was he driven to save humankind from itself?" Herbert, *Heretics of Dune*, 72.

3. Sapolsky, *Behave*, 3.

4. *Ibid.*, 388–389.

5. *Ibid.*, 116–117.

6. *Ibid.*, 494.

7. *Ibid.*, 526.

8. *Ibid.*, 674.

9. *Ibid.*, 3.

10. Herbert, *God Emperor of Dune*, 70.

11. Sapolsky, *Behave*, 621–626.

12. Herbert, *God Emperor of Dune*, 163.

13. Leto refers to rebels as "closet aristocrats" that are easily converted (*Ibid.*, 27). Later, he admits that his most trusted administrators like Moneo were once rebels (*Ibid.*, 226).

14. Sapolsky, *Behave*, 102–107.

15. Herbert, *God Emperor of Dune*, 206.

16. *Ibid.*, 209–210.

17. Herbert, *Chapterhouse: Dune*, 230.

18. For example, see Rothman, "Common Threads Run Through Many of History's Worst Dictatorships" on North Korea and Kandel, "Education in Nazi Germany" on education in Nazi Germany. Similar techniques were also used in Albania, Mao Zedong's China, and Stalin's Russia.

19. Herbert, *God Emperor of Dune*, 238.

20. Sapolsky, *Behave*, 580–613.

21. See "The Sands of Time," in this volume on the nature of prescience as experienced by Paul and Leto II.

22. Herbert, *God Emperor of Dune*, 323.

23. Sapolsky, *Behave*, 674.

24. For commentary on the serpent in Judaism, see Murison, "The Serpent in the Old Testament."

25. For discussion on medieval Christianity and the syncretism of Scandinavian paganism, see Rauer, *Beowulf and the Dragon: Parallels and Analogues*.

26. Herbert, *God Emperor of Dune*, 236.

27. Herbert, *Heretics of Dune*, 138.

28. Philips. *The Fundamentals of Tawheed*, 234.

29. van der Toorn, Becking, and van der Horst, eds. *Dictionary of Deities and Demons in the Bible*, 744–747.

30. Herbert, *Chapterhouse: Dune*, 62.

31. *Ibid.*

32. Mendelsohn, "Unburied: Tamerlan Tsarnaev and the Lessons of Greek Tragedy."

33. Sapolsky, *Behave*, 574.

34. Herbert, *God Emperor of Dune*, 185.

35. *Ibid.*

36. Bolingbroke, *Letters on the Spirit of Patriotism and on the Idea of a Patriot King*, 85.

37. Herbert, *God Emperor of Dune*, 128.

38. But even Leto breaks rules of the Butlerian Jihad as he secretly endorses the Ixians. They created several machines for him in his Sareer. He also allows the Ixians to create no-chambers and use axolotl tanks to create artificial mélange.

39. Elias, *The Civilizing Process*, 441–447.

40. Of course, one could argue that what the Honored Matres and Face Dancers do is far worse.

41. Similar to Leto II's metamorphosis, in *Sandworms of Dune*, Duncan Idaho merges with Erasmus to become the ultimate Kwisatz Haderach and now is in charge of directing humanity's future.

42. Aristotle, *Poetics*, 14.

43. Leto himself is a descendant of King Agamemnon, son of Atreus, in Greek mythology (Herbert, *God Emperor of Dune*, 13).

44. Fjellman, "Prescience and Power," 50.

45. *Ibid.*

46. Herbert, *Children of Dune*, 400.

47. *Ibid.*

48. Herbert, *God Emperor of Dune*, 175.

49. *Ibid.*, 244.

50. *Ibid.*, 181.

51. *Ibid.*, 182.

52. Aristotle, 18.

53. Herbert, *God Emperor of Dune*, 241.

54. Herbert, *Children of Dune*, 395.

55. *Ibid.*, 396.

56. Herbert, *God Emperor of Dune*, 414.

57. Leto describes it as "A little pearl of my awareness will go with every sandworm and every sandtrout—knowing yet unable to move a single cell, aware in an endless dream." *Ibid.*, 219.

58. *Ibid.*, 417.

59. Herbert, *Children of Dune*, 94.

60. *Ibid.*

61. Zeender, "The 'Moi-peau' of Leto II in Herbert's Atreides Saga," 231.

62. See "Political Prescience," in this volume for more on the threat prescience poses to humanity.

63. Herbert, *God Emperor of Dune*, 418.

64. Herbert, *Children of Dune*, 399.

65. Herbert, *God Emperor of Dune*, 420.

66. Grigsby, "Herbert's Reversal of Asimov's Vision Reassessed," 178.

67. Herbert, *God Emperor of Dune*, 420.

68. Ghanima, however, admits that Leto did so because he is stronger. Herbert, *Children of Dune*, 396, 348, and 408.

69. For another analysis of the reign of Leto II, see "The Greatest Predator Ever Known" in this volume.

Works Cited

Aristotle. *Poetics*. 335 B.C.E. Translated by Malcolm Heath. London: Penguin Books, 1996.

Arrowood, Jim, Scott Hertzog, and David Moulton. "Listener Feedback #13." *Dune Saga Podcast*, November 2, 2018, Podcast audio, 53:52. dunesagapodcast.com/listener-feedback-13/.

Bolingbroke, Henry St. John, Viscount, and Arthur Hassall. *Letters On the Spirit of Patriotism and on the Idea of a Patriot King*. Oxford, UK: Clarendon Press, 1917. HathiTrust Digital Library, Committee on Institutional Cooperation. hdl.handle.net/2027 /mdp.39015 004765239?urlappend=%3Bseq=7

Elias, Norbert, Eric Dunning, Johan Goudsblom, and Stephen Mennell. *The Civilizing Process: Sociogenetic and Psychogenetic Investigations*. Revised edition. Oxford, UK: Blackwell Publishers, 2000.

Fjellman, Stephen M. "Prescience and Power: 'God Emperor of Dune' and the Intellectuals." *Science Fiction Studies* 13, no. 1 (1986): 50–63.

Grigsby, John L. "Herbert's Reversal of Asimov's Vision Reassessed: 'Foundation's Edge' and 'God Emperor of Dune.'" *Science Fiction Studies* 11, no. 2 (1984): 174–80.

Herbert, Frank. *Chapterhouse: Dune.* 1985 New York: Ace Books, 1987.

Herbert, Frank. *Children of Dune.* 1976 New York: Ace Books, 1987.

Herbert, Frank. *God Emperor of Dune.* 1981 New York: Ace Books, 1987.

Herbert, Frank. *Heretics of Dune.* 1984 New York: Ace Books, 1987.

Kandel, I.L. "Education in Nazi Germany." *The Annals of the American Academy of Political and Social Science* 182 (1935): 153–63.

Mendelsohn, Daniel. "Unburied: Tamerlan Tsarnaev and the Lessons of Greek Tragedy." *The New Yorker*, May 14, 2013. www.newyorker.com/books/page-turner/unburied-tamerlan-tsarnaev-and-the-lessons-of-greek-tragedy.

Murison, Ross G. "The Serpent in the Old Testament." *The American Journal of Semitic Languages and Literatures* 21, no. 2 (1905): 115–30.

Philips, Abu Ameenah Bilal. *The Fundamentals of Tawheed Sharh mabādi' Al-tawhīd: Islamic Monotheism.* 2nd ed. Riyadh: International Islamic Publishing House, 2006.

Rauer, Christine. *Beowulf and the Dragon: Parallels and Analogues / Christine Rauer.* Cambridge, UK: D.S. Brewer, 2000.

Rothman, Lily. "Common Threads Run Through Many of History's Worst Dictatorships. Here's One Way North Korea Fits In." *TIME*, January 8, 2019. time.com/5494585/north-korea-dictator-history/.

Sapolsky, Robert M. *Behave: The Biology of Humans at Our Best and Worst.* New York: Penguin Press, 2017.

Toorn, Karel van der, Bob Becking, and Pieter W. van der Horst, eds. *Dictionary of Deities and Demons in the Bible.* 2nd ed. Leiden: Brill Academic Publishers, 1999.

Zeender, Marie-Noelle. "The 'Moi-peau' of Leto II in Herbert's Atreides Saga." *Science Fiction Studies* 22, no. 2 (1995): 226–33. www.jstor.org/stable/4240427.

PART II

History and Religion

Frank Herbert's Byzantium

Medieval-Futurism and the Princess Historians Irulan and Anna Komnene

Maximilian Lau

"You think we have the Byzantine corruption."[1]

This quotation, from the tense meeting between Thufir Hawat and the Fremen after Duke Leto Atreides's death and Paul and Jessica's flight, sees the Fremen use one of the hugely enduring, pejorative meanings of the adjective "Byzantine": treachery. The word is often used in synopses of *Dune* and similar works as the most suitable adjective to evoke the Imperium's corruption, backstabbing politics, and overly bureaucratic complexity. It also evokes both decadence and exoticness. Such stereotypes were common in history books while Frank Herbert was writing. Based on the opinion contained in Gibbon's *Decline and Fall of the Roman Empire*, the medieval, east Roman state referred to as "Byzantium" by him and many others was seen as a diminished, corrupted, form of the Classical Republican and early Imperial Roman state.[2] Though previous studies have highlighted the Classical, Medieval European, and Oriental influences upon Herbert's *Dune*, no study has focused on the empire that lasted over a thousand years between them, geographically and chronologically.[3] This essay will introduce those parallels, and then focus on the character of Princess Irulan Corrino. Her seemingly understated influence on *Dune*'s plot mirrors that of the twelfth-century Byzantine Princess Anna Komnene, and thus understanding the one can yield some surprising conclusions as to the influence of the other upon both Herbert's universe and Byzantine history.

Byzantinisms in Dune

No biography or interview of Herbert reveals what he might have known about Byzantium. Therefore, it is unknown if any mirroring was intentional, but both historical and literary influences from Byzantium are at work in the *Dune* novels, and some can be readily sourced. Beginning with the historical influences—beyond Gibbon and those that followed him—Herbert is likely to have been familiar with the more sympathetic portrayal of Byzantium contained in Steven Runciman's immensely popular 1950s historical works on the Crusades.[4] Within the genre, however, the use of Byzantium in fantasy and science fiction has often been as a paradigm for the corrupt and decaying empire, with the prime example being J.R.R. Tolkien's opinion that the imperial capital of Constantinople was a "Heartless Town"[5] that contained "corrupt worldly politics [and the] forceful crushing of alternative or differing visions," perhaps using it as one possible model for the fallen state of Gondor in *The Lord of the Rings*.[6] Herbert adopts elements of this trope in his portrayal of the old Corrino empire that Paul Atreides overthrows in *Dune* itself. In its sequels, he also echoes Runciman's view that the Crusaders were the true villains in his descriptions of how the Jihad evolves under Paul and Alia.[7]

Although Paul's journey in *Dune* has been compared to historical figures such as Lawrence of Arabia and Napoleon Bonaparte, an arguably closer parallel can be found in the rise of Islam against the old empires of Persia and Rome.[8] The narrative framework of a leader who inspired a desert people with religion, far from the old major centers of power, and then how that people brought down an old order and replaced it with a new one is both directly and indirectly referenced in Herbert's work.[9] In terminology and aesthetics, Herbert's depiction of Paul and the Fremen are heavily influenced by early Islam: the Fremen are referred to as

Figure 1: Portrayals of Byzantine Emperors. *Opposite:* The mosaic of Emperor Justinian I and his court from the Church of San Vitale, Ravenna, Italy (Roger Culos, https://en.wikipedia.org/wiki/Basilica_of_San_Vitale#/media/File:Sanvitale03.jpg); *above:* Emperor Theophilos and his court, from the Madrid Skylitzes Manuscript (Alexander R. https://commons.wikimedia.org/wiki/File:Emperor_Theophilos_Chronicle_of_John_Skylitzes.jpg); *right:* and the mosaic of Emperor John II Komnenos, Hagia Sophia, Istanbul (Magnus Manske, https://commons.wikimedia.org/wiki/File:John_II_Komnenos.jpg).

the "Umma," the term for the Islamic community of believers, whilst Alia Atreides's temple in *Dune Messiah* is covered in hangings in Islamic green and black with the "moon symbol of Muad'Dib" upon them.[10] The city itself contains specific architectural elements such as a "postern out of most ancient Baghdad ... a dome dreamed in mythical Damascus" all under Muad'Dib's moon symbol, whilst the orchards "rival those of fabled Lebanon."[11] This is in addition to many of the Fremen words and names coming directly from Arabic.[12]

The original opponents of the new Islamic empire were Byzantium and pre–Islamic Persia, and Herbert's descriptions of the old empire of the Corrinos is dripping with references to these original rivals. Shaddam Corrino IV's title of "Padishah Emperor" combines the titles of both the Persian Shahs and the Byzantine Emperors. Shaddam is first presented in *Dune* as surrounded by "all the fringe parasites of the Court."[13] Such a scene is heavily reminiscent of the Byzantine court, in particular through its reference to epigrams, as courtiers immortalized great events and victories with such poetry to gain imperial favor (fortunately for us, as these poems form a corpus of sources greatly useful for historians today).[14] Paul himself, after becoming emperor, is described as wearing "the jeweled golden robes of state" while he sits enthroned, which immediately evokes the classic portrayal of the Byzantine emperor in particular, such as in these images in Figure 1.[15]

Furthermore, in *Dune Messiah*, Paul attempts to discredit himself as emperor by allowing himself to be blinded, due to the old Fremen tradition of blindness making him unfit for rulership.[16] This too was a Byzantine tradition; rather than kill their opponents, Byzantine emperors often blinded them so they were left alive, but unable to take the throne.[17] Thus, the specific type of emperor and old empire presented to readers of *Dune* is particularly Byzantine in flavor, as demonstrated by the emperor's court and clothes, and by the empire's politics and antiquity.[18]

Though further parallels can be made, and some specifics will be discussed below, what is perhaps more surprising is that there may also be a Byzantine inspiration to some of the more esoteric and philosophical elements of *Dune*'s plot, via William Butler Yeats's famous 1926 poem *Sailing to Byzantium*. Yeats's poem, written when he was around 60, concerns the struggle to remain alive even as the body dies. The poet leaves the living world for an imagined "Byzantium," where the "singing-masters" of his soul can take him away from his tattered body into an "artifice of eternity."[19] Once there, the poet will be but a golden bird "to keep a drowsy emperor awake," or otherwise to sing to "lords and ladies of Byzantium/ Of what is past, or passing, or yet to come." The parallels with Paul and his son Leto II's struggle with prescience are made plainer by the analysis of San Juan, who described: "the tension [in the poem] between memory and desire, knowledge and intuition, nature and history, subsumed within a vision of eternal order."[20]

The parallel with the Golden Path of Leto II, which Paul fears to tread, is plain. Integral to the plot of the Dune sequels, both Paul and Leto II saw that in all but one future humanity wiped itself out, and there was only one Golden Path where humanity survived. That path required millennia of rule by a tyrant, keeping humanity in sheltered order, until finally that tyrant would be brought down and humanity would scatter out beyond what was safe and known, and as such could never be brought down by a single catastrophic event ever again. San Juan's analysis of Yeats's poem neatly reflects Herbert's portrayal of the tension between humanity's stated desire to be safe and controlled with the necessity of volatility so that humanity would not stagnate and die.[21] Yeats's struggle to remain alive even as the body dies reflects the stagnation of the old empire with its rigid class structures and inward looking—though deadly—politics. The "singing-masters" parallel the ancestors that the mother superiors, Paul, and Leto II encounter after they drink the Water of Life, and particularly when the Atreides father and son are guided into seeing the vision of what "is past, or passing, or yet to come."[22] Attempting "to keep the drowsy emperor awake" is then the struggle to preserve humanity as a whole.[23] Whether the poem directly influenced Herbert is, again, impossible to know, but it once more gives us a taste of the intriguing questions that such parallels allow to be asked of the Dune saga.

Princess Historians: Parallel Disparagement

In the previous section, I focused on Byzantine parallels that feed into the stereotypical preconceptions about Byzantine history. In this section, I focus on a parallel that transcends and subverts those paradigms, and one where scholarship has only recently caught up with Herbert's imagination: the one between Irulan Corrino and the twelfth-century Byzantine Princess Anna Komnene (1083–1153). Anna is the renowned author of the *Alexiad*, a history written in heroic style chronicling the rise of her father, the Emperor Alexios I Komnenos, to the throne and then his subsequent reign.[24] As well as being an engaging work of literature in its own right, it is also the essential source for the time period, telling us more than any other work about both her father's reign, the tribulations of eleventh and twelfth-century Byzantium, and especially the arrival of the armies of the First Crusade into the East from an eastern perspective. Despite the impact of Anna's work in providing the bulk of our knowledge of this time period, opinions on her as a person have traditionally been more negative, similar to opinions of Princess Irulan both within the Dune novels and in Dune scholarship more broadly. That opinion of Anna has only recently begun to be updated, and adopting the same approach with Irulan raises her importance to the Dune novels in unusual ways. This comparison necessitates a re-evaluation of both figures.

The poor reputation of both princesses derives from their portrayal as power-hungry schemers, forced to turn to history-writing to lament their failed ambitions, exacerbated by the gender stereotypes of commentators. While examining the birth and upbringing of Anna and Irulan, we see a number of similarities. Beginning with Anna, in the *Alexiad* she lends authority to her work and status by naming herself as the eldest child of her father, "born in the purple."[25] This was an important Byzantine title, *porphyrogennete*, derived from being born in the *porphyra*, a pavilion of the Great Palace of Constantinople where the wives of emperors gave birth to imperial heirs, giving those born there the ordained destiny to one day rule the ancient Roman Empire. Reinforcing this status, at less than a year old she was betrothed to Konstantine Doukas, the son of one of the previous imperial dynasties. This was intended to unite the warring families, and she tells us that as infants the two were even crowned and acclaimed as future rulers. However, as her father solidified his position and had a son, she and Konstantine were disinherited around 1090. Konstantine then died of natural causes in 1094, depriving Anna of her presumed imperial future.[26] Despite this, Anna was supposedly requested as a bride by Sultan Malik Shah of the Seljuk Turks as a way to make peace between him and Alexios. However, she eventually married Nikephoros Bryennios, a scion of another major family that had sought to make themselves emperor in the chaotic decades at the end of the eleventh century. Nikephoros was then integrated into her father's regime as *Kaisar* and *Panhypersebastos*, old and new titles that put him at the top of the imperial hierarchy alongside Anna.[27]

From her history, we can see how Anna was originally intended to be empress, uniting the empire after its period of civil war. When this plan fell through in the face of a male heir and Konstantine's death, she was still used as an important player in her father's strategic game to solidify both his regime and the empire. Anna herself mentions how she obeyed her parents in all things, and both she and other authors claim she was much like her father.[28]

Irulan plays a similar role in the Dune universe. In one of the many quotations from Irulan's own literary works (21 in total) that frame many of *Dune*'s chapters, we have a work titled "In my Father's House," which is cited four times through the course of the novel. Irulan always refers to her imperial father by his rank and relationship to her ("My father, the Padishah Emperor"), and from these quotations we learn that Shaddam Corrino IV wished Irulan had been old enough to marry Paul's father, Duke

Leto Atreides; thus, the necessity for Shaddam to eliminate House Atreides in order to maintain his power would have been avoided.[29] Equally, Irulan was intended to be a tool of the Bene Gesserit from before birth; Herbert's Jesuit-inspired sisterhood here acted as the power behind the throne with its own designs for the stability of the empire, and for maintaining its power.[30] Irulan notes how her mother, a Bene Gesserit sister, denied Emperor Shaddam IV a son and legal heir so that her superiors could control the succession for their own purposes, although the text is unclear as to what exactly Irulan's role in this plan was.[31] Though *Dune* does not reveal what she might have thought of this plan, Irulan remains loyal to her father. Her first word when she finally appears in the final scene of the final chapter is "Father," which she follows soon after with: "For this I was trained, Father."[32] Here she allows herself to be married to Paul Atreides to give the former the appearance of imperial legitimacy, and thus restabilize the empire of the known universe.[33] Despite her marriage to Paul, the new emperor, she does not fulfill her intended purpose from birth to become empress. Paul remains devoted to Chani, his Fremen lover and the mother of his children. Indeed, he swears as much to Chani in the same scene, saying that while she will be a concubine, and Irulan will be his wife for political purposes, that Irulan will have no child, tenderness or passion from him.[34] With such hands dealt to both Irulan and Anna, it can be appreciated how constructing a narrative of scheming to restore their "rightful" place is very tempting. Equally, we can see how their involvement in such plotting becomes their all but defining characteristic to contemporaries and scholars.

For Irulan, we see this immediately in the opening chapter of *Dune Messiah*, when conspirators gather to discuss hobbling the power of the prescient Emperor Paul Atreides. Here, her desire to be the "founding mother of the royal dynasty" is identified by her co-conspirators. In fact, her treason had already begun. In the face of Paul's resistance to even officially crowning her as empress, she had been secretly administering Chani contraceptives in the hope that he would be forced to turn to her for an heir.[35] Equally, she continues to report on Paul's doings to the Bene Gesserit, and thereby furthers the plot to oust or kill him.[36] Paul's prescience unsurprisingly makes him completely aware of Irulan's plotting, but he forgives her, as he is also aware that Chani is destined to die in childbirth. Therefore, Irulan's drugging of her is unintentionally extending Paul's time with his beloved Chani.[37] Further, he foresees that on Chani's death, Irulan's guilt and devotion to duty will see her become his twin children's adopted mother (alongside her history writing), wholly dedicated to their wellbeing to make up for her past scheming.[38]

For Anna, though it has been implied that she may have been involved in previous plotting, she is only directly named as a conspirator against her brother John in 1119, when she is said to have become involved in a plot to kill him at the imperial hunting lodge of the Philopation, just outside the walls of Constantinople.[39] The conspiracy was unmasked, perhaps because both Anna's husband and mother refused to become involved. Anna and Nikephoros are criticized in strongly gendered terms by the late twelfth-/early thirteenth-century historian Niketas Choniates (whose work will be analyzed more fully below).[40] Though Anna was initially deprived of her property, her brother John later restored it, being supposedly magnanimous in victory.[41] Despite this forgiveness, when Anna's husband died, she finished her days in apparent internal exile in her mother's monastery of *Kecharitomene*, Our Lady Full of Grace. It is here, supposedly a bitter old woman, spiteful in her failure, that she wrote her *Alexiad* about her father's reign.[42]

For those who have studied Anna and Irulan, these plots and their backgrounds form the basis of virtually all interpretations of their characters and significance. Edward Gibbon wrote in 1788 that Anna was "stimulated by ambition and revenge," and his caricature was picked up in the twentieth century.[43] Leonora Neville has outlined how the early twentieth-century view of Anna was summed up in Constantine Cavafy's 1920 poem (named after Anna) in which she is both "a power-hungry woman," and "an arrogant Greek woman" with one "consuming pain" as she never gained the throne "snatched … by impudent John."[44] Neville then picks up on the portrait offered in 1906 in Charles Diehl's *Figures Byzantines*, which described Anna, when her coup attempt failed, as "only thirty-six years old, but her life was over." A failed empress who felt the "Fury of Medea" is contrasted with John's forgiveness, who supposedly hoped "by this chivalrous magnanimity to awaken some remorse in her troubled soul."[45] Although Neville does mention some dissenting voices, she notes that the positive depictions of Anna are sparingly taken up in subsequent literature, if at all, and the negative view remains.[46] In fact this interpretation is so enduring that even in 1996 James Howard-Johnston could still make the argument that Anna barely wrote the *Alexiad* at all, and merely reworked her husband's notes, as she could not possibly have the sources for the military matters contained therein.[47] Though this suggestion has been refuted by subsequent scholarship, the idea of Anna as something other than a woman defined by her thwarted plotting, who became mere historian to bemoan her failure, has been absent until recently, and was never spelled out clearly until Neville's 2016 monograph.[48]

For Irulan, the reaction both within Herbert's universe and by scholarship outside it has been no less damning. In the final paragraph of *Dune* Jessica disparages Irulan's future role, which may be nothing more than "pretensions of a literary nature."[49] Her emphatic reaction is understandable, not only due to Irulan being a member of the former Imperial house which was complicit in her beloved Duke Leto's murder, but also since as a concubine, Jessica was never allowed to legally marry Leto, despite her love for him. Jessica thus comforts Chani as the latter grapples with the sad realization that she will also never marry her own beloved. Jessica does so by telling Chani that social status will be irrelevant, both during her lifetime and beyond it, so long as Chani has Paul's love. This focus on the relative importance of marriage, among other factors, caused Julia List to remark how, despite the rejection of many aspects of traditional organized Christian religion and culture in the science fiction universe of Dune, many features of 1960s American society go unchallenged. She argues that Herbert seemingly pushes a mid-twentieth-century mainline Protestant upper/middle class *Weltanschauung*, with women defined predominantly by their relationships to men, in what many would interpret as a direct continuation of medieval gender norms.[50] As an example, Paul's line in this scene is fairly typical: he remarks, "They've even brought their women…. Ah-h-h, my dear Emperor, how confident you are," making clear how he believes that the emperor would have left them behind had he considered there to have been real danger.[51] Indeed, Luis Meza interpreted the final scene and Irulan's role as symbolizing the Bene Gesserit's fall from the power, as "political power shifts from female to male," in clear echoes of the usual line on Anna—whose fall from empress-elect to mere wife was also due to the successes and failures of her male relatives.[52]

Klára Knězková, building upon the work of Miriam Miller and Jack Hand on the traditionalism of women's roles in *Dune*, draws on the classic models of female characters in literature for her analysis.[53] She notes how positive female characters are usually passive, while active ones are negative. They also are often bipartite, such as the positive "mother/wife" role versus the negative "Old Witch" role played by Jessica. Meanwhile Irulan inhabits the positive "Virgin" role versus the negative "Whore/Fallen Woman" role, again a typology that is very familiar in Byzantine literature and historiography.[54] Knězková notes how Irulan's character appears to absolutely follow this stereotype in the original *Dune*, whereby she is described by Paul in the final scene as a "tall blonde woman, green-eyed, a face of patrician beauty, classic in its hauteur, untouched by tears, completely undefeated. Without being told, Paul knew her—princess Royal, Bene Gesserit-trained."[55] As Knězková notes, this description marks her as a classic untouchable, almost angelic "Virgin" type character. Paul followed this remark with "*There's my key*," which makes plain that he views her a tool by which he can win the throne.[56] To him, in that moment, she is presented as a passive, *female*, a key for *him* to unlock *his* ambitions.[57]

Barbara Silliman's study reinforced this, also noting how neither the empire nor the Fremen are mentioned as having female leaders, and how in general Herbert's female characters are "pre-feminist."[58] Carrie Evans sums up the patriarchal society in *Dune* as one where, for all their powers, the Bene Gesserit and the other "powerful" women in *Dune* "must play by the men's rules if they are to play at all."[59] At the furthest extreme is Susan McLean, who suggests an Oedipus complex between Paul and his mother Jessica, which Paul overcomes by "symbolically splitting her character in two, so that he could love her nurturing side, represented by Chani, while rejecting her powerful, threatening side, represented by Irulan."[60] As an historian too, Irulan has been maligned, described by Benoît Rossignol as a "loser" and a character "buffeted by history, unable to influence or even understand it," which he claims was written in order to demonstrate how Irulan was part of the old dynasty that had now been rejected.[61]

Princess Historians: New Interpretations

Despite these disparaging reviews of Irulan and Anna's roles, more recent research has argued that there is more to these characters, and using the analysis of one on the other advances these conclusions still further. For Anna, Neville's main attack on the conventional view is to note how Anna's role in the supposed coup attempt has been hugely over-emphasized, if not invented. Characterizing her as merely a failed plotter completely disparages her incredible successes as an intellectual and author, on whom we are almost fully dependent for details of this period. The same applies to Irulan: the 1980s works of Colin Manlove and William Touponce, and the more recent work of Kněžková, all remark on how Irulan's influence as the narrator was previously overlooked in assessing her character and role in the novels, with the former highlighting how "it is between the knowledge of her mind and ours that the whole book [Dune] moves."[62]

Beginning with Anna, it is noteworthy that her plotting is only related in Choniates's account, written approximately 90 years later.[63] But the distortion of distance is not the only one: Neville, Alicia Simpson, and Anthony Kaldellis have noted that Choniates's goal in writing his history was to explain the decline of Byzantium as a process where the *taxis* (order) of the world became slowly inverted.[64] The language Choniates uses to describe Anna's plot is also highly sexualized to illustrate this argument. The inversion of the sexes reveals, for him, how "unnatural" the whole thing was. Anna's husband is described as being held back by his "sluggish and flaccid custom" in his desire to become emperor by murdering John, in response to which the "hot desire" of the conspirators was doused, such that Anna "blamed nature most of all," a statement that of course suggests she wished she was male, or at least that her husband was more "masculine" and forceful. This is confirmed by the next section whereby she literally indicts nature for giving Bryennios "a long member and balls" while she was "spread wide and hollowed."[65] Such a sexualized passage sees Choniates demand the reader view Anna as someone attempting to invert "natural law" in both her gender and in her plot to overthrow her brother, symbolic to Choniates of the decline of the empire that Alexios inaugurated. Neville puts forward the strong case that due to these narrative goals, the chronological gap, and the absence of Anna's role in the plot by any other historian, Choniates's account should be taken skeptically at best.[66]

Equally, the idea that she was in internal exile in a monastery was politicized by Diehl and by another influential early twentieth-century historian, Ferdinand Chalandon, who claimed that she never truly wished to write history or philosophy, but only did so because she failed in her plot.[67] However, the idea that Anna was in exile for so many years is untenable because she and her brother are presented as being on good terms at the wedding of her children. Indeed, her husband Nikephoros retains the title of *kaisar* his entire life, remains one of John's generals, and dies on campaign with John in Syria in 1137, suggesting that neither Nikephoros nor Anna were put out into the cold for their supposed plotting. Equally, Anna and her husband become major patrons of the arts and intellectuals, as we can still read philosophical commentaries, novels, histories, and many poems produced at their literary salon, and that material is only what has survived the last eight centuries.[68] Her major achievement is, of course, the *Alexiad*, which, as Neville notes in her conclusion, must be seen as a highly successful work of history that saved the deeds of her father from oblivion, with the whole narrative we know today shaped by her.[69] Though Anna does change and obfuscate events that occur to shape her own narrative goals, as criticized by many of these scholars, for better or worse our window on the history of the era is entirely controlled by her. Larisa Vilimonović adds that the *Alexiad* contains a political program designed to discredit John and his son Manuel, and that her text deliberately attempts to destroy the memory of John, using the classical practice of *damnatio memoriae*.[70] Thus, Vilimonović argues that though Anna knew she would never be emperor when she wrote, she would still have the last laugh as history would remember her father and her brother through her scholarship.

Applying this re-evaluation of Anna to Irulan results in many of the same conclusions. Examining her role during the plot and afterwards, the crucial point is that Irulan defects from the Bene Gesserit for the greater good of the empire, something she sees as essential once Paul produces heirs with Chani. She consistently strives for what she believes is best for the universe, initially by trying to unite the old and the new dynasties by having a child with Paul, but then, once there were heirs, devoting herself to supporting them. Paul's sister Alia remarks that she "reeks of trustworthiness" and that though she had loved Paul in vain, she now lived for the children whom Chani had borne.[71] Indeed, later, Irulan offers to kill her own nephew Farad'n in order to preserve her adopted daughter Ghanima, disclosing how she had taken an oath to guard Ghanima forever against danger, putting her own life at risk as needed.[72] This is despite being goaded by Ghanima earlier in the book, when she called Irulan by the anagram "Ruinal" and advocated that Atreides honor must be preserved for the good of all.[73] Irulan's example could, thus, be considered crucial to Ghanima's turning against Alia's plans when the latter was possessed by Baron Harkonnen, and this ensured the survival of Paul's children and the human race via Leto's Golden Path.[74]

The later Dune books are not analyzed anywhere nearly as much in scholarship as *Dune*, but viewing Irulan's character across them forces us to evaluate her as far more than a passive "key" for Paul's ambition. Indeed, as the novels go on, the role of women in general is strengthened; by *God Emperor of Dune*, Leto II has an entirely female army known as the Fish Speakers, with the Bene Gesserit sisterhood becoming major, positive protagonists.[75] Indeed, with the notable exceptions of the villainous and usually outsmarted Tleilaxu, who follow a repressive, chauvinistic religion, and two male characters who are usually passive tools in the plans of the Bene Gesserit, by the later Dune novels we find an entirely female *dramatis personae*. Thus, the idea that Irulan's becoming Paul's wife symbolizes a transferal of female power to male power is false when viewed across the novels. This is in keeping with the overall plan for the Dune series, and why in many ways the first three novels at least should be read together to analyze Herbert's intentions. Paul's rise is shown as flawed, epitomized by the quote from Liet-Kynes, Herbert's original intended protagonist: "No more terrible disaster could befall your people than for them to fall into the hands of a Hero."[76] As O'Reilly has reanalyzed Paul's rise and fall and thus Herbert's thoughts on the dangers of "heroes" across the novels, so too must Irulan's role be so reassessed to see her full arc and significance.[77]

Taking the broader view of women within the *Dune* novels, and Irulan in particular, Manlove, Touponce, and Knĕzková have already remarked on how she acts as a type of narrator for the books with each chapter opening with a quotation from one of her many books, and indeed as a literal narrator in the Lynch film adaptation.[78] Such a role influences the reader by directing them to the foci she highlights in the extracts from her works, in much the same way as Anna does for historians today, even though it is Herbert's prose that the reader engages with directly. When it comes to Irulan's literary works, the 21 works mentioned in *Dune* alone are fantastically diverse, including *Manual of Muad'Dib, A Child's History of Muad'Dib, In my Father's House, Collected Sayings and Conversations with Muad'Dib, Arrakis Awakening, Muad'Dib: The Religious Issues*, and include more direct writings such as a secret report for the Bene Gesserit on the Arrakeen crisis, and a lecture to the Arrakeen War College on the power of symbols.[79] Again, this hardly suggests a woman merely taking comfort in "pretensions of a literary nature," but one who is a genuine towering academic. Equally, Jessica's epigraphic judgment that "history will call us wives!" becomes a fascinating comment in the context of Irulan's authorship of the overarching historical sequence, as it is Irulan who is writing that history. Thus, within the *Dune* Universe, almost everything that is known about these characters later comes through Irulan's writings. In *Heretics of Dune*, Paul's son Leto II even says, "Historians have great power and some of them know it. They recreate the past, changing it to fit their own interpretations. Thus, they change the future as well."[80] Therefore, it would seem that Herbert himself must have been aware of the inherent ironies of Jessica's final statement, and her judgment of Irulan, as it is Irulan who is the historian supreme of the Dune universe. In this, Herbert has dramatically prefigured the argument only made of Anna by Vilimonović in 2019, whereby the *Alexiad* was Anna's response to John's reign; by controlling how we remember medieval Byzantium, she is still affecting us today.[81]

Though there have been no films of Anna's life, it is striking that in the Sci-Fi Channel's adaptation of *Dune*, Irulan's character is given a larger role.[82] Kněžková notes how in the novel Paul tells the emperor "Majesty, we both know the way out of our difficulty," but in this adaptation Irulan is given this line, highlighting her agency.[83] Equally, a new scene includes her at a dinner on Arrakis before the Harkonnen invasion. In it, when the guards seek to remove her and Paul steps up to say she is under his protection, she reacts with an eye roll and an "Oh, please!" highlighting the fact that she needs no medieval knight in shining armor, being entirely confident in her own power as an imperial princess and scholar.[84] Similarly, she is presented visiting the Harkonnen planet of Giedi Prime, attempting to gain details of the Harkonnen plot from Feyd-Rautha, and arguing with her father about his policies, despite her father and Jessica's earlier dismissals of her as someone whose ambitions are more literary than political.[85] Such a dismissal of both Irulan and Anna as second-rate academics, forced to become intellectuals only by their political failures, is bound up with their disempowerment as women by both contemporaries and scholars, and has held us back in our analysis, both historical and literary.

As a final point on the adaptations, it is noteworthy that Irulan's costume also appears partly Byzantine inspired, particularly in the Sci-Fi Channel adaptation where she is ornately robed in purple and gold. Director John Harrison commented that in his meeting with Theodore Pištěk, the costume designer, he emphasized the feudal and "retro" nature of the Dune universe, rather than the usual tropes of science fiction fashion.[86] Specifically, he notes how they decided on gold and violet for the imperial family, so as to use color as a psychological tool, and that each "tribe" (Atreides, Harkonnen, etc.) should have a distinct look.[87] Such a tool and method was extensively used in Byzantium, recalling how Anna defined herself as a princess "born in the purple," and from sources such as Pseudo-Kodinos's book of ceremonies and offices whereby each dignitary of the court was assigned a set dress and color.[88] Thus, Irulan's connection with the other great princess historian, Anna Komnene, has been made explicit visually, preserving her status as a scholar despite the lack of chapter quotations by Irulan in the adaptations.

To return to the interplay with Byzantium in Herbert's works, the character of a supposedly disempowered royal historian resurfaces in *Children of Dune* in the person of Corrino Prince Farad'n. As mentioned above, Farad'n was involved with a plot to bring the Corrino family back to power, though in fact this plot is truly masterminded by his mother (and Irulan's sister), Wensicia.[89] He eventually becomes consort to Paul's daughter Ghanima, but as Leto II attains near immortality as the God Emperor, he never rises to real power. He is, however, made court historian to Leto, and thus Herbert presents us with yet another supposedly powerless royal historian, but this time a man, gaining status only through being consort to a woman. Leto also renames him Harq al-Ada, which literally means the "one who changes customs" in Arabic, which appears as pointed a hint as possible that Herbert was well aware of what he was doing with gender and historical expectations in his novels. Indeed, it may hint that he was reflecting back upon one who may have been a template for both Irulan and Harq al-Ada: Anna Komnene. The interplay between these characters and their analysis by contemporaries and scholars is, thus, symbolic of changing interpretations of gender. As the paradigm of analysis shifts, their significance as women, as intellectuals, and indeed as political figures, can at last be analyzed without the blinkers of previous orthodoxies.

Whether intended or not, the Byzantine themes in Herbert's novels not only contribute to the rich tapestry of imagery and nuance in his universe, but also to the potential to re-evaluate our understanding of both real historical figures and his own characters. Above all, they provide a fulcrum for Herbert to open the door for his readers to the strange worlds of ecology, philosophy, history, and more, inspiring many to walk roads never dreamed of before.[90]

NOTES

1. Herbert, *Dune*, 246.
2. Gibbon, *Decline and Fall of the Roman Empire*. For those readers unfamiliar with Byzantium, a good starter volume is Herrin, *Byzantium*. For those wishing more academic studies, see *A Companion to Byzantium*, edited by Liz James, and *The Byzantine World*, edited by Paul Stephenson.
3. See Lenz, "Manifest Destiny: Science Fiction and Classical Form," 43–46; Roberts, *Science Fiction*, 40; Silliman, "Conserving the Balance," 34–36. Further examples below.
4. Runciman, *A History of the Crusades*.
5. Quotation in Tolkien, "Ælfwine I," 144.
6. Latter quotation is the analysis by Librán-Moreno, "Byzantium, New Rome!" 110. See also Carpenter, *The Inklings*, 123; Cameron, "Byzantinist and Others," 7. Beyond Tolkien, the use in science fiction of the paradigm presented in Gibbon's *Decline and Fall of the Roman Empire* has been artfully discussed by DiTommaso, "The Articulation of Imperial Decadence and Decline in Epic Science Fiction," 267–91.
7. Runciman controversially claimed several times in his works, and notably less than a decade after the Second World War ended, that the sack of Byzantium by the armies of the Fourth Crusade in 1204 was the greatest crime committed against humanity, though the comment could have referred to 'the humanities' in David Abulafia's view. See Abulafia, "Crusades, Spies, And Cruising."
8. On Lawrence of Arabia, see O'Reilly, *Frank Herbert* 43–44; Harper, *"Going Native" with Dune's Paul Atreides*; Kennedy, "Laurence of Arabia, Paul Atreides, and the Roots of Frank Herbert's *Dune*." On Napoleon, see Howard, "Religious Violence in Frank Herbert's *Dune* Series," 33, citing Said, *Orientalism*, 82. See also the posited mid-nineteenth century inspiration for *Dune* from the narrative history *Sabres of Paradise* by Lesley Blanch, which focuses on an Islamic Holy War against Russian Imperialism in the Caucasus: Collins, "The Secret History of Dune."
9. Though there are a number of scholarly books on the subject, and the context is understandably complex and controversial, for those wanting to be introduced to the world when Islam first arose they could do worse than Holland's *Shadow of the Sword*, though the focus is clearly on the world before it arose rather than on the rise itself (though this is also the case in *Dune*). See Holland, *In the Shadow of the Sword*.
10. Herbert, *Dune*, 528, idem, *Dune Messiah*, 109.
11. Herbert, *Dune Messiah*, 110.
12. O'Reilly, *Frank Herbert*; Csicsery-Ronay, *The Seven Beauties of Science Fiction*, 39–40; Kennedy, "Epic World-Building: Names and Cultures in *Dune*," 99–108. Csicsery-Ronay also notes that a fair number of terms in "Galach," the language of the Galactic Empire, come from Greek, making the contrast with Arabic still more distinct, though some terms also derive from other "power languages of Europe" so the parallel is not perfect. Admittedly Byzantine Greek also has numerous loan words from Latin in particular, 40.
13. Herbert, *Dune*, 527. Byzantine emperors, in continuity from their ancient Roman forebears, were known as Imperator, Augustus, Basileus, and Autokrator, all of which are usually translated as "emperor" or "sovereign."
14. C.f. DiTommaso, "The Articulation of Imperial Decadence and Decline in Epic Science Fiction," 274. See: *Byzantine Court Culture from 829–1204*, edited by Henry Maguire, and on rhetoric in particular see Dennis, "Imperial Panegyric," 131–40, and the court

ceremonies volume cited below. Equally, see the chapters on the court and rhetoric in *The Byzantine World* and *A Companion to Byzantium*. More specifically, the Komnenian dynasty of Byzantine Emperors in particular were known to host lavish courts even when on military campaigns, just as described in this *Dune* description, that being the dynasty to which Anna Komnene belongs, as discussed in the second half of this essay. See: Mullet, "Tented Ceremony," 487–514; Lau, "*Ioannoupolis*," 435–64. It has been noted by Evans that Herbert's Paul is criticizing the emperor for being effeminate as well as overconfident by "even" bringing his women with him on campaign on Arrakis; whether meant positively or negatively, such was the Komnenian practice as noted in the papers above, and see further discussion of this below. Evans, "Women of the Future," 54.

15. Herbert, *Dune Messiah*, 53.

16. Herbert, *Dune Messiah*, esp. 170; Howard, "Religious Violence in Frank Herbert's *Dune* Series," 48.

17. To give just one famous example, Empress Eirene of Athens blinded her son Constantine VI, due to his alleged disastrous rule, in order to take over herself. On blinding in Byzantium, see in particular Stumpf, "On the Mutilation and Blinding of Byzantine Emperors from the Reign of Heraclius I until the Fall of Constantinople," 46–54.

18. Ancient Roman and Holy Roman Imperial themes should still not be discounted, see Kennedy, "Epic World-Building: Names and Cultures in *Dune*," 102; Ower, "Idea and Imagery in Herbert's *Dune*," 129–39.

19. Yeats, *The Tower*, 1–3.

20. San Juan, *Poetics*, 59.

21. These tensions are discussed best by DiTommaso, "History and Historical Effect in Frank Herbert's 'Dune,'" 311–25.

22. Yeats, *The Tower*, 3.

23. *Ibid.*

24. Comnena, *The Alexiad*. For the original Greek text cited in this essay, see *Annae Comnenae Alexias*, edited by Reinsch and Kambylis (subsequently cited as: Komnene, *Alexiad*).

25. Komnene, *Alexiad*, 5.1–11.

26. The exact dating has been debated by historians, but these are still the accepted timings for these events. See Komnene, *Alexiad*, 40.93–4 and 451.31–32; Zonaras, *Ioannis Zonarae Epitome Historiarum libri XIII–XVIII*, 18.21.20; Neville, *Anna Komnene*, 82.

27. Komnene, *Alexiad*, 194.42–195.95; Neville, *Anna Komnene*, 3, esp. n. 10; Kazhdan, *The Oxford Dictionary of Byzantium*, 363, 1570.

28. Komnena, *Alexiad*, 184.97–8, 184.85–6. The former is backed up by the court rhetor Michael Italikos: *Michel Italikos Lettres et Discours*, 107.11–22. The latter point is mentioned in Anna's funeral oration by George Tornikes: Tornikes, *Georges et Dèmetrios Tornikès, Lettres et Discours*, 257–63.

29. Herbert, *Dune*, 127–28, 237, 302–03, 342, with the former being the one referring to Duke Leto.

30. The Jesuit inspiration was noted by Timothy O'Reilly in his biography of Frank Herbert, and this was then echoed by Brian Herbert in his biography of his father. See O'Reilly, *Frank Herbert*, 89; Herbert, *Dreamer of Dune*, 23, 193.

31. Herbert, *Dune*, 302–03, 550. As noted by DiTommaso, "History and Historical Effect in Frank Herbert's *Dune*," 323, n.15, Irulan's original Bene Gesserit purpose is unclear, as the Bene Gesserit did not foresee that the Kwisatz Haderach would come a generation early in the person of Paul. Perhaps this lack of sons and a period of less stable rule by Irulan was intended to create a power vacuum in which the Kwisatz Haderach could rise. Though DiTommaso deems it unlikely that Irulan was originally intended to marry the Bene Gesserit's intended Kwizatz Haderach (the planned son of Feyd-Rautha and Jessica's daughter by Leto), the extended lifespans granted by Spice make this a possibility. Further, in Byzantium there are a few cases of elder empresses marrying younger spouses, such as Zoe of the Macedonian dynasty who was married twice in her 50s to younger men in the early eleventh century.

32. *Ibid.* 550, 561

33. In the Sci-Fi Channel adaption of *Dune*, earlier scenes that discuss this possibility are added to presage this. See below for details.
34. Herbert, *Dune*, 526.
35. Herbert, *Dune Messiah*, 14–15.
36. *Ibid.*, 16.
37. *Ibid.*
38. *Ibid.*
39. Choniates, *Nicetae Choniatae Historia*, 10; Zonaras, *Epitome*, 18.26, 753.
40. Choniates, *Nicetae Choniatae Historia*, 10.
41. *Ibid.* 11.
42. Neville, *Anna Komnene*, 134–39, 163, 168, 171, 218 n119.
43. Gibbon, *Decline and Fall of the Roman Empire*, 231.
44. Cavafy, *Collected Poems*, 109; Neville, *Anna Komnene*, 6.
45. Diehl, *Figures Byzantines*, 190–93; Neville, *Anna Komnene*, 6.
46. For example, Georgina Buckler's 1929 monograph does not in fact believe that Anna disputed the succession at all, and rather argues that Choniates' account was fictional. Buckler, *Anna Comnena: A Study*, 27–31; Neville, *Anna Komnene*, 169–70.
47. Howard-Johnston, "Anna Komnene and the Alexiad," 260–302.
48. See Macrides "The Pen and the Sword: Who Wrote the *Alexiad*?" 63–82, and a general outline in Sinclair, "Anna Komnene and Her Sources for Military Affairs in the *Alexiad*," 143–185.
49. Herbert, *Dune*, 562.
50. List, "Call Me a Protestant," 21–47.
51. Herbert, *Dune*, 516.
52. Meza, "The Bene Gesserit in Frank Herbert's Dune," 32–33.
53. Hand, "The Traditionalism of Women's Roles in Frank Herbert's Dune," 24–28; Miller, "Women of *Dune*," 181–92; Knězková, "Frank Herbert's Heroines."
54. Savitt, "Female Stereotypes in Literature"; Knězková, "Frank Herbert's Heroines," 16–23, 56. For an introduction to the expansive field of study on Byzantine women, start with Herrin, *Byzantium*, esp. 55, or take the dive into the online *Bibliography on Gender in Byzantium* by Dumbarton Oaks.
55. Herbert, *Dune*, 545.
56. *Ibid.*
57. Knězková, "Frank Herbert's Heroines," 52–54.
58. Silliman, "Conserving the Balance," 32, 67–68, 120.
59. Evans, "Women of the Future," 73.
60. McLean, "A Psychological Approach to Fantasy in the Dune Series," 152; Silliman, "Conserving the Balance," 62.
61. "vaincu" and "confirment sa situation de personnage ballotté par l'histoire, incapable de l'influencer, ni même de la comprendre," respectively. Rossignol, "Figures de l'historien dans le cycle de *Dune* de Frank Herbert," 6.
62. Manlove, *Science Fiction: Ten Explorations*, 88; Touponce, *Frank Herbert*, 30–31; Knězková, "Frank Herbert's Heroines," 52.
63. Choniates wrote his manuscript in three drafts: one under Alexios III Angelos in the late 12th or early 13th century before the fall of Constantinople, one shortly afterwards and one a decade later. For an overview in what has taken a considerable amount of scholarship to uncover, see Choniates, *Nicetae Choniatae Historia*, VII-CV.
64. Kaldellis, "Paradox, Reversal and the Meaning of History," 75–99. Neville, *Heroes and Romans in Twelfth Century Byzantium*, 22.
65. Choniates, *Nicetae Choniatae Historia*, 10; Neville, *Anna Komnene*, 108.
66. Neville, *Anna Komnene*, passim, esp. 91–174.
67. Chalandon, *Jean II Comnène, 1118–1143, et Manuel I Comnène, 1143–1180*, 16; Neville, *Anna Komnene*, 163; c.f. Jessica's words above, whereby she hopes: "[Irulan] finds solace in such things [her "pretensions of a literary nature"] as she'll have little else," implying that such pursuits are only ever some sort of consolation prize for failed plotters. Discussed further below.

68. Regarding their role as patrons in general, Tornikes mentions in his funeral oration for Anna how she and her husband made their house "a home of the Muses," and various works, both philosophical, historical and fictional, can be traced to this *theatron*, see: Bryennios, *Nicéphore Bryennios Histoire*, 340–55; Prodromos, *Theodore Prodromos: historische Gedichte*, Poem LIX; Cramer, "Xenedemus," 204–15; Tannery, "Théodore Prodrome sur le grand et le petit," 104–19. Tornikes, *Lettres et Discours*, 267, 283–93; Jeffreys, *Four Byzantine Novels*, 3–156; Italikos, *Michel Italikos Lettres et Discours*, 146–51.

69. Neville, *Anna Komnene*, 178.

70. Vilimonović, *Structures and Features of Anna Komnene's* Alexiad, esp. 16–18, 48, 163–242, 263–66, 307–42.

71. Herbert, *Dune Messiah*, 221.

72. Herbert, *Children of Dune*, 145, 273, 302.

73. *Ibid.*, 275–77.

74. *Ibid.*, esp. 302–03.

75. See Phillips, "The Greatest Predator Ever Known," and Womack, "He Who Controls Knowledge Controls the Universe," in this volume on Leto II.

76. Herbert, *Dune*, 319.

77. O'Reilly, *Frank Herbert*, esp. Chapters 4 and 5.

78. Manlove, *Science Fiction: Ten Explorations*, 88; Touponce, *Frank Herbert*, 30–31; Knězková, "Frank Herbert's Heroines," 56–57.

79. Herbert, *Children of Dune*, 211.

80. Herbert, *Heretics of Dune*, 403.

81. See above, but also especially where she argues that where today we study Alexios and then, if at all, we skip forward to Manuel, "Anna's revenge [on John] could not have been stronger or more pervasive": Vilimonović, *Structures and Features of Anna Komnene's* Alexiad, 337

82. Similarly, the quasi-canonical *Paul of Dune* novel, set in between *Dune* and *Dune Messiah*, also gives Irulan a major role, especially in the final chapter where she explicitly partakes in creating the legend of Muad'Dib. In *The Winds of Dune*, set after *Dune Messiah*, she debates how the empire should evolve after Paul's disappearance. Brian Herbert and Kevin J. Anderson's recognition of the role of Irulan in the saga is thus telling as to how *Dune* has been interpreted over the years in a similar way to the film adaptations. Herbert and Anderson, *Paul of Dune*, and *The Winds of Dune*.

83. Herbert, *Dune*, 549; Knězková, "Frank Herbert's Heroines," 57.

84. *Ibid.*, 57–58.

85. *Ibid.*, 55

86. Hise, *The Secrets of Frank Herbert's Dune*, 92–95.

87. *Ibid.*, 92 and 95.

88. Pseudo-Kodinos, *Traité des offices*, 133–66. For an introduction to Byzantine dress, see: Ball, *Byzantine Dress: Representations of Secular Dress*. Such influence is, indeed, prominent in more recent Czech fashion history, from where Pištěk hails, as the great Art Nouveau artist Alphonse Mucha extensively used the Byzantine aesthetic. See in particular his poster for Sarah Bernhardt as Gismonda or the Byzantine Heads, though also his Slav Epic for the theme in general. See "Gismonda," "Byzantine Heads," and "Slav Epic" in Mucha, "The Mucha Foundation." Similarly, the common association of Byzantine fashion with gold and purple was used in Chanel's "Paris-Byzance" fashion line, the garments from which are of a kind with Pištěk's designs. Quin, "Paris-Byzance Fashion Show."

89. Herbert, *Children of Dune*.

90. Many thanks to my proof-readers, Nathaniel Helms, Melissa Tyler, and Aoife Ní Chroidheáin, for their invaluable feedback.

WORKS CITED

Abulafia, David. "Crusades, Spies, and Cruising the Colourful Life of Steven Runciman: Historian, Scholar-diplomat, and Possibly Spy." *STANDPOINT*, September 27, 2016.

https://standpointmag.co.uk/issues/october-2016/books-october-2016-david-abulafia-outlandish-knight-steven-runciman-minoo-dinshaw/

Ball, Jennifer. *Byzantine Dress: Representations of Secular Dress*. New York: Macmillan, 2006.

Bryennios, Nikephoros. *Nicéphore Bryennios Histoire*, translated Paul Gautier. Brussels: Byzantion, 1975.

Cameron, Averil. "Byzantinist and Others." In *Byzantium in Dialogue with the Mediterranean*, edited by Daniëlle Slootjes and Mariette Verhoeven, 6–23. Leiden: Brill, 2019.

Carpenter, Humphrey. *The Inklings: C.S. Lewis, J.R.R Tolkien, Charles Williams and Their Friends*. London: George Allen and Unwin, 1978.

Cavafy, Constantine. *Collected Poems*, revised edition, translated by Edmund Keeley and Philip Sherrard, edited by George Savidis. Princeton, NJ: Princeton University Press, 1992.

Chalandon, Ferdinand. *Jean II Comnène, 1118–1143, et Manuel I Comnène, 1143–1180,* Reprint 2 vols. Paris: Alphonse Picard et fils, 1912.

Choniates, Niketas. *Nicetae Choniatae Historia*, edited by J. van Dieten, Berlin: W. de Gruyter, 1975. English Translation: H.J. Magoulias, *O City of Byzantium, Annals of Niketas Choniates*. Detroit: Wayne State University Press, 1984.

Collins, Will. "The Secret History of Dune." *Los Angeles Review of Books*. September 16, 2017. https://lareviewofbooks.org/article/the-secret-history-of-dune/

Comnena, Anna. *The Alexiad*, translated by Edgar Sewton and Peter Frankopan, revised edition. London: Penguin, 2009.

Cramer, John. "Xenedemus." *Anecdota graeca e codd. manuscriptis bibliothecarum Oxoniensum*, vol. 3. Oxford, UK: Oxford University Press, 1836: 204–15

Csicsery-Ronay Jr, Isvan. *The Seven Beauties of Science Fiction*. Middletown, CT: Wesleyan University Press, 2008.

Dennis, George. "Imperial Panegyric: Rhetoric and Reality." In *Byzantine Court Culture from 829 to 1204*, edited by Henry Maguire, 131–40. Washington, D.C.: Dumbarton Oaks Research Library and Collection, 1997.

Diehl, Charles. *Figures Byzantines*. Paris: Armand Colin, 1906.

DiTommaso, Lorenzo. "History and Historical Effect in Frank Herbert's *Dune*." *Science Fiction Studies* 19, no. 3 (1992): 311–25.

DiTommaso, Lorenzo. "The Articulation of Imperial Decadence and Decline in Epic Science Fiction." *Extrapolation* 48, no. 2 (2007): 267–91.

Dumbarton Oaks Research Library and Collection. "Bibliography on Gender in Byzantium." Accessed October 10, 2019. https://www.doaks.org/research/byzantine/resources/bibliography-on-gender-in-byzantium#cl=&b_start=0

Evans, Carrie. *Women of the Future: Gender, Technology, and Cyborgs in Frank Herbert's Dune*. Master's Thesis, Université Laval, 2016.

Gibbon, Edward. *The History of the Decline and Fall of the Roman Empire*, edited by David Womersley. London: Penguin, 1994.

Harper, Toby. "'Going Native' with Dune's Paul Atreides." Center for Imperial and Global History, University of Exeter. June 26, 2018. https://imperialglobalexeter.com/2018/06/26/going-native-with-dunes-paul-atreides/#_ftn6

Hand, Jack. "The Traditionalism of Women's Roles in Frank Herbert's *Dune*." *Extrapolation* 26, no. 1 (1985): 24–28.

Herbert, Brian. *Dreamer of Dune: The Biography of Frank Herbert*. New York: Tor, 2003.

Herbert, Brian, and Kevin J. Anderson. *Paul of Dune*. London: Hodder, 2008.

Herbert, Brian, and Kevin J. Anderson. *The Winds of Dune*. New York: Simon & Schuster, 2010.

Herbert, Frank. *Chapterhouse Dune*. London: Gollancz, 1985.

Herbert, Frank. *Children of Dune*. London: Gollancz, 1976.

Herbert, Frank. *Dune*, London: Gollancz, 1966.

Herbert, Frank. *Dune Messiah*. London: Gollancz, 1969.

Herbert, Frank. *God Emperor of Dune*. London: Gollancz, 1981.

Herbert, Frank. *Heretics of Dune*. London: Gollancz, 1984.

Herrin, Judith. *Byzantium: The Surprising Life of a Medieval Empire*. London: Penguin, 2008.

Holland, Tom. *In the Shadow of the Sword*. London: Abacus, 2012.

Howard, Kenton. "Religious Violence in Frank Herbert's *Dune* Series." Master's Thesis, Florida Atlantic University, 2012.

Howard-Johnston, James. "Anna Komnene and the Alexiad." In *Alexios I Komnenos: Papers of the Second Belfast Byzantine International Colloquium, 14–16th April 1989 (Byzantine Texts and Translations 4)*, edited by M. Mullett and D. Smythe, 260–302. Belfast: Belfast Byzantine Enterprises, 1996.

Italikos, Michael. *Michel Italikos Lettres et Discours*, edited by Paul Gautier. Paris: Institut Français d'Etudes Byzantines, 1972.

James, Liz (editor). *A Companion to Byzantium*. Oxford, UK: Blackwell, 2010.

Jeffreys, Elizabeth. *Four Byzantine Novels*. Liverpool: Liverpool University Press, 2012.

Kaldellis, Anthony. "Paradox, Reversal and the Meaning of History." In *Niketas Choniates A Historian and Writer*, edited by Alicia Simpson and Stephanos Efthymiadis, 75–99. Seyssel: la pomme d'or, 2009.

Kazhdan, Alexander. *The Oxford Dictionary of Byzantium*. Oxford, UK: Oxford University Press, 1991.

Kennedy, Kara. "Epic World-Building: Names and Cultures in *Dune*." *Names* 64, no. 2 (2016), 99–108.

Kennedy, Kara. "Lawrence of Arabia, Paul Atreides, and the Roots of Frank Herbert's *Dune*." *TOR.com*. June 2, 2021. https://www.tor.com/2021/06/02/lawrence-of-arabia-paul-atreides-and-the-roots-of-frank-herberts-dune/#more-647150

Knězková, Klára. "Frank Herbert's Heroines: Female Characters in Dune and Its Film Adaptions." Master's Thesis, Masaryk University, 2007.

Lau, Maximilian. "*Ioannoupolis*: Lopadion as 'City' and Military Headquarters under Emperor Ioannes II Komnenos." In *The City and the Cities—Selected Papers from the XVI Oxford University Byzantine Society International Graduate Conference*, edited by Nicholas Matheou, Theofili Kampanaki and Lorenzo Bondioli, 435–64. Leiden: Brill, 2016.

Lenz, Joseph. "Manifest Destiny: Science Fiction and Classical Form." In *Coordinates: Placing Science Fiction and Fantasy*, edited by George Slusser, Eric Rabkin and Robery Scholes, 42–48. Carbondale: Southern Illinois University Press, 1983.

Librán-Moreno, Miryam. "'Byzantium, New Rome!' Goths, Langobards and Byzantium in The Lord of the Rings." In *Tolkien and the Study of his Sources. Critical Essays*, edited by Jason Fisher, 84–115. Jefferson, NC: McFarland, 2011.

List, Julia. "'Call Me a Protestant': Liberal Christianity, Individualism, and the Messiah in 'Stranger in a Strange Land,' 'Dune,' and 'Lord of Light.'" *Science Fiction Studies* 36, no. 1 (March 2009): 21–47.

McLean, Susan. "A Psychological Approach to Fantasy in the Dune Series." *Extrapolation* 23, no. 2 (1982): 150–8.

Macrides, Ruth. "The Pen and the Sword: Who Wrote the *Alexiad*?" In *Anna Komnene and her Times*, edited by Thalia Gouma-Petersen, 63–82. New York: Garland Publishing, 2000.

Maguire, Henry (editor). *Byzantine Court Culture from 829–1204*. Cambridge, MA: Harvard University Press, 2004.

Manlove, Colin, *Science Fiction: Ten Explorations*. Kent, Ohio: Kent State University Press, 1986.

Meza, Luis. *The Bene Gesserit in Frank Herbert's Dune: An Analysis*. Bachelors Dissertation, University of Iceland, 2010.

Miller, Miriam. "Women of *Dune*: Frank Herbert as Social Reactionary?" *Women Worldwalkers: New Dimensions of Science Fiction and Fantasy* (Studies in Comparative Literature), edited by Jane B. Weedman, 181–92. Lubbock: Texas Tech University Press, 1985.

Mucha, Alphonse. "The Mucha Foundation." The Mucha Foundation. December 5, 2019. http://www.muchafoundation.org/

Mullet, Margaret. "Tented Ceremony: Ephemeral Performances Under the Komnenoi."

Court Ceremonies and Rituals of Power in Byzantium and the Medieval Mediterranean Comparative Perspectives, edited by Alexander Beihammer, Stavroula Constantinou, and Maria Parani, 487–514. Leiden: Brill, 2013.

Neville, Leonora. *Anna Komnene the Life and Work of a Medieval Historian*. Oxford, UK: Oxford University Press, 2016.

Neville, Leonora. *Heroes and Romans in Twelfth Century Byzantium*. Cambridge, UK: Cambridge University Press, 2012.

O'Reilly, Timothy. *Frank Herbert* ("Recognitions" Series). New York: Frederick Ungar, 1981. https://www.oreilly.com/tim/herbert/index.html

Ower, John. "Idea and Imagery in Herbert's Dune." *Extrapolation* 15, no. 2 (1974): 129–39.

Prodromos, Theodore. *Theodore Prodromos: historische Gedichte*, edited by Wolfram Hörandner. Vienna: Verlag d. Österr. Akad. d. Wiss., 1974.

Pseudo-Kodinos. *Traité des offices [introduction, texte et traduction par Jean Verpeaux]*. Paris: Centre national de la recherche scientifique, 1976

Quin, Elisabeth. "The Paris-Byzance Fashion Show." Chanel. Accessed December 5, 2019. https://www.chanel.com/en_WW/fashion/news/2010/12/the-paris-byzance-show.html

Roberts, Adam. *Science Fiction*. Abingdon: Routledge, 2000.

Rossignol, Benoît. "Figures de l'historien dans le cycle de *Dune* de Frank Herbert." *Cycnos* 22, no. 2 (2005): 1–19.

Runciman, Steven. *A History of the Crusades*, 3 Volumes. Cambridge, UK: Cambridge University Press, 1951–4.

Said, Edward. *Orientalism*. New York: Vintage Books, 1979.

San Juan, Epifiano. *Poetics: The Imitation of Action*. Plainsboro: Associated University Presses, 1979.

Savitt, Jill D. "Female Stereotypes in Literature (With a Focus on Latin American Writers)." Curriculum units of Yale-New Haven Teachers Institute V, 20 parts (1982). February 26, 2007: http://www.yale.edu/ynhti/curriculum/units/1982/5/82.05.06.x.html

Silliman, Barbara. *Conserving the Balance: Frank Herbert's Dune as Propaganda*. Doctoral Dissertation, University of Rhode Island, 1996.

Sinclair, Kyle. "Anna Komnene and Her Sources for Military Affairs in the *Alexiad*." *Estudios bizantinos* 2 (2014): 143–185.

Stephenson, Paul (editor). *The Byzantine World*. Abingdon: Routledge, 2012.

Stumpf, Jonathan. "On the Mutilation and Blinding of Byzantine Emperors from the Reign of Heraclius I Until the Fall of Constantinople." *Journal of Ancient History and Archaeology* 4, no. 3 (2017) 46–54.

Tannery, Paul. "Théodore Prodrome sur le grand et le petit." *Annuaire des Études Grecques* 21 (1887): 104–19

Tolkien, J.R.R. *The Letters of J.R.R. Tolkien*, edited by Humphrey Carpenter and Christopher Tolkien. London: HarperCollins, 1981.

Tornikes, George. *Georges et Dèmetrios Tornikès, Lettres et Discours*, edited by Jean Darrouzès. Paris: Editions Du Centre National De La Recherche Scientifique, 1970.

Touponce, William. *Frank Herbert*. Boston: Twayne Publishers, 1988.

Van Hise, James. *The Secrets of Frank Herbert's Dune*. London: Simon & Schuster, 2001.

Vilimonović, Larisa. *Structures and Features of Anna Komnene's* Alexiad *Emergence of a Personal History*. Amsterdam: University of Amsterdam Press, 2019.

Yeats, William Butler. *The Tower: Facsimile Edition*. New York: Scribner's, 2004.

Zonaras, John. *Ioannis Zonarae Epitome Historiarum libri XIII-XVIII, CSHB* 49, Vol III, edited by Theodore Büttner-Wobst. Leipzig: Teubner, 1897.

Beside the Sand Dunes

Arab Futurism, Faith, and the Fremen of Dune

R. ALI

Frank Herbert's Dune saga features one of the most prominent uses of Arabic and Islamic material in science fiction history. He drew inspiration from the Middle East, using Arabic terms, such as *Mahdi* ("rightly guided"),[1] and named his charismatic protagonist *Muad'Dib*, meaning "educator, teacher and discipliner."[2] In his biography on Frank Herbert, Touponce recognizes that "the predominant number" of terms in Dune "stem from Arabic language."[3] In *Dreamer of Dune*, another biography of Frank Herbert, Brian Herbert mentions that his father studied the Arabic language and literature so extensively that he was able to "think and write" in it.[4] He mentions that "the books Frank Herbert wanted to keep were almost entirely non-fiction—works of history (especially Arab history)."[5] Herbert drew from several Arabic and Islamic sources for his Dune novels, particularly the Qur'an. Most of these sources are found in the first three Dune books—*Dune, Dune Messiah*, and *Children of Dune*, which Herbert viewed as one complete book.[6]

The influence the Qur'an has had on Dune is important both tonally and stylistically. Herbert clearly studied the Qur'an carefully and found particular interest in subjects pertaining to nature, life, water, faith, and God. The Qur'an uses parables and similes as an explanatory method, which Herbert emulates in the Dune trilogy. He uses the language of the Qur'an as a narrative style when portraying Fremen customs, cultures, and ceremonies. This demonstrates his astuteness at identifying the style of language used within such Islamic texts and utilizing those styles in his own writing. Almost every English translation of the Qur'an is unique, each differing slightly in wording, making it easier to identify one translation from another. This makes it possible to trace which versions Herbert used in his research.

Although other scholars have recognized that Herbert borrowed Arabic and Islamic terms, there has been little work identifying where those terms might have been borrowed from specifically. Herbert himself explicitly says, "I based the terminology in *Dune* on colloquial Arabic."[7] Tim O'Reilly touches upon this in his biography of Frank Herbert.[8] While these themes have been explored, perhaps most extensively by Csicsery-Ronay Jr.,[9] and the etymological roots of the words recognized most accurately in Karin Ryding's *The Arabic of Dune: Language and Landscape*, few have offered insight into Herbert's true sources and the deeper meanings behind their usage.[10] For example, as explored below, most of the specific verses Herbert cites from the Qur'an match the A.J. Arberry and Richard Bell translations, and most of the Arabic terms and phrases he uses match Gustave von Grunebaum's *Medieval Islam*.[11]

This essay begins with a brief discussion on Arab Futurism and the importance of Islamic themes and terminologies in the Dune saga. Quotes from Herbert's works are compared to Islamic texts, analyzing specific instances in which the Dune novels quote Qur'anic verses. I continue by showing how Herbert uses Islamic and Arabic history as a tool for his world-building, providing specific examples of Islamic concepts and quotes that inspired names and ideas in the Dune franchise.

The Arab Futurism of Dune

Dune is arguably the first science fiction story to prominently feature Arab Futurism. Herbert places Arabic words, terms, and phrases from the past into the far future, where the vast majority of their meanings remain the same. The concept of Arab Futurism or "Arabfuturism" is the expression of narratives that explore alternative pasts, and project ideas into a future where the Arab identity thrives.[12] It looks at the past and present condition of the Arab world and envisions a future free of the hardships it faces. Frank Herbert's *Dune* explored this idea in the 1960s with his research of historical Arab events, applied to his futuristic setting.

That these Arabic and Islamic themes become a part of the universal narrative of humanity is arguably one of the most important messages in *Dune*. The story offers a future in which humanity bands together for a common cause, the Butlerian Jihad against thinking machines. Due to the war, all of humanity essentially become refugees and Earth becomes a distant memory in the universe, creating a reality they can all relate to. The book gives the reader a taste of the Middle East, provides a space for "the other," and suggests a future in which ideas of faith and language are shared and adopted among all of human society. It is a future in which the Arabic language and Islamic concepts are not confined to the Muslim world, but rather are widely used and accepted by all of humanity, carrying this shared culture to new worlds.

Most of the Arab Futurism in *Dune* is layered. It is not hidden, nor is it explained in great detail. Herbert found no need to justify it. It is simply a reality in his universe; a universe that embraces the Arabic language and elements of Islamic spiritualism, among other ideas on spirituality. It can be seen in the assimilation of Arabic terms throughout the Imperium. This implies that the future of humanity was shaped with the participation of Arab cultures. For example, in *Dune*, Herbert refers to Chairman Bomoko Toure of the Commission of Ecumenical Translators (C.E.T.) as one of the *ulema*, which means learned and informed scholars in Arabic.[13] Just as the historical *ulema* would translate works from Latin to Arabic, Toure was a translator of the Orange Catholic Bible (O.C. Bible), a prominent religious text in the Imperium.[14]

Arabic and Islamic terms can be found in a variety of contexts. Herbert's "Terminology of the Imperium," the glossary at the end of *Dune*, contains words such as *baraka*[15] meaning "blessing,"[16] which Henri Massé describes the possessor of it as having "the mysterious gift of spiritual power (Baraka)" in his book *Islam*.[17] It is a concept the Bene Gesserit sisterhood studied and taught long before they encountered the Fremen,[18] implying that their interest in Arabic and Islamic culture was an independent endeavor, predating their arrival on Arrakis. The sisterhood is linked to Egypt through the study of the "Azhar Book,"[19] a compilation of great religious secrets seemingly named after Cairo's *Al Azhar*, one of the most prestigious Islamic universities and mosques in the world.[20] The term could specifically be inspired by "The Book" of *Al Azhar*, the "basis of the whole curriculum" of the academy, which is the Qur'an.[21]

Reverend Mothers like Ramallo on Arrakis refer to the Fremen as "the people of Misr,"[22] using the Arabic name for Egypt.[23] This might have been part of the Fremen identity long before they settled on Arrakis, but "Misr" might also be a term implanted by the Bene Gesserit Sisterhood among the Fremen via the Missionaria Protectiva. Jessica's internal thought reveals her knowledge of "dar al-hikman" as a common term among the Sisterhood.[24] Defined as a "school of religious translation or interpretation" in the *Dune* glossary, it is based on Cairo's *dar al-hikmah* (hall of wisdom), built by the Caliph al-Hakim in the tenth and eleventh centuries. Both the dar al-hikmah and al-Azhar were established in Cairo by the Fatimid's. As the Azhar book of the Bene Gesserit relates to the "Misr" of nonfictional Earth history, all of these references are tied to the origins of their order, implying that the Sisterhood are descended from or associated with Egypt.

Patterns and Styles of Sacred Dune Texts

Like the learned Bene Gesserit, Islamic history has a tradition of scholarly women. In the age of the Prophet Muhammad, "writing was taught to women and many names are given of women who knew how to write."[25] They memorized, collected, and compiled the sayings of the times. Much like Irulan's "Collected Sayings of Muad'Dib," these women collected sayings of Muhammad, which are called *hadith*. These respected female scholars, also called *ulema*, were held in high esteem and taught *hadith* sayings to those who sought them. The writings of Princess Irulan echo that of a compiler of *hadith*. The epigraphs Herbert places at the beginning of each chapter emulate the structure of *hadiths*, which include commentaries on prophethood collected in books by scholars and scribes, offering insight into past and future events.

Herbert actually uses the term *hadith* in the Dune novels, such as when Stilgar describes Fremen ways as "our science of tradition, our hadith."[26] Herbert equates a *hadith* to the beauty of song, referring to Gurney Halleck's ability to "play" them on his baliset, describing them as an "old Fremen song" with an "internal narrative" and a "voice which invoked those patterns required for survival on Arrakis."[27] This description mirrors the structure and format of a *hadith*.

The narrative style of a Qur'anic chapter is presented to the reader as though written outside the limitations of time. The Qur'an often tells stories of past events that are relevant to the immediate experiences of the Prophet and his companions at the time of its revelation, but the verses can be relatable to the current reader and offer insight into future events, often as an informative lesson or warning. This resembles the epigraphs of the Dune novels and how they are often set many years after the events of the story, yet seem relevant to the current themes and events of each chapter.

The Dune novels cite actual Qur'anic verses to perform a similar function. The verses quoted from the Qur'an occur in significant moments of the narrative, and also refer to past, present, and future events that relate to the current situation of the characters. For example, the word *kalima*—which means "word" in Arabic and is used to describe religious scripture[28]—occurs several times throughout the Dune trilogy. The term also refers to the Islamic declaration of faith: "*Ash-hadu an la illaha illAllah, wa Ash-hadu an-na Muhammadan rasul-ullah*" (which translates as "There is no God but God and Muhammad is The Messenger of God"). Those who believe this statement and declare it are Muslim. In *History of the Arabs*, Philip Hitti mentions, "The child's education began at home. As soon as he could speak it was the father's duty to teach him 'the word' (*al-kalimah*): *La ilaha illa-l-Lah....*"[29]

In *Dune*, Dr. Wellington Yueh teaches the "Kalima" to a young Paul Atreides, instructing him to open the Orange Catholic Bible "to four-sixty-seven Kalima,"[30] using the word in the context of a holy book. It seems that Herbert understood *kalima* to mean "word," especially in the Islamic sense of a divine message. In *Medieval Islam*, one of the few books in which the versions of terms and Qur'anic quotes that Herbert uses in the Dune novels are found, Gustave von Grunebaum talks about "Jesus as a Word (*kalima*)." He quotes from chapter 4 of the Qur'an, called "The Women" which says: "The Messiah Jesus, son of Mary, is only the messenger of Allah, and His Word (*kalima*) which He cast upon Mary, and a spirit (*ruh*) from Him."[31] Herbert spells *kalima* similarly to Grunebaum, whereas other scholars tend to use different spellings, such as *kalimah*. The Fremen concept of the "Ruh-spirit" is another term Herbert likely formulated from this Qur'anic verse found in Grunebaum's book.[32]

While trying to determine the Qur'anic translations Herbert used, Yueh's "467" kalima reference number may offer clues. If one applies that number to the Qur'an, chapter "46" is called "The Sand Dunes," the only chapter to mention dunes in the translations available to Herbert at the time. It speaks of a prophet who warns "his people beside the sand-dunes...."[33] The verse resembles the origins of Herbert's idea for his Dune trilogy, particularly in relation to *Children of Dune*, when Muad'Dib becomes The Preacher and brings his warnings from the desert.

Herbert was interested in patterns of poetry for his writing style, especially the *haiku* form[34]; therefore, he might have found patterns in the Qur'an to be of interest. "The Sand Dunes," Chapter 46 of the Qur'an, begins with "Ha-Mim," a mysterious set of letters with unknown meaning found at the beginning of some chapters of the Qur'an. They occur exactly seven times in the Qur'an, chapter 46 being the final instance in which it is found. These seven chapters are collectively called the "*Hawamim*," which all begin with the Arabic letters Ha and Mim, and are particularly known for the beauty and elegance of their literary style. Herbert seems to have been inspired by the *Hawamim* pattern because throughout his Dune trilogy, characters quote from seven different Qur'anic chapters of Herbert's own choosing. Curiously, Richard Bell's translation of the Qur'an dedicates an entire introduction to the *Hawamim* "rhyme," which is discussed and analyzed in great detail on page 467, the same number as Yueh's religious text reference.[35] This could be the formula from which Herbert derives his "467" kalima.

Applying Dr. Yueh's number "four-sixty-seven" specifically to the Arberry and Bell translations of the Qur'an leads to chapter 4 again, "The Women," and verse 67 which reads:

We sent not ever any Messenger, but that he should be obeyed, by the leave of God. If, when they wronged themselves, they had come to thee, and prayed forgiveness of God, and the Messenger had prayed forgiveness for them, they would have found God turns, All-compassionate.[36]

In other words, this numerical value leads to a verse on seeking forgiveness, which is relevant in light of Dr. Yueh's subsequent betrayal of House Atreides. Yueh teaches the 467 Kalima verse to Paul as an act of healing, which he does to "salve his own conscience."[37] He wrongs himself by betraying the Atreides, due to the Harkonnen imprisonment of his wife Wanna, perhaps the woman most important to him.

Another quote that originates from "The Women" occurs during a conversation between the Sardaukar officer Tyekanik and Corrino Princess Wensicia in *Children of Dune*. When she issues orders, he replies, "I hear and obey, Princess." "We hear and obey" (4:46) is found most prominently in N.J. Dawood's translation of the Qur'an, as well as several others with variant wording.[38] It is a definitive saying from Qur'anic scripture that does not seem to occur similarly in any other scriptural texts. It also appears extensively throughout *The Thousand and One Nights*, which Dawood translated for Penguin books. It is a phrase adopted from the Qur'an and featured in several versions of *The Arabian Nights*. There is little evidence of this phrase being present in other literature or scripture to suggest it came from elsewhere, and those sources do not feature an individual or group explicitly saying the phrase "I" or "we" "hear and obey." Therefore, the Qur'an is the likely source of Herbert's phrase.

The style of language in the Qur'an is applied later on in *God Emperor of Dune* to the speech of Leto II. The "God Emperor" encourages his subjects to recall the past by saying, "remember your own past" and "recall how I treated you,"[39] similar to how God prompts the reader in the Qur'an: "Remember how We delivered you from Pharaoh's people,"[40] and "Recall the brother of 'Ad when he warned his people in the sand-dunes."[41] Leto II encourages Sister Chenoeh to recite a "chorus" reminiscent of a Qur'anic verse: "Why didn't someone warn me?" He then adds, "But I did warn you. I warned you by example...."[42] This resembles a verse in "The Prophets" where God teaches the Prophet Muhammad "verses" to say to disbelievers: "If they give no heed, say: 'I have warned you...'"[43]

The Qur'anic Verses of Dune

Before *Dune* was published in August 1965, it was released in serialized form in *Analog* magazine, the second part titled "The Prophet of

Dune." Herbert was inspired to write *Dune* while researching an article about the movement of sand dunes and the threat of desertification:

> I hit on the idea of a desert planet while researching a magazine article about efforts to control sand dunes. This led me to other research avenues too numerous to detail completely here, but involving some time in a desert (Sonora) and a re-examination of Islam.[44]

Most of the historical Arab texts, available to Herbert at the time he was writing the first three Dune novels discuss various Qur'anic verses. In his trilogy, Herbert draws from several chapters of the Qur'an. His chosen Qur'anic verses are not confined to chapter headings like his epigraphs in the style of *hadiths*, but they are woven into the plot itself. Individual verses of the Qur'an are called *ayat*, a word Herbert uses in *Dune* to describe the information contained within a Fremkit manual, vital for survival on the desert planet of Arrakis. The manual reads: "Here are the ayat and burhan of Life. Believe, and al-Lat shall never burn you."[45] The glossary in the appendices to *Dune* describes "ayat" as "the signs of life," which is also defined as a sign in Arabic.[46] The word "*burhan*" means "proof,"[47] the same definition as listed in the glossary. The *Ayat* of the Qur'an written in the Arabic language urges individuals to reflect upon "signs" and "proofs" pertaining to the stars, planets, life, and creation. These matters seem appropriate for the Fremen people of Arrakis and are likely topics which mattered to Herbert himself.

Herbert's Fremkit manual is called the *Kitab al-Ibar*, the title of a real historical book written by the Tunisian Sunni scholar Ibn Khaldun. Often called his magnum opus, it is widely praised by academics. When Jessica convinces the Fremen that she represents the fulfillment of their legend, she sees a "Fremen with the book of examples" in her waking vision.[48] Ibn Khaldun himself refers to his book as "the Book of Examples, Kitab al-'ibar."[49] Herbert describes it as a "survival handbook-religious manual,"[50] which is essentially what the Qur'an is to a Muslim. Examples of characters uttering the style of the Qur'an are numerous. For example, Stilgar's invocation: "may their faces be forever black"[51] towards "the cursed Guild" is based on a Qur'anic verse from "The Family of Imran" (3:106). Described as "a traditional Fremen curse"[52] in *The Winds of Dune*, it relates to a punishment on the day of Judgment where the faces of the damned shall be blackened by the fires of hell.[53] Stilgar is perhaps the most knowledgeable of Naibs, a deeply religious Fremen who has carefully studied the ayat of the Kitab al-ibar. Paul quotes from the *Kitab al-Ibar*: "Travel by night and rest in black shade through the day."[54] Though there isn't a specific quote completely identical to this in the Qur'an, it follows the Qur'anic method of always placing the night before the day. The following sections are based on each of the seven chapters of the Qur'an featured in Dune and discuss the various references that relate to Herbert's writings.

The Announcement

In "Dune World," the first part of the serialized version of *Dune* published in *Analog* magazine, Jessica and Paul open "The Manual of 'The Friendly Desert'" or Fremkit to read: "God give us water in torrents that we may bring forth vegetation and grain and gardens luxuriant."[55] This quote comes from a chapter of the Qur'an called "The Announcement" (78:14–16) and is worded in precisely the same way in Bell's translation:

> We have sent down from the rain-clouds water in torrents,
>   That We may bring forth thereby grain and vegetation,
>   And gardens luxuriant.[56]

Described as a handwritten prayer in an unpublished version of this *Dune* chapter,[57] Jessica likens the writing in the Fremkit manual to the Azhar Book, with Paul adding that on Arrakis "they call it the Kitab al-Ibar."[58] The "prayer" in fact appears in the real *Kitab al-Ibar* of Ibn Khaldun. In his section on poetry, Ibn Khaldun discusses poetical methods of inquiry. One method of greeting others was "in the form of praying for rain," such as: "Let a pouring rain water the traces of their abandoned camps, And let them be covered by luxuriant verdure."[59]

Herbert takes this verse and turns it into a prayer, just as the Prophet Muhammad, his companions, and the Arabian poets who honored and observed the strictures of Islam would do. Seeing this verse used in poetry in the real *Kitab al-Ibar*, and finding the full verse in translations of the Qur'an seems to have led Herbert to associate Ibn Khaldun's book as a prominent scriptural source for the Fremen. The quote is also found in Grunebaum's book on Islam.[60] In *The Road to Dune*, Brian Herbert explains that the chapter this came from was trimmed for the *Analog* issue, "and then never restored when the novel was published in book form."[61] Although this quote did not appear in the final version of *Dune*, it displays Herbert's initial vision for his version of the Kitab al-Ibar to contain Qur'anic quotes. If we strictly exclude this verse from the idea of seven featured Qur'anic chapters in Dune, then the quote by Tyekanik from "The Women" is the most likely substitute. Ultimately, the Hawamim pattern of "seven chapters" finds its way into the Dune trilogy.

The Prophets

In *Dune*, Paul "recalled the words of 467 Kalima in Yueh's O.C. Bible. He said: 'From water does all life begin.'"[62] A similar quote appears in a chapter of the Qur'an called "The Prophets" (21:30), where all life is also said to originate from water ("And we made from water every living thing...").[63] This scriptural belief is known to come from the Qur'an alone and such a quote would clearly be of interest to Herbert. It would seem more appropriate to place this quote in the Fremkit manual, found on a desert planet obsessed with water for survival. However, Herbert chooses to place this Qur'anic verse, which declares the origin of all life originating from water, among the Atreides, a noble House residing on the oceanic world of Caladan. This demonstrates yet another example of Arab Futurist themes and the Qur'anic influences on the Imperium and the Orange Catholic Bible: these Islamic beliefs are not just for one group, but ideas shared among all people.

The Inevitable

In *Children of Dune*, when Chani warns her daughter Ghanima of danger, she says "enter here and you will eat the fruit of the Zaqquum, the food of hell!"[64] The warning comes from a chapter of the Qur'an called "The Inevitable" (56:52), which warns the damned by saying, "you shall eat the fruit of the Zaqqum-tree,"[65] an "infernal tree" that "the damned shall surely eat of...."[66] It is a touching moment due to Chani never having had the chance to mother her daughter, protect her from physical harm, or form a maternal bond in reality, existing only as a spiritual guide.

When Paul visits his father's tomb, he touches it "with his right hand on the rock shrine enclosing his father's skull (the right hand of the blessed, not the left hand of the damned)."[67] This description comes from the same chapter (56:9) referring to the people on The Day of Judgment and is explained by George Sale's translation of the Qur'an:

> The companions of the right hand and of the left hand. That is, the blessed, and the damned; who may be thus distinguished here, because the books wherein their actions are registered, will be delivered into the right hands of the former, and into the left hands of the latter.[68]

H.A.R. Gibb's book *Mohammedanism* also says, "His deeds will be weighed in the Balance, and his book will be placed in his hand, the right hand of the blessed, the left hand of the damned."[69] It is common for Muslims to use their right hand for "blessed" and pure acts such as eating and greeting, while the left hand is used to cleanse impurities. Paul honors and respects his father's tomb by touching it with his right hand, demonstrating his Qur'anic knowledge which he obtained from the Fremen through the Kitab al-Ibar or the gift of his sight.

The Bee

A saying ascribed to Muad'Dib in *Dune* says: "eat what God has provided thee: and when thou are replenished, praise the Lord."[70] This originates from a Qur'anic chapter called "The Bee" (16:114), which says "eat what God has provided you lawful and good; and be you thankful for the blessing of God...."[71] Herbert specifically states that the narration is from the O.C. Bible and that "The Azhar Book traces this in slightly different form to First Islam,"[72] which implies a direct connection back to contemporary Islam.

In *Children of Dune*, Stilgar contemplates taking the lives of Leto and Ghanima in the cradle, a terrible thought he later comes to regret. He reflects on verses of the Qur'an—a moment Herbert describes as reverting "to primary Fremen beliefs"—which says: "God's command comes; so seek not to hasten it" and "God's it is to show the way, and some do swerve from it." These two quotes are taken verbatim from "The Bee," 16:1 and 16:9.[73] Meditating on these verses, Stilgar stays his hand and chooses to remain loyal, rather than compromise his Fremen beliefs and lose the virtue of loyalty. Later, when Leto II is older, facing the threat of death from Namri, Herbert quotes "The Bee" again. When Leto answers a question about what is wrong with his ministry he says: "God's it is to show the way."[74] The threat is then averted. This verse keeps him safe and implies that he was aware of Stilgar's threat when he was a child in the cradle. The repeated use of "The Bee" as a source of inspiration seems to show that this Qur'anic chapter was of particular interest to Herbert.

Stilgar starts his soul-searching by saying "And my master is God the Merciful, the Compassionate,"[75] which is taken from the opening phrase recited before "The Bee" and almost every other chapter of the Qur'an: "In the Name of God, the Merciful, the Compassionate."[76] This implies the Fremen are closely linked to Muslims, with the overwhelming majority of references to the origins of their faith found in Islam.

Ya-Sin

Stilgar further reflects on another chapter of the Qur'an, which stops him from committing the terrible act he contemplates in *Children of Dune*. He recalls a verse from the chapter "Ya Sin" exactly as it is written in Arberry's translation (36:8–9)[77]:

> Surely, we have put on their necks fetters up to the chin, so their heads are raised; and we have put before them a barrier and behind them a barrier; and we have covered them, so they do not see.[78]

The chapter "Ya Sin" talks about the unaware and the punishable, which Herbert might have used to reveal Stilgar's current state of thought on the innocence of the twins and his fear of punishment. According to Thomas Hughes's *Dictionary of Islam*, the *Kalima* or the declaration of faith, known fully as the *"Kalimatu 'sh-Shahadah,"* and the chapter "Ya-Sin" are to be recited over those who are dying.[79] As this chapter relates to death, this could be why Herbert uses it in this moment, to signify the deadly danger surrounding the twins or, alternatively, the death of Stilgar's intention to take their lives.

The Cow

Before Paul's sandrider test in *Dune*, he recalls a quote that Chani once said to him: "You told me once the words of the Kitab al-Ibar.... You told me: 'Woman is thy field; go then to thy field and till it.'"[80] This implies a tender and loving moment that occurred between the two. It comes from the longest chapter of the Qur'an called "Al-Baqarah," or "The Cow" (2:223), and was likely taken from Lesley Blanch's *The Sabres of Paradise*, due to the precise wording of the verse not found in other translations of the Qur'an. It states: "Did not the Koran say, 'Woman is thy field, go then to thy field and till it'?"[81] Herbert uses this metaphorical verse for a metaphor of his own with riding sandworms, likening Arrakis to a female. Notably, the word for "earth" which is "tilled" is feminine in the Arabic language.[82]

The Elephant

In Jessica's waking vision, when she convinces the Fremen that she is the Bene Gesserit mother of legend who has come with the Mahdi, she recites verses from Herbert's Kitab al-Ibar: "Mine enemies are like green blades eaten down."[83] This description of the enemy is found exclusively in Bell's Qur'an.[84] It comes from a chapter called "The Elephant" (105:5), concerning the defeat of the Aksumite general Abraha al-Ashram and his army of elephants, after his attack on the Ka'bah in Makkah. Jessica goes on to say:

> Hast thou not seen what our Lord did?
>   He sent the pestilence among them
>   That did lay schemes against us.
>   They are like birds scattered by the huntsman.
>   Their schemes are like pellets of poison....[85]

A particular trait of the Qur'an is that it often addresses the reader directly with a question. Herbert uses this literary method here with Jessica paraphrasing "The Elephant" for this crucial moment. This is the five-versed chapter, also found exactly as it is written in Grunebaum's *Medieval Islam*,[86] presented in its entirety from Bell's translation:

Hast thou not seen how thy Lord did with the fellows of the elephant?
Did He not put their scheme awry?
He sent upon them birds in flocks,
Which pelted them with stones and baked clay,
And made them like green blades eaten down.[87]

Herbert mentions the final verse first and continues through the chapter. This almost mirrors a type of arabesque writing style in literature, interweaving stories together and using the last verse of "poetry" as the beginning of the poem in an endless cycle. Both quotes begin with a question concerning an act of God, then the plotting and scheming of others. Birds are then mentioned, followed by dangerous pelting and pellets. His writing mimics the style of Qur'anic scripture which often uses similes. Herbert creates a simile of his own, likening the Qur'an's pellets of hard-baked clay, which destroyed the wrongdoers as the poisonous schemes of Fremen enemies. As for Herbert's addition of the word "pestilence," the event in "The Elephant" is discussed and explored in various works, including Hitti's *History of the Arabs*,[88] which say that Abraha "died of a shocking pestilence"[89] after being pelted with stones.

Herbert's World-Building with Islamic History

Frank Herbert not only draws from the Qur'an as inspiration for the quotes in his Dune books, he also uses the scholarly and historical events related to the Qur'an, as well as famous Islamic texts and figures by embedding them in Fremen culture and other aspects of the Dune universe. In *The Seven Beauties of Science Fiction*, Csicsery-Ronay Jr. asks, "Do these words indicate that the Fremen speak Arabic all the time, and that the narrative merely emphasizes the religious Terms?" It seems very likely to be the case. While some ceremonial phrases may have been derived from a Romani language, the majority of the terms the Fremen use day-to-day are Arabic in origin. Their "survival handbook-religious manual," the Kitab al-Ibar, with its links to Arab history and the Qur'an, is perhaps the strongest evidence to suggest that the Fremen do in fact speak Arabic because such a vital book would need to be written and read in a language accessible to the Fremen people. The ayat of the Fremen Kitab al-Ibar and the hadiths "required for survival on Arrakis"[90] further add to the evidence that the Kitab al-Ibar likely contains the Arabic language that the Qur'anic *ayat* and the historical books of *hadith* are written in. The true nature of language evolution does not apply to Dune when arguing against the use of a preserved form of Arabic in the distant future, due to the author's intentions: "I wanted to hold it close enough to the present, colloquial

Arabic—which is the language that survives."[91] The Bene Gesserit Sister-hood with their influence—in a position as high up as the Emperor's Impe-rial Truthsayer and their extensive access to past memories—makes it possible for such knowledge from the past to thrive in the future.

The Muadh Quran

On Caladan, the ancestral home of House Atreides, the Muadh Quran with its pure "Ilm and Fiqh" has been "preserved among the pundi rice farmers."[92] The word *Muadh* means "preserved," stressing the fact that it is a "preserved Qur'an."[93] This reflects a verse from the Qur'an itself, from a chapter called the "Constellations" (85:21–22), stating: "It is a glorious Qur'an. In a tablet preserved."[94] This is one of two verses in separate chap-ters that speak of a preserved Quran, making it quite rare. It is also found in Hughes's dictionary of Islam,[95] and Grunebaum features the Qur'anic quote in his book: "Yet it is a glorious Koran, written on the Preserved Table."[96] Therefore "Constellations" could have inspired the "preserved Quran" of Caladan. The second verse in which it appears is found in the chapter "The Inevitable," from which Herbert quotes in *Children of Dune*.

The Muadh Qur'an is a part of the culture of Caladan and it seems that Paul's fate was always tied to the religion of a people he would later continue to inspire. Paul is comfortable with many of the terms of Arrakis, which implies that they became part of "Galach," the common tongue of the Imperium, similarly to how the English language has assimilated Ara-bic words like lemon (*"laymoon"*) and algebra (*"al-Jabr"*). Another expla-nation could be that Paul's education includes many languages, among them the Fremen Chakobsa, through his mother's teachings. Hence his familiarity with foreign terms. As the power of his prescient vision grows, it grants him the ability to assimilate himself into Fremen culture more easily through the familiarity with Fremen history and the Fremen future.

Clement Huart's *A History of Arabic Literature*, which talks exten-sively about "preserved" Arab texts, notes that *"Mu'adh* ibn Jabal" was one of the four disciples of Muhammad who "preserved" the Qur'an.[97] Addi-tionally, a book on the teachings of Prophet Muhammad offers an interest-ing insight into the possible origins of the term:

> Nothing better exemplifies the spirit of freedom preserved in the teach-ings of Islam, than the following tradition:—Mohammed whilst deputing Sad-ibn-*Muadh* [emphasis added] as a delegate to some tribe, asked him how he would judge between contending parties if they came to him for decision.[98]

He replies "First I will look to the Koran, then to precedents of the Prophet, and lastly rely upon my own judgment."[99]

Given this context, the reference to *Muadh* in *Dune* suggests that the Qur'an is still a protected book in humanity's future as depicted in the Dune universe, fulfilling and affirming its own prophetic nature. "Muadh Qur'an," the term Herbert creates, implies that the original Qur'an has been preserved. This leads to the assumption that the original form of Islam is still practiced on Caladan by the rice farmers at least, implying a peaceful synergy between the Atreides and Islam on Caladan before contact with the Fremen. This implies that not only is the Qur'an itself preserved, but also the Arabic language through which it was revealed. Herbert's inclusion of the "Muadh Quran" in *Dune* suggests that orthodox Islam has survived as far as 10,191 years into the future, on Caladan no less. Hearkening back to the themes of Arab Futurism, not only are Arab culture and Islam included in the future, but there, they thrive.

Hadiths on Justice

Herbert also draws inspiration from several *hadith* narrations, one of which was spoken by Lady Jessica herself. When Jessica confronts Alia in *Children of Dune* and sides with the Fremen Ghadhean al-Fali, who raises his concerns before the court, she says: "'Onsar akhaka zeliman aw maslumen!' *Support your brother in his time of need, whether he be just or unjust!*"[100] This Arabic narration appears in most of the prominent *hadith* books of collected sayings. In the *hadith*, the Prophet Muhammad says: "Help your brother, whether he is an oppressor or he is an oppressed one," but when people asked how they could help a person who is an oppressor, "The Prophet said, 'By preventing him from oppressing others.'"[101] There is a *hadith* that says "The best of jihad is a just word spoken to an unjust ruler."[102] The Fremen al-Fali and Jessica both "speak truth to power" and challenge an oppressor akin to the challenge of Moses towards Pharaoh. In the case of Dune, the pharaonic figure is Alia through the madness of her abomination. This carefully selected *hadith* alludes to al-Fali and Jessica trying to aid Alia, rather than destroy her. They fulfill the prophetic teachings of Muhammad found in these *hadiths*, speaking just words and helping and supporting Alia in her time of need by preventing her oppression.

Nisai: The Scholar

The *hadith* pertaining to the best jihad being "A word of truth spoken before an unjust ruler" is also found in the collected *hadith* of An-Nisa'i,[103] a Persian Sunni scholar who wrote one of the six canonical *hadith* books called "*Sunan an-Nisa'i.*" In Arabic, the name Nisai could be a surname or imply a place of origin (for example, from Nisa, an ancient settlement in Turkmenistan). Herbert alludes to "Nisai" as being the true leader of the original Fremen belief system. The glossary in *Dune* notes that while scholars regard Ali Ben Ohashi as the schism leader, some evidence suggests that he was actually the spokesman for his wife Nisai.[104] This could imply that Ohashi's wife is a descendant of the Persian scholar or from Nisa.

Mohalata Partnership

In *Children of Dune*, Herbert uses the concept of Mohalata describing it as a form of Atreides government. Jessica notes, "The Mohalata was natural to us. To the Atreides, government was always a protective partnership: Mohalata."[105] This term is found in the travel journal *Mogreb-el-Acksa* by R.B. Cunninghame Graham—seemingly the only source available with the term at the time Herbert wrote the novel. Graham describes a "curious system known as 'protection,' and called by the Arabs 'Mohalata,' which for at least a hundred years has existed in Morocco, as something to be proud of. The word in Arabic means partnership...."[106]

Herbert also takes the Arabic term and adds a new meaning, using it creatively to describe a partnership in which conscious memories and the host protect against other, more aggressive personas within. For example, when Ghanima ventures inwardly, "she first called upon the Mohalata, a partnership of the benign which might protect her."[107] In *Mogreb-el-Acksa*, Graham also writes, "I have heard an Arab say, 'Can I not get away from his cursed "Mohalata"?'"[108] This phrase might have birthed the concept of abomination, when a personality overpowers a person from within.

Gurney the Valorous

Gurney Halleck is given the name "Gurney the Valorous"[109] by Paul Atreides after recalling a saying spoken to him by the Reverend Mother: "A world is supported by four things ... the learning of the wise, the justice of the great, the prayers of the righteous and the valor of the brave."[110] The exact quote is written in Arabic above the portals of the University of Granada, established during Islamic Spain,[111] which is where Gurney Halleck's nickname originates. This also shows that the Bene Gesserit have knowledge pertaining to Islamic history.

Tahaddi al-Burhan: The Ultimate Test

The fateful fight between Jamis and Paul in *Dune* is called the tahaddi challenge, or the "tahaddi al-burhan," which is essentially a Fremen challenge to mortal combat. Herbert uses the concept of *tahaddi* in other parts of the book to signify nonviolent struggles. In Islamic history, the real *tahaddi* challenge was not so violent, involving words, not weapons. When the Muslims struggled against the pagans throughout the Prophet Muhammad's lifetime, the Qur'an presented an open challenge to the Arab community, to see if they could produce "the stylistic uniqueness"[112] of the Qur'an (52:34): "Let them produce a scripture like it, if what they say be true!"[113] The challenge established the Qur'an's superiority over all other works in the region because the best among the pagan Arabs could not produce anything like it. The tahaddi is rooted in deeply theological discussions about miracles and proofs, the beauty of the Arabic language, and the unique style of the Qur'an, one which bested the greatest of Arabian poets. Herbert clearly displays an understanding of the core concept through the use of the word alone and its placement throughout *Dune*, despite turning the term into a literal challenge and the besting of an opponent in combat.

The word *tahaddi* is introduced early in the book, preparing the reader for Paul's own tahaddi challenge, which Stilgar refers to as the boy's "tahaddi al-burhan." For example, in a letter to Paul and Jessica, Dr. Yueh writes:

> Do not try to forgive me. I do not want your forgiveness. I already have enough burdens. What I have done was done without malice or hope of another's understanding. It is my own tahaddi al-burhan, my ultimate test.[114]

Dr. Yueh uses the term as though it is part of his own vernacular, yet another example of the Arab Futurist spread of the Arabic language throughout the known universe. This use by Dr. Yueh not only implies incorporation, but also an affirmation of the concepts these terms are linked to. The scene also shows that Jessica and Paul, the original recipients of the message, are familiar with this type of terminology. Perhaps at some point in its history, the Imperium recognized how challenging the *tahaddi* of the Qur'an truly was. In a universe without thinking machines, it is easy to believe that humanity returned to a time of poetical and literary debates without digital distractions, to answer questions long asked and to reconcile with challenges delivered long ago.

Test of the Mihna

The "Mihna" in *Dune* is the testing of Fremen youth who wish admittance into manhood.[115] For example, Stilgar says, "We'll give you a name, manling ... in the time of the mihna, at the test of aql."[116] The historical *mihna* was a testing time for Islamic scholars too. It was an inquisition against anyone who did not believe that the Qur'an was created, but was knowledge from God, which resulted in punishment, imprisonment, or death, unless they conformed. Herbert likely came across the term in M. Patton Walter's *Ahmed Ibn Hanbal and the Mihna*, which refers to it as "a 'testing' or 'trial' in a general sense, but is often used in reference to a religious test in order to obtain assent to a particular belief or system of beliefs."[117] It was an ordeal for Islamic scholars who were persecuted for remaining loyal to the fundamentals of their faith and opposing the opinions of the Abbasid Caliph al-Ma'mun. Many did not yield and their courage was truly tested. Those who passed were "admitted into manhood," which resulted in their deaths; thus, the Fremen test of manhood is named after this event.

One of the tests in the Mihna of the Dune universe is the test of *aql*. In Arabic, *aql* means "reason, intellect and intelligence."[118] Herbert uses the two together to imply that the Mihna was a true test of intellect. One legendary figure who passed the "time of the Mihna" was Ahmed ibn Hanbal, a prominent Islamic scholar who in Walter's introduction is described as "the most remarkable figure."[119] During the *Mihna*, he "did more than other individuals to strengthen the resistance of his party to the repressive efforts of the Khalifs and their officers. He stood for the standing or falling of orthodoxy in its time of trial...."[120] It is said that Ibn Hanbal would put his opponents to great embarrassment with his intellectual arguments. God's knowledge was never seen to be a created thing among the people, but rather something that could not be created. The Qur'an declared itself to be knowledge from God, something they all agreed upon. Ahmad Ibn Hanbal would say "If this knowledge is uncreated then the Quran must be uncreated," leaving his opponents defeated. There was a saying that "God had cast Ahmed ibn Hanbal into the crucible and he had come out pure gold."[121]

The Bi-la Kaifa Formula

Another link to Ahmed ibn Hanbal is found in a phrase among the Fremen, "bi-la kaifa," which is described as the equivalent of "amen."[122] The true meaning in Arabic translates as "without asking/knowing how" and was called Ahmed Ibn Hanbal's "formula,"[123] written in exactly the same way. Another source credits ibn Hanbal as the original creator of the *bi-la kaifa* doctrine. It was used to settle debates on anthropomorphic texts pertaining to God. Using the phrase resolved theological questions over certain verses of the Qur'an, such as "God's possession of hands and eyes," when there are "no means of specifying their modality (*bi-la kaifa*)."[124] The Fremen say "bi-la kaifa" for various spiritual reasons, including at the ceremonies of the deceased. They tell positive stories of moments they shared with the departed and when dealing with the water of the dead and the terraforming of Arrakis "without asking how," they reply in unison, "bi-lal kaifa."[125]

Gom Jabbar: The High-Handed Enemy

The *gom jabbar*, weapon of the Bene Gesserit Sisterhood, seems to be a colloquial form of the Arabic "Qawm Jabbar" used in the original Arabic of a Qur'anic verse (5:22), which speaks of Moses suggesting that his people enter the holy land of a mighty people. Abdul Majid Daryabadi's *The Glorious Qur'an*, a translation which first appeared in 1941, reads: "They said: 'O Moses! Verily therein are a people *high-handed...* '"[126] Herbert describes the gom jabbar as a "high-handed enemy" in the *Dune* glossary, which aligns with the Qur'anic narrative.[127] Alia boasts, "You've met the Atreides gom jabbar" when she executes her fateful blow against her Harkonnen grandfather the Baron, the Atreides being the high-handed enemy and greatest adversary to the Harkonnens.[128] Just as the test of the *mihna* centers on a debate to determine whether the Qur'an is itself a creation or purely knowledge from God, the gom jabbar is a test to determine if the subject is human or animal.[129] Just as Ibn Hanbal's "*bi-la kaifa*" settles the doubts of anthropomorphism, the gom jabbar test is the high-handed antithesis to this answer.

Conclusion

The concepts in the Dune novels relating to Arabic and Islam are not merely used to add a sense of exoticism; they add a dimension and growth to the characters and narrative in fascinating ways. Herbert weaves Qur'anic verses throughout his Dune trilogy in key moments, such as when Jessica must prove she is the mother of a Mahdi, fulfilling a legend to ensure their survival. They are used to portray morality and faith when the lives of Leto II and Ghanima hang in the balance of Stilgar's blade, facing his greatest moral dilemma as a character. They help build empathy for Stilgar and add an air of suspense and wonder between Jessica and the Fremen. They warn Ghanima through the memory of her mother, who could not physically protect her but could utter Qur'anic scripture to help her daughter avoid danger.

These quotes occur not only in times of peril, but also times of peace, safety, and learning away from the pressures of eager Fremen eyes yearning for a messiah. They occur in the comfort of a Caladan castle through trusted teachers, or in a "Manual of The Friendly Desert" on Arrakis. With these examples, Herbert offers a vision of humanity in which Islam and Arabic terms not only exist in the future, but gain widespread acceptance, bringing a sense of normality to a subject so often misrepresented and misunderstood throughout history. As a key work of science fiction that prominently integrates Arabic and Islam into the future of humanity, the Dune novels exemplify Arab Futurism. In his re-examination of Islam, Herbert seems to have found a respect and sense of commonality, which he conveys throughout his saga. Given the rising Islamophobia of the early twenty-first century, this makes Dune perhaps all the more relevant to readers today.

NOTES

1. Wehr, *Dictionary of Modern Written Arabic*, 1024.
2. *Ibid.*, 10.
3. Touponce, *Frank Herbert*, 26.
4. Herbert, *Dreamer of Dune*, 167.
5. *Ibid.*, 164.
6. Waldentapes, "Dune: A Recorded Interview."
7. O'Reilly, *Frank Herbert: The Maker of Dune*, 105.
8. O'Reilly, *Frank Herbert*, 30.
9. Csicsery-Ronay, *The Seven Beauties of Science Fiction*.
10. Ryding, "The Arabic of *Dune*."
11. Most of the Qur'anic translations Herbert draws from are orientalist in nature. For those wishing to explore the Qur'an further, the English translations generally considered to be the strongest and most sound are the Sahih International and Muhsin Khan translations.
12. Majali, "Towards Arabfuturism/s." *Novelty*, November 23, 2015.
13. Wehr, *Dictionary of Modern Written Arabic*, 636.
14. See Brierly, "A critical moment," in this volume.
15. Herbert, "Terminology of the Imperium," *Dune*, 636.
16. Wehr, *Dictionary of Modern Written Arabic*, 54.
17. Massé, *Islam*, 213.
18. Herbert, *Dune*, 626.
19. Herbert, "Terminology of the Imperium," *Dune*, 621.
20. Wehr, *Dictionary of Modern Written Arabic*, 384.
21. Hitti, *History of the Arabs*, 127.
22. Herbert, *Dune*, 430.
23. Hughes, *A Dictionary of Islam*, 108.
24. Herbert, *Dune*, 361.
25. Azami, *Studies in Early Hadith Literature*, 6.
26. Herbert, *Children of Dune*, 354.
27. *Ibid.*, 267.
28. Wehr, *Dictionary of Modern Written Arabic*, 838.
29. Hitti, *History of the Arabs*, 408.
30. Herbert, *Dune*, 49.
31. Grunebaum, *Medieval Islam*, 84.
32. Herbert, "Terminology of the Imperium," *Dune*, 651.
33. Arberry, *The Koran Interpreted*, 217.

34. Herbert and Anderson, *The Road to Dune*, 223.
35. Bell, *The Qur'an*, 467.
36. Arberry, *The Koran Interpreted*, 82. Due to various editorial or categorical mistakes, this verse should not be placed in 4:67, but is found in 4:64 of subsequent translations of the Qur'an.
37. Herbert, *Dune*, 49.
38. Dawood, *The Koran*, 359.
39. Herbert, *God Emperor of Dune*, 39–40.
40. Dawood, *The Koran*, 327.
41. Bell, *The Qur'an*, 510.
42. Herbert, *God Emperor of Dune*, 128.
43. Dawood, *The Koran*, 294.
44. Herbert and Anderson, *The Road to Dune*, 223.
45. Herbert, *Dune*, 236.
46. Wehr, *Dictionary of Modern Written Arabic*, 56.
47. *Ibid.*, 36.
48. Herbert, *Dune*, 362.
49. Grunebaum, *Medieval Islam*, 22.
50. Herbert, "Terminology of the Imperium," *Dune*, 645.
51. Herbert, *Dune*, 358.
52. Herbert and Anderson, *The Winds of Dune*, 238.
53. Sale, *The Koran*, 45.
54. Herbert, *Dune*, 301.
55. Herbert, "Dune World," 168.
56. Bell, *The Qur'an*, 630.
57. Herbert and Anderson, *The Road to Dune*, 287.
58. Herbert, "Dune World," 168.
59. Khaldun, *The Muqaddimah*, 377.
60. Grunebaum, *Medieval Islam*, 75.
61. Herbert and Anderson, *The Road to Dune*, 239.
62. Herbert, *Dune*, 49.
63. Palmer, *The Qur'an*, 48.
64. Herbert, *Children of Dune*, 285.
65. Dawood, *The Koran*, 109.
66. Hughes, *A Dictionary of Islam*, 702.
67. Herbert, "The Religion of Dune," *Dune*, 624.
68. Sale, *The Koran*, 394.
69. Gibb, *Mohammedanism*, 61.
70. Herbert, "The Religion of Dune," *Dune*, 625.
71. Arberry, *The Koran Interpreted*, 299.
72. Herbert, "The Religion of Dune," *Dune*, 625.
73. Arberry, *The Koran Interpreted*, 287.
74. Herbert, *Children of Dune*, 247.
75. *Ibid.*, 6.
76. Arberry, *The Koran Interpreted*, 29.
77. *Ibid.*, 144.
78. Herbert, *Children of Dune*, 6.
79. Hughes, *Dictionary of Islam*, 102.
80. Herbert, *Dune*, 474.
81. Blanch, *The Sabres of Paradise*, 118.
82. Wehr, *Dictionary of Modern Written Arabic*, 13.
83. Herbert, *Dune*, 362.
84. Bell, *The Qur'an*, 678.
85. Herbert, *Dune*, 362.
86. Grunebaum, *Medieval Islam*, 66.
87. Bell, *The Qur'an*, 678.

88. Hitti, *History of the Arabs*, 64.

89. Bengalee, *The Life of Muhammad*, 21; Moore, *The History of the Small Pox*, 48.

90. Herbert, *Children of Dune*, 267.

91. O'Reilly, *Frank Herbert: The Maker of Dune*, 106.

92. Herbert, "The Religion of Dune," *Dune*, 618.

93. Baalbaki, *Al-Mawrid: A Modern English-Arabic Dictionary*, 720.

94. Bell, *The Qur'an*, 647.

95. Hughes, *A Dictionary of Islam*, 285.

96. Grunebaum, *Medieval Islam*, 106.

97. Huart, *A History of Arab Literature*, 40.

98. Ameer, *The Life and Teachings of Mohammed*, 289.

99. *Ibid.*, 289.

100. Herbert, *Children of Dune*, 164.

101. Al-Bukhari, *Sahih al-Bukhari*, 3:362.

102. Ibn Majah, *Sunan Ibn Majah*, 5:217.

103. An-Nasa'i, *Sunan An-Nasa'i*, 5:140.

104. Herbert, "Terminology of the Imperium," *Dune*, 658.

105. Herbert, *Children of Dune*, 165.

106. Graham, *Mogreb-el-Acksa*, 43.

107. Herbert, *Children of Dune*, 285.

108. Graham, *Mogreb-el-Acksa*, 49.

109. Herbert, *Dune*, 55.

110. *Ibid.*, 37.

111. Hitti, *History of The Arabs*, 563.

112. Grunebaum, *Medieval Islam*, 97.

113. Dawood, *The Koran*, 115.

114. Herbert, *Dune*, 231.

115. Herbert, "Terminology of the Imperium," *Dune*, 647.

116. Herbert, *Dune*, 353.

117. Walter, *Ahmed Ibn Hanbal And The Mihna*, 1.

118. Wehr, *Dictionary of Modern Written Arabic*, 630.

119. Walter, *Ahmed Ibn Hanbal And The Mihna*, 2.

120. *Ibid.*, 2.

121. *Ibid.*, 125.

122. Herbert, "Terminology of the Imperium," *Dune*, 637.

123. Watt, *Free Will and Predestination in Early Islam*, 140.

124. Grunebaum, *Medieval Islam*, 101.

125. Herbert, *Dune*, 392.

126. Daryabadi, *The Glorious Qur'an*, 216.

127. Herbert, "Terminology of the Imperium," *Dune*, 642.

128. Herbert, Dune, 572.

129. For more on how various factions in *Dune* view humanity, see Weyant, "I suggest you may be human," in this volume.

Works Cited

Al-Bukhari, Muhammad ibn Isma'il. *The Translation of the Meanings of Sahih Al-Bukhari*. Translated by Muhammad Muhsin Khan. Riyadh: Dar us Salam, 1997.

Ali, Syed Ameer. *A Critical Examination of The Life and Teachings of Mohammed*. London: Williams and Norgate, 1873.

An-Nasa'i, Ahmad bin Shu'aib. *English Translation of Sunan An-Nasa'i*. Translated by Nasiruddin Al-Khattab. Riyadh: Dar us Salam, 2007.

Arberry, A.J. *The Koran Interpreted: A Translation*. London: Allen & Unwin, 1955.

Azami, M.M., *Studies in Early Hadith Literature: With A Critical Edition of Some Early Texts*. Indianapolis, IN: American Trust Publications, 1978.

Baalbaki, Munir. *Al-Mawrid: A Modern English-Arabic Dictionary*. Beirut: Dar El-Ilm Lil-Malayin, 1981.

Bell, Richard. *The Qur'an: Translated with a Critical Re-arrangement of the Surahs*. Edinburgh: T. & T. Clark, 1937.

Bengalee, Mutiur Rahman. *The Life of Muhammad*. Chicago: Moslem Sunrise Press, 1941.

Blanch, Lesley. *The Sabres of Paradise*. London: John Murray, 1960.

Csicsery-Ronay Jr, Isvan. *The Seven Beauties of Science Fiction*. Middletown, CT: Wesleyan University Press, 2008.

Dawood, N.J. *The Koran: A New Translation*. Baltimore: Penguin Books, 1959.

Daryabadi, Abdul Majid. *The Glorious Qur'an: Text, Translation and Commentary*. Leicestershire: Islamic Foundation, 2001.

Gibb, H.A.R. *Mohammedanism: An Historical Survey*. London: Oxford University Press, 1949.

Graham, R.B. Cunninghame. *Mogreb-el-Acksa: A Journey in Morocco*. London: W. Heinemann, 1898.

Grunebaum, Gustave E. Von. *Medieval Islam: A Study in Cultural Orientation*. Chicago: University of Chicago Press, 1946.

Herbert, Brian. *Dreamer of Dune: The Biography of Frank Herbert*. New York: Tor, 2003.

Herbert, Brian, and Kevin J. Anderson. *The Winds of Dune*. New York: Simon & Schuster, 2010.

Herbert, Brian, and Kevin J. Anderson. *The Road to Dune*. New York: Tor, 2005.

Herbert, Frank. *Children of Dune*. 1976. New York: Berkley Books, 1981.

Herbert, Frank. *Dune*. 1965. Ace Books, 2019.

Herbert, Frank. "Dune World." *Analog Science Fact/Science Fiction* 72, no. 6 (1964).

Herbert, Frank. *God Emperor of Dune*. 1981. New York: Berkley Books, 1983.

Herbert, Frank, and David Lynch. "Dune: A Recorded Interview." Audiocassette. Stamford: Waldentapes, 1983.

Hitti, Philip K. *History of the Arabs*. New York: Macmillan, 1951.

Huart, Clement. *A History of Arabic Literature*. New York: D. Appleton and Company, 1903.

Hughes, Thomas Patrick. *A Dictionary of Islam: Being a Cyclopaedia of the Doctrines, Rites, Ceremonies, and Customs, Together with the Technical and Theological Terms, of the Muhammadan Religion*. New York: Scribner's, Welford & Co., 1885.

Ibn Khaldun, 'Abd al-Rahman ibn Muhammad. *The Muqaddimah: An Introduction to History*. Translated by Franz Rosenthal. New York: Pantheon Books, 1958.

Ibn Majah, Muhammad bin Yazeed. *English Translation of Sunan Ibn Majah*. Translated by Nasiruddin al-Khattab. Riyadh: Dar us Salam, 2007.

Majali, Sulaiman. "Towards Arabfuturism/s." *Novelty*, November 23, 2015. noveltymag.com/towards-arabfuturisms/.

Massé, Henri. *Islam*. Halide Edib, ed. New York: G.P. Putnam's Sons, 1938.

Moore, James Carrick. *The History of the Small Pox*. London: Longman, Hurst, Rees, Orme, and Brown, 1815.

O'Reilly, Timothy (editor). *Frank Herbert: The Maker of Dune: Insights of a Master of Science Fiction*. New York: Berkeley, 1987.

O'Reilly, Timothy. *Frank Herbert* ("Recognitions" Series). New York: Frederick Ungar, 1981. https://www.oreilly.com/tim/herbert/index.html.

Palmer, E.H. *The Qur'an*. Oxford, UK: The Clarendon Press, 1880.

Patton, Walter M. *Ahmed Ibn Hanbal and the Mihna: A Biography of the Imam Including an Account of the Mohammedan Inquisition Called the Mihna*. Leiden: E.J. Brill, 1897.

Ryding, Karin C. "The Arabic of Dune: Language and Landscape," In *Language in Place: Stylistic Perspectives on Landscape, Place and Environment*, edited by Daniela Francesca Virdis, Elisabetta Zurru, and Ernestine Lahey, 106–123. Amsterdam: John Benjamins Publishing, 2021.

Sale, George. *The Koran: Commonly Called the Alcoran of Mohammed, Translated into*

English Immediately from the Original Arabic; with Explanatory Notes, Taken from the Most Approved Commentators. To which is Prefixed a Preliminary Discourse. London: W.H. Allen & Co, 1838.

Touponce, William. *Frank Herbert.* Boston: Twayne Publishers, 1988.

Watt, W. Montgomery. *Free Will and Predestination in Early Islam.* London: Luzac, 1948.

Wehr, Hans. *Dictionary of Modern Written Arabic.* J. Milton Cowan, ed. New York: Cornell University Press, 1961.

"A critical moment"

The O.C. Bible in the Awakening of Paul Atreides

N. Trevor Brierly

The betrayal of House Atreides in *Dune*, and subsequent flight from the Harkonnen and Sardaukar hunters, is a crisis that acts as a catalyst for the awakening of Paul Atreides's hyper-awareness and prescient abilities. This complex transformation occurs in phases, with each phase arising suddenly, triggered by some experience, internal or external. Paul is acutely aware of what is happening to him and sees the origins of his transformation in the early training and development of his talents, but also in "exposure to the O.C. Bible at a critical moment" and the ever-present spice on Arrakis.[1] As the son of a Duke, Paul received training in "sophisticated disciplines" from some of the best tutors in the universe in order to improve his mental acuity and become a "formidable Mentat duke."[2] However, heavy intake of the mélange spice acts as the major trigger for Paul's awakening. Use of mélange is common in the Imperium among those who can afford its very high price because it extends human lifespans and provides resistance to poison and illness.[3] Dr. Wellington Yueh calls it "the prolonger of life, the giver of health."[4] However, for a few, such as Guild Navigators and Paul Atreides, heavy intake of mélange enhances natural prescient ability to see into the future, or rather multiple possible futures, to see beyond sight. Paul is aware of the potential for such change, the awakening of "prescient awareness," when Chani gives him a morsel of food with a heavy concentration of spice.[5]

Less clear, however, is the role the Orange Catholic Bible (O.C. Bible) plays in his transformation. Paul notes that exposure to it "at a critical moment" seems to have played a part in his transformation commensurate in importance with his training and the mélange spice.[6] What does he mean by "exposure" to the O.C. Bible? To which "critical moment" does he refer, and why is it "critical"? The O.C. Bible is mentioned infrequently in the text of *Dune*, and rarely in the other books in the Dune saga. In the narrative there are only a handful of confirmed passages from the O.C. Bible and the associated Commentaries, as well as another handful of passages, mostly from Gurney Halleck, that might originate from the O.C. Bible. With one exception, the O.C. Bible seems to play a very small part in the narrative as a whole, yet Paul mentions it as one of the most important catalysts in his transformation. This essay takes a close-reading approach to the *Dune* novel in order to better understand the role of the Orange Catholic Bible in the religious ecosystem of the Imperium, and specifically the role it plays in preparing Paul for some of the terrifying changes he will undergo.[7]

The question of the role of the O.C. Bible in Paul's transformation does not appear to have been considered within Dune scholarship. As well, little scholarly attention has been paid to the O.C. Bible and, more broadly, to religion in the Imperium (other than that of the Fremen) or to Paul Atreides' religious formation before Arrakis. Herbert provides some data to work with in the "Appendix II: The Religion of Dune" and "Terminology of the Imperium" appendices of *Dune* and scattered throughout the novels. But these raise as many questions as they answer, and there is still much to be learned and considered on these topics (which could be a fruitful field for future Dune scholars).

What Is the O.C. Bible?

The narrative in *Dune* provides little information about the origin of the Orange Catholic Bible or its contents. This is in keeping with the small role it seems to play overall in the lives of the members of the Imperium elite. Duke Leto never quotes from it. Lady Jessica calls to mind a passage from it once.[8] Among their important retainers neither Thufir Hawat nor Duncan Idaho refer to the O.C. Bible. Gurney Halleck has some familiarity with it, but seems to use it primarily as a source of appropriate quotes. Dr. Wellington Yueh will be shown to possibly have some belief in the reason-based religion of the O.C. Bible, but he describes it as merely having "much historical truth in it as well as good ethical philosophy."[9] Most of the information about the Orange Catholic Bible is found in Appendix II of *Dune*, which covers "The Religion of Dune." This appendix discusses the origin and impact of the O.C. Bible on the Imperium and even on Fremen culture, but leaves many unanswered questions, such as the meaning of the name.

Frank Herbert himself apparently never explained why he chose the title "Orange Catholic Bible" for this religious text, but there are some possible clues in the text and in real-world history. The color "orange" is often associated with Protestantism, because of the support for the Protestant cause by William of Orange, who became king of England, Scotland, and Ireland after the Glorious Revolution of 1688.[10] (To this day, the flag of the Republic of Ireland includes an orange stripe to represent the Protestant part of the Irish population.) The term "Catholic" is usually associated with the Roman Catholic Church. Perhaps the combination of these two terms was meant to indicate a book that would combine religions that are different and even had a history of mutual animosity. Herbert's son Brian Herbert provides some support for this idea in a biography of his father, noting, "An Orange Catholic Bible is in the book, suggesting a future merging of Protestantism and Catholicism."[11] But the Orange Catholic Bible is not an amalgam of Protestantism and Catholicism, as it includes passages from sacred texts of many religions, such as "Maometh Saari, Mahayana Christianity, Zensunni Catholicism and Buddislamic traditions."[12]

In the Dune universe, the impetus for the creation of the O.C. Bible came from the Butlerian Jihad, when humanity fought a terrible "crusade against computers, thinking machines and conscious robots" that lasted for two generations and led to a hostility toward thinking machines still present in the Imperium thousands of years later.[13] The violence of this period caused humanity to look closely at the religious beliefs that had fueled the Jihad, and so the "Commission of Ecumenical Translators" (C.E.T.) was formed from representatives of all religions with more than one million adherents. The representatives were tasked with preparing a text that would remove "the claim to possession of the one and only revelation" from the participating religions, what they referred to as "pathological symptoms" of religious thought.[14] They desired to create a single text which would be acceptable to all participating religions, a text which would be "an instrument of Love to be played in all ways."[15] To remove the claims to unique revelation by these religions would mean replacing their sacred texts with a new text that would at the same time also be acceptable to all other religions.

It is not entirely clear how the members of the C.E.T. hoped to accomplish this monumental task. The final product would need to be more than a compilation of the "best of" each religion; it would have to go beyond the vague, universally accepted belief that "there exists a Divine Essence in the universe."[16] The C.E.T. would need to create a text that would reconcile and harmonize the beliefs of these religions, and then hope the results would be accepted by their adherents. The members worked at this task in secret for seven years and then released the O.C. Bible, accompanied by the Commentaries and the Liturgical Manual.

Given the vast differences between the religions of humanity in the twenty-first century, it seems difficult to imagine that a single religious text could somehow ever supplant or replace or even supplement the sacred texts of such varied belief systems and worldviews. But the history of the Imperium includes many efforts to consolidate control over human endeavors in as few organizations as possible. The obvious example is the monopoly on space travel by the Spacing Guild. The Imperium itself is ruled by a single emperor and a small number of Great Houses in the Landsraad. The CHOAM company has a monopoly on Galactic commerce. Mentats control the functions of forecasting, accounting, strategy, etc. The Bene Gesserit order controls eugenics and "politics." The citizens of the Imperium are organized into the single "faufreluches" social structure. So, it is not entirely surprising that there would be attempts to fit the entirety of human religion into one structure. DiTommaso notes that the result of the "faufreluches" system (and it could be argued the other elements mentioned above) was to "[impose] the artificial stability needed to maintain the rigid structure of the Imperium."[17] DiTommaso claims that religion is not a part of that rigid structure,[18] but the process and results of the creation of the O.C. Bible indicate otherwise, resulting in the creation of a religion based on reason and science, designed to end harmful disputation and encourage stability.

The C.E.T appears instead to have essentially created a new religion with "new symbols" and a new revelation.[19] The members claimed to have been inspired by God to rediscover "great ideals" and "moral imperatives."[20] The religion of the O.C. Bible appears to privilege human reasoning over revelation, as the opening of the Commentaries suggests: "Men, finding no answers to the *sunnan* [the ten thousand religious questions from the Shari-ah] now apply their own reasoning."[21] This boldly rejects the claims of other religions to have answers to the most important religious questions. This new religion is one that relies on Science to find what Religion fits humanity into: "Scientists seek the lawfulness of events. It is the task of Religion to fit man into this lawfulness."[22] The O.C. Bible deemphasized revelation by claiming that adherents would recognize correct teachings "because it awakens within you the sensation which tells you this is something you've always known."[23] For a religion in which the truth is within the believer, perhaps buried but already known, there is no need for revelation, just reminders. The religion of the O.C. Bible is a religion of reason and rediscovery rather than of revelation.

It is not surprising that the O.C. Bible was not received well at first, given its apparent focus on reason over revelation. It was accused of being the result of the "hubris of reason" and "filled with a seductive interest in logic."[24] Religions that emphasize the importance of their own revelations over human reason would likely find the O.C. Bible inadequate, perhaps finding it to really be another religion altogether. Revisions replaced the new symbols it presented with familiar ones, such as "Cross, Crescent, Feather Rattle, the Twelve Saints, and the thin Buddha, and the like."[25] The C.E.T. failed to produce something that would unite the main religions since the Appendix II indicates they still exist as the "Ancient Teachings" at time of the events in *Dune* thousands of years later.[26] Most of the members of the Commission of Ecumenical Translators who produced the book were either murdered or recanted. The few who did not recant were called the "Fourteen Sages" and were ultimately vindicated: "Ninety generations later, the O.C. Bible and Commentaries permeated the religious universe."[27] At the beginning of Appendix II, there are listed five "major forces" which shape the beliefs of the people of the Imperium:

> 1. The followers of the Fourteen Sages, whose Book was the Orange Catholic Bible....
> 2. The Bene Gesserit....
> 3. The agnostic ruling class (including the Guild)....
> 4. The so-called Ancient Teachings....
> 5. [and] SPACE TRAVEL![28]

Note that the O.C. Bible is listed first, signifying its importance to the religious universe of the Imperium.

   Given the importance of the O.C. Bible to religion in the Imperium, it is somewhat surprising that Paul appears to not have read it before receiving Yueh's copy before the trip to Arrakis.[29] When he later quotes from it ("From water does all life begin") Jessica is startled: "Where did he learn that quotation? ... He hasn't studied the mysteries."[30] The term "mysteries" in the context of religion or the occult can mean something which is hidden, and only open to initiates. It can also have connotations of being beyond reason, mysterious.[31] Since the O.C. Bible is commonly available, and its emphasis is on reason, the term "mysteries" is striking. Jessica would certainly know it from her Bene Gesserit training, but it is possible that Paul did not. Yueh gives Paul the O.C. Bible as something that would be new to him and Paul shows no indication of familiarity with it. Before the gift, he is familiar with one precept from it, which he quotes to the Reverend Mother after the *gom jabbar* test: "Thou shalt not make a machine in the likeness of a man's mind."[32] But, given the fear and loathing of machines in the Imperium, it would not be surprising if Paul learned this one saying from the O.C. Bible through common knowledge or some other source. Gurney Halleck was known for quoting from the O.C. Bible, but Paul shows no indication of knowing where the quotes come from until after he receives a copy of the O.C. Bible from Yueh.[33]

What Is Paul's Religion?

When considering the theme of religion in Dune, the Fremen and their religion often receive most of the attention.[34] This is not surprising, since Herbert paints a vivid picture of a complex Fremen culture in which religion is intimately tied to Fremen survival in a harsh environment, their longing for revenge against Harkonnens, and their desire to transform the arid Arrakis into a paradise. But Paul is a product of the Imperium, and enters the Fremen culture as an outsider with an existing religious formation from his upbringing among Imperium elites. A full understanding of the character of Paul Atreides and of the novel itself means coming to grips with his exposure to religion in the Imperium before encountering the Fremen. Paul joins the Fremen community and eventually becomes their Lisan al-Gaib, their messianic leader and deliverer. Yet, his context remains the Imperium. As he tells the Fremen "I rule here! I rule on every square inch of Arrakis! This is my ducal fief whether the Emperor says yea or nay!"[35] He is their Mahdi, but he is Duke of Arrakis first. His goal is to get rid of the Harkonnen occupiers, retake Arrakis, and reclaim a high position in the Imperium. This happens to coincide with the goals and desires of the Fremen, which makes Paul's efforts to recover his throne significantly easier. But it is the Imperium from which he comes, and it is the Imperium which continues on with Paul as Emperor, though he reigns from Arrakis instead of Salusa Secundus, and also retains his rule over the Fremen.

Paul's lack of exposure to the O.C. Bible before the events of the first novel might be less surprising when considering the third "major force" mentioned in Appendix II, namely the "agnostic ruling class (including the Guild) for whom religion was a kind of puppet show to amuse the populace and keep it docile."[36] As a member of the "ruling class" with a tendency toward agnosticism, Paul might not have been brought up in any religious tradition. He would likely have learned about religion as part of his general education, but perhaps only as an academic or theoretical subject, instead of as beliefs to be accepted and practices to be undertaken. It is possible that neither Paul nor his parents had a belief in any particular religion. There is little indication in the text that any of them believed in a divine power, an afterlife, or a sacred text. Although Duke Leto Atreides muses at one point, "I may think of Arrakis as a hell I've reached before death,"[37] this does not necessarily indicate that he actually believes in an afterlife.

The religion of the Imperium includes the "Great Mother," which the "Terminology of the Imperium" glossary in *Dune* defines as "the horned goddess, the feminine principle of space."[38] Jessica references this deity, but usually only in exclamations and expressions of surprise (e.g., "Great Mother! He's drunk!"[39]), except for when she tries to impress and manipulate the Shadout Mapes. Several other characters refer to the Great Mother—including Gurney Halleck, Thufir Hawat, Yueh, even the Emperor Shaddam Corrino IV—but only as an exclamation, such as Thufir Hawat's surprise at the fighting skill of the Fremen: "Great Mother! What a fighting force we'd have had!"[40] Only Liet-Kynes seems to speak of the Great Mother entirely sincerely, when he urges Paul to leave their hiding place: "Hurry now, and the Great Mother give you speed and luck."[41] It is less clear whether Jessica also believes in the Great Mother, or simply uses her name as an exclamation or when cynically trying to manipulate the native Fremen with beliefs planted long ago by the Bene Gesserit's Missionaria Protectiva.

If Paul's upbringing did not include the O.C. Bible, what other religions might he have encountered? While the O.C. Bible permeated the religious universe, there were other religions still in existence at the time. The fourth "major force" in the religious universe was the "Ancient Teachings," which—despite their often-improbable syncretism (Zensunni, Buddislamic, Navachristianity)—still traced their roots back to Old Earth. The "pundi rice farmers" of Paul's homeworld of Caladan appear to have preserved the "Muadh Quran with its pure Ilm and Fiqh."[42] "Ilm" and "Fiqh" refer to primary teachings of Islam. "Muadh" refers to Muadh ibn Jabal, a very early convert to Islam and an associate of the Prophet Muhammad who helped compile the original Qur'an.[43] The implication is that the common people of Caladan have preserved a form of Islam that could be considered pure and unchanged. Paul might have had some exposure to this religion, and as such it is interesting to consider that the religion and culture of the Fremen, with its roots in Islam, might not have been entirely unfamiliar to the Atreides. This is speculation, however, since there is no indication in the text that Paul was familiar with this form of Qur'anic religion, particularly since he was not allowed "play or companions his own age" from among the pundi locals who might have exposed him to their faith.[44]

Why Does Yueh Give Paul an O.C. Bible?

Before they leave for Arrakis, Dr. Yueh gives Paul a miniature traveler's version of the O.C. Bible. A striking aspect of this scene is Yueh's determination that Paul take the book. When Paul seems about to return it, Yueh says to himself "I must catch his mind as well as his cupidity."[45] He instructs Paul to open the book in order to engage him with the book as text, as well as a desirable physical object. It is not entirely clear why Yueh wants Paul to have the O.C. Bible. He says to himself as Paul is opening the book: "I salve my own conscience. I give him the surcease of religion before betraying him. Thus I may say to myself that he has gone where I cannot go."[46]

There is much that is curious about this passage. It seems difficult to believe that Yueh thought a small gift such as this could compensate to any degree for the monstrous betrayal he was about to inflict on House Atreides. Was Yueh a believer in the religion of the Fourteen Sages and the O.C. Bible himself? He tells Paul the book was given to him when he was young, and one of the markings may have been his, the passage from 467 Kalima ("From water does all life begin"), which he asks Paul to read. The book was also used by his wife, who had also marked a favorite passage. Since it appears to have been used to some extent by Yueh and his family, it is possible that Yueh was a believer in the religion of the O.C. Bible in some way.

Yueh believes that he will be giving Paul the "surcease of religion," which is strange considering the term "surcease" actually means "cessation" or "a temporary respite or end."[47] Does Yueh think he is giving Paul "cessation of religion" or "cessation from religion" in the sense of an end to religious belief? As a member of the "agnostic elite," Paul might not even have a religion to surcease. Approached from a different angle, there are a number of ways in which religion and faith themselves have been considered a "surcease." Many have found in religion an end to—or at least relief from—fear, doubt, confusion, uncertainty, or suffering. Perhaps it is religion that is offering the "surcease." Perhaps Yueh hopes that somewhere in the O.C. Bible or religion of the "Fourteen Sages" Paul will find some solace or strength during his upcoming trial, some surcease from suffering. This would make Yueh's next thought more understandable: "Thus I may say to myself that he has gone where I cannot go."[48] Yueh expects to find none of this kind of surcease himself. The note he includes in the *fremkit* for Paul and Jessica says: "Do not try to forgive me, I do not want your forgiveness. I already have enough burdens."[49] So perhaps from Yueh's point of view he was offering Paul the consolation of religion that he would never have, with some hope of salvation or an afterlife.

What little is available of the contents of the O.C. Bible in the Dune saga texts offers scant support for this idea. Yueh mentions that the miniature O.C. Bible has 1,800 pages, which suggests it was an enormous book; not surprising given its origins in an attempt to reconcile or include texts from many religions. Very little of the text of the O.C. Bible is quoted throughout the Dune saga—fewer than 300 words are quoted in *Dune*—so conclusions about its overall contents can only be tentative. What we have consists primarily of aphorisms, proverbs, and commandments. There appears to be some concept of an afterlife expressed in at least one of the passages, the *sirat*: "Paradise on my right, Hell on my left and the Angel of Death behind."[50] But no information is available about how one obtains the afterlife. It does not appear to contain any sort of spiritual diagnosis of the human situation such as sin, attachment, or karma, or anything like a "Plan of Salvation" or "Four Noble Truths" that would offer a spiritual solution. There is one passage that mentions sin ("Any sin can be ascribed, at least in part, to a natural bad tendency that is an extenuating circumstance acceptable to God"),[51] but no indication of what sin is and what can be done about it. Yueh's own description of the O.C. Bible further suggests its contents were primarily informational and inspirational, rather than diagnostic: "It has much historical truth in it as well as good ethical philosophy."[52] We can only guess at the contents of the O.C. Bible, but it seems difficult to believe that Yueh thought that providing Paul with merely "historical truth" and "good ethical philosophy" would give him solace sufficient to salve Yueh's conscience.

How Does the O.C. Bible Affect Paul's Awakening?

Dr. Yueh asks Paul to turn to a passage in the O.C. Bible, but Paul accidentally turns to a different one, one which was a favorite of Yueh's wife. Paul begins to read but is cut off by Yueh:

> Think you of the fact that a deaf person cannot hear. Then, what deafness may we not all possess? What senses do we lack that we cannot see and cannot hear another world all around us? What is there around us that we cannot—....[53]

The passage affects Paul powerfully, but he is not sure how or why: "Yet it contained a mystery ... something had happened while he read from it."[54] Whatever it was, it was connected to his "terrible purpose." Paul experiences frequent intimations of the "terrible purpose" he is meant to fulfill, beginning with the test of the *gom jabbar* when he is 15 years old, when his prescience is little more than glimpses and vague dreams.[55] Why does this passage in the O.C. Bible "stir" his "terrible purpose"? At this point, Paul's understanding of his "terrible purpose" is very rudimentary, as are his prescient abilities. But the passage is one of a number of experiences that feed into the transformation that takes place later in the novel.

It appears that Paul was influenced from that point onwards by the O.C. Bible. He recognizes a quote from it by Gurney Halleck: "I have been a stranger in a strange land."[56] He quotes it on impulse himself when he accepts the gift of the stillsuits from Kynes: "The gift is the blessing of the giver."[57] The passage he read with Yueh comes back to him as he and Jessica flee the sandstorm and it rings in his mind.[58] The vivid "sirat" passage from the O.C. Bible comes to him when approaching the Cave of the Birds: "Paradise on my right, Hell on my left and the Angel of Death behind."[59] So it is clear that Paul's exposure to the O.C. Bible has at least contributed to his religious education. This would be useful on Arrakis, where he enters a world very different than his homeworld, a religiously complex one on which faith and belief have an urgency and fervor Paul might not have seen before on lush Caladan.

At this point, it might be possible to answer the question of why "exposure to the O.C. Bible at a critical moment" was such an important part of Paul's awakening. That transformation was a complex process, taking place in several phases.[60] In some of the phases, the changes seem to force themselves upon him, indeed overall the process is something over which he has little control. For the most part, it is happening to him, rather than something he controls. At each phase Paul needs to accept the extraordinary changes that have happened to him in order to pass successfully through to the next phase.

Perhaps the most significant period of change takes place when Jessica and Paul are hiding in the stilltent. The trauma of fleeing from the joint Imperial and Harkonnen attack has triggered a level of prescience within him. But it is a level still very much tied into his Mentat abilities:

> Something had happened to his awareness this night—he saw with sharpened clarity every circumstance and occurrence around him. He felt unable to stop the inflow of data or the cold precision with which each new item was added to his knowledge and the computation was centered in his awareness. It was Mentat power and more.[61]

Paul's new level of ability is still based on "computation" of an "inflow[s] of data." It is more than "Mentat power," but it appears to be an extension of that power. The language of computation is frequent in the next part of the text. He refers to incoming information as "another datum to be entered in his mind," to his mind as "adding sense impressions, extrapolating, computing," and to the "cold precision of his being."[62]

Paul appears to be relatively accepting of this expansion of his Mentat abilities. It is an expansion of a capability he was comfortable with, perhaps attributable to the spice that was everywhere in his environment. But the next phase in his transformation is more unusual, and distressing:

> Abruptly, as though he had found a necessary key, Paul's mind climbed another notch in awareness. He felt himself clinging to this new level, clutching at a precarious hold and peering about. It was as though he existed within a globe with avenues radiating away in all directions ... yet this only approximated the sensation[63]

From this point onwards, Paul's prescience is described most often as a sense, which was similar to sight, but only "approximated the sensation." Paul thinks to himself: "I have another kind of sight. I see another kind of terrain: the available paths."[64] His prescience is no longer experienced as computation, it has become another sense. If there is still computation taking place, it is taking place outside of his consciousness and is presented to his consciousness visually. Paul found that "[t]he awareness conveyed both reassurance and alarm."[65] At that moment he understands better what is happening to him, and finds it at least partially reassuring, though the lack of visibility into some parts of the "terrain" is troubling. The reassurance doesn't last long though and Paul then experiences terror:

> He felt that something must shatter. It was as though a clockwork control for a bomb had been set to ticking within him. It went about its business no matter what he wanted…. The emptiness was unbearable…. And he could see ahead, the most terrifying direction….[66]

It is shortly after this change that Paul realizes the awakening of his prescience has been set in motion by "exposure to the O.C. Bible at critical time," as well as by his training and the mélange.[67] He includes the O.C. Bible in the list because the passage he read with Yueh has prepared him for some of the changes he is undergoing, in particular for understanding what had just happened to him. The O.C. Bible asks the reader: "What senses do we lack that we cannot see and cannot hear another world all around us?"[68] Something that was just a "mystery" when he first read it would have made more sense now: he says, "I have another kind of sight."[69]

The passage Paul read with Yueh appears to have stayed with him, as it appears twice more in the original six Dune novels, more often than any other O.C. Bible passage. The second time occurs when Paul and Jessica escape in an ornithopter through a sandstorm.[70] As they pass through, Paul recites the Litany against Fear, a short Bene Gesserit text recited to calm oneself and remain focused during perilous experiences. The words of the Litany have a powerful effect on him:

> They were out of the storm … and Paul sensed himself trembling on the verge of a revelation … he found himself caught on the question of what caused this trembling awareness. Part of it, he felt, was the spice-saturated diet of Arrakis. But he thought part of it could be the litany, as through the words had a power of their own.[71]

Paul is about to pass through another phase-change: "he felt himself poised on a brink of self-awareness that could not have been without the litany's magic."[72] Then the text from the O.C. Bible comes upon him suddenly: "What senses do we lack that we cannot see or hear another world all around us?"[73] If the words of the Litany against Fear have a "power of their own," do the words from the O.C. Bible also have a power to cat-alyze Paul's transformation? There are other examples of the power of words to effect changes in Paul. For example, later in the Fremen sietch Jessica quotes from the Fremen "book of examples." This causes turmoil within Paul: "His mother's words had locked onto the working of the spice essence."[74]

The text immediately switches to a more active scene as Paul and Jessica wrestle the damaged 'thopter to the ground, so the effect of the passage from the O.C. Bible is unclear. Sometime later, when they are observing a sandworm up-close, Paul speaks of crossing a kind of barrier: "He could sense the darkness ahead, nothing revealed to his inner eye."[75] But this does not frighten him: "the sensation of time-darkness forced a hyper-acceleration of his other senses."[76] This phase in his transformation accelerates his other senses, and reminds him that even without prescience he has "other senses."[77] The rhythm of Paul's transformation appears to slow significantly at this point, until he takes the Water of Life much later. The O.C. Bible has played its part in Paul's awakening, preparing him for a reality in which he has sometimes-disturbing senses that most other humans lack.

Conclusions

Appendix II on "The Religion of Dune" contains a large amount of information about the O.C. Bible, which might seem disproportionate to the importance of the O.C. Bible within the Dune saga. It is the source of a handful of quotes and references (mostly in *Dune*) and plays a brief though "critical" role in awakening Paul Atreides to his full capabilities with pre-science and hyper-awareness. It has "historical truth" and "good ethical philosophy,"[78] and seems to teach a religion based on reason, which might elicit interest and devotion, but not passion. As a religion that was meant to absorb "the ancient superstitions and beliefs"[79] it failed. Instead, a new religion was created, one suitable for an Imperium that prized order and lawfulness.

Herbert was famously suspicious of "superheroes" because of their inevitable transformation into tyrants, and the ensuing catastrophe of their rule.[80] *Dune*, and its sequel *Dune Messiah*, is ultimately the story of the rise of a religious tyrant. Herbert was also suspicious of religions and other systems: "It's the systems themselves that I see as dangerous.... Sys-tems take over and grind on and on."[81] Faith in religion or a charismatic leader allows individuals to surrender their critical faculties and sense of morality to someone or something else. The Fremen religion seems vibrant and passionate, but, it must be remembered, also violent and murderous as it swept across the Known Universe in a bloody Jihad. The religion of the O.C. Bible might not have seemed as dangerous as the religion of the Fremen, but it still contributed to the rise of a religious tyrant.

Notes

1. Herbert, *Dune*, 191.
2. *Ibid.*, 46.
3. *Ibid.*, 507.
4. *Ibid.*, 63.
5. *Ibid.*, 287.
6. *Ibid.*, 191.
7. This essay focuses on the O.C. Bible as portrayed by Frank Herbert in his six Dune novels. The novels by Brian Herbert and Kevin J. Anderson in the expanded Dune universe contain additional information about the O.C. Bible and the C.E.T., but that is beyond the scope of this essay.
8. Herbert, *Dune*, 190.
9. *Ibid.*, 40.
10. "William, III of Orange."
11. Herbert, *Dreamer of Dune*, 187.
12. Herbert, *Dune*, 508.
13. *Ibid.*, 505.
14. *Ibid.*, 486.
15. *Ibid.*, 487.
16. *Ibid.*
17. DiTommaso, "History and Historical Effect in Frank Herbert's *Dune*," 314.
18. *Ibid.*
19. Herbert, *Dune*, 489.
20. *Ibid.*, 488.
21. *Ibid.*
22. *Ibid.*
23. *Ibid.*
24. *Ibid.*
25. *Ibid.*
26. *Ibid.*, 484.
27. *Ibid.*, 489.
28. *Ibid.*, 484–85.
29. *Ibid.*, 39–40.
30. *Ibid.*, 303.
31. See for example: "Mysteries," *The Oxford Dictionary of Phrase and Fable.*
32. Herbert, *Dune*, 191.
33. *Ibid.*, 90.
34. For example, Howard, *Religious Violence in Frank Herbert's Dune*; Touponce, *Frank Herbert*, 68–72, 76–79; and DiTommaso, "History and Historical Effect in Frank Herbert's *Dune*," 316–317.
35. *Ibid.*, 415.
36. *Ibid.*, 484.
37. *Ibid.*, 78.
38. *Ibid.*, 503.
39. *Ibid.*, 145.
40. *Ibid.*, 210.
41. *Ibid.*, 222.

42. *Ibid.*, 484.

43. See Ali, "Beside the Sand Dunes," in this volume for a discussion of the meaning of Muadh as it relates to the Dune saga.

44. Herbert, *Dune*, 4.

45. *Ibid.*, 39.

46. *Ibid.*

47. *Merriam-Webster*, "surcease." One possibility is that "surcease" is a textual error and that some other word such as "solace," "relief" or "release" was meant instead. However, Herbert appears to be aware of the correct meaning of the archaic term "surcease," since he uses it correctly in several other locations in the Dune saga (*Children of Dune*, 232, 259; *Heretics of Dune*, 498). Consulting earlier editions of the text of *Dune* confirms that this term is present back to printings in 1965 at least. Additionally, *Dune* was first published in serial form in *Analog* magazine in 1963–1965, and the original version of this passage also has "surcease." If this is an error it goes far back in the text, and it is probably better to try to wrestle with its meaning than to assume a textual error.

48. Herbert, *Dune*, 39.

49. *Ibid.*, 185.

50. *Ibid.*, 281.

51. *Ibid.*, 490.

52. *Ibid.*, 40.

53. *Ibid.*, 39.

54. *Ibid.*, 40.

55. *Ibid.*, 11–12, 26.

56. *Ibid.* 90, probably originally from Exodus 2:22 in the Bible.

57. *Ibid.*, 108.

58. *Ibid.*, 237.

59. *Ibid.*, 281.

60. DiTommaso provides an expanded precis of this process, though without touching upon the possible role of the O.C. Bible. "History and Historical Effect in Frank Herbert's *Dune*," 319.

61. *Ibid.*, 184.

62. *Ibid.*, 185. See also Nardi, "Political Prescience," in this volume on the use of computational language to describe prescience.

63. Herbert, *Dune*, 190.

64. *Ibid.*, 190.

65. *Ibid.*

66. *Ibid.*, 191.

67. *Ibid.*

68. *Ibid.*, 39.

69. *Ibid.*, 190.

70. The third use of the passage occurs in *Dune Messiah* (180), when Paul contemplates the metal Tleilaxu eyes of the ghola Duncan Idaho.

71. Herbert, *Dune*, 237.

72. *Ibid.*, 237.

73. *Ibid.*

74. *Ibid.*, 287.

75. *Ibid.*, 260.

76. *Ibid.*

77. *Ibid.*, 237.

78. *Ibid.*, 40.

79. *Ibid.*, 488.

80. Herbert, "Dune Genesis," 72.

81. *Ibid.*, 74.

Works Cited

DiTommaso, Lorenzo. "History and Historical Effect in Frank Herbert's *Dune*." *Science Fiction Studies* 19, no. 3 (1992): 311–325.

Herbert, Brian. *Dreamer of Dune: The Biography of Frank Herbert*. New York: Tor, 2003.

Herbert, Frank. *Dune*. 1965. New York: Ace Books, 1999.

Herbert, Frank. "Dune Genesis." *OMNI* 2, no. 10 (July 1980): 72–76.

Howard, Kenton Taylor. *Religious Violence in Frank Herbert's Dune*. Master's Thesis, Florida Atlantic University, 2012.

Merriam-Webster. s.v. "surcease." Accessed April 11, 2020. https://www.merriam-webster.com/dictionary/surcease.

Touponce, William F. *Frank Herbert*. Boston: Twayne Publishers, 1988.

"William, III of Orange." *Historic World Leaders*, edited by Anne Commire. Detroit: Gale, 1994. Accessed 4 July 2021. link.gale.com/apps/doc/K1616000617/WHIC?u=fairfax_main&sid=bookmark-WHIC&xid=3e219275.

PART III

Biology and Ecology

Locations of Deviance

A *Eugenics Reading of* Dune

LEIGHA HIGH MCREYNOLDS

In his *Reader's Guide* to Frank Herbert, David Miller observes that Herbert's novels "form a remarkably unified treatment of two complementary problems."[1] The first, of course, deals with ecology.[2] The second deals with humanity: "If man freezes an achieved balance, decadence sets in and life yields to entropy. Thus, the problems to be solved by Herbert's characters require that chaos be organized and stasis disturbed."[3] The entropy of *Dune* is one of genetic stagnation; the society of the imagined empire is a product of eugenics. Underlying the *bildungsroman* of one of the most powerful superheroes ever written—Paul Muad'Dib Atreides, Duke of Arrakis, Kwisatz Haderach, Lisan al-Gaib—is the story of a breeding program hundreds of years old. As a result, Paul's fate and his relationship to his society are attributed as much to his genetic makeup as to his environment and education. Behind this breeding scheme are the Bene Gesserit. A religious/scientific school of women with intimate genetic knowledge, as well as the ability to control their own impregnation and the sex of their children, they have spent years breeding for the "perfect" human, the Kwisatz Haderach, the man who can also be a Reverend Mother. Paul was not intended to be this legendary figure, and the narrative of *Dune* is driven by the fact that his Bene Gesserit mother, Jessica, has disobeyed orders and borne a son instead of a daughter. Therefore, Paul is a genetic deviant, making him infinitely dangerous to a society built on eugenics and genetic control.

Focusing on the importance of eugenics to the narrative allows one to read *Dune* in generative new ways. While scholars have previously recognized the eugenic and evolutionary themes in Herbert's work, there has not been a sustained consideration of how this might augment our understanding of the narrative.[4] In order to theorize its impacts, I turn to the work of disability studies, which draws attention to the presence and function of disability in cultural productions. In their work *Cultural Locations of Disability*, foundational disability studies scholars Sharon Snyder and David Mitchell argue that "disability [is] a concept of deviant variation"[5] and trace this conflation of disability and deviant variation "back to the eugenics era, when disability began to be counted as an undesirable deviation from normative existence."[6] If, as Snyder and Mitchell explain, the "eugenics movement ... equate[d] ... disabled bodies with undesirable biological deviances,"[7] then undesirable biological deviances, such as Paul's entire, unauthorized genome, can be equated with disabled bodies. In other words, disability studies shifts our understanding of disability from a physical impairment to a cultural attitude. Disability in this model is constructed by and relative to society's ideology. Thus, I propose that, because he is a genetic deviant in a eugenics system, we can read Paul as disabled. It follows that *Dune*'s narrative, as far as it is a narrative of eugenics, is a narrative of disability.

For many readers, the concept of "disability" may connote lack of ability, which clearly does not apply to Paul. While disability studies works to separate the experience of disability from assumptions about an individual's ability to function, it is true that neither Paul nor a number of other disabled characters in the text fit comfortably into the American historical eugenics narrative where "disability [is] the foundation of biological ideologies of inferiority."[8] Paul is, in spite of his genetic deviance, a superior person. In fact, because of his deviance, he is the most superior. However, in his reading of disability in science fiction, Michael Bérubé asserts, "There are also texts in which exceptionality—of all things—is rendered as disability."[9] Bérubé, and others, frequently turn to the X-Men films to support this reading of disability as extraordinary ability. While some X-Men, like Professor X, are visibly disabled, Bérubé argues, "[T]he X-Men films render mutant exceptionality as disability even when mutants discover their power to change their shape or to heal their wounds in seconds."[10] This essay will show how, in a similar vein, Paul's exceptionality contributes to his disabled-ness by the way it reveals his deviance.

Martin Mantle extends Bérubé's work in his article on superhero films from the early 2000s by exploring what drives this correlation between exceptionality and disability in science fiction. Mantle calls attention to the genetic explanations underlying the hero's exceptional abilities and argues that "extra-ordinary ability, and the anxieties expressed about those abilities, parallels ... and gives rise to the anxieties about deviation and deviance."[11] In other words, the extreme difference of these characters from the norm, regardless of whether that difference might be an exceptional or useful thing, creates a disability narrative. Mantle argues that this is because "[t]he films' focus on extra-ordinary ability can be taken as a sign of the extent of the anxiety about what we might consider normal."[12] Disability is defined in opposition to the norm, and extra-ordinary ability functions the same way: Paul is definitely not normal. Mantle is not claiming that extra-ordinary ability is the same as an impairment, but rather that we are limited in how we can talk about bodies that deviate from the norm: "These superhero films demonstrate that, in order to talk about super-ability as a deviation from a normal body, they rely on disability scripts as the language of deviation."[13] Using a disability script can help assess the significance of Paul as deviant in a eugenic regime.

A Diagnostic Regime

In a disability reading of *Dune*, the Bene Gesserit function as a "*diagnostic regime* [emphasis]" original.[14] . While the monetary and military power of *Dune*'s universe is divided between the male-dominated Imperial Household, the Landsraad (the aristocratic houses), and the Spacing Guild (which controls interstellar travel), the Bene Gesserit wield reproductive power. As eugenicists, they do not work to improve or make viable the genetic patterns/families that they view as unfit, but rather focus on managing the reproduction of genomes. The eugenics movement in this society is so powerful that it controls, in essence, who may or may not sit on the throne. For example, one of the reasons that Paul can demand the throne at the end of the first novel is that the Emperor has been denied an heir by his Bene Gesserit wife who, unlike Jessica, obeys the orders of her superiors. With their sexual reproduction in the hands of a higher authority, although they remain unaware, the reader can see how the entire aristocratic society of *Dune* is participating in a disability narrative. Snyder and Mitchell's interpretation of the eugenics movement supports such a reading: "The eugenicists thus installed a binary coding system into which all human beings could be slotted ... in the reproductive sphere [as] those 'fit' and 'unfit' to breed."[15] In this model, being unfit to breed automatically classifies one as defective and, therefore, disabled.

Markers of Disability

Under this diagnostic regime, embodiment is understood in terms of visible genetic markers. In a world where one's genetic makeup and one's ancestry can be read by a society trained to notice these genetic markers, Paul's genetic deviance becomes a *visible* disability. This is illustrated by how the characters describe and understand themselves and others. For example, at their first meeting, the Reverend Mother assesses Paul's ancestry through his facial structure:

> face oval like Jessica's, but strong bones ... hair: the Duke's black-black but with browline of the maternal grandfather who cannot be named, and that thin disdainful nose; shape of directly staring green eyes: like the old Duke, the paternal grandfather who is dead.[16]

With the awakening of his gifts, Paul gains the insight necessary to imitate the Reverend Mother and read the genetic deviance that marks him as exceptional. Paul reveals this ability to his mother in an exchange that follows his revelation: "We carry our past with us ... *we* are Harkonnens ... when next you find a mirror, study your face—study mine now. The traces are there if you don't blind yourself" (emphasis original).[17] So omnipresent is the role of genetics in one's ancestry that characters are as much a sum of their genetic parts as they are unique individuals. As a result, Paul's visible markers cannot be separated from his sense of self.

Paul's deviancy is also identified—by himself and others—through language commonly associated with disability in fiction and in social reality: the language of monsters and freaks. Though Paul is a genetically crafted superhuman, he is still, for most of the novel, only fifteen, and his awakening gifts, his exceptionality, are as bewildering and complicated as any adolescent's entrance into puberty. Readers are drawn into Paul's self-awareness at the moment of his awakening:

> The emptiness was unbearable. Knowing how the clockwork had been set in motion made no difference. He could look to his own past and see the start of it.... And he could look ahead—the most terrifying direction—to see where it all pointed.
> *I'm a monster!* he thought. *A freak!*[18]

This idea of monstrosity, this feeling of freakishness, however it may be linked to an understanding of more traditional and visible disability, is rooted in his genetic deviance. And this reading of Paul bears out throughout the novel. While he might intimidate and be admired, he also incites the abject fear, disgust, and curiosity associated with a monster or a freak.

However, the more obvious "freak" of the text is not Paul, but rather his sister, Alia Atreides. Her presence in the text is marked by linguistic signifiers of disability and difference. Not only is Alia a genetic deviant—Jessica has again conceived without orders from her Bene Gesserit superiors—she is also a genetic mutant, altered in the womb when Jessica goes through the Fremen ritual to become a Reverend Mother. While Paul develops race consciousness at the time of his awakening, Alia is born with the feminine race consciousness characteristic of all Reverend Mothers,

Bene Gesserit or otherwise. Though Alia's doubly deviant status is, like her brother's, a result of genetic differences, her deviance is, more so than his, located in her body. Jessica draws attention to Alia's "subtle differences…. The child … carried herself with a calmness and awareness beyond her years."[19] Even a mother's love cannot keep Jessica from wondering, *"What have I borne?"* when presented with the embodied differences between her daughter and other children.[20] In articulating her self-awareness of her strangeness, Alia, like her brother, turns to a common label for physical difference: "'I know I'm a freak,' Alia whispered."[21] This identification of her "abnormality," the self-labeling as freak—a title which carries associations with deformity, disability, and sensations of disgust—demonstrates how the exceptional body can functionally be read as impaired.

What ultimately sets Alia apart from her brother is the Bene Gesserit's diagnostic assessment that her existence is not only unplanned, but unnatural. When Alia meets the Reverend Mother Gaius Helen Mohiam after the Emperor's failed invasion, Alia tries to make a connection by referencing their shared mental access to their female predecessors. In response, the Reverend Mother exclaims, "That child is an abomination!"[22] Within a diagnostic regime, this labeling of Alia as an abomination attempts, in the words of Snyder and Mitchell, "to salvage the danger that deviance poses generally, [by using] designations of disability … to place some populations as not only anomalous to, but nearly outside of, cultural adjudications of functional, aesthetic, and biological value."[23] Designating Alia as an abomination relies on the child's status as genetic deviant and mutant, forcing her into a disabled state where she lacks value—in fact carries negative value—in a system where her embodiment is deemed undesirable.

While Paul and Alia are deviant bodies because of their presence outside of or adjacent to the diagnostic regime, Count Hasimir Fenring demonstrates that the Bene Gesserit's eugenic project can fail even when they control reproduction. When the Count and Paul finally meet, Paul understands, "Fenring was one of the might-have-beens, an almost-Kwisatz Haderach, crippled by a flaw in the genetic pattern—a eunuch, his talent concentrated into furtiveness and inner seclusion."[24] As a man, Fenring is literally *impaired* in the sense of reproductive functionality. But in the socio-political structure of *Dune*, a genetic flaw is "crippling": Fenring is *disabled* because he cannot fully contribute to society. In a eugenics paradigm, his usefulness is thus limited to eliminating genetic errors: he cannot make life, but he is mentally and physically engineered to take it. Thus, Jessica labels him: "Count Fenring…. A genetic-eunuch … and a killer."[25] His destiny has been scripted by his genomic sequence and the resulting disability.

Deviants Are Dangerous

Paul's genetic deviancy, in contrast to Fenring's genetic flaw, is what gives him the freedom to subvert the structures of a society that so rigidly defines him by his genetic potential. While Fenring might be the deadliest person in the empire, Paul is the most dangerous. His dangerousness may take many forms, but it stems from his existence in opposition to the controlled breeding that defines the society he occupies. Through his very existence, Paul threatens the diagnostic regime of the Bene Gesserit: because of his gender, the faithful patience of ninety generations may fail and crucial bloodlines may never be passed down. The knowledge he gains from his hyper-awareness, an exceptionality enabled by his unique genetic makeup, undermines the secrecy surrounding their plans. We see this, for example, in the moment where he realizes the truth about his maternal grandfather, the one never meant to be named. His outsider status also gives him a vantage point from which to scrutinize—not just understand—the Bene Gesserit's program.

Though the narrative does not make this explicit, it is implied that Paul is the only character to publicly resist the eugenic paradigm that is the background of his society. At the end of the text, when Paul confronts the Reverend Mother a second time, his life experience and exceptional cognitive powers as a genetic deviant provide him with the knowledge to condemn the eugenic work of the Bene Gesserit in front of the Emperor himself: "'I'll give you only one thing,' Paul said. 'You saw part of what the race needs, but how poorly you saw it. You think to control human breeding and intermix a select few according to your master plan! How little you understand.'"[26] Ultimately, Paul's subversion of Bene Gesserit authority lies not in his understanding or condemnation of the system, but his adamant refusal to be a participant in it at the same decisive meeting. Paul confronts the Reverend Mother Mohiam and tells her that the Bene Gesserit have patiently waited ninety generations for their Kwisatz Haderach, only to find that he will not obey them.[27] Through his embodied performance of genetic deviance, Paul is the ultimate disruption of their eugenic narrative. He understands that his role as Kwisatz Haderach is to disrupt genetic entropy: "The race of humans had felt its own dormancy, sensed itself grown stale and knew now only the need to experience turmoil in which the genes would mingle and the strong new mixtures survive."[28] When he enables this genetic rampage across the universe by unleashing the jihad, the carefully structured genomes and Bene Gesserit regime are both at risk.

As a genetic deviant and an outsider, Paul is also dangerous to the more traditional political regime, namely the Emperor Shaddam IV. He recognizes this disruptive potential within himself: "I am an embarrassment to the Emperor.... As I live, I shall continue to be such an embarrassment that I stick in their throats and choke them to death!"[29] When Paul makes this vow, the overt meaning is that he is an embarrassment because he has foiled the Emperor's plans, both by being born in the first place and in surviving the attack on the Atreides household. And he makes good on his threat, ultimately defeating the Emperor and placing himself on the throne. However, in the context of the larger eugenics narrative that encapsulates their society, Paul functions more subtly as an embarrassment through his genetic deviance, not just because it provides him with the exceptionality that makes him superhuman, but because his deviance from the system of genetic control allows him to embody the Emperor's greatest desire: a male heir. As a genetic deviant, Paul is both the unauthorized heir of his father and fathers an heir outside of Bene Gesserit control.

But it would be overly simplistic to assert that Paul's deviancy can be summed up in the story of an exceptional human being who subverts the corrupt authorities of his society by virtue of his outsider status, for Paul is literally dangerous. His deviancy, both genetic and societal, is the direct cause of—and often an excuse for—death and violence. In the space between the end of *Dune* and the beginning of the next book in the series, *Dune Messiah,* Paul will lead his Fremen army across the universe in a jihad, killing billions. In *Dune,* deviancy is not simply cast as redemptive; it is not, like a clichéd narrative of disability, a character-development device that enables a hero to overcome all odds. The deviant figure is inherently both necessary and dangerous as, in Herbert's personal views and fiction, "evolutionary priorities take precedence over man's desires for an ideal world."[30] The evolutionary priority underlying *Dune* appears to value variation in the human genome and casts deviation as a healthy and desirable form of embodiment.[31]

In *Dune,* we see an empire founded on eugenics in which one's ability to contribute to society is determined by one's adherence to or deviance from a desired genetic sequence. Returning to Snyder and Mitchell provides a historical eugenics context for the effects Paul has on his society. They argue that eugenics is dangerous because it threatens the biological variability and vitality of humanity: "Our ability to erase organically embedded characteristics that are integral to the functioning of bodies and minds ultimately threatens the very core of our viability as biologically based beings in the first place."[32] Herbert himself obviously held this view in the context of his beliefs about evolution, and it takes on additional significance framed by a disability studies approach to variation:

> [according to Herbert] adaptability in all its forms—from engineering improvisation to social mobility to genetic variability—is essential. Improvisation is the only security. It is not an absolute security, but relative. Life is always changing and demanding new adaptations.[33]

Conclusion

In this essay, I have discussed *Dune* within the context of Snyder and Mitchell's *Cultural Locations of Disability* because the two books—one with fiction and the other with history—are performing similar cultural projects, though the illumination of that project in *Dune* might not occur without the framework of the other. Snyder and Mitchell essentially argue that the eugenics history they trace persists into the present moment, under the rubric of genetics, which often seems (reading into what Snyder and Mitchell argue) almost intentionally designed to obscure its dark historical roots in eugenics: "The updated eugenics of the present day, often called genetics, examines conditions in bodies that are classed as 'mutant,' 'tragic,' 'coding errors,' 'suffering,' 'unhealthy,' 'deviant,' 'faulty,' and 'abnormal.'"[34] The Bene Gesserit project, and therefore the underlying narrative of *Dune*'s society, is also located in and around this cusp between eugenics and genetics; a disability studies reading of the novel exposes that cusp as illusory. If *Dune* is a white savior narrative, as some have argued,[35] then Paul would be an uncritical super-crip[36] perpetuating harmful disability tropes. But, if we read the novel as a critique of great men and overreaching institutions, then Paul's subversive deviance functions as a condemnation of certain forays in genetic science.

This reading aligns with Herbert's larger political perspective and his stated motivation for telling Paul's story. According to Herbert:

> Dune was aimed at this whole idea of the infallible leader because my view of history says mistakes made by a leader (or made in a leader's name) are amplified by the numbers who follow without question.... That's how Germany said "Sieg Heil!" and murdered more than six million of our fellow human beings.[37]

The invocation and critique of a eugenics paradigm naturally suggests Hitler's diagnostic regime and the resulting Holocaust. But, while it is easy to apply a great-man theory of history and blame charismatic leaders, a eugenics reading of *Dune* brings equal attention to the culpability of the systems, institutions, and technologies that produce and prop up great men. In *Dune*, this is the diagnostic regime of the Bene Gesserit, but these institutions proliferate later in the series, including the massive religious apparatus that springs up around Paul and his jihad.

It is important to read *Dune* with an awareness of the eugenics—and resulting disability—narrative at the center of the text. Reading through this lens brings attention to disabled figures and disability narratives as more than just signifiers of difference. At the same time, it highlights how *Dune* allows readers to imagine different experiences of embodiment and to reflect on the social and political value of bodily deviance in a regime informed by eugenics.[38] The latter is a crucial perspective in our current world where so much value is put on institutions of ranking—such as IQ tests and SAT scores—that are results of the mindset we inherited from the eugenics era. In addition, there is the development and gradual acceptance of recent technologies that might enable eugenic practices, like "preimplantation genetic diagnosis" and CRISPR-cas9. As science fiction scholars become more broadly aware of disability studies and as disability studies scholars are encouraged to turn to works of science fiction, such readings will become more commonplace.[39] Although this essay only covered the first novel in the Dune saga, the sequels include additional material, including Paul's literal impairment in *Dune Messiah*, that would prove of interest to scholars of disability studies. The varieties of embodiment and genetic experimentation proliferate as the series continues. However, all subsequent progress in the Dune universe originates in Paul's genetic deviance.

NOTES

1. Miller, *Frank Herbert: Starmont Reader's Guide 5,* 9.
2. See Reef "From Taming Sand Dunes to Planetary Ecology," in this volume.
3. Miller, *Frank Herbert: Starmont Reader's Guide 5,* 9.
4. See Hart, "From Silver Fox to Kwisatz Haderach"; Field, "Evolution by Any Means on Dune"; and Semler, "The Golden Path of Eugenics."
5. Snyder and Mitchell, *Cultural Locations of Disability,* 31.
6. *Ibid.,* 3.
7. *Ibid.,* 13.
8. *Ibid.,* 12.
9. Berube, "Disability and Narrative," 569.
10. *Ibid.*
11. Mantle, "Have You Tried Not Being a Mutant?"
12. *Ibid.*
13. *Ibid.*
14. Snyder and Mitchell, *Cultural Locations of Disability,* 71.
15. *Ibid.,* 79.
16. Herbert, *Dune,* 6.
17. *Ibid.,* 198.
18. *Ibid.,* 194–195.
19. *Ibid.,* 394.
20. *Ibid.,* 395.
21. *Ibid.,* 397.
22. *Ibid.,* 462.
23. Snyder and Mitchell, *Cultural Locations of Disability,* 5.
24. Herbert, *Dune,* 487.
25. *Ibid.,* 473.
26. *Ibid.,* 478.
27. *Ibid.,* 477.
28. *Ibid.,* 482.
29. *Ibid.,* 223.
30. O'Reilly, *Frank Herbert,* 167.

31. This perspective plays out more explicitly in the later book *God Emperor of Dune* when Paul's son Leto develops the Golden Path.

32. Snyder and Mitchell, *Cultural Locations of Disability*, 99.

33. O'Reilly, *Frank Herbert*, 115.

34. Snyder and Mitchell, *Cultural Locations of Disability*, 19.

35. See Asher-Perrin, "Why It's Important to Consider Whether *Dune* is a White Savior Narrative" on tor.com for a thoughtful and nuanced exploration of this question.

36. "Super-crip" is a disability studies term that's becoming more broadly used in popular writing about disability narratives. When talking about "real-world" representations of disability, it refers to narratives about people with disabilities heroically overcoming their impairments—a common narrative about Paralympic athletes. When applied to science fiction and similar genres, the term expanded to included disabled characters who function through a special ability—Professor X of the X-Men is a prime example. See Hamilton, "The Transcontinental Disability Choir" on bitchmedia.org for an accessible discussion of the term. Schalk, "Reevaluating the Supercrip," published in the *Journal of Literary and Cultural Disability*, offers an academic literature review of the term's use.

37. Herbert, "Introduction" in *Eye*.

38. In her book *Disability, Literature, Genre: Representation and Affect in Contemporary Literature*, Ria Cheyne argues that genre fiction, science fiction included, is uniquely capable of offering these "reflexive representations" (19) of disability.

39. The first collection at the intersection of disability studies and science fiction, *Disability in Science Fiction: Representations of Technology as Cure*, edited by Kathryn Allan, was only published in 2013. While the current volume has been in production, *MOSF Journal of Science Fiction* and *The Journal of Literary and Cultural Disability Studies* have added substantively to this area of scholarship by publishing special issues. As Kathryn Allan and Ria Cheyne note in their introduction to the latter, while it is currently possible to make an exhaustive list of the published work on disability and science fiction, the field is on a trajectory to expand significantly.

Works Cited

Allan, Kathryn, ed. *Disability in Science Fiction : Representations of Technology as Cure*. New York: Palgrave Macmillan, 2013.

Allan, Kathryn, and Ria Cheyne. "Science Fiction, Disability, Disability Studies: A Conversation." *Journal of Literary & Cultural Disability Studies* 14, no. 4 (2020): 387–401. doi: 10.3828/jlcds.2020.26.

Asher-Perrin, Emmet. "Why It's Important to Consider Whether *Dune* is a White Savior Narrative." Tor.com, March 6, 2019. www.tor.com/2019/03/06/why-its-important-to-consider-whether-dune-is-a-white-savior-narrative/.

Bérubé, Michael. "Disability and Narrative." *Publications of the Modern Language Association of America* 120, no. 2 (2005): 568–76. www.jstor.org.proxygw.wrlc.org/stable/25486186.

Cheyne, Ria. *Disability, Literature, Genre: Representation and Affect in Contemporary Fiction* Liverpool: Liverpool University Press, 2019.

Field, Sandy. "Evolution by Any Means on Dune," In *The Science of Dune: An Unauthorized Exploration into the Real Science Behind Frank Herbert's Fictional Universe*, Science of Pop Culture, edited by Kevin R. Grazier, 67–81. Dallas: BenBella Books, Inc, 2009.

Hamilton, Anna. "The Transcontinental Disability Choir: Disability Archetypes: Supercrip." bitchmedia, December 18, 2009. www.bitchmedia.org/post/the-transcontinental-disability-choir-disability-archetypes-supercrip.

Hart, Carol. "From Silver Fox to Kwizatz Haderach: The Possibilities of Selective Breeding Programs." In *The Science of Dune: An Unauthorized Exploration into the Real Science Behind Frank Herbert's Fictional Universe*, Science of Pop Culture, edited by Kevin R. Grazier, 59–65. Dallas: BenBella Books, Inc, 2009.

Herbert, Frank. *Dune.* New York: Ace Books, 1965.

Herbert, Frank. "Introduction" in *Eye.* New York: Berkley Books: 1985.

Mantle, Martin. "'Have You Tried Not Being a Mutant?': Genetic Mutation and the Acquisition of Extra-ordinary Ability." *M/C Journal* 10, no. 5 (2007). journal.media-culture. org.au/0710/10-mantle.php.

Miller, David M. *Frank Herbert: Starmont Reader's Guide 5.* Mercer Island, WA: Starmont House, 1980.

O'Reilly, Timothy. *Frank Herbert.* New York: Frederick Ungar Publishing Co., 1981.

Schalk, Sami. "Reevaluating the Supercrip." *Journal of Literary & Cultural Disability Studies* 10, no. 1 (2016): 71–86. muse.jhu.edu/article/611313.

Semler, Stephanie. "The Golden Path of Eugenics." In *Dune and Philosophy: Weirding Way of the Mentat,* Popular Culture and Philosophy Book 56, edited by Jeffery Nicholas, 13–35. Chicago: Open Court, 2011.

Snyder, Sharon L., and David T. Mitchell. *Cultural Locations of Disability.* Chicago: The University of Chicago Press, 2006.

From Taming Sand Dunes to Planetary Ecology

Historical Perspectives on Environmental Thought and Politics in the Dune Saga

PAUL REEF

At first, the Dune saga might seem like a stereotypical space opera starring rival galactic dynasties. Yet Frank Herbert used this setting to reflect upon larger questions like the mechanisms behind power and authority, as well as the human exploitation of nature. Retroactively, Herbert has stated that *Dune* "was to be an ecological novel, then, with many overtones...."[1] Certainly, he intended to introduce his readers to ecology and raise environmental awareness.[2] Published in 1965, *Dune*'s warning against human interference with nature resonated with a general public increasingly aware of environmental problems and concerned about nuclear waste, extinctions of animal species, acid rain, mass deforestation, toxic chemicals, and water pollution. As such, *Dune* became a pivotal work of ecological science fiction: "*Dune*'s influence on environmentalism cannot be overstated ... in its willingness to imagine ecology on a global scale, *Dune* opened up new horizons for environmental literacy in the realm of SF."[3]

Herbert's initial inspiration to write *Dune* drew on an older and more utilitarian strand of nature conservation and applied ecological science. In 1957, then journalist Herbert visited a project to stabilize shifting sand dunes in Florence, Oregon, which were threatening farmland and towns. It was managed by the U.S. Soil Conservation Service (SCS), an off-shoot of the federal government's responses to soil erosion and the Dust Bowl in the 1930s.[4] This visit sparked Herbert's interest in the interaction between humans and nature and ecological science in particular, eventually resulting in *Dune*—which he even dedicated to "the dry-land ecologists, wherever they may be...."[5] Initially, the novel mirrors Herbert's fascination with taming Oregon's dunes and portrays Arrakis's terraforming into a lush, green agricultural planet positively.

Only later in the Dune series do the disastrous consequences of large-scale human tampering with Arrakis's ecosystem become apparent. The multi-layered nature and suspense of this realization was meant to make readers ponder their societies' unintended yet harmful impact on Earth. Building on ecologists' insights, Herbert declared that "ecology is the science of understanding consequences," and "one of the purposes of this story was to delineate consequences of inflicting yourself upon a planet, upon an environment."[6] The somewhat simplified setting of a desert planet enabled Herbert to create a parable of humanity's hubris in seeking to control and exploit nature while touching on other environmental issues.[7] In fact, Herbert later stated he deliberately named his novel "Dune" for its onomatopoetic similarity to Doom.[8]

This chapter embeds the initial Dune trilogy within the longer history of American environmentalism and contemporary shifts in ecological thought and politics. Without this historical perspective, it is hard to appreciate why Herbert rooted his story in a government effort to stabilize dunes for human utility. Previous scholars have mainly discussed Herbert's work in relation to 1960s counterculture and ecological activism, (science fiction) literature, or climate change ("cli-fi," or climate fiction in the Anthropocene).[9] Yet, to fully understand the message and thinking behind Dune, I argue that it needs to be contextualized within two paradigm shifts in postwar environmental thought and governance within and beyond the United States. Moreover, this contextualization explains how and why Herbert's own views on environmental politics changed.

The first development is the emergence of a new political concept of the "environment" rooted in ecological science around 1970. That is not to say no one was concerned about nature before: there was a long history of advocacy for wilderness preservation and conservation of natural resources under state guidance. At the same time, there were protests and regulations against smog, polluted drinking water, or deforestation[10] However, after 1945, scientific advances, international cooperation, and research on nuclear fallout and ecological warfare during the Cold War gave rise to a new ecological notion of the environment, which highlighted how all living organisms are intricately interconnected with their physical surroundings. Furthermore, photographs of "spaceship Earth" from space further nurtured this imagining of global inter-dependence—and ecological vulnerability.[11] This novel concept of the environment integrated many different aspects of environmental issues that were previously perceived separately. It moreover enabled people to holistically envisage humanity's problematic relation with nature and devise new policies or mobilize people.[12]

The second change concerned growing criticism of the postwar belief in scientific prowess and state planning of society. Western societies generally had a confident belief in modernization and the state's—as well as science's—ability to improve society. Examples range from President Franklin Roosevelt's New Deal and the Marshall Plan to widespread optimism around nuclear energy, automation, and technologies like the refrigerator and air-conditioning that seemed to promise a more comfortable future. The economic crises of the long 1970s, failures of modernization policies, and the ascendancy of neoliberalism would bring about a paradigm shift in political thought. There was more criticism of technocratic practices and the application of scientific expertise. Related to this, citizens and new social movements, including many environmentalists, demanded more direct participation in politics and an end to paternalistic, top-down governance.[13]

Both shifts profoundly shaped Herbert's thinking as an environmentalist and critical citizen. This chapter takes a historical approach to analyzing how Herbert conceptualized the environment and ecological politics in the initial Dune trilogy: Dune, Dune Messiah (1969), and Children of Dune (1976). The first section analyzes how the Dune saga intersects with state-orchestrated, scientific environmental management and Herbert's own environmental views and criticism of Western planning of nature. The second section illustrates how the Dune novels are entangled with the history of environmentalism and in which ways they reflect Herbert's understanding of ecology.

Herbert as Conservative Environmentalist

The terraforming and social engineering of Arrakis closely resembles what anthropologist James C. Scott has defined as high modernist ideology. Social engineering in this context refers to how experts, corporations, and governments sought to systematically organize and restructure societies for the better using scientific methods and planning between circa 1880 and 1970.[14] In Scott's view, states endeavor to *see* the societies and domains which they govern in specific ways. They make these legible by imposing specific techniques of observation, ranging from geological surveys to population censuses, which reduce a complex reality to easily legible data. By his definition, high modernist ideology denotes a utopian belief in progress and the willingness to plan—or enforce—societal change via grand schemes grounded in technocratic rationalism.[15]

Historically, the rise of the welfare state and wartime planning during the First World War opened up new areas for state interference in regulating and disciplining society. The New Deal illustrates how states aimed to manage the economic crisis during the 1930s, which included large-scale environmental and agricultural projects. Moreover, scientific advances, including computers and new statistical models, enabled ever more detailed planning. Scientific management permeated postwar reconstruction and welfare states. It was a belief in the possibilities of engineering society—including eugenics in its most extreme form—held by fascist and communist states, but also by Western democracies and newly independent countries.[16] Already in the 1930s and 1940s, liberal critics like Friedrich Hayek and Karl Popper, and science fiction writers like George Orwell and Aldous Huxley, had warned of the dangers of social engineering by all-powerful states.[17]

Building on longstanding state practices in nature conservation, the introduction of environmental policies nonetheless indicated a shift in conceptions of the environment. Partly following from public concern over toxic substances in food, nuclear fallout, and industrial pollution, the federal government created the Environmental Protection Agency in 1970 and passed a range of environmental laws. Most scientific experts, policy-makers, and environmentalists shared a self-evident view that, as a holistic problem, the environment was best dealt with collectively, preferably federally.[18] New insights from the biological sciences, backed up by computer models and statistics, buttressed confidence in scientific environmental management.[19]

In the United States and Western Europe, widespread optimism about the capability of states to plan society for the better would not wane until the 1970s. The economic crises of the 1970s and difficulties with modernization efforts demonstrated the limits of state planning in a globalizing world. Simultaneous disputes over the expanding costs of public welfare and especially the rising influence of neoliberalism and market logic tied into older conservative critiques of increasing state interference. Increasingly, scientists, politicians, and citizens alike criticized the goals and effectiveness of technocratic rationalism and the application of expertise as expertise itself became more contested and pluralized. Moreover, conservative arguments against governmental encroachment and progressive calls for more direct forms of democracy and transparency further undermined the authority of distant technocratic modes of governance.[20] Counterculture environmentalists, Native American protesters, and labor union activists were skeptical of government programs for not being radical enough or shielding vested interests,[21] while conservative environmentalists argued that federal regulation and bureaucracy were ultimately detrimental to nature's best interests.[22]

Herbert's political ecology was rooted in conservative politics and a strand of grassroots liberal ecological activism. For a long time, he had been fascinated with nature protection in Oregon, as well as off-shore resource extraction and environmental management like dryland ecology. Inspired by ecological science, by the 1960s Herbert embraced an over-arching ecological conception of the environment in which it is impossible to distinguish between society and nature, or politics and economics. In a 1969 interview, he stated he was not a "classical conservationist" and instead wanted to explore "ways of living with our planet and not against it."[23] For Herbert, this did not entail a utopian vision of symbiosis between humans and nature. Although he participated in the first Earth Day of 1970, he kept his distance from such counterculture environmentalism and was not against industrial capitalism or resource extraction per se. He disliked the influential report *Limits to Growth* (1972), which warned about the consequences of economic and population growth to the world's natural resources. In his view, the book postulated "growth must be selective, oriented, governed—that is, *planned*," yet it did not tackle the root of the problem, namely a continued belief in "technology worship, endless economic growth ... the limitless powers implied by scientific investigation,"[24] which Herbert had also called the "technological toy syndrome."[25]

Rather, Herbert advocated a more ecologically minded society aided by green innovations, preferably in a community setting without too much state interference. Calling himself a "technopeasant," Herbert saw technology as a means to create a sustainable society more in line with ecology. His "Ecological Demonstration Project" with solar panels and recycling on his Oregon farm resembled the eclectic *Whole Earth Catalog*, which lauded *Dune* as an environmental novel. Herbert's practices also fit a strand of West Coast liberal grassroots environmentalism, which prioritized American ingenuity and technological entrepreneurship.[26]

As an environmentalist, Herbert's views oscillated between conservatist critiques and radical ecology, between eco-capitalism and a rejection of Western exploitation of nature. During the 1950s, Herbert worked for Republican Senate campaigns, and his criticism of bureaucracy and state interference became even more pronounced later in life, especially when he became embroiled with the IRS.[27] His dystopian novel *The Green Brain* (1966) enmeshes ecological concerns over the use of pesticides and extinction with a condemnation of scheming bureaucrats.[28] In a 1981 interview with environmental entrepreneur John Elkington, Herbert argued in favor of aligning capitalism and resource extraction with ecology and against conservationism. Subsequently, Herbert compared a "managed bureaucracy" approach to ecological protection to the "autocratic" Soviet Union.[29] In 1984, Herbert added that while disapproving of President

Ronald Reagan's foreign policy, "as long as he's paranoid of the bureaucracy I'll stand aside and applaud."[30] However, although Herbert agreed with the Republican critiques of government, his ecological vision and critique of Western modernity and its exploitation of nature and indigenous peoples had more in common with left-wing (environmental) movements.[31] Herbert was close friends with a Quileute tribe member who in 1958 explained to him the environmental destruction and deforestation of his native lands. Although Herbert did not believe the myth of native Americans living in harmony with pristine pre–Columbian wilderness, this was another ecological influence behind *Dune*.[32] The next section of this essay analyzes how the Dune series reflects Herbert's ecological criticism of Western modernity.

Seeing Like a Planetologist

In line with building a rational modern state, the Atreides seek control over Arrakis's people and natural resources far beyond harvesting spice. Previously, the Corrino emperors ordered Imperial planetologists to map the planet's development potential. After arrival, Duke Leto Atreides dispatches expeditions to chart Arrakis's resource capabilities and study the Fremen—of whom he desired to field five battalions as soon as possible.[33] Hardened by their environment, the nomads could be turned into a powerful, disciplined fighting force. At the same time, Paul aims to rapidly alter this environment by fast-forwarding the Fremen terraforming effort. This reflects Herbert's warnings against the messianic impulses of all-powerful individuals and older tropes of heroic individualism in science fiction.[34] On a deeper level, Paul's ideal of reshaping Arrakis highlights an instrumental view of not only nature, but also the planet's population. Ultimately, this terraforming project becomes a grand social and bio-engineering project conducted in a strictly top-down manner.

The terraforming effort on Arrakis mirrors how Western states and empires sought to control nature and populations for productive means. By making Arrakis legible via censuses and maps, Imperial scientists envisaged the planet as a colonial resource. Planetologist Pardot Kynes's vision of a terraformed planet embodies this Western gaze. Arrakis is merely an expression of energy, a machine driven by the sun requiring modification to become productive and inhabitable.

Interestingly, Kynes's botanical station network to test vegetation suitable for Arrakis resembled the Soil Conservation Service's efforts to tame Oregon's dunes, which will be discussed in more detail below. Kynes aims to transform the Fremen into a tool within his terraforming scheme by imprinting on them "that basic source of civilization—agriculture."[35] Similarly, Leto and Paul habitually perceive Arrakis as a planet inhabited by "barbarians," a "dry wasteland," an "uncharted dirty wilderness."[36] Theirs and Kynes's visions are couched in a dual discourse of social engineering and imperialism and reflect an imperative to reshape social and ecological structures to the model of Western modernity, that is, an efficiently governed agricultural state with productive subjects.[37]

Over the course of the Dune trilogy Paul comes to regret both his imperial rule and acceleration of Arrakis's terraforming. Previously, all Fremen *sietches* had meticulously gathered water to fulfill Kynes's plan for a green Arrakis over the course of centuries in line with their own ecological practices to make the desert more habitable. Paul drastically accelerates terraforming by securing independence for the Fremen, but this also served his personal ambitions.[38] As transformation begins affecting Fremen society, Paul realizes he forced an alien way of living onto the Fremen. A sense of hubris creeps into his consciousness: "is it not presumptuous, he wonders, to think he could make over an entire planet… ?"[39] Still, he longed for Caladan's seas, calling Arrakis an "ugly, barren land."[40] Nevertheless, confronted with what he has inflicted upon the planet as messianic dictator, Paul steps down after deliberately having become blind in an assassination attempt. It forebodes the dire effects of the planet's transformation, which come to light fully in *Children of Dune*. Decades after the events of the first novel, Fremen openly resent the influx of off-worlders and their ways until traditionalist tribes revolt. Even Stilgar, once Paul's right-hand man, begins questioning the changes to the point that he and his tribe reject civilization. However, the terraforming process has become irreversible: the desert along with its sandworms and spice will disappear, and the Fremen will never regain their freedom to roam the desert under the Atreides regime.[41]

For Herbert, Paul and Kynes symbolize the shortsightedness of "Western man." Paul's penance and epiphany are deliberate plot turns to make the reader realize the folly of state-orchestrated planning of nature. It demonstrates the perhaps unintended yet very real consequences of humankind inflicting itself upon a planet.[42] This is a fundamentally ecological critique of the economic and industrial structures behind human-caused environmental degradation in line with more radical environmental activism.[43]

Herbert claims he wrote the Dune novels as a critique of scientized Western notions of ecology, condemning Western culture's "control disease" which has been forced upon "underdeveloped" peoples across the globe.[44] However, some scholars have read *Dune* as an apology for Western exploitation of developing countries and a fictional representation of expansionist American foreign policy during the Cold War. Consequently, they argue that the Fremen embody negative Orientalist tropes and point out that Paul reasserts imperial control over the native peoples.[45] These analyses raise important questions about ethnic representation and underlying (neo)imperialist discourses even in a work allegedly criticizing "Western man," but they engage relatively little with Herbert's authorial intentions and—more importantly—overlook *Dune*'s sequels. Especially in solely focusing on *Dune*, this line of scholarship overlooks how *Dune Messiah* and *Children of Dune* more explicitly question Paul's messianic rule, including the resistance of Fremen to terraforming. In addition, these scholars downplay the characteristics Herbert ascribes to the Fremen, whose relationship with the Atreides is much more ambiguous and layered than a straightforward imperial hierarchy. The Fremen are not passive victims, but rather have some agency; they had been pursuing the terraforming project before Paul's arrival on Arrakis and they had been bribing the Spacing Guild to help hide satellite imagery that would reveal their efforts. Lastly, these critics disregard the ecological and environmental dimensions of the critical subtexts of Dune, which I expand upon in the next section.

Emergence of Modern Environmentalism

Dune's indebtedness to ecological activism has been well documented, but its connection to earlier strands of environmentalism and the emergence of a new concept of the environment less so.[46] Herbert drew notably on natural resource management and applied ecology stretching back to the 1930s. At the same time, he was inspired by the postwar emergence of an overarching ecological concept of the environment. The birth of modern environmentalism is often tied to biologist Rachel Carson's *Silent Spring* (1962), especially in an American context. She and other activist scientists contributed to disseminating an understanding of nature as an ecological system and raised critical questions about the application of science to exploit nature, and the government's role in supporting this exploitation.[47] However, a single book did not bring about either this notion or the emergence of a mass—and indeed a global—movement. Carson's message built on older concerns over nature and existing environmental movements.[48]

Since the nineteenth century, partially in reaction to the Industrial Revolution, Americans had increasingly cared about preserving nature for its pristine beauty and conserving natural resources. The preservationist effort to protect "wilderness" was influenced by Romantic notions of nature as pure, unspoiled by civilization, and as spiritual renewal vis-à-vis industrialization.[49] Almost simultaneously, a broad conservation movement of scientists, loggers, politicians, industrialists, and farmers argued for the rational management of natural resources to prevent unsustainable exploitation. By 1900, national parks, wildlife preserves, and nature conservation agencies had been established. During the New Deal, the federal government greatly expanded its role in developing agricultural land, harnessing rivers, and natural resource planning in a spirit of modernization and state-led scientific planning.[50] Preservationism and conservationism did not constitute coherent movements so much as colliding clusters of nature management discourses under an overarching anthropocentric perception of nature.[51]

During the American Progressive Era, local movements emerged to counter the worst threats to public health from industrial pollution, as they had in Europe. In industrial cores like Pittsburgh, well-off citizens pressured local governments to take measures against smog. As in conservationist nature management, an elite-based mode of anti-pollution regulation emerged, which mitigated the worst effects of smog, but rarely infringed upon elite interests.[52] Additionally, governments responded to environmental damage like floods and soil erosion via new forms of expert management. Particularly after 1945, however, popular dissatisfaction with the impacts of excessive industrialization grew. Moreover, the protest of sections of society beyond urban white middle-classes gained traction, ranging from Mexican farmworkers' struggle against pesticides in southern California to citizens fighting open-pit coal mining in the Appalachians. A growing mainstream concern and protest about environmental pollution challenged the older cooperative mode of regulation dominated by politicians and business leaders.[53]

The increasing environmental awareness of the 1960s represented a new holistic notion of the environment as a comprehensive problem requiring immediate political action. Far from a sudden environmentalist awakening, there was much continuity of conservationist ideals, Romantic notions of nature, and grassroots activism. Certainly, modern environmentalism emerged against the backdrop of worsening natural conditions due to acid rain and smog and a newfound sensitivity to the negative-side effects of consumerism and industrial society. However, most important was the social construction of an (imminent) environmental crisis, shaped by the actions of specific actors and their perceptions of ecological problems.[54] From the 1920s onwards, biologists, geologists, ecologists, and other scientific disciplines began comprehending life on earth as being interconnected within larger systems, further stimulated by postwar cybernetic system analysis. Developments in the earth sciences drastically improved the understanding of geological preconditions for life, particularly within a Cold War context of state-sponsored research on global nuclear fallout and ecological warfare. Weather satellites and photographs of "Spaceship Earth" contributed to a planetary understanding of environmental matters. Moreover, new mass media and a dense web of international organizations, as well as scientific cooperation, facilitated the transfer of these ideas.[55] Environmental historians Paul Warde et al. have argued that these scientific advances, data accumulation, internationalization, and the Cold War rendered the environment legible and established it as a concept between circa 1948 and 1972, during which this new knowledge also began spilling over to society and politics.[56]

By 1970, the environment transformed into a transnational political issue by social movements, activist scientists, and the establishment of environmental political bodies on the national and global level. Industrial pollution and deforestation were no longer separate issues of hygiene and agriculture, but had entered the political mainstream as threats to an overarching ecological system.[57] Moreover, the ethical or ecocentric argument that nature did not exist solely to serve growing human needs and had its own rights became more pronounced. Environmental historian Jens Ivo Engels has identified four defining characteristics of this "ecological turn": (1) a holistic notion of *the* environment; (2) a global perspective; (3) scientific expertise or a science-based discourse concerning the environment; (4) large-scale politicization of the environment as well as mass-mobilization of environmentalist protest groups.[58] The 1960s and 1970s are perhaps best understood as a transformative period for how modern society conceives its relationship with nature—or rather the environment. The new ecological concept of the environment became the paradigm in which to conceive of nature and human-nature relations, as well as the normative notion in which our present debates about climate change and the Anthropocene have been embedded.

Environmental and Ecological Thought in Dune

Ecological discourse and environmental themes permeate the Dune trilogy. Herbert narrated complex ecological issues and theories to his audience, integrating the ecological narrative with other themes. One of these messages was humanity's overexploitation of nature, which was embedded in existing worries over the scarcity and finiteness of natural resources. Herbert had become interested in natural resource management while working on marine resources as an aide to a Republican senator. His first novel, *The Dragon in the Sea* (1956), focused on oil scarcity and dangerous off-shore mining in a Cold War setting. Herbert took this issue to a new level in *Dune*, which "famously transmogrifies oil imperialism into a battle for control of the 'spice' that makes interstellar navigation possible" in a desert setting anticipating later developments surrounding oil and the Middle East.[59] Similarly, Herbert has stated, "the scarce water of *Dune* is an exact analog of oil scarcity" but water also played a more fundamental ecological role.[60] In this sense, the Dune series was a way for Herbert to move from resource scarcity to an ecological discussion of the global problem of how humans inflicted themselves upon nature.

The very title "planetologist" indicates a shift from a local understanding of damage to nature to a global environmental one. To compress the complexity of an actual ecosystem, Herbert devised a micro-ecology revolving around the sandworm.[61] Sandtrout are sandworms in the larval stage whose function is encysting large bodies of water to terraform a planet into a desert, as water is lethal to sandworms. When the fungal excretions of sandtrout mix with water, they form a pre-spice mass. This pre-spice mass comes to the surface, exploding under Arrakis's intense heat, creating the *mélange* spice. Surviving sandtrout hibernate in a cyst and emerge as small sandworms. Sand plankton feed upon *mélange* traces, which are subsequently—together with sand and other creatures—food for the giant sandworms. Spice is a byproduct of a sandworm cycle, but requires a hot and completely dry environment, which the sandtrout ensure. Herbert even made the sandworm metabolism produce atmospheric oxygen, which a planet without forests would otherwise lack.[62] The sandworm ecosystem encompasses the entire planet, except for the area around the northern pole demarcated by the Shield Wall mountain range. The sandworm life cycle and desert world-building served to elucidate ecological interdependence and the risks of interference with nature in a subtle parable. Nevertheless, Herbert's world-building has been criticized as stimulating but environmentally impossible and a representation of an outdated "balance of nature" model of ecology.[63] It has also been criticized as an oversimplified mediation of Western notions of "Arabia" invoking imperial adventure tropes, while also intersecting with older narratives of American frontiers and wilderness—even though Herbert and other New Wave science fiction authors wanted to distance themselves from such earlier romanticized visions.[64]

In *Dune*, Liet-Kynes provides a further introduction to ecology. It is no coincidence that his botanical testing station network mirrored the Soil Conservation Service's efforts to tame Oregon's dunes for farmland development and its ethic of scientific resource management. The SCS needed to plant vegetation on dunes with sand poor in nutrients. It was aware of aquifers beneath the dunes, but there were no local plants which could reach this ground water. The SCS tested hundreds of plants before settling for European beach grasses, essentially invasive species, to counter erosion by wind. Additionally, because of his work as an investigative journalist on the West Coast during the 1950s, Herbert must have been aware of other dryland ecology projects and desert farming efforts in California.[65] *Dune*'s appendix further explains to the audience the ecology of plant succession and nutrient availability. During a banquet, Kynes discusses the possibility of open water on Arrakis by an orderly cycle, "a rule of ecology." He does so by delving into the science behind terraforming: "if we can get three per cent of the green plant element on Arrakis involved in forming carbon compounds, we've started the cyclic system."[66] This quote is appropriated from ecologist Paul Sears's *Where There Is Life* (1962). Sears had worked on countering soil erosion during the Dust Bowl and was a major influence on Herbert.[67] Subsequently, Kynes explains how he has established pilot projects to rapidly gather results according to the Tansley Effect's positive feedback loop—a non-existent theory Herbert named after British botanist and ecological pioneer Arthur Tansley. It is a vision that had become imprinted on Fremen culture. At Stilgar's *sietch*, Paul and Jessica witness an almost religious ritual canting of the plan's steps. Stilgar knows every detail by heart, precisely including the quantity of water that would be needed for the transformation.[68]

Initially, *Dune* narrates terraforming as a successful way of making nature productive for humankind and even an act of Fremen emancipation. However, later it is revealed how Kynes's gaze is fixed on science-based development, agriculture, and the subjugation of individuals and nature.[69] Only when facing death after his banishment into the desert does Kynes realize his hubris. Entranced, he hears his father reiterating the entire process of terraforming. Pardot Kynes attempts to comfort his son: terraforming is a noble undertaking. They will use the Fremen "as a constructive ecological force" to compensate for the fact that "men and their works have been a disease on the surface of their planets before that."[70] Suddenly, however, "it occurs to Kynes that his father and all the other scientists are wrong, that the most persistent principles of the universe are accident and error."[71] Herbert discusses the modernizing principles underpinning the expert-planned transformation project in several publications and interviews. In one interview shortly before *Dune Messiah*'s release, the author highlighted this scene as a pivotal plot point, saying "I thought it was very important that the planet killed the ecologist."[72] This conveys a wry but important lesson in Herbert's message to the public: nature consists of a range of carefully balanced ecological interdependencies linked to a global ecosystem. Upsetting this will ultimately cost humans sorely and in *Dune*, the expert dies by the hands of the very desert he set out to tame.

Arrakis as Gaia

As the title *Dune* already foreshadows, Arrakis's ecosystem is an active, almost sentient factor in shaping the environment and its dwellers. Herbert's narration of a planetary ecological system was embedded in a newfound planetary awareness stimulated by space-born photographs of Earth—not coincidentally, the *Whole Earth Catalog*'s first front cover.[73] More fundamentally, Herbert took cues from biologists' study of ecology as an inter-related biological system. Echoing ecologist and activist Barry Commoner, Herbert believed the only way to stave off ecological destruction was by dispelling belief in technological progress and bringing society's functioning in line with ecological considerations.[74] Subsequently, Herbert went further than most contemporary scientists would have agreed with in envisaging a planet whose ecosystem actively sustains a desert biosphere. Literature scholar Bruce Clarke has argued that *Dune* reflects a philosophical and political conceptual shift from this scientific understanding of ecology towards the need to foster a form of eco-citizenship, a broader awareness of socio-ecological interdependence and ecological ethics.[75] The ecocentrism of Dune, its apocalyptic undertones, allusions to eco-mysticism, and emphasis on human society's profound interconnectivity with a planetary biosphere contradicted contemporary mainstream biological science.

The concept of a planet as a living organism strongly anticipated new currents in environmental systems thought, particularly the Gaia hypothesis, Earth system modeling, and astrobiology.[76] Developed around 1970 by chemist and former NASA scientist James Lovelock and microbiologist Lynn Margulis, the Gaia hypothesis proposes that there is an interaction or rather co-evolution between living things and the inorganic elements of Earth in which living things have played a role in altering Earth so that it can continue to sustain life. It postulates a complex system of a planetwide biosphere that reinforces a specific chemical and physical environment, ranging from seawater salinity to atmospheric oxygen.[77] There are clear similarities between Herbert's ecological thought and the Gaia hypothesis, but Herbert never explicitly referred to it, even though *Children of Dune* came out after the hypothesis was more widely disseminated. It is quite possible that he was aware of Lovelock's ideas, especially given his interest in ecology and because many science fiction writers, including Ursula K. Le Guin and Isaac Asimov, had appropriated the Gaia thesis.[78] Moreover, Katherine Buse has demonstrated how Herbert's imagining of planetary ecology embedded in biological science and cybernetics not only anticipated advances in Earth system modeling and astrobiology, but has also inspired a great number of climate scientists and astronomists in thinking along planetary lines.[79]

Arrakis's biosphere proactively sustained a physical and chemical environmental suitable for the sand plankton-to-sandworm cycle, albeit more aggressively than Lovelock's Gaia concept had outlined. In fact, after sandtrout had been introduced on Arrakis, they encysted all surface water deep under the sand dunes and turned a lush, green planet into a dry desert fit for sandworms. Subsequently, sandworms produced the oxygen for life that plants could no longer provide, while they and their spice became essential aspects of Fremen culture. The increasing abundance of atmospheric humidity because of the coopted terraforming project, however, poses an existential threat to Arrakis's biosystem, which starts fighting back. Not only do sandworms and sandtrout start attacking water installations, but human tampering with nature also provokes storms. Paul's son Leto has a dystopian vision of the threat water poses, which "filled him with foreboding for the cataclysmic changes which human intervention was bringing."[80] Later, Leto senses the coming of a storm rare in magnitude, reflecting, "it was as though the planet fought them [the ecological transformation teams] with a conscious fury out here, the fury increasing as the transformation took in more land."[81] Even Paul's daughter Alia is alarmed at the signs of the planet itself rallying against her regime:

> She shudders. Forty qanats had been breached, their waters loosed into the sand.... Sandtrout leaped into qanats and shattered to become hosts of small replicas. Worms deliberately drowned themselves. Blood ripped from Second Moon and fell to Arrakis, where it stirred up great storms. And the storm frequency is increasing![82]

The passage represents human-wrought environmental apocalypse turned upside down: the environment itself wreaking havoc in revenge on humans.

Leto becomes very critical of the environmental changes caused by his father. While being held captive in Jacurutu, he embraces the Golden Path his father had refused to embark on. Following his vision, Leto consumes an enormous amount of spice in order to fool sandtrout to cover his body and becomes a sandworm-human symbiote. Subsequently, Leto conducts a guerrilla war against the man-made water infrastructure. His embrace of the Golden Path and environmental vision makes Leto his father's antithesis. In a way, Leto's revolt against human terraforming and his amalgamation with the sandtrout symbolizes a sentient, self-regulating Gaia-like planet. However, it also relates to how Herbert ascribes agency to the Atreides rather than the Fremen in shaping Arrakis.[83]

There remains a tension between a positive portrayal of the Fremen living in symbiosis with nature and environmental determinism. The Fremen are represented as fully adapted with stillsuits for living in balance with Arrakis's barren nature. Yet their yearning for a greener planet is seized by Paul Muad'Dib with a promise of independence. Ultimately, however, the Fremen remain without notable agency as a new imperial and ecological structure erasing their freedom is imposed. On Arrakis, it turns out that humans have to submit themselves to the desert; large-scale terraforming would destroy both the indigenous culture and biosphere.[84] Fremen and Sardaukar are both produced by harsh planets (the Imperium even consciously used Salusa Secundus as a training ground for Sardaukar soldiers). The Fremen realize this as well. At the opening of *Children of Dune*, Stilgar discovers how "as his planet changes, he knew he had changed."[85] In one interview, Herbert discussed that humans do not exist in a vacuum from nature, while the Fremen "were in their system. Even when the environment changed, the people did not...."[86] At the trilogy's very end, Stilgar and other Fremen refuse to change and wish to return to the old ways, even though they are told the desert is irreversibly dying. Yet Herbert did not perceive the ecological ways of the Fremen entirely negatively. He once told his son Brian he most identified with Stilgar—which Brian interpreted as a self-identification with a Native American leader protecting "the time-honored ways that did not harm the ecology of the planet."[87]

Conclusion

At the heart of the Dune trilogy lies a slowly unraveling but urgent realization of the dire consequences of human interference with nature. From a historical perspective, *Dune* and its first two sequels are pivotal science fiction books which embody the tenets of modern environmentalism. At the same time, Dune narrates older concerns over resource scarcity and management or the relationship between nature and humanity in such an imaginative way that they still speak to today's audiences. In the words of science fiction scholar Rob Latham, *Dune* "probably did more than any other single book to bring ecological awareness into the center of the genre."[88] The trilogy embraces the new, holistic notion of the environment as a global biosphere and introduces readers to the complex mechanisms behind ecology. In fact, it could be argued that by postulating the fundamentally global nature of ecosystems, Herbert's imagination was ahead of its time. To Herbert, any scientific or governmental schemes for managing the natural world to sustain an unreformed mass consumerist society are a form of hubris, of which we can scarcely know the ultimate consequences.

Dune provides preciously few answers on how exactly to live more in line with ecology, but perhaps its strength lies in its capacity to make us question and ponder over environmental challenges from new angles. The impact of the novels' ecological subtext lies in the fact that both readers and protagonists only become aware of the grave effects of human-caused environmental change when it is too late. Herbert's message that many human incursions into complex ecological systems are undertaken too hastily or too carelessly without reflecting upon their possible outcomes holds just as true as 50 years ago. If anything, *Dune*'s layered discussion of environmental politics and the long-term consequences of environmental ignorance remain unquestionably relevant today. For, even though Herbert along with activists and scientists have succeeded in raising environmental awareness, optimism in technological progress alone continues to prevent the structural change needed to tackle our planet's current environmental challenges, particularly human caused climate change.

NOTES

1. Herbert, "When I Was Writing Dune," v–vi.
2. Herbert, "Dune Genesis," 74; Ellis, "Frank Herbert's *Dune*," 104–105.
3. Evans, "New Wave Science Fiction," 434.
4. The SCS still exists and was renamed to Natural Resources Conservation Service in 1994.
5. Kratz, "Frank Herbert's Ecology," 3–8; Landa, "In a Supporting Role," 99–101; also documented by Frank Herbert's son: Herbert, *Dreamer of Dune*, 123–127,
6. Herbert and Herbert, interview by McNelly.
7. Roberts, "Frank Herbert," 104–105.
8. Herbert, "Introduction," 5.
9. Ellis, "Frank Herbert's *Dune*,"; Stratton, "Environmental Action in *Dune*,"; Pak, *Terraforming*, 116–124; Gough, "Speculative Fictions,"; Trexler, *Anthropocene Fiction*, 8–9; Callaway, "Speculative Ecosystems," Rumpala, *Écologie, science-fiction et éthique du futur*, 22, 37–38, 84–86.
10. Uekötter, *Age of Smoke*; Hays, *Environmental Politics in the United States*.
11. Höhler, *Spaceship Earth*.
12. Engels, "Modern Environmentalism"; Mahrane et al., "De la nature à la biosphère"; Meyer, "From Nature to Environment."
13. Van Laak, "Planung," 317–325; Brückweh et al., *Engineering Society*; Patel, *The New Deal*; Herbert, "Europe in High Modernity"; Egan, *Barry Commoner*, 7–10.
14. Etzemüller, *"Social engineering,"* 20–37.
15. Scott, *Seeing Like a State*, 4–5.
16. Couperus et al., "Planning in High Modernity,"; Escobar, "Planning."
17. Van Laak, "Planung," 315–317.
18. Rome, "'Give Earth a Chance,'"; Meyer, "From Nature to Environment," 34–35.
19. E.g., Hutter, "Ecosystems Research and Policy Planning."
20. Herbert, "Europe in High Modernity," 15–20; Brückweh et al., *Engineering Society*; Gilcher-Holtey, "Political Participation and Democratization in the 1960s," Niall Ferguson et al., *The Shock of the Global*; Escobar, "Planning," 157–160.
21. Montrie, *The Myth of* Silent Spring, 99–137; Woodhouse, "The Politics of Ecology."
22. Drake, *Loving Nature, Fearing the State*.
23. Herbert and Herbert, interview by McNelly; similarly Herbert, "Dune Genesis."
24. Herbert, "Science Fiction and a World in Crisis," 77.
25. Herbert, "Frank Herbert."
26. Kirk, *Counterculture Green*, 1–12, 187–191; Herbert, *Dreamer of Dune*, chapter 23.

27. Herbert, *Dreamer of Dune*, 80–86, 112, 118, 134; Immerwahr, "Heresies of 'Dune.'"

28. See O'Reilly, *Frank Herbert*, chapter 5.

29. Herbert, "Profile of Frank Herbert."

30. Herbert, "Futurist Meditations."

31. Woodhouse, "The Politics of Ecology," 73–77; on this: Herbert, *Dreamer of Dune*, 161–166, esp. chapter 19.

32. Herbert, *Dreamer of Dune*, 132, chapter 19; Immerwahr, "Heresies of 'Dune'"; Allard, *Dune*, 100–101; Cronon, "The Trouble with Wilderness." Herbert would also become more engaged with the emancipation of native Americans and wrote a novel on this topic: *Soul Catcher* (1972). Also Smith, *Hippies, Indians, and the Fight for Red Power*.

33. Herbert, *Dune*, e.g., 5, 90–92, 108.

34. Pak, *Terraforming*, 118–119; on this also Callaway, "Speculative Ecosystems," 249–251.

35. Herbert, *Dune*, 291.

36. *Ibid.*, 84–85.

37. Escobar, "Planning."

38. Otto, "Science Fiction and the Ecological Conscience," 49–52; Sullivan, "Petro-Texts, Plants, and People," 158–159.

39. Herbert, *Dune Messiah*, 40–41.

40. *Ibid.*, 266.

41. On Herbert's critical narration of terraforming: Pak, *Terraforming*, 120–124.

42. Herbert and Herbert, interview by McNelly.

43. Zelko, "Challenging Modernity," 26–34; Woodhouse, "The Politics of Ecology."

44. Herbert, "Science Fiction and a World in Crisis," 83; Herbert, "Futurist Meditations." On *Dune* as an emancipatory postcolonial novel: Gaylard, "Postcolonial Science Fiction."

45. E.g., Zaki, "Orientalism in Science Fiction"; Kennedy, "Epic World-Building"; Hoberek, "*Dune*, and Post-1960 U.S. Foreign Policy"; Higgins, "Psychic Decolonization."

46. Stratton, "Environmental Action in *Dune*"; Otto, "Science Fiction and the Ecological Consciousness"; Ellis, "Frank Herbert's *Dune*." For a similar argument: Kratz, "Herbert's Ecology."

47. Thomas, "A Call to Action"; Zelko, "The Politics of Nature," 729–731. Herbert's other environmental novel *The Green Brain* (1966) takes it focus on pesticides from Carson, O'Reilly, *Frank Herbert*, chapter 5.

48. McNeill and Engelke, *Environmental History of the Anthropocene*, 184–186.

49. Nash, *Wilderness and the American Mind*.

50. Patel, *The New Deal*, 85–86, 97–103, 209–218, 294–298.

51. Hays, *Environmental Politics in the United States*, 1–28; Egan and Crane, "Introduction."

52. Uekötter, *Age of Smoke*; Uekötter, "A Twisted Road to Earth Day."

53. Montrie, *The Myth of Silent Spring*, 1–22.

54. Engels, "Modern Environmentalism,"; McNeill and Engelke, *Environmental History of the Anthropocene*, 184–190, 203–205.

55. Hamblin, *Arming Mother Nature*; Robertson, "Total War and the Total Environment"; Höhler, *Spaceship Earth*; Egan, *Barry Commoner*.

56. Warde et al., *The Environment*, chapters 3 and 5.

57. Schulz-Walden, *Anfänge globaler Umweltpolitik*; Warde et al., *The Environment*, 109–132; Rome, "'Give Earth a Chance.'"

58. Engels, "Modern Environmentalism," 124–125.

59. Canavan, "Retrofutures and Petrofutures," 340; also Pak "Oil and Energy," 473–474; Herbert, *Dreamer of Dune*, 83–85, 154–155.

60. Herbert, "Dune Genesis," 74; O'Reilly, *Frank Herbert*, chapter 3.

61. Pak, *Terraforming*, 120; Herbert and Herbert, interview by McNelly.

62. Herbert, *Dune*, Appendix I: Ecology of Dune; Herbert, *Children of Dune*, 48–49.

63. Geologically, it is virtually impossible for a planet to be covered almost entirely by kilometer tall sand dunes, while fluctuations in Arrakis's axis or orbit would enforce

climatic changes. See: Lorenz, " The Planetology of Arrakis," 53–54; Steyer, "Arrakis et les vers géants"; Callaway, "Speculative Ecosystems," 241–243.

64. Roberts, "Frank Herbert," 104; Hoberek, "*Dune*, and Post-1960 U.S. Foreign Policy," 95; Pak, *Terraforming*, 98–102; Ellis, "Frank Herbert's *Dune*," 117–121.

65. Kratz, "Frank Herbert's Ecology"; Hays, *Environmental Politics in the United States*, 18–21; Landa, "In a Supporting Role," 99–101.

66. Herbert, *Dune*, 149.

67. Buse, "The Working Planetologist," 67–68; Ellis, "Frank Herbert's *Dune*," 108–109; on Sears: Warde et al., *The Environment*, 69–70.

68. Herbert, *Dune*, 342.

69. Pak, *Terraforming*, 124; Anderson, "Critical Bioregionalist Method in Dune," 230–232.

70. Herbert, *Dune*, 293–294.

71. *Ibid.*, 296.

72. Herbert and Herbert, interview by McNelly.

73. Höhler, *Spaceship Earth*; Clarke, "The Planetary Imaginary."

74. Egan, *Barry Commoner.*

75. Clarke, "The Planetary Imaginary," 153–160.

76. Pak, *Terraforming*, 120.

77. In 1975, they first published this for a broader audience: Margulis and Lovelock, "The Gaia Hypothesis."

78. Stableford, *Science Fact and Science Fiction*, 142.

79. Buse, "The Working Planetologist"; Clarke, "The Planetary Imaginary," 155; Gough, "Speculative Fictions," 6.

80. Herbert, *Children of Dune*, 48.

81. *Ibid.*, 449.

82. *Ibid.*, 498–499.

83. Higgins, "Psychic Decolonization."

84. Mellamphy, "Terra & Terror Ecology."

85. Herbert, *Children of Dune*, 3–6.

86. Herbert, "Frank Herbert."

87. Herbert, *Dreamer of Dune*, 166.

88. Latham, "Biotic Invasions," 87.

Works Cited

Allard, Nicolas. *Dune: Un chef-d'œuvre de la science-fiction*. Malakoff: Dunod, 2020.

Anderson, Daniel Gustav. "Critical Bioregionalist Method in Dune: A Position Paper." In *The Bioregional Imagination. Literature, Ecology, and Place*, edited by Tom Lynch, Cheryll Glotfelty, and Karla Armbruster, 226–242. Athens: University of Georgia Press, 2012.

Brückweh, Kerstin, Dirk Schumann, Richard F. Wetzell, and Benjamin Ziemann, editors. *Engineering Society: The Role of the Human and Social Science in Modern Societies, 1880–1980*. Basingstoke UK: Palgrave Macmillan, 2012.

Buse, Katherine. "The Working Planetologist. Speculative Worlds and the Practice of Climate Science." In *Practices of Speculation. Modelling, Embodiment, Figuration*, edited by Jeanne Cortiel, Christine Hanke, Jan Simon Hutta, and Colin Milburn, 51–76. Bielefeld, Germany: Transcript Verlag, 2020.

Callaway, Elizabeth. "Islands in the Aether Ocean. Speculative Ecosystems in Science Fiction." *Contemporary Literature* 59, no. 2 (2018): 232–260.

Clarke, Bruce. "The Planetary Imaginary: Gaian Ecologies from *Dune* to *Neuromancer*." In *Earth, Life, and System. Evolution and Ecology on a Gaian Planet*, edited by Bruce Clarke, 151–74. New York: Fordham University Press, 2015.

Couperus, Stefan, Liesbeth van de Grift, and Vincent Lagendijk. "Experimental

Spaces—Planning in High Modernity." *Journal of Modern European History* 13, no. 4 (2015): 475–479.

Cronon, William. "The Trouble with Wilderness or, Getting Back to the Wrong Nature." In *Uncommon Ground: Rethinking the Human Place in Nature*, edited by William Cronon, 69–90. New York: W.W. Norton, 1995.

Drake, Brian Allen. *Loving Nature, Fearing the State. Environmentalism and Antigovernment Politics before Reagan*. Seattle: University of Washington Press, 2013.

Egan, Michael. *Barry Commoner and the Science of Survival. The Remaking of American Environmentalism*. Cambridge, MA: MIT Press, 2007.

Egan, Michael, and Jeff Crane. "Introduction." In *Natural Protest. Essays on the History of American Environmentalism*, edited by Michael Egan and Jeff Crane, 1–16. New York: Routledge, 2009.

Ellis, R.J. "Frank Herbert's *Dune* and the Discourse of Apocalyptic Ecologism in the United States." In *Science Fiction Roots and Branches. Contemporary Critical Approaches*, edited by Rhys Garnett and R.J. Ellis, 104–23. Basingstoke, UK: The Macmillan Press, 1990.

Escobar, Arturo. "Planning." In *The Development Dictionary. A Guide to Knowledge as Power. Second Edition*, edited by Wolfgang Sachs, 145–60. London: Zed Books, 2010.

Etzemüller, Thomas. "*Social engineering* als Verhaltenslehre des kühlen Kopfes. Eine einleitende Skizze." In *Die Ordnung der Moderne. Social Engineering im 20. Jahrhundert*, edited by Thomas Etzemüller, 11–40. Bielefeld, Germany: Transkript Verlag, 2009.

Engels, Jens Ivo. "Modern Environmentalism." In *The Turning Points of Environmental History*, edited by Frank Uekötter, 119–31. Pittsburgh, PA: University of Pittsburgh Press, 2010.

Evans, Rebecca. "New Wave Science Fiction and the Dawn of the Environmental Movement." In *The Cambridge History of Science Fiction*, edited by Gerry Canavan and Eric Carl Link, 434–446. Cambridge, UK: Cambridge University Press, 2019.

Ferguson, Niall, Charles S. Maier, Erez Manela, and Daniel J. Sargent, editors. *The Shock of the Global: The 1970s in Perspective*. Cambridge, MA: Harvard University Press, 2010.

Gaylard, Gerald. "Postcolonial Science Fiction: The Desert Planet." In *Science Fiction, Imperialism, and the Third World: Essays on Postcolonial Literature and Film*, edited by Ericka Hoagland and Reema Sarwal, 21–36. Jefferson, NC: McFarland, 2010.

Gilcher-Holtey, Ingrid. "Political Participation and Democratization in the 1960s. The Concept of Participatory Democracy and its Repercussions." In *Democracy in Modern Europe. A Conceptual History*, edited by Jussi Kurunmäki, Jeppe Nevers, and Henk te Velde, 257–280. New York: Berghahn, 2018.

Gough, Noel. "Speculative Fictions for Understanding Global Change Environments: Two Thought Experiments." *Managing Global Transitions* 1, no. 1 (2003): 5–27.

Hays, Samuel P. *Beauty, Health, and Permanence. Environmental Politics in the United States, 1955–1985*. Cambridge, UK: Cambridge University Press, 1987.

Hamblin, Jacob Darwin. *Arming Mother Nature: The Birth of Catastrophic Environmentalism*. Oxford, UK: Oxford University Press, 2013.

Herbert, Brian. *Dreamer of Dune: The Biography of Frank Herbert*. New York: Tor, 2003.

Herbert, Frank. *Children of Dune*. 1976 New York: Ace, 2008.

Herbert, Frank. *Dune: 50th Anniversary Edition*. 1965 London: Hodder & Stoughton, 2015.

Herbert, Frank. "Dune Genesis." *OMNI* 2, no. 2 (July 1980), 72–74.

Herbert, Frank. *Dune Messiah*. 1969 London: Hodder & Stoughton, 2017.

Herbert, Frank. "Frank Herbert. Science Fiction's 'Yellow Journalist' Is a Homesteading 'Technopeasant.'" Interview by Pat Stone. *Plowboy* (May/June 1981): 17–23.

Herbert, Frank. "Futuristic Meditations from Dune's Frank Herbert." Interview by Jean Marie Stine. Los Angeles, 1984. *The Los Angeles Reader* (1984), digital version: http://futurespast-editions.blogspot.com/2013/10/lost-interview-futuristic-meditations.html.

Herbert, Frank. "Introduction." In *New World or No World*, edited by Frank Herbert. New York: Ace Books, 1970.

Herbert, Frank. "Profile of Frank Herbert." Interview by John Elkington. London. *The Environmentalist* 1, no. 3 (1981): 229–234.

Herbert, Frank. "Science Fiction and a World in Crisis." In *Science Fiction, Today and Tomorrow*, edited by Reginald Bretnor, 69–97. New York: Ace, 1975.

Herbert, Frank, and Beverly Herbert. Interview by Willis E. McNelly. Fullerton. February 3, 1969, http://www.sinanvural.com/seksek/inien/tvd/tvd2.html.

Herbert, Ulrich. "Europe in High Modernity. Reflections on a Theory of the 20th Century." *Journal of Modern European History* 5, no. 2 (2007): 5–21.

Higgins, David M. "Psychic Decolonization in 1960s Science Fiction." *Science Fiction Studies* 40, no. 2 (2013): 228–245.

Hoberek, Andrew. "*Dune*, the Middle Class and Post-1960 U.S. Foreign Policy." In *American Literature and Culture in an Age of Cold War: A Critical Reassessment*, edited by Steven Belletto and Daniel Grausam, 85–108. Iowa City: Iowa University Press, 2012.

Höhler, Sabine. *Spaceship Earth in the Environmental Age, 1960–1990*. London: Routledge, 2015.

Hutter, Michael. "Ecosystems Research and Policy Planning: Revisiting the Budworm Project (1972–1980) at the ISSA." In *Planning in Cold War Europe. Competition, Cooperation, Circulations (1950s-1970s)*, edited by Michel Christian, Sandrine Kott, and Ondrej Matejka, 261–84. Berlin: De Gruyter, 2018.

Immerwahr, Daniel. "Heresies of 'Dune.'" *The Los Angeles Review of Books*, November 19, 2020. https://lareviewofbooks.org/article/heresies-of-dune/.

Kennedy, Kara. "Epic World-Building: Names and Cultures in *Dune*." *Names* 64, no. 2 (2016): 99–108.

Kirk, Andrew G. *Counterculture Green. The Whole Earth Catalog and American Environmentalism*. Lawrence: University Press of Kansas, 2007.

Kratz, Veronika. "Frank Herbert's Ecology, Oregon's Dunes, and the Postwar Science of Desert Reclamation." *SLE: Interdisciplinary Studies in Literature and Environment* (2021). Advance online version: https://doi.org/10.1093/isle/isab026.

Laak, Dirk van. "Planung. Geschichte und Gegenwart des Vorgriffs auf die Zukunft." *Geschichte und Gesellschaft* 34, no. 3 (2008): 305–326.

Landa, Edward R. "In a Supporting Role: Soil and Cinema." In *Soil and Culture*, edited by Edward R. Landa and Christian Feller, 83–105. Dordrecht: Springer, 2010.

Latham, Rob. "Biotic Invasions: Ecological Imperialism in New Wave Science Fiction." In *Green Planets. Ecology and Science Fiction*, edited by Gerry Canavan and Kim Stanley Robinson, 77–95. Middletown: Wesleyan University Press, 2014.

Lorenz, Ralph D. "Dunes of Dune: The Planetology of Arrakis." In *The Science of Dune: An Unauthorized Exploration into the Real Science Behind Frank Herbert's Fictional Universe*, edited by Kevin R. Grazier, 49–58. Dallas: Benbella Books, 2008.

Mahrane, Yannick, Marianne Fenzi, Céline Pessis, and Christophe Bonneuil, "De la nature à la biosphère. L'invention politique de l'environnement global, 1945–1972." *Vingtième Siècle. Revue d'Histoire* 1, no. 113 (2012): 127–141.

Margulis, Lynn, and James Lovelock. "The Atmosphere as Circulatory System of the Biosphere—The Gaia Hypothesis." *CoEvolution Quarterly* 6 (1975): 32–40.

McNeill, J.R., and Peter Engelke. *The Great Acceleration. An Environmental History of the Anthropocene since 1945*. Cambridge, MA: Belknap Press of Harvard University Press, 2014.

Mellamphy, Nandita Biswas. "Terra & Terror Ecology: Secrets from the Arrakeen Underground." *Design Ecologies* 3, no. 1 (2011): 39–59.

Meyer, Jan-Henrik. "From Nature to Environment: International Organizations and Environmental Protection Before Stockholm." In *International Organizations & Environmental Protection. Conservation and Globalization in the Twentieth Century*, edited by Wolfram Kaiser and Jan-Henrik Meyer, 31–73. New York: Berghahn, 2017.

Montrie, Chad. *The Myth of Silent Spring. Rethinking the Origins of American Environmentalism*. Berkeley: University of California Press, 2018.

Nash, Roderick Frazier. *Wilderness and the American Mind. Fourth Edition*. New Haven: Yale University Press, 2001.

O'Reilly, Timothy. *Frank Herbert*. New York: Frederick Ungar, 1981. https://www.oreilly.com/tim/herbert/index.html.

Otto, Eric. "Science Fiction and the Ecological Conscience." Doctoral Dissertation, University of Florida, 2006.

Pak, Chris. "Oil and Energy Infrastructure in Science Fiction Short Stories." In *The Palgrave Handbook of Twentieth and Twenty-First Century Literature and Science*, edited by the Triangle Collective, 469–482. London: Palgrave Macmillan, 2020.

Pak, Chris. *Terraforming: Ecological Transformations and Environmentalism in Science Fiction*. Liverpool: Liverpool University Press, 2016.

Patel, Kiran Klaus. *The New Deal. A Global History*. Princeton: Princeton University Press, 2016.

Roberts, Adam. "Frank Herbert (1920–86)." In *Fifty Key Figures in Science Fiction*, edited by Mark Bould, Andrew M. Butler, Adam Roberts, and Sherryl Vint, 101–105. London: Routledge, 2009.

Robertson, Thomas. "Total War and the Total Environment: Fairfield Osborn, William Vogt, and the Birth of Global Ecology." *Environmental History* 17, no. 2 (2012): 336–64.

Rome, Adam. "'Give Earth a Chance': The Environmental Movement and the Sixties." *The Journal of American History* 90, no. 2 (2003): 525–554.

Rumpala, Yannick. *Hors des décombres du monde. Écologie, science-fiction et éthique du futur*. Seyssel France: Champ Vallon, 2018.

Schulz-Walden, Thorsten. *Anfänge einer globalen Umweltpolitik. Umweltsicherheit in der internationalen Politik (1969–1975)*. Munich: Oldenbourg, 2013.

Scott, James C. *Seeing Like a State: How Certain Schemes to Improve the Human Condition Have Failed*. New Haven: Yale University Press, 1998.

Smith, Sherry L. *Hippies, Indians, and the Fight for Red Power*. Oxford, UK: Oxford University Press, 2012.

Stableford, Brian. *Science Fact and Science Fiction: An Encyclopedia*. New York: Routledge, 2006.

Steyer, Jean-Sébastien. "Arrakis et les vers géants, un écosystème global." In *Dune : Exploration scientifique et culturelle d'une planète-univers*, edited by Roland Lehoucq, 53–76. Saint-Mammès: le Bélial, 2020.

Stratton, Susan. "The Messiah and the Greens: The Shape of Environmental Action in *Dune* and *Pacific Edge*." *Exploration* 42, no. 4 (2001): 303–316.

Sullivan, Heather I. "Petro-texts, Plants, and People in the Anthropocene: The Dark Green." *Green Letters. Studies in Ecocriticism* 23, no. 2 (2019): 152–167.

Thomas, Sarah L. "A Call to Action: Silent Spring, Public Discourse and the Rise of Modern Environmentalism." In *Natural Protest: Essays on the History of American Environmentalism*, edited by Michael Egan and Jeff Crane, 185–204. New York: Routledge, 2009.

Trexler, Adam. *Anthropocene Fictions. The Novel in a Time of Climate Change*. Charlottesville: University of Virginia Press, 2015.

Uekötter, Frank. "A Twisted Road to Earth Day: Air Pollution as an Issue of Social Movements after World War II." In *Natural Protest: Essays on the History of American Environmentalism*, edited by Michael Egan and Jeff Crane, 163–83. New York: Routledge, 2009.

Uekötter, Frank. *The Age of Smoke: Environmental Policy in Germany and the United States, 1880–1970*. Pittsburgh, PA: University of Pittsburgh Press, 2009.

Warde, Paul, Libby Robin, and Sverker Sörlin. *The Environment. A History of the Idea*. Baltimore: Johns Hopkins University Press, 2018.

Woodhouse, Keith M. "The Politics of Ecology: Environmentalism and Liberalism in the 1960s." *Journal for the Study of Radicalism* 2, no. 2 (2009): 53–84.

Zaki, Hoda M. "Orientalism in Science Fiction." In *Food for Our Grandmothers: Writings by Arab-American and Arab-Canadian Feminists*, edited by Joanna Kadi, 181–187. Boston: South End Press, 1994.

Zelko, Frank. "Challenging Modernity: The Origins of Post-War Environmental Protest in the United States." In *Shades of Green: Activism to Protect the Environment Around the Globe*, edited by Christof Mauch, Nathan Stoltzfus, and Douglas Weiner, 13–40. Lanham, MD: Rowman & Littlefield, 2006.

Zelko, Frank. "The Politics of Nature." In *The Oxford Handbook of Environmental History*, edited by Andrew C. Isenberg, 716–742. Oxford, UK: Oxford University Press, 2014.

Shifting Sands

Heroes, Power, and the Environment
in the Dune Saga

WILLOW WILSON DIPASQUALE

Frank Herbert's *Dune* has been a commercial and critical success since its publication in 1965. Its treatment of politics, power, and religion has garnered it consistent interest in popular culture and academic circles in the subsequent decades. Much of its appeal seems to be grounded in its depiction of its young hero, Paul Atreides, and his unlikely rise to power as the leader of the story's free people. Despite the original novel's massive success, though, subsequent Dune books have received less critical and popular attention, perhaps because Herbert dismantles the victory Paul achieved in the first book. Thus, this essay explores how Herbert purposefully subverts the success of Paul and his mission as "savior," calling into question the efficacy of power structures, as well as the reader's desire for such a savior. In doing so, I demonstrate that while the Dune sequels are certainly worthy of reading for pleasure, they more importantly provide a rich glimpse into Herbert's creative vision; without these sequels, the world of Dune is incomplete, our understanding of the author's perspective hindered.

Much of the first novel's strength lies in how well Herbert has employs the epic genre. Paul is a quintessential monomythic hero. Born into a noble family, possessed of unusual talents and charisma, reluctant to assume his role as leader (endearing himself more so to readers), ultimately successful in his quest to vanquish evil forces and take his place as brave champion—all these elements play out with breathtaking style and nuance to captivate readers, even those familiar with the monomythic pattern.[1] Paul's hesitation to be the hero that others demand of him, as well as Herbert's obvious hints at how tenuous this success is, serves to make his ultimate victory even more satisfying and inevitable. In other words, readers want Paul to succeed, expect him to do so, and to some extent perhaps refuse to acknowledge the possibility of his failure. Thus, when Herbert enacts the careful undoing of all Paul's successes, it is understandable that readers might resist this narrative shift. It would be remiss, however, to allow this discomfort to obscure the potential these sequels have to provide a more nuanced understanding of the world Herbert created. In addition, the themes Herbert introduces in the first book only emerge more completely over the course of the series; they can be analyzed and appreciated in each book separately, but their full impact cannot be realized without the context of the entire Dune series. Throughout these works, Herbert uses tension and contradiction to underscore how complete political power harms its citizens and damages the environment.

In fact, Paul's own ambivalence in the first two books contributes to this core tension: his motivation to do good and "deliver" the Fremen from outside forces is at the same time perpetuating the Fremen's dependence on an outside force to aid in their deliverance, reinforcing a problematic power dynamic between leader and led.[2] As the books continue, this tension is repeated, mirrored, and expanded in several ways. What remains constant, however, serving as both backdrop and fundamentally important "character," is the planet Dune itself, also known as Arrakis. While the messiness of Atreides and Bene Gesserit politics unfolds over millennia, Herbert suggests that a healthy ecosystem—one which thrives on change, dynamism, and the respectful care of its co-inhabitants—is fundamental to a healthy humanity. In his own life and through various ecological "projects," Herbert "developed a deep respect for the natural rhythms of nature. The ecology message, so prevalent in much of his writing, is one of his most important legacies."[3]

As much as Herbert saw Western culture and white men in particular as generally destructive environmental forces, his devotion was always to "the survival of humanity" as inherently valuable, and he saw the caretaking of nature as a contribution to humans' "quality of life."[4] In order to convey these values, he collected ideas that would later inform the Dune series, set on a distant planet but with fully human concerns: "[B]orrowing from the American Indian's opinion of white culture, he would describe how man inflicts himself upon his environment, usurping it and failing to live in harmony with it."[5] This format works especially well in these novels because it "demonstrates effectively with the simplified ecology of the planet Arrakis how important and surprising the connections among things in an ecosystem can be,"[6] while "Herbert also uses the cognitive estrangement of an alien planet and its indigenous people to unwrap for his readers some aspects of the relationship between nature and culture."[7]

Thus, Herbert was able to combine his own ecological concerns with his spiritual beliefs, showing that interconnections between people and ecosystems are present in our real world as much as in Arrakis, and that human culture has a profound impact on nature (both key tenets in ecocriticism). Therefore, to read the sequels is to understand Herbert's ecocritical point of view.[8]

Dune Messiah: *Purposeful Vacillation*

Set 12 years after the events in *Dune*, the perhaps ironically titled *Dune Messiah* continues the subtle work begun in the first novel of dismantling Paul's position as absolute hero, particularly through Herbert's use of Paul's ambivalence and his seemingly unavoidable fate. At the opening of this work, Paul rules as emperor over an increasingly fertile planet, enacting the work of ecological transformation he promised the Fremen. At the same time, a cosmic jihad rages across the universe, spreading the Atreides' political power, ensuring control of the spice (and thus of space travel), and killing over 60 billion people ("at a conservative estimate"[9]) in Paul's name. Despite his role as emperor, Paul hesitates to fully take on the identity of messianic leader, vacillating between the needs of the planet, the Fremen, and himself. His frequent interior, reflective moments reveal this indecisiveness: he "taste[s] the smoke of a devastated future and the voice of another kind of vision commanding him to disengage,"[10] while "[s]ince the day of his first encounter with terrible purpose, he had peered at the future, hoping to find peace."[11] Indeed, his relationship with his prescient visions contributes to this ambivalence. He sees many possible futures but feels increasingly trapped between two choices: to take on "godhead," ensuring the survival of humanity at the cost of his own, or to give up the mantle of leadership, preserving his own identity but losing his literal and prescient sight. Paul's thoughts reveal his ambivalence: "There existed a way [to find peace] ... a rote future, strict in its instructions to him: disengage, disengage, disengage."[12] The cost of this ambivalence is one of ineffectiveness, as he "felt that he occupied an inhospitable middle zone, a wasted place where his emotions drifted, swayed, swept outward in unchecked restlessness."[13] The juxtaposition of sight and blindness, growth and stagnation, giving and taking all arise to underscore Herbert's larger creative vision and invite readers to dismantle their expectations of an epic hero.

From its opening pages, *Dune Messiah* tells readers that Paul's fate is contested: "We know this moment of supreme power contained failure. There can be only one answer, that completely accurate and total prediction is lethal."[14] The tension between "supreme power" (suggesting success) and "failure" subverts our desire for Paul's prescience to be used for a conventionally satisfying ending. Paul, too, doubts his own success in using his near-mythological status to lead the Fremen. Edric, a Guild Navigator, confronts Paul on this matter: "It seems to most observers, however, that you conspire to make a god of yourself. And one might ask if that is something any mortal can do … safely?"[15] Paul acknowledges that he has weighed this question himself, "time and again. But he had seen enough alternate Timelines to know of worse possibilities than accepting godhead for himself. Much worse."[16] Paul has to justify a "lesser of two evils" metric for decision making, but Herbert (again through Edric) raises complicated questions about the uses of power: "Religion, too, is a weapon. What manner of weapon is religion when it becomes the government?"[17] The very thing the Bene Gesserit worked over generations to "implant" (myths, religion, a figure to be worshipped) in the Fremen culture is coming to pass, emphasizing its artificiality. Paul's intentions may be noble, but the system of power he operates in is not.

Another way Herbert highlights tension in this book is through the terraforming of Arrakis. The planet shifts from a desert land of trials and danger to a verdant place of water, safety, and plenty. The consequence of this plenty, though, is that the Fremen become weaker and more reliant on the Atreides/organized government. In later novels, their identity devolves into that of "museum Fremen"—that is, they carry out diluted rituals from their cultural past, but without the same firsthand knowledge and experience of their ancestors. As the name suggests, they become a passive fixture instead of a powerful, active people. Paul, however, recognizes the contradictory nature of his presence on Arrakis, and of his ecological goals. Early in the novel, Paul has solitary reflective moments in which he can simultaneously appreciate the beauty of Dune's terraforming but also see how vulnerable to conflict and chaos it is: "He stood naked and oddly attuned to his world. Dune was a world of paradox now—a world under siege, yet the center of power. To come under siege, he decided, was the inevitable fate of power."[18] This scene combines Paul's literal exposure (his nakedness) with the environment's exposure to political strife, a problem that Paul's messianic leadership has not altogether solved.

Perhaps even more so than in the first book, Paul is "attuned" to the needs of Arrakis, to its vitality as its own place, its existence outside of and in spite of all the struggles for control of its resources. He sees the consequences of his ecological plan, but also recognizes the inherent problems of trying to change the planet: "Was it not presumptuous, he wondered, to think he could make over an entire planet—everything growing where and how he told it to grow? Even if he succeeded, what of the universe waiting out there? Did it fear similar treatment?"[19] This final question suggests that Paul's noble plan to terraform Dune is a "fear"-ful form of manipulation, of interference. Similarly, his leadership suggests a type of absolute control that can only lead to "human resistance,"[20] implying that citizens will need to question and reform the systems of authority ruling over them. Paul is clearly pulled by competing forces, impelled by his visions to save humanity but also confronted by his intuitive understanding that nature does not need humanity to dictate its boundaries. Here, Herbert reveals an inherent connectedness between environment and government, one which becomes more intricate as the narrative unfolds.

Herbert's descriptions of the planet itself further reinforce the binary tensions at play in his novels. It has at once "ecstasies of tranquility and wild motion."[21] Paul recognizes his own tenuous grasp on the planet, implying that no one person has absolute control: "This planet beneath him which he had commanded be remade from desert into a water-rich paradise, it was alive. It had a pulse as dynamic as that of any human. It fought him, resisted, slipped away from his commands."[22] In the face of this resistance and conflict, Paul decides to renounce his leadership and his "vision," entering the desert in the Fremen way. This decision is yet another way duality operates in the story. Paul succumbs to double-blindness, losing his physical eyesight and his prescient visions, contrasting with dramatic tension from the first book, which tracked Paul's emerging prescient power. This second volume unravels the "terrible purpose" he has taken on as emperor. While the story does not resolve in a way that answers all the questions raised by Herbert's characters, *balance* emerges as a potential solution to the conflicting forces throughout the narrative. As Paul says to Stilgar, "you urgently need a sense of balance which can come from an understanding of long-term effects."[23] Ultimately, "balance" becomes Paul's way through his struggle.

Paul balances his needs against those of his leadership by actively choosing to be blinded and to walk into the desert. This sacrifice destabilizes Arrakis's power structure, as control is taken up by his sister Alia (herself an emotionally and psychologically unstable character) and then later his son, then even later the Bene Gesserit, the Honored Matres, and, ultimately, the Fremen again (even if temporarily). In other words, Herbert creates a dynamic, ever-changing world, one in which ultimate power cannot thrive, however upright its leader's intentions are. While clearly not a perfect solution, the ending of *Dune Messiah* suggests that there is no one singular answer to the problems of power. Rather, it is a medium between opposing forces. Paul has "failed," but failed nobly, in a way that allows us to both sympathize with his position and to recognize how Herbert questions and subverts the very model of leadership set forth in *Dune*. The tragic ending underscores Herbert's vision in his series: to ennoble Paul as a selfless hero and leader while simultaneously showing how such heroism and leadership are inherently problematic.

As *Dune Messiah* concludes, readers are left with a few elements to examine: balance in an unstable world; respect for nature's power and independence; and a surprising need for love. In the closing pages, Paul's sister, Alia, asks Duncan Idaho (a "ghola" or clone of the loyal Atreides retainer from *Dune*) to love her. Herbert suggests that there is power in human connection, however that humanity is defined. The Atreides' search for love reemerges throughout the series, and it finds many different forms. Rather than trusting in heroes, Herbert suggests, perhaps the characters would do better to trust in life and cultivate authentic relationships with each other and with their planet. Herbert's characters enjoy the greatest happiness and success when they form interpersonal connections, both romantic and platonic (Paul and Chani, Duncan Idaho and Alia, Darwi Odrade and Sheeana, to name just a few), as well as with Arrakis itself. The Atreides' greatest success is perhaps in stewarding and preserving the planet's physical space, or, if this becomes impossible, in stewarding the spirit of the Fremen people. As Paul enjoins, "If you need something to worship, then worship life—all life, every last crawling bit of it! We're all in this beauty together!"[24] Through Paul, Herbert urges readers to pivot from looking to leaders for salvation and instead to consider how our own relationship with "all life" can create stronger bonds than political loyalty.

Yet, despite these lofty ideas, Herbert grounds us in the reality facing his characters, a reality that continues beyond the end of this book. As Prieto-Pablos notes:

> In the end, [Paul] is glad to give his "water to the desert" as a way of escaping his affliction, and glad, too, we may infer, to leave the floor to his son. But at the conclusion of *Dune Messiah*, the reader is aware that the novel gives an end to the story of Muad'Dib while everything else continues as ever and even threatens to grow worse.[25]

While Paul lays aside his leadership, unable to see the Atreides plan through to its end, the novel's conclusion suggests that all these tensions remain for the next generation to grapple with. In other words, Herbert has dismantled the idea of a superhero introduced in the first book, but he then raises more problems than he resolves. Not only is this ambiguity intentional, but, as I maintain, it is essential to understanding the Dune series.

Children of Dune: *Binary Tensions*

The sequel to *Dune Messiah*, *Children of Dune*, takes place nine years later and continues the theme of ambivalence begun in the first two novels. As critics have noted,[26] *Dune* and *Dune Messiah* have a fugal quality: the main themes in book one are picked up and inverted in book two, point and counterpoint positioned to reveal the unstable relationship between power and its uses, and the same is true in book three. Perhaps even more than its predecessors, this entry puts duality visibly into focus. Alia struggles between the lure of political power and her own sanity. The remembered lives that Paul also had within him, a side-effect of prescient vision, vie for dominance inside Alia, supplanting her sense of self.

Like Janus, looking backward and forward, Paul and Alia must balance the competing voices in their lives—their memories of ancestors, the advice of their followers, and their own desires. Paul escapes these voices by relinquishing his prescience (though he returns in this book as the mysterious "Preacher"). Alia cannot find balance, and her fate seems yet another warning from Herbert. While *Dune Messiah* ends with Alia appealing to Duncan for love, a humanizing quality which offers readers some hope for her future, here she descends into the madness and "failure" that comes from any absolute system. Intelligence, "breeding," talent—none of these qualities can offset the corrupting influence of power, in Herbert's worlds. Alia's desperate act of "resolution" (suicide) suggests a frightening outcome for those who cannot find equilibrium in a world of change and surprise.

The planet's terraforming also reveals binary tensions, as its transformation from desert into verdant land has changed the dynamics between the Fremen and Arrakis. The planet's harsh climate and limited resources were a kind of "testing ground" for generations of Fremen, shaping their identity and culture, their entire way of life. As the planet softens, so too do the people. The book explores unintended consequences this change brings. What begins as a noble plan to provide abundance and resources has an unfortunate side effect: the Fremen more than ever need others to take power, to use political influence to shape their futures. They lack independence and resilience, and many have succumbed to corruption. Their lush planet will eventually be their destruction.

At the same time, Arrakis's ecological transformation has also affected resource dependence. Without wide swaths of desert, the sandworms and their spice production are restricted. Thus, a tension arises between resource abundance (water and greenery) and resource scarcity (spice, needed for prescience, space travel, and trade). Out of this tension, Herbert positions the idea that a better relationship with one's environment can in fact improve the moral character of that person:

> The Fremen must return to his original faith, to his genius in forming human communities; he must return to the past, where that lesson of survival was learned in the struggle with Arrakis. The only business of the Fremen should be that of opening his soul to the inner teachings. The worlds of the Imperium, the Landsraad and the CHOAM Confederacy have no message to give him. They will only rob him of his soul.[27]

Herbert's "message" is again planet-centered. If the characters treat land primarily as a resource for their own comfort and stability, they will ultimately be disappointed. Their moral character suffers in proportion to their disconnect with nature. On the other hand, their connection to the planet can provide an existential reward, as the "agricultural work" on Arrakis has "the Fremen implication that this labor occurred simultaneously in Another World where it symbolized cultivating the richness of the soul."[28] In Herbert's creative vision, nature and humanity are inextricably linked. Thus, systems of power must be "cultivated" to encourage a soul-enriching relationship with the planet and the people, not one that removes power from people or sacrifices the resources of earth.

Paul and Chani's twin children, too, are a fitting physical representation of the conflicting pulls of the Atreides family's legacy. Leto II and Ghanima are finding their place within a Paul-less Arrakis. Both are faced with their father's unfinished Golden Path, the centuries-long journey to environmental and biological transformation that will ensure humanity's survival (and its absolute control). The decisions they wrestle with amplify themes of duality/tension, and these themes' resolutions are distorted, even when resolved. Ghanima rejects the Golden Path, moving in one direction; Leto moves in another, enacting the terrible purpose his father rejected. Yet their destinies remain intertwined as their paths simultaneously diverge and converge. They marry each other, but their union is more symbolic than literal, as they will not have offspring. Their choices provide a strange resolution of binaries, an unsteady sense of closure to the question of who will take power for the next generation. Power rests again in the Atreides' hands, but it will need to unfold through Herbert's sequels for readers to understand its impact.

God Emperor of Dune: An Intentionally Contradictory Hero

Set 3,500 years after the last book, *God Emperor of Dune* further explores the contradictions and ironies of its prequels. We see clearly the consequences of Leto II's decision to set in motion the Golden Path. He has evolved into a sandworm "godhead," calling into question his relationship with humanity as he becomes less human, and with nature as he becomes more a part of his environment. He often considers how his less human side can be "callous" and "calculating."[29] At the same time, he feels an enormous burden towards humanity, seeing "every living thing [as his] responsibility."[30] As much as Leto's body and identity have been places of transformation, Arrakis, too, has been more thoroughly terraformed. The planet is now forested, save for a controlled space which Leto reserves for sandtrout (all other sandworms are gone). He has absolute control of the spice, the planet, and the Fremen. Through this terraforming of planet and people, Leto hopes to test humanity, to ensure they are resilient enough to survive into the future. Paradoxically, Herbert has turned Leto into an extremist leader to warn the Fremen of extremism. At the same time, Leto himself wrestles with his gradual loss of humanity and empathy, prone to uncontrollable, instinctual outbursts of anger, yet eventually undone by his strong desire for love. Like his ancestors (especially Paul and Jessica), in some ways he has "failed" because of his love. And because of love, he ultimately sacrifices himself to further the needs of humanity, allowing history to see him as a tyrant even though he is what has allowed humans to have a history.[31]

In this book, Herbert both continues the pattern of an ambivalent hero and more closely examines ecocritical principles, including animism and interrelatedness. Through his union with the sandworms and his ultimately selfless sacrifice, Leto demonstrates these concepts which were in fact introduced in book one. Through animism (the "assum[ption] that the world all around us is alive, and that all beings have the ability to communicate"[32] if people just listen), Leto's status as sandworm/deity gives a quite literal "voice" to nature, proving it to be capable of "conversation" with humankind. At the same time, his evolution from human to worm (and the sandworms' life cycle more generally) implies a connection between people and the natural world, a blurring of boundaries between the two.[33] Finally, Leto's leadership philosophy (though rife with contradiction) reveals an intriguing perspective on what a ruler owes to their people and planet. For example, Leto believes that leaders are fallible, and that it is neither realistic nor productive to think otherwise: "How persistent it is, this demand that our gods be perfect. The Greeks were much more reasonable about such things."[34] Yet, while the unspoken implication is that Leto too is imperfect, he still feels an unerring sense of responsibility to humanity. As Leto's servant Moneo says, "The Atreides art is the art of ruling without hysteria, the art of being responsible for the uses of power."[35] While Leto is a "tyrant," for better or worse, he still strives toward a larger humanitarian vision, one which ensures that the Fremen will thrive and be independent, and one which further promotes the well-being of nature.

The book ends with an appeal to history, to learn from the past as a means of understanding the future. In light of finding Leto's journals, historians suggest that the joy of surprise is one which has been preserved through Leto's Golden Path. Leto worked to breed an Atreides descendant who was immune to prescience, thus introducing a new element of uncertainty and change into humanity's opportunities. This element of unpredictability (again, unstable, incomplete, another tension) ensures there will be a chance for the Fremen—and indeed for humanity itself—to discover what kind of future they want to build, perhaps even apart from the political machinations of those in power:

> [H]istorians must listen to that voice from our beginnings. If it is only the journals, we must listen. We must listen across at least as many years into our future as those journals lay hidden in our past. We will not try to predict the discoveries yet to be made within those pages. We say only that they must be made. How can we turn our backs on our most important inheritance? As the poet, Lon Bramlis, has said: "We are the fountain of surprises!"[36]

Herbert ends this story on a note of hope and potential, yet again, though with the possibility that such a "fountain of surprises" could take us into unresolved territory.

Heretics of Dune: *Scattered Power*

Another 1,500 years have passed by the time of *Heretics of Dune*, and a diaspora has scattered trillions of inhabitants across the universe as part of Leto's plan to ensure humanity's survival. Instead of control being focused in one ruler or city, Leto's death has intentionally destabilized the prior model of power. In this work, "scattering" is a theme that plays out literally in humankind's situation and figuratively in how the many different factions act upon each other. Here, again, Herbert shows readers the inherent tension in any form of government or power. The Fish Speakers (female warriors that Leto used as security forces during his rule) have evolved into something different: the Honored Matres, a distorted reflection of the Bene Gesserit. If the Bene Gesserit are a religious order intent on training and perfecting humanity, the Honored Matres are a matriarchal society intent on training for the purpose of violence, aggression, and force. In essence, they represent control of two different kinds: intellectual versus physical. *Heretics of Dune* reiterates a fugal pattern, playing out themes introduced previously in new ways—sometimes harmonizing, but often cacophonous.

The Bene Gesserit want to create another "god-like" figure for the scattered people to worship and for the Bene Gesserit to control (and thus to control the scattered, by extension). However, in this iteration, Herbert achieves an unusual, destabilizing effect because the different factions and individuals have special abilities that were previously reserved only for the Bene Gesserit or the Atreides. Because so many "players" have power and ability, Herbert suggests that they need to cultivate new tools to survive and assert (or decline) power. In essence, characters have to nurture more human rather than superhuman qualities,[37] particularly love and empathy. The Reverend Mother Darwi Odrade, who emerges as a quasi-heroic figure in the last two books, is unique in the Bene Gesserit for seeing love as both strength and weakness: "Love, damnable love, weakening love."[38] She knows it can weaken, but she cannot give up her love for her "natural" father Miles Teg, her empathy for humanity, or her compassion for the planet. Throughout this book and *Chapterhouse: Dune*, Herbert puts in conversation the binary between political alliances and un-politicized love. Within that conversation, he suggests that each person has a responsibility to improve their shared human experience: "Life cannot find reasons to sustain it, cannot be a source of decent mutual regard, unless each of us resolves to breathe such qualities into it."[39] This sentiment is at odds with Paul's initial mission to be a superhero; an admirable goal, perhaps, and one which reveals a certain selflessness, but in light of *Heretics of Dune*, Herbert's later model of leadership requires some measure of contribution and cooperation, not absolute rule.

One of the failures of Bene Gesserit leadership seems to be in their attitude towards nature. Rather than valuing it for its own sake (consistent with deep ecology principles, which promote living closely with nature through embedded practices[40]), they instead have an artificial version of nature to fulfill functional needs. Their buildings and rooms are designed to mimic nature, as Odrade observes a particular room filled with windows intended to let in soft evening light, "spice-fiber hangings," and "[s]ilver-yellow glowglobes hover[ing] near the ceiling, all tuned to match the sunlight."[41] But this mimicry is always in a crafted sense, evocative of how they create the appearance of many things, but merely for their own ends. They cannot value nature, life, love, or any "human" or organic qualities in and of themselves (which contradicts, among other things, the principles of deep ecology). Even in the horticultural imagery that pervades *Heretics of Dune* and *Chapterhouse: Dune*, there is a certain sense of order and control that implies a larger "plan" for how nature should be *used*. (As Miles Teg concludes, "Manipulation. That was their mark. They manipulated everyone and everything."[42])

In contrast, the Fremen and the Atreides have always placed the natural, organic, and human as central needs. Against this tension of artificiality and authenticity, Odrade's transformation from Bene Gesserit tool to independent being is satisfying. Like Jessica, she helps forge a new and different path for humanity. Her moments of revelation play out dramatically, particularly when she uncovers the messages buried by Leto II for the Sisterhood to find. Leto II calls out the Sisterhood for putting the burden of the Golden Path on his shoulders, allowing him millennia of suffering instead of answering the call themselves. Ultimately, he appeals to her own higher morals, pleading with her to help humanity to a better place:

> WHAT IS SURVIVAL IF YOU DO NOT SURVIVE WHOLE? ... WHAT IF YOU NO LONGER HEAR THE MUSIC OF LIFE? MEMORIES ARE NOT ENOUGH UNLESS THEY CALL YOU TO NOBLE PURPOSE.[43]

Odrade is moved by these questions, ultimately recognizing that she is willing to sacrifice the Sisterhood and unseat harmful systems of power. She recognizes the "language" of Leto II, reassessing his status as tyrant.

Unlike the Bene Gesserit, who procreate and control procreation for their own power, Odrade sees a genetic line that is not tied to self-serving extremists. As Odrade tells yet another Duncan Idaho ghola, "No single force will rule all of our futures completely, never again."[44] Her way of thinking has evolved, enough so as to set in motion a new path for Rakis and even for the Bene Gesserit and Honored Matres. Herbert closes this book with Odrade's pledge to help Duncan lead the life he wants to, to contribute to that "noble purpose" begun by the Atreides so long before. In the face of Duncan's doubt, Herbert leaves Odrade with an independence that has emerged out of centuries of control. She asks Leto rhetorically if all of what has happened is part of his design: "There was no answer but then she had not really expected an answer."[45] In other words, she must discover the future for herself. Only at this point of the series are Herbert's characters truly able to begin the difficult work of moving beyond being a piece of an organized group to self-actualized, emotionally independent individuals.

Chapterhouse: Dune: *Cultivating Compassion (and Nature)*

Herbert's final Dune novel, *Chapterhouse: Dune*, takes place immediately after the events of the previous book. Planet Dune has been destroyed. Some of the Bene Gesserit decide to take sandworms to reestablish the ecosystem of Arrakis rather than keeping them for political power. The Bene Gesserit and Honored Matres, two warring factions—potentially complementary but opposite—remain. Another cycle of terraforming begins, as the Bene Gesserit work to transform the planet Chapterhouse to recreate a Dune-like environment for the worms, the spice, space travel, and thus control over resources. However, this time they want to avoid prescience and the subsequent power structures created by Paul and his son. The cliffhanger ending, left unresolved in part because of Herbert's death in 1986, leaves open an important interpretation: while history is in large part cyclical, progress can be made only when that cycle is disrupted. Herbert's warning to avoid absolutes emerges yet again, as different characters and groups strive for balance, or fail to do so. Murbella, a convert from the Honored Matres to the Bene Gesserit, crosses the territory between the two factions to create something new—a unifying possibility.

Interestingly, the imagery throughout this work is that of horticulture. The book opens with a garden, a symbol of control compared to the wildness of Paul's world (the desert), and yet it suggests a model of stewardship. Odrade again seems to embody a better understanding of humanity's place within the natural world: "Ownership is an interesting question.... Do we own this planet or does it own us?"[46] She even more explicitly makes the connection to environmental caretaking in this scene, telling Miles Teg (another Atreides descendent), "My Sisterhood believes we are stewards of the land."[47] While readers can interpret this as yet another instance of Bene Gesserit control (a reciprocal relationship rather than selfless motivation), Odrade's influence on her order suggests that their view of nature has evolved.

Odrade and Sheeana (an Atreides descendent who is immune to prescience) represent interesting models for human/nature relations. Odrade has learned the radical and secret act of loving herself, something she must hide from the Bene Gesserit. (Again, love is a potential weakness, a belief that apparently has not left the Sisterhood.) Sheeana has embraced a life as an artist and sculptor. She fashions her own artistic statements about life, acting on her personal creative impulses. Odrade wants food, companionship, an orchard. In other words, here Herbert builds a world in which the ordinary desires of humanity, in concert with a productive relationship with nature, are to be cherished. These acts can take on a radical quality in the face of such grand struggle. Odrade sees herself as part of a complex conversation, understanding the language of Chapterhouse as the planet speaks to her in a personal way. As the verdant land shifts into desert, she sees it as different from before, but still vibrant.[48] The rhythms of nature have become part of her identity. In fact, after her death, she is buried in an orchard, achieving her goal in a tragically ironic detail.

The book itself ends with two mysterious people gardening, a returning image of horticulture. Herbert's final work is more and more about nature, stewardship, and looking to the ordinary things in life as a salvation from the exhausting nature of cosmic political control. Amidst the doubling, binaries, and ironies that play out in complex, fascinating ways, the Dune series ultimately suggests that renewal (personal, political, environmental, even spiritual) could be a reward for a life well-lived, one in pursuit of a "noble purpose." Herbert does not prescribe one version of that noble purpose, but rather suggests that each of his characters can search out this pattern for themselves, questioning systems of corrupt or absolute authority and encouraging productive relationships between humankind and the environment.

Conclusion

Ultimately, reading the Dune series requires a meaningful and engaging interaction between text and reader. If readers keep the whole saga in frame as they parse Herbert's authorial vision, they can better understand the various elements introduced in *Dune* but not fully explored until the closing pages of *Chapterhouse: Dune*. Among many other things, Herbert shows readers the need for reform of power structures and watchfulness over the environment, themes that emerge only at their strongest when viewing the series in its entirety. Herbert's antidote to Paul, though at times difficult to swallow, is to deconstruct such figures of power and transfer authority and, indeed, responsibility back to the people. These ideas emerge in Herbert's own beliefs and in his fictional writings. Herbert's son Brian details what role his father saw for himself and other real-world citizens: "For an individual to be in harmony with the universe, my father believed, he needed to place himself in synchronization with the changing state of nature and human society. He needed to take risks."[49] In *Children of Dune*, Paul (now the blind "Preacher") asserts, "It is not always the majestic concerns of Imperial ministers which dictate the course of history, nor is it necessarily the pontifications of priests which move the hands of God."[50] Through this passage, Herbert implies that the everyday citizen, not the Superhero, can "dictate the course of history" and "move the hands of God." Another chapter's epigraph asserts that, no matter what progress is made in human civilization, "*the very future of humankind, depends on the relatively simple actions of single individuals.*"[51]

Such an interpretation positions the Dune saga as a work readers can view through their own cultural lens, questioning contemporary systems of power, their impact on ecosystems, and the folly of placing trust in a political "savior." Herbert's chronicle of the Atreides family's influence on the course of the universe is nuanced, messy, and complicated. But these complications should not be dismissed. By dismissing the sequels as too dense or intricate, some readers are depriving themselves of rich ground for analysis. Scholars and readers alike would do well to revisit these works, leaving open the possibility that they can be moved by the turmoil of these characters, and convinced not to look to Paul as their rescuer but as a supremely fallible and relatable character, a representative of the enormous potential and failure bound up in human nature.

NOTES

1. See Palumbo's articles on monomyth and chaos theory in the Dune series, "The Monomyth as Fractal Pattern in Frank Herbert's *Dune* Novels."
2. Prieto-Pablos, "The Ambivalent Hero," 68.
3. Herbert, *Dreamer of Dune*, 33.
4. *Ibid.*, 142.
5. *Ibid.*
6. Stratton, "The Messiah and the Greens," 307.
7. *Ibid.*
8. The majority of this essay's analysis focuses on *Dune's* five sequels, as there is a small but rich repository of scholarship on the first book already. Many critics recognize the elements of *Dune* that have made it so successful (the hero's journey, mythopoeic fiction elements, the fractal nature of Herbert's narrative), and they also acknowledge that Herbert intended to deconstruct the narrative he built in the first book. Thus, little space will be devoted to textual scrutiny of the first volume and proving that intention.
9. Herbert, *Dune Messiah*, Kindle location 1819.
10. *Ibid.*, Kindle location 613.
11. *Ibid.*
12. *Ibid.*
13. *Ibid.*
14. *Ibid.*, Kindle location 269.
15. *Ibid.*, Kindle location 1687.
16. *Ibid.*
17. *Ibid.*, Kindle location 1740.
18. *Ibid.*, Kindle location 535.
19. *Ibid.*, Kindle location 751.
20. *Ibid.*
21. *Ibid.*, Kindle location 1036.
22. *Ibid.*, Kindle location 1162.
23. *Ibid.*, Kindle location 1809.
24. *Ibid.*, Kindle location 3848.
25. Prieto-Pablos, "The Ambivalent Hero," 70.
26. See O'Reilly, *Frank Herbert*, 151–175; Herbert, *The Maker of Dune*, 97–101; and Kucera, "Listening to Ourselves" among other sources, for a discussion of the fugal, polyphonic nature of Herbert's Dune novels.
27. Herbert, *Children of Du e*, Kindle location 555.
28. *Ibid.*, Kindle location 1632.
29. Herbert, *God Emperor of Dune*, Kindle location 4158.
30. *Ibid.*, Kindle location 5585.
31. *Ibid.*, see Phillips, "The Greatest Predator Ever Known," and Womack, "He Who Controls Knowledge Controls the Universe," in this volume for more on Leto.
32. Brawley, *Nature and the Numinous in Mythopoeic Fantasy Literature*, 22.
33. *Ibid.*, 23.
34. Herbert, *God Emperor of Dune*, Kindle location 4980.
35. *Ibid.*, Kindle location 6426.
36. *Ibid.*, Kindle location 7918.

37. Kennedy, "The Softer Side of *Dune*: The Impact of the Social Sciences on World-Building," 2.

38. Herbert, *Heretics of Dune*, Kindle location 2331.

39. *Ibid.*, Kindle location 2614.

40. Howarth, "Some Principles of Ecocriticism," 74.

41. Herbert, *Heretics of Dune*, Kindle location 2928.

42. *Ibid.*, Kindle location 2561.

43. *Ibid.*, Kindle location 5724.

44. *Ibid.*, Kindle location 8827.

45. *Ibid.*

46. Herbert, *Chapterhouse: Dune*, Kindle location 412.

47. *Ibid.*

48. *Ibid.*, Kindle location 7629.

49. Brian Herbert, *Dreamer of Dune*, 155.

50. Herbert, *Children of Dune*, Kindle location 1856.

51. Herbert, *Dune Messiah*, Kindle location 2707.

Works Cited

Brawley, Chris. *Nature and the Numinous in Mythopoeic Fantasy Literature.* Jefferson, NC: McFarland, 2014.

Herbert, Brian. *Dreamer of Dune: The Biography of Frank Herbert.* New York: Tor, 2003.

Herbert, Frank. *Chapterhouse: Dune.* 1985 New York: Ace, 2009. Kindle.

Herbert, Frank. *Children of Dune.* 1976 New York: Ace, 2008. Kindle.

Herbert, Frank. *Dune.* 1965 New York: Ace, 2008. Kindle.

Herbert, Frank. *Dune Messiah.* 1969 New York: Ace, 2008. Kindle.

Herbert, Frank. *Frank Herbert: The Maker of Dune: Insights of a Master of Science Fiction*, edited by Timothy O'Reilly. New York: Berkeley, 1987.

Herbert, Frank. *God Emperor of Dune.* 1981 New York: Ace, 2008. Kindle.

Herbert, Frank. *Heretics of Dune.* 1984 New York: Ace, 2009. Kindle.

Howarth, William. "Some Principles of Ecocriticism." In *The Ecocriticism Reader*, edited by Cheryll Glotfelty and Harold Fromm, 69–91. Athens: University of Georgia Press, 1996.

Kennedy, Kara. "The Softer Side of *Dune*: The Impact of the Social Sciences on World-Building." In *Exploring Imaginary Worlds: Essays on Media, Structure, and Subcreation*, edited by Mark J.P. Wolf, 159–174. New York: Routledge, 2020.

Kucera, Paul Q. "Listening to Ourselves: Herbert's Dune, 'the Voice,' and Performing the Absolute." *Extrapolation* 42, no. 3 (2001): 232–245.

O'Reilly, Timothy. *Frank Herbert* ("Recognitions" Series). New York: Frederick Ungar, 1981. https://www.oreilly.com/tim/herbert/index.html.

Otto, Eric C. *Green Speculations: Science Fiction and Transformative Environmentalism.* Columbus: The Ohio State University Press, 2012.

Palumbo, Donald E. "The Monomyth as Fractal Pattern in Frank Herbert's *Dune* Novels." *Science-Fiction Studies* 25, no. 3 (1998): 433–58.

Palumbo, Donald E. "The Monomyth and Chaos Theory: 'Perhaps We Should Believe in Magic.'" *Journal of the Fantastic in the Arts* 12, no. 1 (2001): 34–76.

Palumbo, Donald E. "'Plots Within Plots… Patterns Within Patterns': Chaos-Theory Concepts and Structures in Frank Herbert's Dune Novels." *Journal of the Fantastic in the Arts* 8, no. 1 (1997): 55–77.

Prieto-Pablos, Juan A. "The Ambivalent Hero of Contemporary Fantasy and Science Fiction." *Extrapolation* 32, no. 1 (1991): 64–80.

Stratton, Susan. "The Messiah and the Greens: The Shape of Environmental Action in *Dune* and *Pacific Edge*." *Extrapolation*, 42, no. 4 (2001): 303–316.

PART IV

Philosophy, Choice, and Ethics

The Sands of Time

Dune *and the Philosophy of Time*

NATHANIEL GOLDBERG

"In the week before their departure to Arrakis, when all the final scur-rying about had reached a nearly unbearable frenzy, an old crone came to visit the mother of the boy, Paul."[1] That opening sentence of Frank Her-bert's *Dune* introduces individuals who between them can see the past, the future, and (like the rest of us) the present. The old crone is Gaius Helen Mohiam, a Bene Gesserit Reverend Mother. Like all Reverend Mothers, Mohiam possesses her female ancestors' memories. Since these memories include those formed as events occurred, Mohiam can in that sense see the past. The boy, Paul, son of Duke Leto Atreides and the Lady Jessica, will become the Kwisatz Haderach, akin to a male Reverend Mother, possess-ing his male and female ancestors' memories.[2] Paul can therefore see the past, too. He can, however, also see the future[3]; the mélange spice, com-bined with his Mentat training, grants Paul prescience.[4]

The powers that Paul particularly displays make us question the nature of time in *Dune*.[5] Specifically, what does it mean that Paul can see the future, and does it differ from how he can see the past or present? Gen-erally, what does all that mean for *Dune*'s metaphysics of time? In this essay, I answer these questions by appealing to textual evidence from Her-bert's novel and conceptual resources from philosophy.

Past, Present, Future

Metaphysics concerns the nature of existence. There are three meta-physical views (or "metaphysics") of time. First, according to *presentism*, only the present, or "now," is real. Time exists as a single moment like a single grain of sand. While only the present does exist, however, the past did exist and future will exist. Second, according to *the growing-universe theory*, only a moment that is or was present ("now") is real. Time accumulates like grains of sand as the universe grows. While only the past and present do exist, the future will exist. Third, according to *eternalism*, all moments of time are real and there is nothing metaphysically noteworthy about "now." Neither like a single grain nor accumulating like grains, all moments of time exist and so are analogous to positions in space, laid out like all the sand in a desert. Because no moments did or will exist while all moments do exist (eternally), eternalism eschews grammatical tense, instead employing the tenseless present.[6]

Determining the metaphysics of time in *Dune* requires determining whether in the novel the past, present, and future exist and are treated as real. It might be obvious, but in *Dune* the present exists. It is treated as real rather than as illusory. The plot really happens when described as happening, *viz.*, in the novel's present. Actions do not occur in simulations or as ruses. While there are dreams and drug-induced states, these are distinguished as such. Admittedly, the present seemingly passes more slowly for Jessica and for Paul when each changes the Water of Life, the poisonous exhalation of a drowned sandworm, into a potable liquid.[7] After this, Jessica becomes a Bene Gesserit Reverend Mother and Paul something like a male version. The present passes normally for other characters, however; the seeming slowness for them is due to the drug's psychological effects. As explained below, Paul later perceives the past, present, and future all in the present and is confused about which is really present.[8] Yet, Herbert's description of Paul's confusion indicates that there is an objective "now" in which events occur. The present exists, as Paul ultimately sorts things out.[9]

In *Dune*, the past also apparently exists and is treated as real. Mohiam explains that the Truthsayer drug, having the same effect as the Water of Life, enables a Reverend Mother to "look down so many avenues of the past."[10] One can look down only those avenues that are really there. Looking down something, rather than merely thinking that one is looking down something, is what philosophers call "factive," because it tracks the facts. One can *think* that one is looking down something that does not exist. The brain can even cause a person to engage in processes indistinguishable from those involved in actually looking down something. But one cannot *actually* look down something that is not *actually* there. (I return to this below when discussing Paul's "seeing" the future.) Further, after Jessica imbibes the liquid, Ramallo, a Reverend Mother on Arrakis, explains that Jessica now possesses memories of the past, and Jessica sees events in Ramallo's own life as they occur. Hearing Jessica's thought, "*This is hallucination*,"[11] Ramallo responds: "You know better than that."[12] While

Jessica might suspect that she is experiencing a memory of the past rather than the past *qua* past, either way she is perceiving something real; even if a memory, Jessica is perceiving events as they unfold. So, there is reason to read *Dune* as committed to the existence of the past.[13]

The existence and reality of the future is less clear. On the one hand, some passages in *Dune* suggest that the future has neither. Paul's initial glimpses into it happen in dreams, as when on Caladan he tells Mohiam about his dream in which a strange girl on Arrakis will say to him: "Tell me about the waters of your homeworld, Usul."[14] Although this dream later becomes reality, dreams generally are of things that do not (now) exist, even if eventually they will—as often happens for Paul. This suggests that future events do not exist either, but might *come* to exist when they be*come* present. The future *qua* future is not real. Soon Paul's glimpses of the future pervade his waking hours. When he and Jessica flee into the desert after the Harkonnen attack, "[w]ithout even the safety valve of dreaming, he focused his prescient awareness, seeing it as a computation of most probable futures."[15] Computations can attempt to predict futures that do not—and will not—exist, as talk of "probable" futures indicates. What is probable, as a species of what is possible, need never become actually real. This suggests that Paul's access to the future is not to something real but rather merely to computations—hypotheses based on present data and trends—of what could become real. Paul later describes his prescience as a "waking dream,"[16] and so presumably of events that are not yet real. After Paul and Jessica are found by the Fremen and Jamis challenges Paul to a fight, Paul thinks: "Anything could tip the future here."[17] Anything could tip it, presumably, because future events do not exist unless they become present. The future *qua* future again is not real. Paul observes: "There would come an instant when [the future] could be unraveled."[18] Amidst a sea of possibilities, none is real until the "instant" when it "becomes present" by coming into existence.

On the other hand, other passages in *Dune* suggest that the future does exist and is treated as real. Paul reveals to Jessica: "[W]e are Harkonnens"—sworn enemy of the Atreides, whose *paterfamilias*, Baron Vladimir Harkonnen, orchestrated Paul's father's death—"[Y]ou are the Baron's own daughter."[19] He knows this not because he has the Baron's memories—Paul has yet to imbibe the Water of Life—but rather because "I've walked the future, I've looked at a record, I've seen a place, I have all the data." Although one can dream and see a computation of things that do not exist, one cannot look at or walk something that does not exist. Furthermore, when the strange girl of his dreams, now revealed as Chani, daughter of the Imperial Planetologist Liet-Kynes and Fremen Faroula, feeds Paul spice-laced food:

> Awareness flowed into that timeless stratum where he could view time, sens-
> ing the available paths, the winds of the future … the winds of the past:
> the one-eyed vision of the past, the one-eyed vision of the present and the
> one-eyed vision of the future—all combined in a trinocular vision that permit-
> ted him to see time-become-space.[20]

A timeless stratum would be without time and therefore outside it. From
the perspective of something outside time, all moments are metaphysically
on par. Hence, since the present and (likely) the past exist in *Dune*, the
future does too.

Admittedly, Paul can sense "the available paths" of the future, and
their availability suggests that they are not real, only becoming so if they
become present. Yet, those paths are "the winds of the future," just as there
are "winds of the past," which there is reason to think exist. Indeed, Paul
has "one-eyed vision" of the past, present, and future. He can see them all
"in a trinocular vision." As with looking at and walking, one can think that
one sees something that does not exist, but one cannot actually see it. This
passage therefore treats the past, present, and future collectively as real.
Such trinocular vision also "permitted [Paul] to see time-become-space."
Eternalism, recall, analogizes time with space. Just as all positions in
space are all laid out, all moments in time are too. Paul's trinocular vision
apparently grants him an eternalist perspective.[21] Paul "tried to focus on
[Chani], but past and future were merging into the present, blurring her
image."[22] Past and future can merge into the present, which in *Dune* is
treated as real, only if all three are so treated. Indeed, for Paul, past, present, and future "mingled without distinction"[23]—including, presumably,
without distinction in their existence.[24]

Eternalist or Growing-Universe?

Dune's handling of the future seems inconsistent. There is evidence
that only the past and present are treated as real, making its metaphysics of time growing-universe. There is also evidence that the past, present,
and future are all treated as real, making its metaphysics eternalist. Which
metaphysics fits better overall?

There is reason to think that in *Dune* the future, along with the past
and present, exist, and that the novel's metaphysics is eternalist. As already
suggested, Paul can *see* the future.[25] And seeing, like looking down, and
walking, is factive. Indeed, seeing is visual knowing. Because Paul can see
the future, he knows that certain events will occur. If I *see* that someone is
reading *Dune*, rather than merely *think* that I see that someone is reading
it, then (whether articulated explicitly or not) I *know* that someone is doing

so. Seeing and knowing are both factive. Both track the facts. Both therefore require truth. I cannot *know* that someone is reading *Dune* unless it is *true* that someone is doing so. Absent truth, what I might think is knowledge is instead incorrect belief. Moreover, the relationship between knowledge and truth applies as much to the present as to the future. I cannot know that someone will be reading *Dune* unless it is true that someone will do so. Otherwise, I would again have an incorrect belief.

No matter how unlikely, it is possible that one does not have any true beliefs about the future. One would therefore lack knowledge of it. Paul, however, does have true beliefs and, with it, knowledge about the future. His belief that a strange girl will say to him, "Tell me about the waters of your homeworld, Usul," is true. So are his beliefs mentioned throughout the novel about the galactic jihad that will be fought in his name.[26] Each belief counts as knowledge. In *Dune* at least, each is factive. Finally, truths track reality. Whether about the actual world or about a fictional one such as *Dune*'s, truths describe what really happens. Putting all this together, for there to be knowledge of the future, the future must be real. Hence Paul's knowing that certain events will occur entails that future events are treated as real in *Dune* and do exist. Eternalism, rather than the growing-universe theory, is apparently *Dune*'s metaphysics of time.

Yet passages remain that do not treat the future as real. They seem committed to the growing-universe theory instead. Three strategies for handling this apparent inconsistency suggest themselves. First, concede that *Dune* has an inconsistent metaphysics. Although paying much attention to ecology, politics, and religion, Herbert pays little to philosophy. Second, contend that, although Herbert does not narratively distinguish them, some of *Dune*'s descriptions are metaphorical. It is not literally true that Paul "sees" the future and that his "[a]wareness flowed into [a] timeless stratum," that he has "trinocular vision," or that he could see "time-become-space." Third, contrast metaphysical views (or "metaphysics") of time, concerning the nature of its *existence*, from epistemological views (or "epistemology") of time, concerning the nature of *knowledge* of it. Even if literally true that Paul can see the future and that his awareness flows into a timeless stratum, these describe the nature of Paul's knowledge rather than the nature of time itself. If either the second or the third strategy succeeds, then *Dune*'s metaphysics could be consistently growing-universe.

The first two strategies are wanting. Each reconciles the apparent inconsistency at the expense of ascribing to Herbert philosophical or narrative carelessness, respectively. Let me set these strategies aside for the moment (I return to them below). Instead, I pursue the third by finding an epistemology that is supported by the text and enables *Dune*'s metaphysics to be consistently growing-universe. In Herbert's own spirit of relying on religious themes, I borrow from a *magnum opus* in the philosophy of religion: sixth-century Roman philosopher Boethius's *Consolation of Philosophy*.[27]

Borrowing from Boethius

Although I have no evidence that Herbert knowingly borrowed from Boethius,[28] *Dune*'s descriptions of Paul's knowledge of the future are strikingly similar to *Consolation*'s descriptions of God's knowledge thereof. Boethius is concerned with reconciling God's prescience (and indeed omniscience) with human free will. Pursuant to that reconciliation and relevant here, Boethius maintains that God's having knowledge of the future does not require that the future exist or be treated as real. As discussed below, by parity of reasoning, Paul's having knowledge of the future does not require the same either. Those passages apparently committing Herbert to the metaphysics of eternalism can instead commit him to Boethius's epistemology, itself consistent with presentism and the growing-universe theory. Since Herbert is committed to either the growing-universe theory or eternalism, borrowing Boethius's epistemology of time as contrasting any such metaphysics allows Herbert to have a consistently growing-universe metaphysics.

Boethius begins by describing the epistemology of time for beings like us:

> [W]hatever exists in time proceeds as a present thing from the things that have happened into the things that are going to happen… [I]t does not yet gain what is tomorrow's, but has already lost what is yesterday's.[29]

Because human beings exist "in time," proceeding "as a present thing" from past to future, we do not "yet gain"—or know—the future, having "already lost"—and so no longer (at least directly) knowing—the past. Our epistemology of time is time-bound. Our perspective is inside time, specifically the present. In that sense, Boethius later explains, human epistemology "endures the conditions of time."[30]

According to Boethius, God's epistemology of time differs:

> his knowledge … has passed beyond all the motion of time and is stable in the simplicity of its own present; it embraces the infinite reaches of what has passed and what is to come and, in its own simple perception, it looks at all things as if they are being carried out *now*.[31]

Rather than acquiring knowledge during the passage of time, God's knowledge passes "beyond all the motion of time." God's epistemology of time is not time-bound. God's perspective is outside time, neither past, present, nor future. Embracing "the infinite reaches of" past and future, to God all things seem "as if they are being carried out *now*." Although we exist only in the present, God's *now*—God's "present"—*is* as if it is the past, present, and future, because God accesses them timelessly. God's "present" is the philosopher's tenseless one. Yet Boethius is not saying that the past, present, and future exist. Indeed, his view is apparently that the metaphysics of time is presentist. Something proceeds "as a present thing," existing *now*, "from things that *have happened*," in the past, "to things that are *going to happen*," in the future. Thus, only the present exists, although the past did and the future will exist.

So, although Boethius's *metaphysics* of time is presentist, God's *knowledge* of time—i.e., God's *epistemology*—accesses all three, because God "*looks* at all things as if" they are present. While human knowledge "endures the conditions of time, God has an ever-eternal and ever-present-moment condition."[32] God's epistemology is "ever-eternal," and so eternalist, because the conditions of God's experience of time are that of an "ever-present-moment." Hence, "should you want to ponder the foresight by which God distinguishes all things, you will more accurately determine that it is not a foreknowledge as of something that is to come."[33] God does not see or know the future *qua* future, as if God's perspective were internal to time. It is "as if ... it is *now*" but in reality is timeless (and so talk of "now" is tenseless). "From these considerations God's knowledge of the future ... is not named Previdence ... but Providence." God's knowledge is not "Previdence," literally seeing before, as in time, but "Providence," literally seeing forth, as if in space.[34] For God "looks out at all things"—past, present, and future—"as if from some lofty head."[35] This is so even for those events that have not yet come into being and so do not yet exist.

Because God knows the future without the future being real (which is apparently Boethius's view), God's epistemology is consistent with a growing-universe metaphysics. Because God also knows the past without the past being real (which is also apparently Boethius's view), God's epistemology is consistent with a presentist metaphysics also. Because it is consistent with both, I can choose which to borrow. Since in *Dune* the past is apparently treated as real, I choose the growing-universe metaphysics. Thus, like Boethius's God, Paul's "awareness"—the nature of his epistemology—"flowed into that timeless stratum." While, for Boethius, a human being "endures the conditions of time," Paul's perspective is akin to God's, timeless and in that sense "ever-eternal," or eternalist. What for Boethius is God's epistemology is for Herbert Paul's epistemology. The Bene Gesserit "sought in Paul ... a human with mental powers permitting him to understand and use higher order dimensions."[36]

Herbert's idea of "higher order dimensions" resembles Boethius's idea of "some lofty head." As *Consolation* describes God's knowing events in "an ever-eternal and ever-present-moment condition" and God's "embracing all things by its present-moment knowledge,"[37] *Dune* describes Paul's experiencing events as "past and future were merging into the present" and "mingled without distinction." As for Boethius's God, so too for Herbert's Paul, the future does not need to exist for Paul to see it as if present. Paul's knowledge of the future, in Boethius's terms, is not "Previdence," seeing before, as in time, but "Providence," seeing forth, as if in space. Indeed, Paul's "[a]wareness ... permitted him to see time-become-space."[38] According to Boethius, God "in its own simple perception ... looks at all things as if they are being carried out *now*."[39] According to Herbert, Paul's "[a]wareness flowed into that timeless stratum where he could view ... past, ... present, ... and ... future ... all combined in a trinocular vision,"[40] making them look as if they are also being carried out *now*. This is so even for those events that have not yet come into being and so do not yet exist.

Objections

Whether or not Boethius's God exists in the world, Herbert's Paul exists in *Dune*. If my borrowing from Boethius succeeds, then *Dune*'s metaphysics can be consistently growing-universe. Its sands are neither a single grain (as with presentism) nor all laid out like all the sand in the desert (as with eternalism). *Dune*'s sands accumulate like grains as the novel progresses (as with the growing-universe theory). But does my borrowing succeed? I close by considering four objections.

First, Boethius argues that God—and I argue that Paul—can know the future without the future's existing because God and Paul's epistemology is timeless. The future has not come into existence because it is not present, although God and Paul still see it from outside time. Yet, recall, seeing implies knowing. That in turns implies the existence of what is seen and therefore known. Even if God and Paul each have timeless knowledge, therefore, each nevertheless sees the existence of things in a time-bound manner. So, knowledge of the future apparently still entails its existence. Therefore, *Dune*'s metaphysics cannot be consistently growing-universe.

This objection ignores the timeless nature of God and Paul's knowledge. Those whose perspectives are not in time know events without being constrained by time. While human knowledge, for Boethius, "endures the conditions of time," God's knowledge, for Boethius—and, I am suggesting, Paul's knowledge, for Herbert—do not. Admittedly, *at the moment that* God were to see the future, the future would exist. But—and here is the timelessness of God's epistemology—there is no moment *at* which God sees anything. God does not see in time or *at* any moment. The conditions of God's knowledge are "ever-eternal," or eternalist, although the nature of time is not. That events did, do, or will exist—and therefore regardless of whether they do exist—does not constrain God's ability to see them. Nor does God's ability to see (or know) them imply that they exist. Likewise, Paul would not see in time or *at* any moment. Instead, his vision is "trinocular." The fact that events did, do, or will exist—and therefore regardless of whether they do exist—does not constrain Paul's ability to see them. Nor does Paul's ability to see (or know) them imply that they exist. Neither God's nor Paul's epistemology of time entails an eternalist metaphysics. *Dune*'s metaphysics can be consistently growing-universe.

The second objection is that the conditions of God's knowledge can be timeless because God created time. That is how God sees events "as if from some lofty head." Obviously, Paul did not create time. So, it is unclear what allows him to "use higher order dimensions" to see events in time "in a trinocular vision." It is thus unclear how Paul's epistemology of time could be like God's.

Dune's Appendix III, "Report on Bene Gesserit Motives and Purposes," offers something of a response. Discussing how the Bene Gesserit lost control of the Kwisatz Haderach, it explains: "one is led to the inescapable conclusion that the inefficient Bene Gesserit behavior in this affair was a product of an even higher plan of which they were completely unaware!"[41] The book never reveals anything more about this plan or the nature of its planners. While one might read the passage as a Bene Gesserit attempt to skirt blame for mishandling Paul, one might also read it as evidence that some aspects of *Dune* are mysterious. Perhaps the something or someone "higher" at work is responsible for Paul's ability. Perhaps that ability is itself mysterious. Because *Dune* is science fiction, it veers toward scientific-sounding explanations, generally articulating underlying mechanisms to account for features of its world-building. Herbert does so for such things as ecology, eugenics, physical and mental training, and space travel—even if he does not always do so for psychopharmacology. Regardless, Appendix III suggests that mystery might be at the novel's heart.

Third, thoughts occur linearly. They are sequential. Yet linearity and sequentialism presuppose time. Thinking therefore seems impossible independently of it. God and Paul's epistemology, however, I am suggesting, is timeless. If neither "endures the conditions *of* time," then neither's thoughts would be formed *in* time. Neither God nor Paul could apparently therefore have thoughts. Hence, neither could have knowledge, including of the future. This dissolves the apparent inconsistency in *Dune*'s passages. Because Paul has no knowledge of the future—or of anything else—whether or not such knowledge implies the existence of the future is irrelevant. But it also falsifies many more passages. Herbert repeatedly ascribes knowledge to Paul just as Boethius does to God.

There is little reason to think that God's or Paul's thoughts or knowledge have to be linear or sequential. Perhaps God and Paul think thoughts all at once, "as if," according to *Consolation*, "they are being carried out *now*," in "an ever-eternal and ever-present-moment condition." God is meant to be omniscient and omnipotent; denying God's ability to think timelessly denies each. Similarly, Paul's thoughts are not always linear or sequential, as, according to *Dune*, past and future for him are "merging into the present ... mingled without distinction." Although Paul is neither omniscient nor omnipotent, his epistemology of time is more like God's than like ours. If it is difficult for us to understand how thoughts could fail to be linear or sequential, then that might be because, unlike God or Paul, we ourselves are "endur[ing] under the conditions of time" (as per Boethius), lacking "trinocular vision" (as per Herbert).

Fourth, perhaps one need not borrow from Boethius at all. Recall that three strategies handle the apparent inconsistency in *Dune* between commitment to eternalism and to the growing-universe theory. Setting the first two strategies aside, I borrowed from Boethius the contrast between the epistemology and the metaphysics of time. That is because the first two strategies—that *Dune* has an inconsistent metaphysics and that some of *Dune*'s descriptions are metaphorical even though Herbert never signals which—ascribe to Herbert philosophical and narrative carelessness, respectively. Perhaps, however, I too quickly dismissed the second strategy. Maybe one could regard unsignaled metaphorical meaning less as narrative carelessness and more as literary license. As already observed, Herbert's describing Paul's prescience as "seeing ... a computation of most probable futures" does not require that an *actual* future exist. But then Herbert's suggesting that Paul can see *the* future could metaphorically mean that Paul can see *one* of those *probable futures*.[42] So it need not be literally true that Paul's "[a]wareness flowed into [a] timeless stratum," that he has "trinocular vision," or that he could see "time-become-space." Moreover, regarding Herbert as taking literary license still permits reading *Dune* as committed to a growing-universe metaphysics.

There are three reasons against reading these passages metaphorically. First, while Herbert's description of Paul's "computation of most probable futures" is evidence that Herbert's descriptions of the future as real are metaphorical, the language of "computation" fails to explain some of Paul's abilities, including his prescient dream while still on Caladan about a strange girl on Arrakis who will say to him: "Tell me about the waters of your homeworld, Usul." Absent impossibly specific data, which

Paul *ipso facto* cannot possess, there is no way in which Paul could compute (in a dream or otherwise) that this exact event will occur. But then "computation" language cannot ground a metaphorical reading of those later passages. Second, literary license differs from narrative carelessness only by degree. Given that Boethius's contrast between the epistemology and metaphysics of time reconciles Herbert's apparent textual inconsistencies, borrowing from Boethius avoids ascribing to Herbert anything approaching carelessness. So, it is the more charitable option. Finally, descriptions of Paul's assuming a "timeless stratum," with his "trinocular vision," from which "time-become[s]-space," are so consonant with Boethius's characterization of God's perspective—and therefore fit so well with contrasting Paul's epistemology of time from any such metaphysics—that Ockham's razor suggests Herbert is in fact contrasting them. Borrowing from Boethius when reading Herbert has explanatory simplicity on its side.

Conclusion

While textual evidence from *Dune* supports both a growing-universe and an eternalist metaphysics of time, conceptual resources from *Consolation of Philosophy* permit that metaphysics to be consistently growing-universe. Herbert's Paul, like Boethius's God, sees the future without the future's existing or being treated as real. In each case, that is because each one's epistemology is timeless.

As explained above, Boethius contrasted God's epistemology of time with the metaphysics of time to reconcile God's prescience with human free will.[43] It is worth observing in closing that Herbert raised the subject of free will when depicting Paul's seeing a galactic jihad that will be fought in his name. For much of *Dune*, Paul wishes to prevent what he sees occurring from actually occurring,[44] later acknowledging that he cannot.[45] One reading of this is that Paul comes to believe that his prescience is incompatible with his and his Fremen's (and the rest of the known universe's) free will. Because he cannot avoid seeing the jihad, it is determined that it will occur.[46]

Paul is not Herbert's only prescient protagonist. In *Dune Messiah*, Paul and Chani's son, Leto II, is born, who in *Children of Dune* and *God Emperor of Dune* transforms himself into a "God Emperor," whose effects are felt in *Heretics of Dune* and *Chapterhouse: Dune*. Although not omniscient like Boethius's God, Leto II is more godlike than Paul. If Paul's prescience is incompatible with free will, then the God Emperor's certainly is. Yet, Leto II breeds into human beings a gene preventing them from appearing in his or any similar prescience. One reading of this is that Leto II agrees with Paul that his prescience is incompatible with free will. Hence Leto makes his prescience impossible.

If Boethius is right, however, then human beings can act freely in the present because the future does not exist, even though God sees and knows those actions from a perspective outside time. So divine prescience is compatible with human free will. Insofar as Paul and Leto II can assume their own timeless perspective, with or without Leto's breeding program, their prescient abilities would be compatible with human free will too.[47]

Notes

1. Herbert, *Dune*, 3.
2. Though *Dune* considers only two genders, Reverend Mother Mohiam and Paul's abilities are consistent with other genders whose memories neither possesses. See Hart, "From Silver Fox to Kwisatz Haderach," for discussion in terms of real-world genetics of the Bene Gesserit selective breeding program whose goal was to produce the Kwisatz Haderach.
3. There are two cases where *Dune* seems inconsistently to suggest that (female) Reverend Mothers can see the future also. First, in their subsequent scene, Jessica says to Mohiam: "I ask only what you see in the future with your superior abilities" (Herbert, *Dune*, 23). Such "sight," however, could come from superior abilities honed through experience rather than from actual prescience. Indeed, Mohiam responds: "I see in the future what I've seen in the past. You well know the pattern of our affairs, Jessica." That strongly suggests that experience rather than prescience informs her. Second, shortly before his climatic confrontation with the Padishah Emperor, Shaddam IV, Paul:

> gave his thoughts over to this day's accumulated discoveries—the mixed futures and the hidden *presence* of Alia within his awareness.
> Of all the uses of time-vision, this was the strangest. "I have breasted the future to place my words where only you can hear them," Alia had said. "Even you cannot do that, my brother. I find it an interesting play." (368)

Unlike the first, this second case is harder to dismiss. That may not be because of any inconsistency so much as Alia's extraordinary biography. Alia became a Reverend Mother before she was born—Mohiam therefore calls her an "abomination" (462, 477, 483)—when Jessica, unknowingly pregnant with Alia, transformed the Water of Life into a potable liquid. Jessica and her unborn child then both became Reverend Mothers together (explained below). Moreover, Alia is Paul's sister, sharing nearly identical genes with the Kwisatz Haderach. Though female, and so incapable of being the Kwisatz Haderach, Alia nevertheless inherits enormous abilities. Finally, the Bene Gesserit had originally commanded Jessica to bear a daughter instead of Paul, who would become the mother of their intended Kwisatz Haderach. So, Alia, or someone like her, was to be a parent of the most powerful being in existence. That Alia has an ability that even her brother lacks is further evidence that Alia's case is singular.
4. Csori claims that Paul's "ability of prescience was twofold: first, to see individual lines of possible futures in stark details, and second, to know precisely which actions would lead to which future" ("Prescience and Prophecy," 112). If Paul saw individual lines "in stark detail," however, then he would *ipso facto* see points constitutive of those lines, "precisely" representing which actions lead to which future. Csori's twofold distinction collapses. Csori nevertheless correctly summarizes: "Three factors converged in the life of Muad'Dib to give him his special power of prescience: genes," from the Bene Gesserit breeding program, "training," from his Mentat education, "and drugs," *viz.*, the spice (121).

5. Insofar as *Dune* makes its readers think about the philosophy of time, it serves as a philosophical thought experiment. See Gavaler and Goldberg, *Superhero Thought Experiments*, for an argument that superhero comics do likewise.

6. See Prior, "The Notion of the Present," 129–30, and "Changes in Events and Changes in Things," 131–40, for discussion of presentism; Williams, "The Myth of Passage," 149–60, for eternalism; and Broad, "The General Problem of Time and Change," 141–48, for the growing-university theory. Eternalism and presentism are related to McTaggart's B- and A-theory, respectively ("The Unreality of Time"; see Goldberg, "McTaggart on Time").

7. Herbert, *Dune*, 354 and 443, respectively.

8. *Ibid.*, 360.

9. Kevin Williams fails to distinguish time from the experience of time in *Dune* (Williams, *Wisdom of the Sand*, 173–84). The recording of time is also distinct from time, yet Williams ignores that too when asking: "'What could time possibly mean before the church bell, the alarm clock and the wrist watch marked the time, inscribed time in numbers, located it in space or gave it direction'?" (50). While Williams asks this question rhetorically, time "means" whatever the church bell, alarm clock, and wristwatch were designed to mark.

10. Herbert, *Dune*, 13.

11. *Ibid.*, 355.

12. *Ibid.*, 356.

13. That the past is seen through memories poses a problem for seventeenth-century English philosopher John Locke and twentieth-century English philosopher Derek Parfit, who argue that memories are constitutive of personal identity. In such views, Jessica and Paul are not the same persons before and after imbibing the worm exhalation. Separately, Adam Ferner ("Memories Are Made of Spice") does not recognize the implication of his own Lockean view that the new "person" that Jessica and Paul each becomes contains other "persons" within it.

14. Herbert, *Dune*, 25.

15. *Ibid.*, 193. The text continues: "[Time] was a spectrum of possibilities from the most remote past to the most remote future." As I read this, not the past but time's movement from the past to the future is a possibility.

16. *Ibid.*, 196.

17. *Ibid.*, 302.

18. *Ibid.*, 405.

19. *Ibid.*, 198.

20. *Ibid.*, 295.

21. When Jessica transformed the Water of Life into a potable liquid, Paul "realized suddenly that it was one thing to see the past occupying the present, but the true test of prescience was to see the past in the future" (*Ibid.*, 360). Not only would seeing the future entail that there is a future, but seeing the past in it would be to see the future *qua* past. So, there is more reason to think that the past exists in *Dune*.

22. *Ibid.*, 361.

23. *Ibid.*, 380

24. Kevin Williams writes: "Paul enters a Picasso time" (Williams, *Wisdom of the Sand*, 51). Less cryptically, he describes what he takes to be Paul's "diaphanous, manifold, and integral time awareness the *at-once*" (*Ibid.*, 66).

25. Paul's prescience is not omniscience, as he does not always know that certain events will occur. There are "limits of his power... A kind of Heisenberg indeterminacy intervened: the expenditure of energy that revealed what he saw, changed what he saw" (Herbert, *Dune*, 218, 296). During his confrontation with the Padishah Emperor, Shaddam IV, Paul acknowledges that neither he nor the Spacing Guild (whose members have limited prescience) see the outcome of the confrontation (*Ibid.*, 447, 476), which the Guild acknowledges too (*Ibid.*, 465). Paul also sometimes sees probable futures. I address this below.

26. See notes 44 and 45 below.

27. See Sharples, "Fate, Prescience and Freewill," for interpretations of *Consolation*.

28. Nor apparently does anyone else. Jennifer Simkins observes only that *Dune* "draws on the philosophical works of Martin Heidegger (1889–1976) and Karl Jaspers (1883–1969)" concerning myth, tradition, and lived experience (Simkins, *The Science Fiction Mythmakers*, 121). Several authors in Jeffery Nicholas's edited volume (*Dune and Philosophy*) and Williams (*Wisdom of the Sand*) use these and other philosophers (but not Boethius) to explain *Dune*, yet do not claim that Herbert borrowed from any.

29. Boethius, *Consolation*, 5.6.5.

30. *Ibid.*, 5.6.15.

31. *Ibid.*, 5.6.15–16.

32. *Ibid.*, 5.6.15.

33. *Ibid.*, 5.6.16–17.

34. *Ibid.*, 5.6.17.

35. *Ibid.*

36. Herbert, *Dune*, 508.

37. Boethius, *Consolation*, 5.6.43.

38. Herbert, *Dune*, 295.

39. Boethius, *Consolation*, 5.6.15–16.

40. Herbert, *Dune*, 508

41. Herbert, *Dune*, 510.

42. If Paul can see a probable future, then such a probable future exists. It is treated as real. But it exists as merely probable, one of a series of futures all of which are possible, none of which is actual. Eternalism requires that there exists an actual future.

43. See Zagzebski, *The Dilemma of Freedom and Foreknowledge*, for discussion of Boethius's and others' solutions to its titular dilemma.

44. Herbert, *Dune*, 199, 309, 320, 321, 347, 350 (twice), 386, 388 (twice), 405.

45. *Ibid.*, 467, 469 (twice), 482 (thrice).

46. See Nardi, "Political Prescience" in this volume for an alternative interpretation of prescience.

47. Thanks go to the editors and an external reviewer for helpful suggestions and to Alan Sisto and Shawn E. Marchese of the *Prancing Pony Podcast* on J.R.R. Tolkien's works for introducing this philistine philosopher to Boethius's view.

Works Cited

Boethius, Anicius Manlius Severinus. *Consolation of Philosophy*. 524 CE. Translated by Joel C. Relihan. Indianapolis, IN: Hackett Publishing Company, 2001.

Broad, C.D. "The General Problem of Time and Change." In *Metaphysics: The Big Questions*, edited by Peter van Inwagen and Dean W. Zimmerman, 141–48. New York: Wiley, 2008.

Csori, Csilla. "Prescience and Prophecy." In *The Science of Dune: An Unauthorized Exploration into the Real Science Behind Frank Herbert's Fictional Universe*, Science of Pop Culture, edited by Kevin R. Grazier, 111–25. Dallas: Benbella Books, 2008.

Gettier, Edmund L. "Is Justified True Belief Knowledge?" *Analysis* 23 (1963): 121–23.

Ferner, Adam. "Memories Are Made of Spice." In *Dune and Philosophy: Weirding Way of the Mentat*, Popular Culture and Philosophy Book 56, edited by Jeffery Nicholas, 161–73. Chicago: Open Court, 2011.

Goldberg, Nathaniel. "McTaggart on Time." *Logic and Logical Philosophy* 13 (2004): 71–6.

Goldberg, Nathaniel, and Chris Gavaler. *Superhero Thought Experiments*. Iowa City, IA: University of Iowa Press, 2019.

Hart, Carol. "From Silver Foxes to Kwisatz Haderach: The Possibilities of Selective Breeding Programs." In *The Science of Dune: An Unauthorized Exploration into the Real Science Behind Frank Herbert's Fictional Universe*, Science of Pop Culture, edited by Kevin R. Grazier 59–65. Dallas: Benbella Books, 2008.

Herbert, Frank. *Chapterhouse: Dune*. 1985. New York: Ace Books, 2007.

Herbert, Frank. *Children of Dune*. 1976. New York: Ace Books, 2007.
Herbert, Frank. *Dune*. 1965. New York: Ace Books, 2007.
Herbert, Frank. *Dune Messiah*. 1969. New York: Ace Books, 2007.
Herbert, Frank. *Heretics of Dune*. 1984. New York: Ace Books, 2007.
McTaggart, John McTaggart Ellis. "The Unreality of Time." *Mind* 17 (1908): 457–74.
Nicholas, Jeffery, ed. *Dune and Philosophy: Weirding Way of the Mentat*, Popular Culture and Philosophy Book 56. Chicago: Open Court, 2011.
Prior, A.N. "Changes in Events and Changes in Things." In *Metaphysics: The Big Questions*, edited by Peter van Inwagen and Dean W. Zimmerman, 131–40. New York: Wiley, 2008.
Prior, A.N. "The Notion of the Present." In *Metaphysics: The Big Questions*, edited by Peter van Inwagen and Dean W. Zimmerman, 129–30. New York: Wiley, 2008.
Sharples, Robert. "Fate, Prescience and Free Will." In *Cambridge Companion to Boethius*, edited by John Marenbon, 207–27. New York: Cambridge University Press, 2009.
Simkins, Jennifer. *The Science Fiction Mythmakers: Religion, Science and Philosophy in Wells, Clarke, Dick and Herbert (Critical Explorations in Science Fiction and Fantasy 54)*. Jefferson, NC: McFarland, 2016.
Williams, D.C. "The Myth of Passage." In *Metaphysics: The Big Questions*, edited by Peter van Inwagen and Dean W. Zimmerman, 149–60. New York: Wiley, 2008.
Williams, Kevin C. *Wisdom of the Sand: Philosophy and Frank Herbert's Dune*. New York: Hampton Press, 2013.
Zagzebski, Linda. *The Dilemma of Freedom and Foreknowledge*. New York: Oxford University Press, 1996.

The Choices of Muad'Dib

Goods, Traditions, and Practices in the Dune Saga

Jeffery L. Nicholas

Paul Atreides, Muad'Dib, the hero of *Dune*, is a tragic figure, a figure whose downfall is a result of his own actions. What is this downfall? We see it in two pivotal scenes at the end of *Dune*. In the first scene, Paul must turn away from the one he loves, Chani, and marry Princess Irulan Corrino in order to become the legitimate emperor with less loss of life and destruction. Of course, Paul assures Chani that he will never sleep with Irulan, nor show her any kindness. Yet, in the context of his family's history, the readers know that this choice is a heavy burden to carry, a burden shown by an interaction with his father, Duke Leto Atreides. Duke Leto had one regret: that he never married Paul's mother, the Lady Jessica. He loved her, yet he never married her so that the other Houses might think a union with House Atreides still possible. His inability to be true to his own desires weighed on Duke Leto. The second pivotal scene which highlights Paul's downfall occurs when Paul looks at Stilgar, the Fremen leader, and sees something pass over his eyes. Paul recognizes that he has gained a follower, but lost a friend. We can mention other sad moments in Paul's life—when he is blinded in *Dune Messiah* or when he walks into the desert leaving behind his young children to be raised by someone else— but these two moments, I believe, signify Paul's loss of humanity in a way other moments do not.

These reflections lead to the question that drives this essay: namely, what choices led Paul to these situations? Paul's younger sister Alia explains, "For the love of heaven.... Paul's entire life was a struggle to escape his Jihad and its deification. At least he's free of it. He chose this!"[1] Indeed, Paul had choices, as he reminds us over and over. He chooses those paths that he thinks will allow him to control the chaos that would follow his victory, only to discover that he never had any possibility of control.

His choices were always limited, however, because of his education in the particular traditions to which he belonged. Traditions, as I shall define them, center on the pursuit of goods. The term "goods" here encompasses not only possessions and the kinds of things that allow human beings to achieve their goals, but also non-subjective goods. By "non-subjective," I mean goods that are such regardless of how the individual subject identifies them (e.g., as good or not), that are valuable in themselves. The sandworm, Shai-Hulud, is a non-subjective good, valuable for itself, as well as a means of transport. It is valuable in-itself because it is a living being. Paul's primary traditions come from the Great Schools of the Mentats, who focus on computation and manipulation, and of the Bene Gesserit, which focus on political power.[2] In contrast, the Fremen tradition offers alternative goods, such as those that come from the funeral practice or riding the sandworm or transforming the ecology of Arrakis. Yet, Paul was overdetermined to prize power over these goods.

I begin with a discussion of *Dune* as a response to Friedrich Nietzsche. A number of authors have discussed *Dune* in relation to Nietzsche,[3] but I clarify the theme in relation to the discussion of goods. The second section discusses Alasdair MacIntyre's theory of practices and traditions as a response to Nietzsche's concept of the Will to Power. Where MacIntyre reads Nietzsche as rejecting non-subjective goods that individuals pursue, he proposes non-subjective goods that agents identify in practices and traditions. Elsewhere, I have demonstrated the power of MacIntyre's philosophy for responding to Nietzschean themes in popular culture.[4] This essay extends that work by focusing on goods and power. Finally, I examine the three primary sources of Paul's education in the Dune saga—the Mentats, the Bene Gesserit, and the Fremen. The Mentats and the Bene Gesserit are Machiavellian to the core, focused on power and the pursuit of self-preservation. In contrast, the Fremen tradition offers a set of non-subjective goods that vie with self-preservation. My focus is on Paul and Leto II in *Dune, Dune Messiah, Children of Dune,* and *God Emperor of Dune.*

Dune *as a Response to Nietzsche*

Roy Jackson reads Paul as a Nietzschean Hero. Nietzsche, according to Jackson, judges values not in terms of truth but in relation to whether or not they "are life-enhancing"; that is, whether they make more living things or create more life.[5] To be life-enhancing, history must be willing to recast the values of the past into something new so that life does not stagnate. Religion can be dangerous in this situation because it tends toward stagnation.[6] Against this stagnation, Jackson points out, Muad'Dib always "fought the temptation to choose a clear safe course."[7]

On Jackson's reading, Fremen values are not true. They are shaped, in part, by the Bene Gesserit Missionaria Protectiva, a religious-seeding program, and by the Orange Catholic Bible (O.C. Bible), and the Maometh Saari, one of the religious elements of the O.C. Bible.[8] Through their Missionaria Protectiva, the Bene Gesserit imprint or spread various superstitions on planets throughout the Imperium, connecting to religious beliefs already found among the population. They do so in order to provide opportunities to protect sisters who might be lost or find themselves trapped on planets where the Bene Gesserit cannot act directly, for example, because they do not have a group of sisters there "guiding" events. Paul, in refusing the safer path, destroys the Fremen and their old values and ways. What he did to the Fremen sickens him. Paul becomes one of Nietzsche's heroes, "prepared to put aside comfort and security in the quest for greatness, for to go beyond good and evil as understood by the masses is to take risks and even put their own life in danger."[9]

Brook Pearson also reads the Dune saga through a Nietzschean lens. He describes Leto II's Golden Path as an attempt to remake humanity so that it "will never again allow itself to be dominated by a monolithic vision or single individual."[10] More than Jackson, Pearson brings out the sacrifice required of the hero: "the personal development of Leto II into the sandworm-human hybrid is not one that he wishes any other human to undergo."[11] The end result of Paul's prescience and Leto II's Golden Path is "the destruction of the cultural and other limitations inherent in this system."[12]

Elisabeth Frisby notes a number of similarities between *Dune* and Nietzsche's philosophy. For instance, the goal of the Bene Gesserit breeding program is similar to Nietzsche's goal "to create a being higher than ourselves."[13] Likewise, Nietzsche's Superman and the Kwisatz Haderach are bridges which overcome the divide between past and future by remaking the past. Nietzsche sees himself embracing the chaos of the universe, while Paul sees himself as a vector of the chaotic jihad that would prevent human stagnation.[14] These parallels allow Paul to speak for life: "If you need something to worship, then worship life."[15] Like Pearson, Frisby also recognizes the loss of humanity that Leto II suffers in becoming "no longer human,"[16] which enables him to impose on humanity "the greatest evil" so that humanity does not stagnate or die out.[17] Here, Frisby takes "the greatest evil" from Nietzsche's *Thus Spoke Zarathustra*: "The greatest evil is necessary for the overman's best."[18] Leto II makes himself inhuman—the greatest evil—in order to save humanity.[19] Paul asks his son if the chaos of death and destruction is necessary. Leto II answers: "It's that or humans will be extinguished."[20]

Jackson, Pearson, and Frisby reveal the Nietzschean themes in Frank Herbert's *Dune* series. Paul and Leto II recreate the past to prevent the human species from stagnating. In the process, Paul and Leto cause atrocities, destroying Fremen culture and killing billions with their jihads. While Jackson makes passing mention that Paul suffers, the books place greater emphasis on the suffering of Leto II, who gives up his humanity. These articles, however, say nothing about the good or the goods involved. Nietzsche seeks a morality beyond good and evil. That is, Nietzsche believes that "good" and "evil" function in ways, not to determine moral goods, but to exercise power. As a moral psychologist, Nietzsche is interested in how morality functions psychologically in human life and culture as a mask for the Will to Power. Morality "bears decided and decisive witness to *who he is*—that is, what order of rank the innermost drives of his nature stand in relation to each other."[21] These terms tell one something about the psychology of the person who holds them, nothing more.

Frank Herbert is concerned with this drive for power. The Dune series cautions against those who are attracted to power because "such people are imbalanced, in a word: insane."[22] Throughout *Children of Dune*, Leto II denies that he has a personality of his own. He has multiple people living in his head. So too do his aunt, Alia Atreides, who was possessed, and his sister, Ghanima Atreides, who overcame the inner lives aroused within her. Leto II, instead, bargains. In a sense, he is insane (if not clinically). He goes so far in his quest for power that he is "no longer human" but a human-sandworm hybrid. He does so in order to control the universe: ultimate power for 3,500 years. Paul is also insane. He does not have the voices in his head (even if he feels the Baron's presence within himself) that Leto II, Alia, and Ghanima do. Yet, Jessica admits that she "twisted" and "manipulated" him.[23] His attempt to control the future through his prescience and his purposefully becoming a religious figure bespeak a narcissism in Paul.

If Paul and Leto II are insane in their quest for power, they serve the purpose for which Herbert wrote *Dune*, as a warning against the hero. In interviews, Herbert admonished readers, "Don't give over all of your critical faculties to people in power."[24] It seems difficult to argue that Paul or Leto II lacked critical powers. They were Mentats, the ultimate thinkers, able to make calculations in their heads faster than our computers and to let logic guide their guesses to accurate predictions. The mélange spice enhances this ability in Paul and Leto II. Yet, even the Mentat can give over his or her critical thinking to people in power. While Piter de Vries prefigures this by allowing Baron Vladimir Harkonnen to control him through spice addiction, the ghola Mentat of Duncan Idaho in *Children of Dune* embodies loyalty to a ruler. This Idaho sacrifices his life, a second time in service of the Atreides.

Herbert's *Dune* is an argument against Nietzschean heroes. It is an argument about seeking power; we can ask, however, what other goods can we choose from. In the next section, I explore the Fremen through the eyes of Alasdair MacIntyre's concepts of practice and tradition as a way of proposing an alternative path for Paul.

Practices and Traditions

In *After Virtue*, MacIntyre claims, "the defensibility of the Nietzschean positions turns *in the end* on the answer to the question: was it right in the first place to reject Aristotle?"[25] For MacIntyre, Nietzsche accurately diagnosed the failure of modern moral theories to provide a rational foundation for ethics and concluded from that insight that all moral values are covers for a Will to Power.[26] For MacIntyre, in contrast, it was the dissolution of Aristotle's moral philosophy which led directly to a society that treats moral rules like taboos and consider them masks for subjective will. This modern approach followed the breakdown of community brought on by the rise of capitalism.

Likewise, in the Dune universe, society also suffers a breakdown, not with the rise of capitalism, but with the Butlerian Jihad against thinking machines. If we imagine that the Butlerian Jihad occurs in our universe, that we form a continuum with the future depicted in *Dune*, then our time now—the time of MacIntyre and Nitzsche's failed moral theory—constitutes the past for Paul and the other characters. The Great Schools, primarily the Bene Gesserit and the Mentats, arise in our future, their past. They see moral rules as masks for power and, in their own ways, attempt to create an *übermensch*.

In short, Great Schools cannot see moral rules as non-subjective, as something more than taboos. True, the Bene Gesserit and the Mentats differ in their approaches. As Joshua Pearson discusses, Bene Gesserit training is more multifaceted than that of the Mentats.[27] For Pearson, the Mentat is limited in focusing only on computation and logic, whereas the Bene Gesserit look at the nuances of speech and emotion.[28] He claims that this difference makes the Bene Gesserit more accomplished and able to exercise power.[29] Both, however, understand the real goal to be the exercise of power and the ability to manipulate. Pearson understands this point and praises the Bene Gesserit for better understanding their task, as reading emotion and speech is necessary for manipulating others.[30]

Neither Great School intends to make the Kwisatz Haderach an *übermensch*. The Bene Gesserit do not train Paul to be the Kwisatz Haderach and the Mentats do not understand Paul as the Kwisatz Haderach. Insofar as the Bene Gesserit train their sisters to be obedient to the order and to the Reverend Mother, they fail to create an *übermensch* among themselves. In breaking free from the Reverend Mother's order to produce a female child, Lady Jessica may herself claim a role as Nietzsche's *übermensch*. Her claim to that title lies in her breaking free from them and imposing her will on the world. Of course, she uses the tools for manipulation that her school provides to accomplish this feat, especially reading the faces of the Fremen and drawing on the legends placed among them by the Missionaria. The Mentat, in contrast, seek to make someone who can impose their will on the world through computation, yet, like the Bene Gesserit, the Mentat is often in the service of some other master. Both ultimately aim for the Will to Power, the ability to manipulate others and impose their will on the world. The Bene Gesserit seek to accomplish this task, at least among the Fremen, through the imposition of a moral language, which requires seeing all moral language as manipulative.

In a world of fragmented language, moral rules as taboos operate in service to the exercise of power. For the Bene Gesserit, "the purpose of argument is to change the nature of truth."[31] The Bene Gesserit, through argument or through the Missionaria Protectiva, obliterate the distinction between manipulative and non-manipulative social relations. A fragmented moral language "entails the obliteration of any genuine distinction between manipulative and non-manipulative social relations."[32]

In contrast, the Fremen, driven from planet to planet until they end up as outcasts on Arrakis and persecuted by the Harkonnen, stand outside this large tapestry. Belonging to the Zensunni tradition, Fremen can trace their culture to Sunni Islam. In our own history, Islamic civilization kept Aristotle's texts alive for centuries when they had been lost to Europeans. The Zensunni tradition provides for the Fremen and Paul what Islamic philosophy provided for medieval Europeans like Thomas Aquinas: access to a coherent tradition of the virtues and of goods for human flourishing.[33] I am not claiming, of course, that Herbert intentionally wrote the Fremen as Aristotelians. Rather, I propose a particular reading of the Dune saga that sees in the Fremen a culture of moral values, in contradistinction to the culture of success and manipulation of the Mentats and the Bene Gesserit.

Paul, then, is cast, as it were, into the midst of these three conflicting traditions. As such, Paul's choices are the choices all European-American peoples face between adopting a modern moral theory marred by fragmented moral language, adopting Nietzsche's stance on morality and seeing it as merely a means to power, or returning to the traditions of the virtues. Herbert recognized this fact and as Irulan notes in the epigraph to the first chapter of *Dune*, Muad'Dib must be understood within his time and place (the 57th year of the reign of the Padishah Emperor Shaddam IV and the planet Arrakis).[34] We are also told by the historian Bronso of Ix that Paul "was an Atreides first and he was trained by a Bene Gesserit adept."[35] To understand why Paul chose as he did, we need to understand his history and the sociocultural context in which he lived.

The Fremen of Arrakis present Paul with the third possibility of returning to the traditions of the virtues. Paul is so steeped in the moral fragmentation of the Bene Gesserit and the Mentat traditions that his choices are inhibited in such a way that he cannot choose the goods offered by Fremen society. To identify these goods, we must understand the practices and larger tradition of the Fremen. On this point, I go beyond Pearson. Pearson reads Paul as purposefully trying to use the Fremen ecological philosophy as a means of manipulation.[36] In contrast, I argue that he is introduced into the Fremen tradition for its own sake and falls in love with Chani because of that adoption of the Fremen tradition. Lady Jessica, in contrast, can only see the Fremen as a source of power, which is why she leaves Arrakis when Paul takes power.

Practices

Of central importance for us is the concept of "goods." Internal goods, or goods of excellence, are things that we achieve through specific activities called practices. The baliset player, for instance, achieves the good of "expressing one's self through music created by strumming a nine stringed instrument" or the good of "beauty found in strumming a nine-stringed instrument." Playing the baliset produces a different beauty than playing the guitar or piano. External goods, or goods of efficiency, do not require specific practices and can be achieved through any activity, luck, or other external goods. Gurney Halleck, for instance, has the good of fame from playing the baliset; however, he could gain fame in other ways, such as by killing Duke Leto or being the consort of Lady Jessica.

Goods of excellence are goods we desire mostly for themselves, whereas goods of efficiency are things we desire for what else they gain for us. This distinction hearkens back to Aristotle's discussion of the good in the *Nichomachean Ethics*. Importantly, if the good can be stated in three words or less, it is not an internal good. The reason for this proviso is that it helps maintain the distinction between internal and external goods. Internal goods must make some reference to the practice. "Self-expression through music," for instance, is not related to a specific practice. Self-expression through music created on the baliset refers to a specific practice of playing the baliset. Playing the baliset and playing the piano do not produce the same music or the same goods.

My discussion of practices follows that of Alasdair MacIntyre in *After Virtue*:

> By a "practice" I am going to mean any coherent and complex form of socially established cooperative human activity through which goods internal to that form of activity are realized in the course of trying to achieve those standards of excellence which are appropriate to, and partially definitive of, that form of activity, with the result that human powers to achieve excellence, and human conceptions of the ends and goods involved, are systematically extended.[37]

According to this definition, playing the baliset is a practice: it involves strumming and plucking or picking, making chords, pressing finger-tips on the string just behind a fret, tuning, stringing an instrument, etc. A variety of standards of excellence exist for playing baliset, including not only where to place your finger so as to produce the right note, but also excellence in rhythm, in tuning, and in holding a note or chord, as well as the ability to play across nine strings, as opposed to the six strings of the guitar. By meeting these standards of excellence, the baliset player realizes a number of goods internal to playing guitar. In addition, human powers develop—such as creativity and expression of meaning. Finally, the conception of the human end is extended, so that the person who plays the baliset comes to a deeper understanding of the place of music in human flourishing. Gurney's good would be nothing without the baliset, and we see his understanding of the good flow out to Paul, who chooses Jamis's baliset in the funeral ceremony.

In order to achieve the development of human powers and extend the human good, practices should prioritize internal over external goods. Yet, external goods are necessary to maintain the practice. Institutions facilitate the pursuit of external goods. Playing the baliset is a practice; a baliset club is an institution. Institutions are:

> characteristically and necessarily concerned with ... external goods ... in acquiring money and other material goods ... structured in terms of power and status ... they distribute money, power, and status as rewards. Nor could they be otherwise if they are to sustain not only themselves, but also practices.[38]

Without institutions, practices cannot survive; without external goods, institutions cannot survive. As such, the temptation to prioritize external over internal goods is strong. Thus, institutions have a "corrupting power."[39] One can, for instance, play the baliset without ever thinking about external goods, but one cannot manage an institution without considering the external goods. The Great Schools are institutions of different varieties within the Dune universe. Mentat training does not happen in a traditional school, the way Bene Gesserit training does, but Mentats still are institutionalized in the sense of having rules for being promoted, recognized, and tested that are approved by other Mentats. Born in a universe of fragmented moral language, they are subject to corruption as much if not more than institutions in our world, including universities, which pursue external goods like money and recognition, sometimes at the cost of education.

A discussion between Leto II and Stilgar in *Children of Dune* reveals the struggle between the pursuit of internal and external goods. Leto says to Stilgar, "How beautiful the young women are this year."[40] This comment leads to Stilgar's mind racing, to identify these beautiful women with water richness, with the decline of water discipline in the tradition of the Fremen, to the final idea that the tradition could blind one to the need for change. The Sietch, as an institution, guarded against change; yet, in doing so, it opened up an opportunity for Alia to weaken the Fremen and strengthen her own power. That meant overturning the internal goods of the Fremen practices of water rationing and water discipline.

Tradition

MacIntyre defines a tradition as an "historically extended, socially embodied argument ... precisely in part about the goods which constitute that tradition."[41] Traditions are living, and yet at the same time historically and social contained. The "living" aspect is captured in the notion that traditions are active arguments with insiders and outsiders. For instance, science fiction is a tradition that involves arguments among insiders and with outsiders. Insiders argue over what counts as science fiction. For instance, Darko Suvin holds that *Frankenstein* and *Star Wars* are not science fiction, whereas others, like myself, hold that they are. Yet, science fiction theorists, such as Suvin and Frederick Jameson, might argue over what the best society looks like with utopian theorists, such as Ruth Levitas, or over what counts as good fiction with classicists. The insiders will argue over points in their internal agreements—what counts as science fiction or who the best science fiction writers are—while sharing certain assumptions. With outsiders, though, they will not necessarily agree on any fundamental assumptions.

For this essay, we are considering three traditions within the Dune universe: the Bene Gesserit, Mentat, and Fremen traditions. These three traditions do have some shared ideas: all three recognize the importance of the Butlerian Jihad, for instance. Generally, however, their agreements are disparate. The table below, adopted from previous work,[42] suggests some primary differences. Exemplars are standards of reasons which give guidance in how to think through a situation or come to some conclusion.

Symbolic generalizations are key definitions central in defining the universe and the tradition. Values and goods are the objects which members of the traditions desire as good for human life. Practices are, for our purposes, what MacIntyre defines as practices.

Table 1: Three Traditions in *Dune*

Tradition	Bene Gesserit	Mentat	Fremen
Cosmology	Scientific-Mystical	Scientific-Logical	Mystical-Scientific
Exemplars	• "The mind can go either direction under stress ... strongly influenced by training" (*Dune*, 333). • "The purpose of argument is to change the nature of truth" (*Children*, 62).	• "There's no real mystery about this at the moment. This is what we want now." (*Children*, 221)	• "When God hath ordained a creature to die in a particular place, He causeth that creature's wants to direct him to that place" (*Dune*, 159). • "Be prepared to appreciate what you meet" (*Dune*, 251).
Symbolic Generalizations	• *Kwisatz Haderach* • Abomination • Truthsayer	• Supra-logical • The Naïve Mind	• *Lisan Al-Gaib* • Possession • Crysknife • The Maker
Values/Goods	• Diplomacy • Human genes	• Logic	• *Amtal* Rule • Water • Discipline • Strength
Practices	• *Gom Jabbar* • *Prana Bindu*	• Computation	• Test of *aql* • Burial Rite • Sandworm Riding

The cosmology listed for the three traditions is general. We could also list here other key aspects that would be partially defined in the symbolic generalizations. That level of detail is not needed for the argument I am making. The Bene Gesserit and the Fremen share a cosmology that allows for mystical elements alongside science. From my reading of the Dune series, Mentats do not have that mystical view, although Duncan Idaho, as a Zensunni philosopher, might embrace some mystical elements in his cosmology. I have listed science before mysticism for the Bene Gesserit because they are focused primarily on protecting the genetic strain and manipulating it. The mysticism serves that primary goal. By contrast, mysticism is listed first for the Fremen. This prioritizing recognizes that the science of ecology that drives Fremen work in transforming Arrakis is late to their tradition, brought in by Pardot Kynes. The mysticism associated with Zensunni, however, reaches back perhaps to the beginning of the Fremen culture.

Goods and Power

A World of Power

The traditions and practices within the Dune setting provide the characters with a number of goods to pursue, as well as means for navigating their way toward those goods. Just as in real life, power, a quintessential external good, is often necessary for the pursuit of other goods. Indeed, as seen in Table 1, the exemplars in row three suggest that power is a dominant external good for both the Bene Gesserit and the Mentats. These traditions of the Great Schools are part of the larger milieu that Paul finds himself in and must navigate. In that milieu, power is of paramount importance, so that the drive for power of the Great Schools complements the milieu. In short, Herbert's *Dune* magnifies what MacIntyre warns against in *After Virtue*: "if in a particular society the pursuit of external goods were to become dominant, the concept of the virtues might suffer first attrition and then perhaps something near total effacement."[43] In our world, power dominates to such an extent that it prevents human flourishing. In our world and the world of *Dune*, internal goods tend to serve external goods, especially power.

In the Dune saga, power is the overwhelming concern, particularly power in the service of self-preservation, whether that preservation is for the individual, the House, or humanity. House Atreides serves a particular role, defending justice, especially of the Lower Houses; Duke Leto is even called "the Just." The Atreides are contested by House Harkonnen, which is a hedonistic, power-hungry house out only for profit. Thus, at several times, characters reflect on the fact that Duke Leto considered his men more important than resources or equipment, such as ornithopters or spice factories. Duke Leto's rescue of men from a sandworm even caused Liet-Kynes to begin to like the man he was being paid to betray. In addition, the Padishah Emperor Shaddam Corrino IV aligned with Baron Harkonnen in order to defeat House Atreides. Leto was becoming too popular, and Shaddam feared the threat to his rule.

The Mentats and the Bene Gesserit are sources of power that arise after the Butlerian Jihad to serve particular functions, primarily political, one more overtly than the other. The Bene Gesserit serve and pursue power through their breeding program, their training of initiates as concubines, their Truthsayer powers, and machinations in the royal court. Mentats function primarily as strategists for the Great Houses. Their ability to make not only mathematical computations but also gain insight into motivations and activities surpasses even that of the thinking machines destroyed during the Butlerian Jihad. For the Bene Gesserit, politics covers the "need for a thread of continuity in human affairs."[44] The Bene Gesserit serve their own agenda by farming out members to "serve" the needs of the Imperium and the Great Houses. The Bene Gesserit Truthsayer, for instance, is necessary for Shaddam IV to maintain his power. Mentats serve the more immediate function of political self-preservation for individual houses and other associations. Both Mentats and Bene Gesserit focus on developing power for self-preservation.

Paul is trained in the Bene Gesserit and Mentat traditions, which serve the larger social milieu of the semi-feudalism of the Imperium. For his first fifteen years, Paul's education focuses on power: its uses, the possibility of loss, and the machinations that might force one Great House to abandon its home or go rogue. When Duke Leto reveals that Paul could become a Mentat, he tells Paul that being a Mentat would make him a formidable duke. Paul's training in Bene Gesserit prana-bindu gives him power as well, both as a fighter and as a person able to read others. Training in the Voice also provides a significant power, one that must be used with caution. By the time Paul flees to the Fremen, he can see the Fremen only as another source of power. This view of the Fremen defined House Atreides's strategy on Arrakis. Duke Leto sought to turn the Fremen into a fighting force against the Harkonnen.

A Second First-Language

Just as Paul could only become the Kwisatz Haderach as a Bene Gesserit, so too could he only become the Lisan al-Gaib as a Fremen. In this context, Paul must learn to be Fremen; he learns a second first-language and adopts the ways of the Fremen. A first-language is what we are born into, what shapes our perception of the world. Learning to speak Chakobsa, for instance, might let one interact with other speakers. Only when one adopts it as a second—that is, not original—first-language can one understand the nuances of the poetry and the idioms, thus grasping a view of the world as it differs from the original view one has. Paul is baptized by fire, so to speak, with the Test of Aql and becomes fully Fremen when he rides Shai-Hulud as a Fremen man. In learning this second first-language, Paul must necessarily learn the different aspects of the Fremen tradition, including the values and goods of Fremen society, as well as the various practices of the Fremen.

The Fremen funeral ceremony is a practice that involves internal goods. One such good is preserving the dignity of the dead. This yields a variety of external goods, such as peace and friendship among Fremen who, like any human group, have friends who might be angry that a friend or loved one was killed. The ceremony also distributes property in a way that prevents accumulation by a few while making sure that necessary items are put to use by those who can use them. Yet, despite these secondary benefits, the dignity of the dead itself is not an external good. While balisets and coffee services can be gained through other means, providing dignity to the dead can only be achieved, for the Fremen, through the specific funeral practice we observe after the death of Jamis in *Dune*. Thus, when Paul reaches out to lift the baliset and call himself a friend of Jamis, "Paul felt the diminishment of his *self* ... as though he lost a fragment of himself and sought it here."[45] In seeking the fragment of himself in Jamis's belongings, Paul gives dignity to the dead.

Another important practice for Paul is riding the sandworm. Sandworm riding is a rite of passage for Fremen. Their ability to lead the tribe is limited if they cannot ride a sandworm. Obviously, the sandworm provides a means of travel for the Fremen, which helps them escape detection from those from whom they wish to hide. Yet riding a sandworm involves internal as well as external goods. One such internal good is respecting the sandworm as only a rider would. Before Paul captures a sandworm to ride, he has only ridden on the smaller ones that the Fremen use to make the Water of Life. In capturing his own sandworm, he will meet "an old man of the desert."[46] When Paul calls a large maker, he "understood why Stilgar had warned him once about the brashness of young men who danced and played with these monsters."[47] By capturing his first sandworm and riding it, Paul comes to respect them in a way that was not possible beforehand. Another internal good is the particular teamwork of sandworm riders that cannot be gained through other means. As Stilgar instructs Paul, "Remember that we work together. That way, we're certain."[48] For example, Stilgar advises to always leave room for someone else to take the sandworm if the primary rider cannot.

While these goods are internal to practices, Paul is exposed to the overarching goods from the Fremen tradition. These goods entail the transformation of Arrakis into a planet where Fremen need not die from thirst or live such harsh lives. They develop many of their practices guided by the planetologist Pardot Kynes. Kynes and Liet, his son, sought to transform the Arrakeen desert into a water-rich planet, ending the suffering of the people there. Their work and educational efforts made the Fremen allies and helped to mold the tradition of the Fremen, who took over the dream of transforming Arrakis. Liet understood what his father taught: "To the working planetologist, his most important tool is human beings.... You must cultivate ecological literacy among the people."[49] The sophistication of the Fremen can be seen in the design of the stillsuit, which recycles the body's water. By *Children of Dune*, the poor design of stillsuits is a sign of the decay of the Fremen virtues.

Despite learning this second first-language, Paul's first language—the language of power—ultimately determines his choices. Paul chooses power over the goods of community and love that he learned from the Fremen. First, he chooses Irulan, daughter of Shaddam IV, as his bride, and relegates Chani to the role of concubine. Matrimony in this case is not a practice with an internal good; rather, the desire for power drives this choice. He tells his mother, "[Irulan is] my key to the throne, and that's all she'll ever be."[50] Paul's concern here is self-preservation, but of an odd kind. He is not seeking to preserve himself through children; he chooses to do that with Chani. Rather, Paul seeks the self-preservation of the Atreides household. Shaped early on by his Bene Gesserit and Mentat training, he sees the way forward as rooted in revenge and in preserving House Atreides. As he tells Jessica, "Mistake? You think because I'm what you made me that I cannot feel the need for revenge?"[51] Even if as Usul he loves Chani, as Duke he cannot forsake the power he has been trained to crave.

Paul faces a similar choice in *Dune Messiah*: either let Chani die so that he can try to maintain some control over humanity's survival, or run away with Chani and let humanity dwindle to weakness and death. Trained as a Bene Gesserit, he understands the lesson the Reverend Mother Mohiam taught through the gom jabbar practice, the difference between animals and humans. Animals might seek nothing more than escape from a trap, but a human might have the foresight to stay, despite the pain, to deceive and kill a trapper who was a danger to other humans.[52] Paul sees the trap of his choices, knows that he will go blind and lose Chani. Yet, he remains in the trap to free the threat to his kind; self-preservation, in this case of the human species, wins out over other goods. Alia recognizes this fact: "He's the bait in his own trap. He's the servant of power and terror."[53]

In relation to the ecological goods of the Fremen, Paul pursues it in the primary way he knows: through power. He abandons the goods of Liet-Kynes, the ecological literacy of the Fremen. Under Paul, power and wealth become the primary means of attaining the goods of the Fremen tradition. This use of power comes with a cost. First, it lessens the Fremen culture. Even in *Dune Messiah*, some Fremen have abandoned the discipline necessary for preserving water, a change that takes full effect in *Children of Dune*. As noted above, the quality of stillsuits has declined. More importantly, power and wealth provide the means for Alia to gain control over the Mahdinate and abandon Muad'Dib's ways. The Fremen abandon their traditional ways, which is why The Preacher returns to Arrakeen to denounce Alia and the Mahdinate. In pursuing absolute power, Alia grows insane, turning into that which the Atreides hate—the Baron Harkonnen. The Fremen turn into something weak, a caricature of their traditions. The changes to Arrakis threaten to destroy the sandworm and the spice, until Leto II's Golden Path corrects the problem.

Conclusion

Frank Herbert crafted *Dune* and its sequels as a response to the Nietzschean hero. While much scholarship has examined this aspect of the trilogy, focusing on Paul and Leto II as heroes and the threats they pose to humanity, the literature has not addressed the alternative that must be present if we turn away from hero worship. This essay examined Paul, Leto II, and the Dune saga to explore the non-subjective goods that stand in contrast to a Will to Power. I do not, of course, argue that Nietzsche is wrong; nothing so daring could be tried in such a short piece. In taking on that argument, Herbert's *Dune* stands out both for its length—not only in the original novel but through the series—and its philosophical richness. Rather, I have suggested that something underlies the choices that Paul and Leto II make: an alternative to the path of power. That underlying framework is the goods of practices and traditions as defined by MacIntyre in *After Virtue*. Paul is taught a number of practices within three traditions. While the practices of the Bene Gesserit and Mentat traditions focus on grasping power within a milieu devoted to the pursuit of power, the practices of the Fremen focus on internal goods, which can enhance human abilities and develop human conceptions of the good. Although he learns the Fremen ways as a second first-language, Paul's primary language is that of power. All of his choices are guided by self-preservation—whether of himself, of House Atreides, or of humanity. The pursuit of power transforms Paul into a Kwisatz Haderach—a monster that destroys from within. Perhaps the ultimate question this narrative asks, then, is whether it is the pursuit of the Will to Power that leads to the weakening of the species until it dies off.

NOTES

1. Herbert, *Dune Messiah*, 277.
2. Reverend Mother Mohiam refers to the "Mentats" as a class of citizens rather than a

school, which some might infer to mean that the Mentat do not constitute a school. Such would be a misinterpretation. Brian Herbert and Kevin J. Anderson call the Mentats a school, and their *Mentats of Dune* novel make clear that the current canon considers them thus. Mentats are also listed as a Great School in the academic literature (for example, Csori, "Prescience and Prophecy," 114), as does, for that matter, the Dune Fandom wiki. The institutionalization of each school might be different, but that could also be said of many Greek schools of philosophy.

Paul is not trained by the other Great Schools, including the Spacing Guild, the Swordmasters of Ginaz, and Suk Doctor Inner School—so I do not discuss them here.

3. For example, Jackson, "Paul Atreides the Nietzschean Hero"; Pearson, *Managing Power*; and Frisby, "Nietzsche's Influence on the Superman."

4. Nicholas, *Reason, Tradition, and the Good*, and Nicholas, "Of Buggers and Gods." MacIntyre's analysis of Nietzsche has faced some legitimate challenges (see Hill "MacIntyre's Nietzsche: A Critique"; Cohen, "In Defense of Nietzschean Genealogy"; and Korkut, "MacIntyre's Nietzsche or Nietzschean MacIntyre"). To summarize, while MacIntyre reads Nietzsche as a moral theorist, Nietzsche is as much a moral psychologist. While I agree with these criticisms, they are not relevant to the main thrust of the argument of this essay.

5. Jackson, "Paul Atreides the Nietzschean Hero," 180.

6. *Ibid.*, 181.

7. *Ibid.*

8. See Brierly, "A critical moment," in this volume.

9. Jackson, "Paul Atreides the Nietzschean Hero," 187.

10. Pearson, "Friedrich Nietzsche Goes to Space," 192.

11. *Ibid.*, 194.

12. *Ibid.*, 202

13. Frisby, "Nietzsche's Influence on the Superman," 87.

14. *Ibid.*, 91.

15. Herbert, *Dune Messiah* 232, quoted in Frisby, "Nietzsche's Influence on the Superman," 95.

16. Herbert, *Children of Dune* 333, quoted in Frisby, "Nietzsche's Influence on the Superman," 101.

17. Frisby, "Nietzsche's Influence on the Superman," 103.

18. Nietzsche, *Thus Spoke Zarathustra*, 288.

19. Frisby does not accept that Nietzsche would have supported Nazism, even if she recognizes some similarities between Zarathustra and Nazism. Rather, the overman achieves greatness by self-overcoming—which is what Leto II does by becoming a human-sandworm hybrid (discussed below). In contrast, Hitler sought to destroy other peoples. Thus, Frisby does not see Leto II as identifiable with Hitler or the Nazis. See Frisby, "Nietzsche's Influence on the Superman," 116–117, especially note 141.

20. Herbert, *Children of Dune* 350, quoted in Frisby, "Nietzsche's Influence on the Superman," 103.

21. Nietzsche, *Beyond Good and Evil*, I §6, 14 (emphasis in original).

22. Herbert, "Dune Genesis," 72–73.

23. Herbert, *Dune*, 553.

24. Herbert, "Dune Genesis," 72.

25. *Ibid.*, 117 (emphasis in original).

26. MacIntyre, *After Virtue*, 109, 113.

27. Pearson, *Managing Power*, 45

28. *Ibid.*, 39.

29. *Ibid.*, 40–41.

30. *Ibid.*, 45

31. Herbert, *Children of Dune*, 62.

32. *Ibid.*, 23. MacIntyre is speaking here about emotivism. The obliteration of non-manipulative and manipulative social relations is endemic to a world of fragmented moral language.

33. Sometimes MacIntyre uses the term "tradition of the virtues" to refer to the specifically Aristotelian tradition of the virtues carried on by Thomas Aquinas. However, I think he is clear that other traditions of the virtues exist, such as the Confucian tradition.
34. Herbert, *Dune*, 3.
35. Herbert, *Dune Messiah*, 4.
36. Pearson, *Managing Power*, 45.
37. MacIntyre, *After Virtue*, 187.
38. *Ibid.*, 194.
39. *Ibid.*
40. Herbert, *Children of Dune*, 116.
41. MacIntyre, *After Virtue* 222.
42. See Nicholas, *Reason, Tradition, and the Good*.
43. MacIntyre, *After Virtue*, 196.
44. Herbert, *Dune*, 14.
45. *Ibid.*, 400.
46. *Ibid.*, 512.
47. *Ibid.*
48. *Ibid.*, 509.
49. *Ibid.*, 347.
50. *Ibid.*, 600.
51. *Ibid.*
52. *Ibid.*, 14–15.
53. Herbert, *Dune Messiah*, 244.

WORKS CITED

Cohen, Andrew Jason. "In Defense of Nietzschean Genealogy." *The Philosophical Forum* XXX, no. 4 (December 1999): 269–288.

Csori, Csilla. "Prescience and Prophecy." In *The Science of Dune: An Unauthorized Exploration into the Real Science Behind frank Herbert's Fictional Universe*, Science of Pop Culture, edited by Kevin R. Grazier, 111–127. Dallas, TX: Ben Bella Books, 2008.

Frisby, Elisabeth Stein. "Nietzsche's Influence on the Superman in Science Fiction Literature." Doctoral dissertation, Florida State University, 1979.

Herbert, Frank. "Dune Genesis." *OMNI* 2, no. 10 (July 1980): 72–76.

Hill, Kevin. "MacIntyre's Nietzsche: A Critique," *Philosophy Faculty Publications and Presentations* (1992): 13.

Jackson, Roy. "Paul Atreides the Nietzschean Hero." In *Dune and Philosophy: The Weirding Way of the Mentat*, Popular Culture and Philosophy Book 56, edited by Jeffery L. Nicholas, 177–188. Chicago: Open Court, 2011.

Jameson, Frederick. *Archaeologies of the Future: The Desire Called Utopia and other Science Fictions*. New York: Verso, 2007.

Korkut, Buket. "MacIntyre's Nietzsche or Nietzschean MacIntyre." *Philosophy and Social Criticism* 38, no. 2 (2012): 199–214.

Lear, Jonathan. *Radical Hope: Ethics in the Face of Cultural Devastation*. Cambridge, MA: Harvard University Press, 2008.

Levitas, Ruth. *The Concept of Utopia*. Oxfordshire, UK: Peter Lang Publishers, 1990.

MacIntyre, Alasdair. *After Virtue: A Study in Moral Theory* (3rd ed.). Notre Dame, IN: University of Notre Dame Press, 2007.

MacIntyre, Alasdair. *Whose Justice? Which Rationality?* Notre Dame, IN: University of Notre Dame Press, 1998.

Merchant, Carolyn. *The Death of Nature: Women, Ecology, and the Scientific Revolution*. New York: Harper One, 1990.

Nicholas, Jeffery. "Bowling Our Way Out of Nihilism," In *The Big Lebowski and Philosophy*, edited by Peter Fosl, 123–135. Hoboken, NJ: Blackwell, 2012.

Nicholas, Jeffery (ed.). *Dune and Philosophy: The Weirding Way of the Mentat*, Popular Culture and Philosophy Book 56. Chicago: Open Court, 2011.

Nicholas, Jeffery. "Of Buggers and Gods: Friendship in Ender's Game." In *Ender's Game and Philosophy*, edited by Kevin Decker, 124–135. Hoboken, NJ: Blackwell, 2013.

Nicholas, Jeffery. *Reason, Tradition, and the Good: MacIntyre's Tradition-Constituted Reason and Frankfurt School Critical Theory*. Notre Dame, IN: University of Notre Dame Press, 2012.

Nietzsche, Friedrich. *Beyond Good and Evil*. Translated by Walter Kaufmann. New York: Vintage Books, 1989.

Nietzsche, Friedrich. *Genealogy of Morals*. Translated by Walter Kaufmann. New York: Vintage Books, 1989.

Nietzsche, Friedrich. *Thus Spoke Zarathustra*. Translated by Walter Kaufman. New York: The Viking Press, 1966.

Pearson, Brook W.R. "Friedrich Nietzsche Goes to Space." In *Dune and Philosophy: The Weirding Way of the Mentat*, Popular Culture and Philosophy Book 56, edited by Jeffery L. Nicholas, 189–206. Chicago: Open Court, 2011.

Pearson, Joshua Danley. *Managing Power: Heroism in the Age of Speculative Capital*. Doctoral Thesis. University of California Riverside, 2018.

Polanyi, Karl. *The Great Transformation: The Political and Economic Origins of Our Times*. New York: Beacon Press, 2001.

Suvin, Darko. *Metamorphoses of Science Fiction*. Bern, Switzerland: Peter Lang, AG, 2016.

"I suggest you may be human"

Humanity and Human Action in Dune

CURTIS A. WEYANT

In Spring 1971 and Fall 1972, Frank Herbert taught a political science class at the University of Washington using utopian and dystopian novels to explore "the myth of the better life." As told by his son Brian, at the start of each course, Herbert asked his students to define what it meant to be human, receiving "a variety of medical and anthropological answers" in return.[1] Throughout the class, Herbert engaged in conversations with his students about how personal psychological myths infiltrated aspects of everyday life. Such myths, Herbert believed, affected individuals' understandings of themselves and others, and they informed actions and decisions—including such things as "selection of clothing, food, homes, cars, politicians"—that in turn contributed "to misunderstandings between ethnic, religious and cultural groups."[2] Herbert's goal for the class was to explore "unexamined linguistic and cultural assumptions" and shatter "myth structures under which we live."[3] As he wrote elsewhere, "No human being on our 'real' planet is completely free of his unexamined assumptions," and "science fiction does better than any other art form" at examining such assumptions.[4] For example, analyzing Isaac Asimov's Foundation stories, Herbert notes, "Asimov ... operates within a surround of assumptions" rooted in "behaviorist psychology ... that would gratify B.F. Skinner." Such assumptions include that "scientist-shamans know best which course humankind should take"; "no surprise will be too great or too unexpected to overcome the firm grasp of science upon human destiny"; and "politics in [the] future can be reduced to the terms, the conflicts and the structures as they are understood on earth today."[5] In the same way, the stories Herbert used as texts in his class provided starting points from which he and his students could examine cultural assumptions and myths from different points of view.[6]

228

Long before his political science classes, questions about how different individuals and groups define humanity, and how those differing definitions lead to conflict, presented themselves as major themes in Herbert's seminal novel *Dune*. According to Bill Ransom, who coauthored several novels with him, Herbert "believed that science fiction was the only genre whose subject matter attempted to define what it is to be human. We use contact with aliens or alien environments as impetus for human interaction."[7] In *Dune* and its sequels, Herbert presented readers with a universe that contains only humans—no aliens—though the capabilities, physical characteristics, dispersion, and division of humans in the *Dune* universe far exceed those of our world.[8] Much like our world, however, some humans in *Dune* do not recognize the humanity of others, and despite the lack of aliens, both actual and perceived differences serve to alienate some groups of humans from others.

This essay explores humanity in *Dune* through the lens of praxeology, the study of human action. Specifically, it presents four prominent perspectives of humanity from different groups in the novel *Dune*, showing how each perspective influences actions of both in-group and out-group individuals. It also demonstrates how Paul Atreides synthesizes these perspectives, effectively expanding the definition of humanity to encompass all of the groups to which he belongs.

Praxeology: Humans and Their Actions

Praxeology is the study of human action, specifically purposeful behavior.[9] Succinctly put, "praxeology deals with the ways and means chosen for the attainment of ... ultimate ends."[10] That is, it is generally concerned with *how* people act rather than *why* people act. While intent is sometimes revealed through action, praxeology is not primarily concerned with psychological motivation. The proposition that human action is purposeful, even if the specific motivation behind it remains unidentified, is known as the action axiom.

In concert with the action axiom are three prerequisites (or preconditions) to human action.[11] To paraphrase, before a person acts, one must have:

- A desire to change the current situation;
- The ability to imagine a better situation; and
- A belief that action will produce the imagined (desired) result.

The second precondition, imagination, is where praxeology intersects with literature: "It is the distinctive feature of human action, that whenever we choose what to do, we imagine an action for ourselves as though we were inspecting it from the outside."[12] When we act, we attempt to bring an imagined world into reality, but it is also possible to imagine worlds without trying to actualize them. Such imagination is not an empty exercise, for "[e]ven imaginary constructions which are inconceivable, self-contradictory, or unrealizable can render useful, even indispensable services in the comprehension of reality."[13]

Speculative fiction is filled with "inconceivable, self-contradictory, or unrealizable" constructions. Such "imaginative acts increase the range and clarity of emotions which can be experienced by the imaginer,"[14] and thus literature is "dedicated to the cultivation of the imagination ... that form of subjectivity that has always allowed humanity to aspire for other, and better, ways of life."[15] By cultivating imagination, readers become better able to imagine "subjunctive worlds"—worlds that could, should, or would exist if a specific action were to be taken—giving them a wider range of potential actions to achieve their goals.[16] Herbert himself was fascinated by "how we influence our surroundings, the impact of human effort on the world around us,"[17] and he believed science fiction stories can "take you through experiences that cannot be achieved through any other means"[18]; "the fine use of conjecture as a literary tool," he argued further, allows readers to "see the codified myths upon which humans of our time place their greatest faith" and helps them envision "a future based on current premises."[19] In other words, fiction—and especially science fiction—improves our ability to imagine actions that have the potential to favorably change present circumstances.

Four Perspectives of Humanity in Dune

One way to expand our available avenues of action is to consider perspectives offered in books like *Dune*. In his novel, Herbert uses an alternating third-person voice that provides insight into the thoughts, concerns, and emotions of certain characters. In addition, a number of characters reveal their personal opinions about humanity (their own and others') through expositional or didactic dialogue. The clearest and best developed perspectives of humanity offered in *Dune* come from the four groups to which the main characters of the story belong: the Bene Gesserit, the Mentats, the Fremen, and the Great Houses. Most conflicts in the novel occur either between same-group members who apply similar perspectives on humanity in different ways—such as the political conflict between House Atreides and House Harkonnen—or between other-group members whose perspectives differ significantly. Some conflicts also arise due to some characters being members of more than one group, giving them blended perspectives. By the end of *Dune*, Paul represents the most complex and expansive synthesis of perspectives on humanity in the story, and much of his character development is concerned with balancing those perspectives to help him achieve his goals.

Bene Gesserit: Sifting People to Find the Humans

Almost immediately, readers are thrown alongside Paul into the horrifying ordeal of the gom jabbar test. After administering the test, The Reverend Mother Gaius Helen Mohiam describes the gom jabbar as a way to "sift people to find the humans,"[20] suggesting humanity has little to do with human genetics. According to her, pain is "the axis of the test," the response to which determines whether one is human. As the Reverend Mother explains, "You've heard of animals chewing off a leg to escape a trap? There's an animal kind of trick. A human would remain in the trap, endure the pain, feigning death that he might kill the trapper and remove a threat to his kind."[21] While it might be possible to imagine other human actions besides enduring pain in order to kill a threat later, the Reverend Mother's primary distinction is that humans respond to environmental stimuli with reason, whereas animals act reflexively.

At the heart of this perspective is a paradox: through control, humans attain freedom. When Paul asks why the Reverend Mother tests for humans, she replies, "To set you free." The ability to ignore one's instinctual response to negative stimuli in favor of a reasoned response is the pinnacle of control for the Bene Gesserit. In *Dune*'s historical past, people developed "thinking machines," and the Reverend Mother claims "men turned their thinking over to machines in the hope that this would set them free. But that only permitted other men with machines to enslave them."[22] After the Great Revolt, schools were established to develop human reasoning capabilities (among other talents) from which the Bene Gesserit and Spacing Guild emerged.

However, freedom-through-control only works with self-control; to control others is to undermine their freedom. The Reverend Mother says "a ruler must learn to persuade and not compel."[23] Likewise, when Dr. Wellington Yueh asks Lady Jessica why she did not make Duke Leto marry her, she replies, "…motivating people, forcing them to your will, gives you a cynical attitude toward humanity. It degrades everything it touches."[24] She reinforces her perspective by telling Thufir Hawat, "If I desired a puppet, the Duke would marry me." The Bene Gesserit *can* control others, as happens occasionally in the story, but only as a last resort. Jessica uses the Voice on

Hawat; however, as she explains, the Bene Gesserit do not seek to shape people into "human tools." Jessica demonstrates her dedication to non-coercion by immediately releasing her power over Hawat, asking him to consider what it means that a human held a knife to his throat, yet not only refrained from killing him, but freed him and gave him a knife to use at will.[25]

Self-control and freedom aside, the long-term goal of the Bene Gesserit was to produce "a human with mental powers permitting him to understand and use higher order dimensions ... a super-Mentat, a human computer with some of the prescient abilities found in Guild navigators."[26] In other words, they wanted to breed someone who held as much control over his mental faculties, and therefore possessed as much freedom, as humanly possible. Through reason and foresight, the Kwisatz Haderach would have more freedom than any other human, because he would be able to calculate all the possibilities of potential actions and anticipate all of the subjunctive worlds that could be actualized from those actions. When Paul discovers that he possesses the abilities for which the Bene Gesserit have long bred, his choices seem to become more limited; although he sees many possibilities, they narrow to a single, inevitable future, leading him to reprimand the Reverend Mother: "You saw part of what the race needs, but how poorly you saw it. You think to control human breeding and intermix a select few according to your master plan! How little you understand...."[27] However, the freedom Paul possesses through self-control also prevents others from controlling him, and he tells the Reverend Mother that he will never do her bidding. Thus, the Bene Gesserit paradox in which control induces freedom comes full circle through Paul's exercise of his freedom from his breeders' control.

Mentats: Seeing Things the Way They Truly Are

The first mention of Mentats comes from Reverend Mother Mohiam, who after administering the gom jabbar test asks Paul if he has "studied the Mentat" in his service.[28] After Paul clarifies that he "studied *with* Thufir Hawat," the Reverend Mother explains, "The Great Revolt ... forced *human* minds to develop. Schools were started to train *human* talents."[29] She then discusses the founding of schools from which the Bene Gesserit and Spacing Guild descended, without mentioning the Mentats any further. However, the proximity of her question about Mentats to her emendation of the Orange Catholic Bible ("Thou shalt not make a machine to counterfeit a *human* mind"), and the subsequent comments about the Great Revolt's role in compelling the development of human minds, suggests that she sees Mentats as at least potential humans. Lady Jessica's confrontation with Hawat reinforces this view, as she refers to herself as "another human" and "this other human," suggesting Hawat himself is as much human as she.[30] Given the Bene Gesserit view that humans are people who can override instinct with reason, it is unsurprising they would consider Mentats' extreme logic capabilities as grounds for potential humanity. (Jessica's contrasting view that emotion makes Thufir *more* human is addressed below.) Appendix III, prepared by Lady Jessica's "agents immediately after the Arrakis Affair" according its own extradiegetic explanation, describes the Kwisatz Haderach eugenics program as an attempt to breed a "super-Mentat,"[31] further suggesting the Bene Gesserit viewed Mentat capabilities as quintessentially human.

The Bene Gesserit view provides an insightful contrast to the Mentat perspective of humanity—which is to say, the Mentat did not likewise see the Bene Gesserit as human, as evidenced by Hawat's use of the dehumanizing term "witch."[32] For example, when Paul insists he can distinguish Hawat's footsteps from a potential imitator, the Mentat thinks, "*That witch mother of his is giving him the deep training,*" and shortly afterward he calls the Reverend Mother a "Truthsayer witch" and "witch-spy."[33] During his confrontation with Lady Jessica, Hawat stops short of using the term, to which Jessica responds, "Go ahead, say it.... Bene Gesserit *witches.*"[34] When Hawat is convinced of Jessica's betrayal, he questions the humanity of her mental processes, thinking "*who knows how a Bene Gesserit witch thinks ... if you can call it thinking?*"[35]

Although Piter de Vries never uses the word "witch," Baron Vladimir Harkonnen uses it in his presence regularly without any objection from de Vries. More significantly, de Vries's enjoyment in torturing Wanna Marcus is certainly dehumanizing.[36] De Vries may lack the empathic capacity to recognize humanity in others at all; the Baron suggests as much when he explains to Feyd-Rautha, "I cause pain out of necessity, but [de Vries] ... I swear he takes a positive delight in it."[37] When the Baron suggests that de Vries might enjoy watching Sardaukar sack the cities of Giedi Prime, the Mentat responds, "Does the Baron need to ask?"—leading the Baron to admonish, "You're too interested in blood and pain."[38] While discussing ways to get the drugged Duke Leto Atreides to answer Baron Harkonnen's questions, de Vries describes one of his favorite torture methods, dripping hot tallow on various parts of the body, asserting there is "a sort of beauty in the pattern of pus-white blisters on naked skin."[39] The prospect of his own death does not even seem to bother de Vries. After admitting his awareness that the Baron will one day have him killed, de Vries says, "Truth without fear surprises the Baron.... I know as a Mentat when you will send the executioner. You will hold back just so long as I am useful."[40] Complete lack of empathy and conscience is not characteristic of all Mentats, but given the displays of antipathy toward the Bene Gesserit by both de Vries and Hawat, it is clear that Mentats have a common capacity for dehumanizing other groups.

Another question that arises for both de Vries and Hawat is that of Mentat accuracy. Baron Harkonnen calls de Vries "emotional and prone to outbursts" and complains that he "consumes too much spice, eats it like candy,"[41] implying that the Mentat's addiction to the mélange spice contributes, at least in part, to errors. However, a few moments before, de Vries had protested his failure to predict that Lady Jessica would bear a son, saying, "I'm not often wrong, Baron.... Give me that: I'm not often wrong," which the Baron does not deny.[42] The only other obvious mistake de Vries makes is his failure to predict Yueh's double treachery and the poison gas capsule in Duke Leto's fake tooth, leading to the Mentat's death.[43] As for Hawat, he also "made few mistakes," according to Gurney Halleck,[44] and it may be those mistakes were likewise tied to emotion. When Jessica confronts Hawat over his suspicion of her, she suggests the Mentat's emotion makes him *more* human, counter to the general Bene Gesserit view. She asks Thufir to examine his emotional involvement in the situation. His use of logic in everything is useful, but unnatural. She points out to him that it is a human trait that it is difficult to bring logic to bear on problems that affect us personally.[45] Baron Harkonnen also viewed Hawat's emotions as a source of mistakes—ones he could exploit. "Hawat has deep emotions," the Baron tells Feyd-Rautha. "The man without emotions is the one to fear. But deep emotions ... ah, now, those can be bent to your needs."[46]

In considering Mentat mistakes, it would be unfair to ignore the Baron's complicity. When Hawat attempts to ascertain the relationship between the Sardaukar and Salusa Secundus, he criticizes his captor-employer for withholding information that could help his analysis, saying, "Any area is open to my speculation if it does what you've hired me to do.... I am a Mentat. You do not withhold information or computation lines from a Mentat."[47] However, the Baron frequently withholds information from his Mentats, admitting to his nephew, "I know what I have in Hawat and how to control it."[48] One controls a Mentat, the Baron tells Iakin Nefud, "through his information. False information—false results"; thus, the Baron requires that Hawat remain ignorant about Yueh's treachery so the Baron can "feed his suspicions against the Lady Jessica,"[49] which he achieves until his own and Hawat's deaths.[50] Likewise, the Baron orders Nefud to secretly administer a poison in Hawat's drinking water, the antidote for which is delivered in the Mentat's daily meals; it is unclear if Hawat ever learns about the secret poison. Ironically, despite withholding important information from Hawat himself, the Baron criticizes Duke Leto for his inability to "afford the most efficient spies to provide his Mentat with the required information."[51]

Summarizing the above, the Mentat perspective on humanity is one that values logic over emotion and irrationality, and comprehensiveness over incompleteness or approximation. The otherness of the Bene Gesserit is due to the mystery behind their powers, which are incomprehensible to the Mentat. *"Does every human have this blind spot?"* Hawat wonders when Lady Jessica freezes him with the Voice, adding, *"Who could stop a person with such power?"*[52] Failure lies in emotional blind spots, inadequate data, and unprecedented events—such as Jessica's choice of a male child. If there is a common ethic among the Mentats, it is in attempting to understand the world so completely that the future is no longer a mystery. As Hawat explains, "I've always prided myself on seeing things the way they truly are…. That's the curse of being a Mentat. You can't stop analyzing your data."[53]

Fremen: Customs Differ, But the Meaning's the Same

The Fremen are the only group of the four analyzed here that do not refer to outside groups as other than human. When Lady Jessica and Paul flee through the desert and come upon a Fremen troop, Stilgar jests, "What have we here—jinn or human?" immediately concluding, "Human, I warrant."[54] This is not to say the Fremen made no distinction between in-group and out-group individuals; indeed, relationship to the tribe is extremely important, as is status within the tribe. In that same encounter, Stilgar questions his expectations about people who survived the desert without knowing Fremen ways, saying of Paul: "He has lived on much water. He has lived away from the father sun. He has not the eyes of the ibad. Yet he does not speak or act like a weakling of the pans. Nor did his father. How can this be?"[55] Lady Jessica does not trigger the same interest, prompting Stilgar to order leaving her behind. However, Jessica uses the Fremen's assumption of her weakness to trick Stilgar and take him hostage until she and Paul convince him to bring them to his sietch.

Through their confrontation, Stilgar reassesses Jessica's worth, saying, "We make our own judgments on value," and other Fremen, such as Jamis, interject with their assessments as well.[56] As Stilgar explains, "Unless you've been deep-trained from childhood to live here, you could bring destruction onto an entire tribe," indicating that his assessment is not of human versus non-human, but the relative value and worth of an individual to the tribe.[57] After Jessica elicits a trade from Stilgar—sanctuary in return for instruction in "the weirding ability of battle"—she feels compelled to reveal Paul's passage of the gom jabbar test, as a way to signal his "ascendancy" and force Stilgar to reassess his earlier judgment.[58] This revelation occurs within the context of Stilgar mentioning "the test of aql" (or "test of reason")[59] that the Fremen use as a rite of adulthood, rather than a test of personhood, as Jamis alludes when he invokes the amtal rule and forces a tahaddi challenge against Jessica with Paul as her champion.[60]

The duality of a person as both individual and tribe member comprises the core of the Fremen perspective of humanity. When Jamis reminds Stilgar of his "duties," the leader replies, "My duty is the strength of the tribe."[61] This Fremen sense of tribal duty is found throughout the story, especially in the ownership of water: the mantra "A man's flesh is his own; the water belongs to the tribe" is repeated several times with slight variation.[62] Water may belong to the tribe, but individuals possess water-counters (currency representing an individual's share of water held in stewardship), even while the physical water remains in a communal pool.[63] The complexity of the water relationship between individual and tribe is initially lost on Hawat and his men when they, along with a troop of Fremen, are hunted by Sardaukar. When Hawat asks if the Fremen can help his soldiers reach some smugglers to escape the Harkonnens, the Fremen inquires whether any of the wounded men in the group "can see the water need of [the] tribe," implying that a sacrifice for the good of the group might be necessary for the journey to have a chance at success.[64] After one of the soldiers dies, the Fremen move to take him to a nearby water reclamation site, but some of the remaining soldiers initially prevent them. Hawat steps in then, not fully understanding the issue but comprehending enough to preserve the unsteady alliance, explaining, "These people respect our dead. Customs differ, but the meaning's the same."[65] What stands out is that, during those tense moments, the Fremen applied their own view of the duality of humans as both individuals and tribe members to their allies. When Hawat admits he would like to be free of the responsibility of choosing whether his wounded men should die, the Fremen leader responds, "How can you be responsible for your wounded? They are their own responsibility. The water's at issue…"—emphasizing both the individuality of the person and the collective claim on the water that person holds in custody.

The duality of individual and tribe member is also observed in the customs around Fremen leadership. In one sense, leadership among the Fremen is Darwinian: the fittest not only survive, they rule as well. However, the leader is not merely the strongest individual; it is the individual who makes the whole tribe stronger, and "[t]he quality of good leadership on Dune includes providing for the welfare and safety of the group."[66] As Stilgar explains to Lady Jessica, "The leader is … the one who brings water and security."[67] When Jessica outwits Stilgar and incapacitates him, she "best[s]" the entire tribe, but according to the leader, even if Jessica were to call him out and beat him in formal combat, the tribe would not follow her, because she is "not of the sand"—that is, she would be unable to provide security and water for the tribe.[68] Thus, there is among the tribe a consent of the governed, since the Fremen have a voice in selecting their leader, even though they do not hold formal elections. Conversely, part of the Fremen leader's duty to the tribe is an obligation to cultivate individuality. As Stilgar says, a leader "maintains the level of individuals. Too few individuals, and a people reverts to a mob."[69] Part of the cultivation of individuality requires allowing those who cannot support themselves to die, as exemplified in the Fremen law that "[o]nes who cannot live with the desert" are left to die,[70] and the custom that wounded individuals "are their own responsibility."[71] The clearest example of this is Jamis, whom Stilgar allowed to remain with the tribe as a useful fighter, even though he would never become leader.[72] Killing is a last resort, and as Stilgar explains to Jessica, "young men who have reached the age of wild spirits ... must be eased through this period" to maintain the strength of the tribe, preferably without maiming or killing them.[73] Thus, a Fremen leader allows others to flourish and helps them grow stronger, even to the point where their ability to provide for the tribe surpasses the leader's own, giving them an eventual path to succession.

On the whole, the Fremen are a live-and-let-live people—or live-and-let-die, in the case of those who venture into the desert without the tools and skills to survive. Fremen generally get along with the other natives of Arrakis, even intermarrying with people of the graben, sink, and pan.[74] They deal with smugglers, and they bribe the Spacing Guild to prevent satellites from being deployed in orbit.[75] The Fremen are wary of the Atreides upon arrival, but they initially agree to stop raiding the villages they had raided during the Harkonnen reign.[76] Furthermore, Duke Leto—having seen and understood the Fremen potential—hires some of them as household servants and forms a tenuous alliance that benefits his family and loyal subjects after his death.[77] The Fremen even respect the Sardaukar for their fighting ability,[78] though respect does not prevent the Fremen from killing them. The only open animosity the Fremen show is toward the Harkonnens, an understandable response to a House that "sneered at the Fremen, hunted them for sport, [and] never bothered even trying to count them."[79] All of this is to say that, while the Fremen never treat all people equally, at least they treat everyone as fellow humans.

The Great Houses: A Place for Every Man and Every Man in His Place

All of the groups analyzed here have their internal conflicts—Jessica and the Reverend Mother among the Bene Gesserit, Hawat and de Vries among the Mentats, Stilgar and Jamis among the Fremen—but the Great Houses are in many ways more contentious and less monolithic than the others. However, despite differences in governing style, moral code, personal bearing, and long-term goals, some generalizations can be made about the perspective of Great House members toward other humans.

The Great Houses are at the top of the faufreluches, the feudal-style class system of the Dune universe.[80] The plot of the novel revolves around three Great Houses: House Atreides, House Harkonnen, and House Corrino. While each House has its own goals, they share in common the use and abuse of the people below them as means to various ends. This is blatantly and obviously true with Baron Harkonnen, who wantonly kills subjects and slaves, manipulates his Mentats, and commits "[e]very degradation of the spirit that can be conceived."[81] The Padishah Emperor Shaddam IV, head of House Corrino, is more discreet, getting others like Count Hasimir Fenring and Baron Harkonnen to carry out his plans, though he himself kept slave-concubines and, according to Princess Irulan, made assassination attempts against his own family.[82] Duke Leto Atreides is cut from the same aristocratic cloth: he orders Hawat to forge certificates of allegiance to justify confiscating the property of Harkonnen allies on Arrakis; he sends a party to raid the Harkonnen storehouses on Giedi Prime; he boasts about the quality of his propaganda corps, which he uses to inform his subjects how well he governs them; and his worst manipulation is to feign and foster distrust against the Lady Jessica, an action he describes as hateful but necessary.[83] Perhaps the clearest evidence that Baron Harkonnen and Duke Leto use similar methods is their parallel considerations of power and fear as the tools of statecraft[84] and embracing of "the twin pillars of inequality and feudal hierarchism."[85]

For anyone who wants to downplay Duke Leto's participation in the manipulation, and at times abuse, of the people he ruled, there is at least the following consolation: ruminating about the recent attempt on his son's life, "[t]he Duke felt in this moment that his own dearest dream was to end all class distinctions and never again think of deadly order," a dream allegedly shared by the Fremen.[86] The irony is that realizing such a dream, if it could be realized, required taking advantage of his position in the very "deadly order" he wished to abolish. The Duke's promise that "one day water will not be a precious commodity on Arrakis"[87] may have endeared him to Liet-Kynes and his Fremen followers, but following through on that promise would require him to use all the available tools of statecraft.

Paul: This Being Has Human Shape

Paul is the synthesis of the four groups reviewed above. From early childhood, he is trained in the traditions of both the Bene Gesserit and the Mentats.[88] He is the son of Duke Leto, and later he discovers he is also the grandson of Baron Harkonnen via his mother, who was unaware of her own paternity.[89] The Fremen bring Paul into their community, and eventually he unites all the Fremen tribes, becoming the prophesied Lisan al-Gaib, the Voice from the Outer World.[90] As the synthesis of these groups, Paul is able to combine the perspective he receives from each one, allowing him to encompass a wider perspective of humanity than any of the individual groups to which he belongs.

Paul's expanded perspective is evidenced in a number of scenes throughout the story. When he dubs the Harkonnens "twisted humans," Lady Jessica chides him for calling them humans, referring to the Bene Gesserit distinction between humans and animals, to which Paul replies, "Don't be so sure you know where to draw the line."[91] Likewise, when Gurney pleads for Paul to let him kill Feyd-Rautha, he calls the recently ascended Baron "a Harkonnen animal," to which Paul responds, "But this being has human shape ... and deserves human doubt."[92] As described above, the Bene Gesserit and Mentat are already more closely aligned in perspective than either group might care to admit, given the Bene Gesserit's breeding of a "super-Mentat"[93] and the Mentat extreme logical computation as a rejection of "animalistic" irrationality. While Paul may be the culmination of the Bene Gesserit eugenics program, he claims he is not the Kwisatz Haderach but rather "something unexpected."[94] His Bene Gesserit training gives him more observational skills than the average person, and his Mentat training helps him analyze his observations. A large part of his foresight and prescience may be explained by the combination of good training and bespoke genetics, rather than godlike powers of prescience and foresight.[95]

It is important to understand that Paul's synthesis of perspectives does not in itself lead to complete clarity, perfect foresight, and unimpeded bliss. As shown in the paragraph above, Paul is better able than other characters to see the world as it is—something Hawat had prided himself on, at times incorrectly—but that ability also presents him with visions that are undesired and even terrifying. Glimpses of a galaxy-wide jihad incited by his own charismatic leadership cause internal anxiety and feelings of failure and futility long before the events he fears transpire.[96] He cannot see everything, and much of what he sees leads to the same result. Each attempt to alter the future further solidifies it until the moment before his kanly duel with Feyd-Rautha. Paul knows then that nothing he could do would change the future. The jihad would continue, even if he opposed the jihad internally. Legions would march out from Arrakis, needing only his legend to sustain them. He had given them what they needed, a way to control the Guild Navigators.[97] In other words, "Everything he does, at least on a certain level of self-deception, is designed to prevent [jihad], but everything he does ends up leading him back along the timeline to the inevitable."[98]

Given Paul's anxiety and impending sense of failure by the end of the book, the question then becomes: is his expanded perspective any more useful than the individual perspectives of the discrete groups? The answer to that may depend on whether the reader stops with *Dune* or continues on to the sequels. What is certain is that Paul comes away with a larger set of tools with which to predict the future and choose an action with the intent of bringing about a desired result.

Giving students a broader toolset was likewise the goal Frank Herbert had in his political science class at the University of Washington, using texts like Aldous Huxley's *Brave New World* and Thomas More's *Utopia* to explore how personal myths often impede understanding between different people. Through the discussions in his class, as well as his own writings, Herbert tried to answer the question of what it means to be human. His own response to that question was: "It means 'just like me.'"[99] Fortunately, through the literary exploration of works like *Dune*, we can synthesize other perspectives of humanity so that "just like me" takes on a broader meaning, giving us a bigger toolset with which to act upon our own world.

Notes

1. Herbert, *Dreamer of Dune*, 244–5.
2. *Ibid.*, 244–5.
3. Herbert, Introduction to *God Emperor of Dune*, xii.
4. Herbert, "Men on Other Planets," 128.
5. *Ibid.* 128–9.
6. Herbert, *Dreamer of Dune*, 245.
7. Ransom, Foreword to *The Road to Dune*, 13.
8. Herbert, Afterword to *Dune*, 526.
9. Mises, *Human Action*, 11.
10. *Ibid.*, 21.
11. *Ibid.*, 13.
12. Davis, Introduction to *Aristotle On Poetics*, xvii.
13. Mises, *Human Action*, 236.
14. Maitre, *Literature and Possible Worlds*, 61.
15. Berman, *Fiction Sets You Free*, 23.
16. Weyant, *Praxeology and Literature*, 27–38.
17. Herbert, Speech at UCLA, 9:08.
18. Herbert, "Men on Other Planets," 126.
19. *Ibid.*, 130, 133; emphasis removed.
20. Herbert, *Dune*, 10.
21. *Ibid.*, 8.
22. *Ibid.*, 11.
23. *Ibid.*, 30.

24. *Ibid.*, 64.
25. *Ibid.*, 153–4.
26. *Ibid.*, 492.
27. *Ibid.*, 463.
28. *Ibid.*, 11.
29. *Ibid.*
30. *Ibid.*, 154.
31. *Ibid.*, 492.
32. Hawat is not the only person to refer to the Bene Gesserit as witches: Paul thinks of the Reverend Mother as a "fatuous old witch" (26), later refers to "the old witches" of the Bene Gesserit school (195), and calls the Reverend Mother a witch just before his duel with Feyd-Rautha (462, 465); the Harkonnen troopers who kidnap Paul and Jessica refer to both the Reverend Mother and Jessica as witches (163–4); the Princess Irulan writes that her father called her "a witch like all the others" (199); Gurney Halleck refers to Jessica as a witch several times (250, 411, 418); when Paul and Jessica are waylaid by Stilgar's band of Fremen, they call her a "Bene Gesserit witch" (277); and the Baron Harkonnen uses the word "witch" in reference to Lady Jessica (16, 18, 229), Wanna Marcus (174), and the Reverend Mother (358). At one point, when Baron Harkonnen meets the Emperor's retinue on Arrakis, the narrator even calls the Reverend Mother "witch" (444–6). That others refer to the Bene Gesserit as witches reinforces the dehumanizing use of the word by the Mentat.
33. Herbert, *Dune*, 28, 30.
34. *Ibid.*, 151.
35. *Ibid.*, 208.
36. *Ibid.*, 173–74.
37. *Ibid.*, 15.
38. *Ibid.*, 15–16.
39. *Ibid.*, 178.
40. *Ibid.*, 15.
41. *Ibid.*, 16.
42. *Ibid.*
43. *Ibid.*, 179–80. This could be considered a double mistake, since it contradicts de Vries's earlier declaration that he knew when Baron Harkonnen would execute him (15). Whether de Vries was correct is a matter for debate. It is possible the Baron could have executed Piter, but it was not a foregone conclusion. After de Vries's death, the Baron routinely admonishes those who suggest he had disposed of his Mentat lightly. For example, the Baron calls de Vries as his "most valuable Mentat" when talking to Iakin Nefud about needing a new Mentat (229), then becomes brusque with Rabban's suggestion the Baron had grown tired of de Vries and had him killed, saying, "You insinuate that I obliterated Piter as one obliterates a trifle... I am not so stupid, Nephew" (231). (In contrast, the Baron reinforces his conscious disposition of Yueh, calling the doctor "a wild sort of weapon to leave about," adding, "I didn't obliterate him casually.") While chiding Feyd-Rautha for a lack of subtlety, the Baron "found himself regretting the loss of Piter, the Mentat. There had been a man of delicate, devilish subtlety" (359). When bluffing Hawat about de Vries' death, the Baron says, "He became too familiar, too demanding of me," to which Hawat replies, "You assure me you don't waste a useful man" (367). Given the tonal shift in the Baron's attitude toward de Vries while alive and after his death, it is unclear whether he would definitely have executed the Mentat. In any case, de Vries's miscalculation about Yueh's ability to attack the Harkonnens obviated the need for the Baron to have him executed.
44. *Ibid.*, 250.
45. *Ibid.*, 151.
46. *Ibid.*, 361.
47. *Ibid.*, 364.
48. *Ibid.*, 361.
49. *Ibid.*, 228.
50. *Ibid.*, 460.
51. *Ibid.*, 229.

52. *Ibid.*, 153.
53. *Ibid.*, 204.
54. *Ibid.*, 272.
55. *Ibid.*, 273.
56. *Ibid.*, 274.
57. *Ibid.*
58. *Ibid.*, 278–9.
59. *Ibid.*, 279, 497.
60. *Ibid.*, 290–3, 497, 514. When Stilgar calls Paul "but a boy," Jamis interrupts, "You named him a man... His mother *says* he's been through the gom jabbar." The implication is that, to the Fremen, the gom jabbar is a test of manhood (or adulthood) rather than personhood, although Jamis may be disingenuous here, considering Stilgar continues to refer to Paul as "child" and "boy," and Jessica likewise thinks of him as a boy throughout the confrontation. Nonetheless, Stilgar allows the fight to happen, a de facto acknowledgement of both Paul's personhood and manhood.
61. *Ibid.*, 273.
62. *Ibid.*, 211, 302, 491.
63. *Ibid.*, 303, 307.
64. *Ibid.*, 207.
65. *Ibid.*, 211.
66. Barton-Kriese, "Exploring Divergent Realities," 212.
67. Herbert, *Dune*, 282.
68. *Ibid.*, 282–83.
69. *Ibid.*, 285.
70. *Ibid.*, 273, 410.
71. *Ibid.*, 207.
72. *Ibid.*, 291.
73. *Ibid.*, 285.
74. *Ibid.*, 38.
75. *Ibid.*, 84–5, 283.
76. *Ibid.*, 50.
77. *Ibid.*, 42–4, 50, 84. This sentiment is reiterated when Duke Leto muses, "If anything could buy a future for the Atreides line, the Fremen just might do it" (78). The nascent alliance between the Atreides and the Fremen is based in part on similarities of leadership values. When Stilgar tells Leto not to unsheathe the crysknife of the courier who died trying to warn Atreides forces about Harkonnen soldiers disguised as Fremen, Stilgar says, "It is said that the Duke Leto Atreides rules with the consent of the governed." Leto responds, "Sir, I honor and respect the personal dignity of any man who respects my dignity. I am indeed indebted to you. And I always pay my debts" (91–2). The Shadout Mapes said something similar to Paul immediately after the hunter-seeker assassination attempt, telling him that "we Fremen pay our debts—be they black debts or white debts" (68). There is no evidence Paul told his father about the Shadout's words, but the Duke's parallel phrasing helps convince Stilgar of the Atreides' worth as allies.
78. *Ibid.*, 210, 213.
79. *Ibid.*, 44.
80. *Ibid.*, 501.
81. *Ibid.*, 44, 127, 313, 357, 362.
82. *Ibid.*, 255.
83. *Ibid.*, 90, 99, 102–04, 182.
84. *Ibid.*, 104, 226. Lady Jessica adds blackmail to the toolbox of statecraft (220); since blackmail is the use of power to instill fear, it could be viewed as an application of the tools Duke Leto and Baron Harkonnen delineate.
85. DiTomasso, "History and Historical Effect in *Dune*," 321.
86. Herbert, *Dune*, 78
87. *Ibid.*, 129.
88. *Ibid.*, 5–6, 26, 45–46.

89. *Ibid.*, 194–95.
90. *Ibid.*, 432, 493.
91. *Ibid.*, 194.
92. *Ibid.*, 466.
93. *Ibid.*, 492.
94. *Ibid.*, 194.
95. For additional discussion of prescience, see Nardi "Political Prescience," and Goldberg, "The Sands of Time" in this volume.
96. Herbert, *Dune*, 340, 377–78, 453.
97. *Ibid.*, 467.
98. Spinrad, "Emperor of Everything," 155.
99. Herbert, *Dreamer of Dune*, 244–45.

Works Cited

Barton-Kriese, Paul. "Exploring Divergent Realities: Using Science Fiction to Teach Introductory Political Science." *Extrapolation* 34, no. 3 (Fall 1993): 209–15.

Berman, Russell A. *Fiction Sets You Free: Literature, Liberty, and Western Culture.* Iowa City: University of Iowa Press, 2007.

Davis, Michael. Introduction to *Aristotle on Poetics*, translated by Seth Benardete and Michael Davis. South Bend, IN: St. Augustine's Press, 2002.

DiTommaso, Lorenzo. "History and Historical Effect in Frank Herbert's 'Dune,'" *Science Fiction Studies* 19, no. 3 (November 1992): 311–325.

Herbert, Brian. Afterword to *Dune*, 40th Anniversary edition, by Frank Herbert, 521–528. New York: Ace Books, 2005.

Herbert, Brian. *Dreamer of Dune: The Biography of Frank Herbert.* New York: Tor, 2003.

Herbert, Brian. Introduction to *God Emperor of Dune*, by Frank Herbert, ix–xv. New York: Ace Books, 2019.

Herbert, Frank. *Dune*, 40th Anniversary ed. 1965. New York: Ace Books, 2005.

Herbert, Frank. "Men on Other Planets." In *The Craft of Science Fiction: A Symposium on Writing Science Fiction and Science Fantasy*, edited by Reginald Bretnor. New York: Harper & Row, 1976.

Herbert, Frank. Speech at UCLA, April 17, 1985. UCLA Campus Events Commission Archive, July 11, 2016. http://youtu.be/5IfgBX1EW00.

Maitre, Doreen. *Literature and Possible Worlds.* London: Middlesex Polytechnic Press, 1983.

Mises, Ludwig von. *Human Action: A Treatise on Economics.* 4th ed. New York: Liberty Fund, 2007.

Ransom, Bill. Foreword to *The Road to Dune*, by Frank Herbert, Brian Herbert, and Kevin J. Anderson, 11–16. New York: Tor, 2005.

Spinrad, Norman. "Emperor of Everything." *Science Fiction in the Real World.* Southern Carbondale, IL: Illinois University Press, 1990: 149–164.

Weyant, Curtis A. *Praxeology and Literature.* Masters thesis, Signum University, 2017.

Belief Is the Mind-Killer

The Bene Gesserit's Transcendental Pragmatism

KEVIN WILLIAMS

"When you believe something is right or wrong, true or false, you believe the assumptions in the words which express the arguments."[1] What does it mean to believe? Right and wrong, true and false, after all, do have meaning. But does a true statement, for example, *represent* a sense that is already there, immutable, just waiting to be found? Or does the statement *make* sense? Are words creative, malleable, historical? One's orientation to knowledge, no matter how reassuring or disorienting, is based on the assumptions placed on words. These assumptions are accessible by looking at language—the structure which makes communication practical, and speech—the living and breathing act of putting language into action. To avoid ignorance of the assumptions that belief engenders, or at least to see the presuppositions for what they are, the Bene Gesserit demonstrate a transcendental pragmatism. This is not so much a theory, but a methodology that examines the presuppositions and practices of ideologies, mythologies, and religions—belief systems that encyst believers. Their own convictions, for all their eloquence, are minimal and founded on a rigorous examination and continuous interrogation of experience. After all, as the Reverend Mother Taraza implored Miles Teg to understand, "The mind of the believer stagnates."[2] The true believer, the person who holds onto belief without continuous, critical interrogation, risks acting on preconceptions, and fails to see through the veil of assumptions a belief casts; the believer gives themselves to the code, creed, law, or myth that the belief propagates.

To counter stagnation, and ever recreate themselves, the Bene Gesserit take up a transcendental awareness. That is, acolytes learn to reflect on pre-reflective experience, and to question tacit presuppositions. Lucilla, when stranded on Gammu, takes up this meditative stance, this Bene Gesserit "naïveté."

Her proctors had called this "the innocence that goes naturally with inexperience, a condition often confused with ignorance." Into this naïveté all things flowed. It was close to Mentat performance. Information entered without prejudgment. 'You are a mirror upon which the universe is reflected. That reflection is all you experience. Images bounce from your senses. Hypotheses arise. Important even when wrong. Here is the exceptional case where more than one wrong can produce dependable decisions.[3]

The Bene Gesserit are, at the same time, pragmatic. As the Reverend Mother Odrade counsels the Honored Matre Murbella, "Look for the consequences.... That's how you ferret out things that work. That's what our much-vaunted truths are all about."[4] Beliefs, and with them, convictions, judgments, truths, and so on, are painted by the Bene Gesserit not as fixed objects of or for thought but as maps for action. They value challenging and undercutting belief-systems by seeing assumptions, borne on the wings of arbitrary signifiers, as guides for action. The Bene Gesserit's transcendental pragmatism is expressed throughout the Dune series, but most poignantly in *Chapterhouse: Dune*, in which they proceed to educate or indoctrinate others into their way of thinking.

The Education of Murbella

At the opening of *Chapterhouse: Dune*, Mother Superior Darwi Odrade resides in Central on Chapterhouse. Odrade takes up the education of the Honored Matre Murbella, who is the only Honored Matre ever captured by the Bene Gesserit. Murbella poses a grave threat because the Honored Matres seek to destroy the Bene Gesserit. Odrade, however, has other plans; she hopes to unify the two sects. If Murbella can be transformed, converted, from Honored Matre to Bene Gesserit, then the two warring factions can potentially be integrated—a hybrid.[5] The means of Murbella's transformation is a complete re-evaluation of her beliefs, her truths—a complete rebuilding of ontological, epistemological, and axiological tenets. This is largely accomplished using words as weapons: "If you believe certain words, you believe their hidden argument."[6] The Bene Gesserit employ a lexical engineering designed to reveal the hidden assumptions in the Honored Matres' philosophy. As Murbella notes, "They're so damned clever with their word-weapons!"[7]

Odrade's linguistic re-education of Murbella follows a system of deprogramming and reprogramming.[8] Words are weaponized to disarm, damage, and destroy Murbella's Honored Matre consciousness (her held beliefs). We can see results when Murbella and Duncan Idaho are residing in a no-ship. Murbella reflects on an encounter with the Reverend Mother, and on how Odrade's words now shape her thoughts, despairing "of ever rooting out all of the cheating in her past."[9] She sees ingrained patterns of how "to simulate a need and gain attention" as cheating; the ability to regurgitate on demand: "That was called education."[10] Murbella immediately takes up a reactive stance to Odrade's teaching about rooting out cheating, wondering, "*Why should I?*" She reflects and quickly realizes, "More cheating!" She recognizes the bad faith in her previous thought. Leto II, the God Emperor of Dune, had considered bad faith: "If you live in bad faith, lies will appear to you like truth."[11] Put another way, Murbella realizes that she is cheating herself in that moment, and sets herself on a path that actually roots out the cheating behavior. In doing so, she internalizes Odrade's lesson: Murbella *should* root out the cheating inherent in her Honored Matre consciousness.[12] Odrade reflects on Murbella's progress: "Words, words, words. Murbella was tangled in questions of philosophy. A dead end if Odrade had ever encountered one."[13]

Word weapons also penetrate Murbella's *un*conscious; they enter and focus her dreams. In a nightmare, she appears microscopic, swimming in an enormous, echoing place; the words "data reservoir" appear around her with animated jaws.[14] A data reservoir is an untapped potential—exactly what Murbella is at that moment. Word weapons appear to have accomplished their task when Murbella can actually laugh at herself; this is something no Honored Matre could do. A Bene Gesserit, on the other hand, likely sees the cosmic humor of the human condition. When Murbella laughs, she is breaking bonds. She becomes free to walk her own path, even if it means becoming complicit in the Sisterhood's plans.[15]

Murbella further realizes, "My oath to Honored Matres was only words. An oath to the Bene Gesserit can be no more."[16] Ultimately, her bond is not founded on any thing, that is, no metaphysical postulate, no God or first cause. If metaphysics consists of belief, of first principles set in an ontological, epistemological, and axiological matrix, then an oath in "words" is essentially groundless, arbitrary, founded on the indeterminacy of communication, and not on a grand narrative or metaphysical postulate. Odrade's methodology works because Murbella believed in an Honored Matre mythos; therefore, she can abandon this position. As Herbert notes in *Dune Messiah*, "Belief can be manipulated. Only knowledge is dangerous."[17]

When Murbella is converted from Honored Matre to Bene Gesserit, she recites an oath—just words. Later, when she has internalized the Bene Gesserit way, the words come back to her. She realizes that not only was her original cynicism recognized by the Bene Gesserit proctor, it was allowed. Indeed, her criticism of the Bene Gesserit was a critical act—she was allowed to be critical of the Bene Gesserit because she must ultimately be critical of everything. She later repeats those same words with an authentic voice. As the words flood her awareness, a tear falls down her cheek:

> I stand in the sacred human presence. As I do now, so should you stand some day. I pray to your presence that this be so. Let the future remain uncertain for that is the canvas to receive our desires. Thus the human condition faces its perpetual tabula rasa. We possess no more than this moment where we dedicate ourselves continuously to the sacred presence we share and create.[18]

Murbella focuses on the moment, the transcendental, pragmatic moment, in which we find ourselves as creative beings. Where the Honored Matres had sown finitude and absolutes, now the Bene Gesserit opened her to infinity.[19] She had ridden different realities to a new potential.

Another basic lesson concerns the understanding and deconstruction of conventions or communication systems. As Murbella sits in repose, Odrade's teaching echoes in her thoughts: "Conventional education? ... Behind that facade of wisdom, the Bene Gesserit were unconventional. They often did not think about teaching; they just did it."[20] Murbella's Honored Matre education stands as an emblem of convention and false consciousness next to the Bene Gesserit's distrust of conventions and search for authentic consciousness. Conventional education teaches the student how to lie and cheat, to repeat knowledge that is not theirs, but is rather the understanding of the master. More importantly, conventional education is based on bad faith. Students are under pressure to adopt a consciousness not their own, thus disavowing their personal freedom, their own being, and their authentic life.

Conventional education is predicated on the semantics of facts and figures. One learns a variety of codes, weights, and measures that are regurgitated to the overseers. Alternatively, the intended relevance is not revealed to or intuited by the student. Such teaching begins and ends with definitions, and proceeds by the method of emulation of adults by children.[21] Herbert gives voice to this critique in *Chapterhouse: Dune*: "[Murbella] learned cheating as an infant.... Many 'how to's' in the cheating pattern. The older she got, the easier the cheating."[22]

The archetypal psychologist James Hillman suggests that the psyche resides neither in some subjective mind nor in an objective reality, but rather in-between, in a relationship of consciousness, intersubjectivity, and the world.[23] He relates diseases of the body to problematics of culture: An educational system, for example, can be bulimic; students are fed prepackaged knowledge and wisdom, and then asked to regurgitate on demand; that is, to repeat knowledge handed down from adults rather than develop their own abilities. Buildings can be depressed, dilapidated, and run-down; people work in fields of cubicles, and dull, lifeless board-rooms. Institutions have no heart; people are tools for the purpose of doing business. Health and retirement plans atrophy. Our education system is increasingly narrowed, clogged by the cholesterol of a common curriculum. Commutes and customer relations are built on hurry-up-and-wait, manic-depressive cycles, stop and go traffic.[24] Hillman suggests that a pragmatic course for authentic living requires overcoming the emphasis we put on the subject and object, and suggests a turn that is intersubjective; the field in which one lives is consciousness, and its significance is generated by persons living in the world.

Odrade rejects such a bulimic education. In fact, she suggests in *Chapterhouse* that the dampening of imagination brought about by the practice of regurgitation is not education, but merely passing down convention and custom—in other terms, ideology, and mythology.[25] This conventional vision imposes false limits; it stunts one's growth because one accepts meanings as given, instead of understanding that significance is created. We can say that knowledge is power, but real power comes from the ability to create what passes for knowledge.[26] One can, however, seek knowledge by testing the limits of the possible; then one can see knowledge as constructed. As Darwi Odrade says:

> Making workable choices occurs in a crucible of informative mistakes. Thus Intelligence accepts fallibility. And when absolute (infallible) choices are not known, intelligence takes chances with limited data in an arena where mistakes are not only possible but also necessary.[27]

Lucilla's (Attempted) Education of Dama

While Lucilla is stranded on Junction, she receives an audience with The Great Honored Matre, Dama.[28] During her interrogation, Lucilla experiments to see how far she can go to understand the Honored Matre, and educates Dama in the ways of the Bene Gesserit at the same time. Lucilla begins by noting that the Bene Gesserit have no conventional government. She explains, "There's no such thing as a social code to meet all necessities."[29] The Bene Gesserit are, in this way, somewhat anarchistic, preferring no overseer (be it person or creed) to delimit their course of action. The discourse settles into an account of bureaucracies, and the difference between law and regulation. "Laws convey the myth of enforced change…. Laws enforce the future."[30] Pass a new law to keep something unwanted from happening ever again. Laws bring about a constant crisis of politics, e.g., "Power in my time! To hell with my descendants!"[31] If laws look to the future, then regulations look to the past. They work to solidify myths, the stories about how we once were. Both laws and regulations work to encyst believers in myths of stability.

Consider the consequences. "[L]aws keep you from adapting."[32] Patterns become entrenched. Lucilla notes, "Isn't it odd ... how rebels all too soon fall into old patterns if they are victorious?" It's not that "power corrupts," and that "absolute power corrupts absolutely," as Dama regurgitates that hackneyed phrase, but rather, as Lucilla corrects, that "power attracts the corruptible."[33] The Bene Gesserit "believe there's a morality above any law, which must stand watchdog on all attempts at unchanging regulation."[34] As Dama fails to grasp the Reverend Mother's argument, Lucilla continues: "Laws are dangerous to everyone.... They have no human understanding in and of themselves."[35] Laws must be interpreted (and thus require a specialist, bureaucratic caste of persons to practice hermeneutics). This remains the case in spite of those who speak in singularities, e.g., "The law is the law."[36] Laws, and reactions to them, set off perilous states of affairs—anarchy, chaos, rebels, terrorists, jihad. At this point in the conversation Dama suggests that the Bene Gesserit practice democracy. Lucilla responds, "with an alertness you cannot imagine."[37] In contradistinction to the Honored Matres, rebels who "originated as terrorists," bureaucrats entrenched in law, the Bene Gesserit, place consciousness in front of any fixed way of conceiving themselves.[38]

How distinct is the difference between the Honored Matre and the Bene Gesserit? How distinct is the difference between Rome and Athens? Latin and Greek? The difference is stark. The Honored Matres' politics of ruling is autocratic bureaucracy and domination, with the Grand Honored Matre as the grand governor. The Bene Gesserit, however, steer themselves, and the sisterhood, through political waters; "Real boats rock," as Odrade says.[39] The Bene Gesserit are the pilots of a pragmatic approach to knowledge, and a transcendental tack to understanding being.

The Education of the Fremen

"The education of the Fremen," refers to the way that the Bene Gesserit sowed mythic images in order to make the Fremen believe in certain phenomena. The myth of the coming of the Mahdi, for example, is planted and takes root until Paul Atreides shows up. He fits the image. He exploits the myth and rides on the back of Fremen belief. The Bene Gesserit weaponized words in the very first book of *Dune*. They had developed the Missionaria Protectiva, an organization that planted the basis of legends and prophecies in the cultures of the worlds of the Imperium. These latent patterns of words could be manipulated later by Bene Gesserit agents who might need to control individuals or populations, for protection or other purposes.[40] Such a program recognizes that persons will submit to pre-constructed beliefs if the patterns are strong enough and properly planted.

When dealing with the Fremen, the Bene Gesserit turn away from rational arguments and toward images and myths. The Missionaria Protectiva, for example, combines words and images, rather than rational arguments, to lay down a pattern for the Fremen to follow. They recognize that the Fremen have an oral culture that is distinct from the literate culture of the Great Houses. This means that the Bene Gesserit can conceive of both literacy and orality as distinct forms of intentionality. Intentionality should not be confused with intention. Rather, intentionality represents the finding that consciousness (i.e., ordinary awareness) is always directed toward an object, toward content.[41] Consciousness is always a consciousness of *something*. These distinct forms of intentionality can be seen because the Bene Gesserit adopt a transcendental reflection that yields mythic awareness distinct from rational consciousness, and, most importantly, allows them to deal with the Great Houses or the Fremen on their own terms—in their own style of communication. To understand the content of myth, one must bracket common beliefs and presuppositions, and instead focus on patterns of practice (i.e., rituals) and stories (i.e., myths).[42] Not everyone is capable of such awareness. Even the Mentat Thufir Hawat has trouble seeing mythical awareness. In *Dune*, Jessica notes that Thufir has a blind spot to this dimension of communication brought on by his intense attention to logical, rational thinking. However, as Jessica notes:

> The *natural* human's an animal without logic. Your projection of logic onto all affairs is *un*natural.... Your problem solutions are concepts that ... are projected outside yourself, there to be studied and rolled around, examined from all sides.[43]

In this observation, Jessica points to the limitations of a wholly rational, conceptual consciousness that works on the objective, measurable, field of experience. Mythical consciousness is, for such a person, only a latent possibility. For the Bene Gesserit, this dimension of communication is a schoolroom in which they learn how to use words to control the thoughts of others.

When consciousness is reduced, phenomenologically, to its essential (its eidetic) structure (its intentionality), then the thought-lines that constitute mythic awareness, as separate from mental-rational thinking, can be seen. Myth, its rhetoric and mode of awareness, is neither mental nor rational. Myth, instead, focuses on imagination and oral communication.

Myth is a form of speech that offers *explanations of phenomena*.[44] Myths are stories, "usually a traditional story of ostensibly historical events that serves to unfold part of the world view of a people or explain a practice, belief, or natural phenomenon."[45] Myths are, essentially, the stories we live by.[46] The Bene Gesserit, by bracketing belief in word-meanings, and by looking to necessary conditions, are prepared to look at the stuff of myth—the words that point to beliefs.

Apprehended by its own terms, myth is not simply some false story about past superstitions. It is more a system of communication, a mode of making beliefs known, and a way of understanding the world.[47] Myths are stories that describe a way of understanding the cosmos; ways of making the senses sensible. To these ends, all religions are mythic, as are even the physical sciences; both spell out ways of believing and understanding the complexities of experience. According to Claude Levi-Strauss, myths, grasped semiotically, are stories that resolve binary oppositions and establish ways of believing.[48] According to Jean Gebser, myth emerged as dominant in Western civilization around the second millennium BCE, and is still manifest today, although it is often obscured by the mental, conceptual, and rational bias of our time.[49] "Myths," says Gebser, "are the collective dreams" of a people.[50] Myths tell us stories about ourselves. They expose the underlying desires and values of our culture. By taking the form of stories, provoking and resolving contradictions, kindling desire and forging dreams, mythical-imagistic awareness favors polarity, undergone experience, and imagery. Persons, as cultural participants, are interpellated by a structuring of consciousness with which we resonate, even if tacitly. Thus, mythic imagery and mythic belief make sense, even when we cannot put our finger on why. If we can grasp the mythic dimension of imagery, as the Bene Gesserit do, we do not have to fall prey to myth's rhetoric. We will be able to see the dreams laid out before us and gain the ability to ask: Whose dreams are these? What power, institution, or interest do they serve? Can these dreams be realized?

Planting stories for the protection of the Bene Gesserit is a kind of manipulation, not persuasion. Persuasive speech puts its cards on the table; it is democratic. By contrast, manipulative speech hides the cards *and the table*; it is autocratic. We can see signs of this same mythic engineering in today's power politics. The "Make America Great Again" slogan, for example, creates a narrative of a savior and redemption. Under the savior's guidance (the slogan suggests), the populace can return to a better time, a simpler time, a time which, in actuality, never existed. The cards are not shown (e.g., What greatness can we expect? How will it be achieved?). Indeed, there is no table (e.g., What period shall we return to? When did America stop being great?). The important thing that the Bene

Gesserit teach us is to be able to see the structure, the signs of the presence of mythic imagination.

The Education of Farad'n

In *Children of Dune*, when the Lady Jessica positions herself as the Sisterhood's plenipotentiary to Salusa Secundus to oversee Farad'n Corrino's education, we are given direct insight into the Sisterhood's transcendental pragmatism. Jessica prepares Farad'n to live an authentic existence—the goal of Bene Gesserit education. Existence is inauthentic when a person lives a life within—but not questioning—the natural attitude and the common discourses of the time. For Martin Heidegger, authenticity meant seeing *through* the natural attitude and activities within a tradition.[51] A transcendental reduction—reflecting on pre-reflective experience—would begin to expose the natural state of affairs as constructed, as being cultural rather than *natural*. That move would open a way toward an authentic engagement with others and with the world. Farad'n's authentic awareness appears when he makes his first academic breakthrough: "My mind controls reality."[52]

After his first eight days of study, the dictates of the real, facticity, and the limits of discourse start to become visible. All notions of the real begin with experience, with a body already encultured, already bathed in language and learning. When Farad'n begins to see his hands grow young and old at will, he learns how to set aside, or bracket out, the social world; to reduce experience to a pre-thematic flow; and then to focus and shift attention intentionally. This is a fundamentally creative act; he creates his reality. He becomes aware of the mechanics of phenomena—intentionality. Farad'n learns that he gives perpetual birth to the known, and that he is capable of re-seeing, re-knowing, and thus, challenging every conception as a preconception or presupposition. As Jessica suggests:

> relative stability.... This is the perspective which you create with your own belief, and beliefs can be manipulated by imagination ... you must make the universe your own creation. This will permit you to harness any relative stability to your own uses, to whatever uses you are capable of imagining.[53]

For example, Jessica notes that Muad'dib "didn't really see the future; he saw the process of creation and its relationship to the myths in which men sleep."[54] Farad'n was prepared with the ability to test any reality against his demands, to challenge any postulate of society.[55] The Lady Jessica tells him, "This is the perspective which you create with your own belief, and beliefs can be manipulated by imagination. You've learned only a limited way of looking at the universe. Now you must make the universe your own creation."[56] Farad'n was positioned to become the authentic man of Jean-Paul Sartre and Heidegger's existential phenomenology. As Jessica tells Farad'n, "If you complete this program of learning, you'll be your own man. Whatever you do, it'll be because that's what you want to do."[57] Odrade's intentions for Murbella are the same: "Excellent, Murbella! You're beginning to think like one of us…. Neither fish nor fowl, but your own true self."[58] And she warns against taking the easy path, against settling into the patterns of belief: "Even there, you're only a steward. Beware, Murbella! If you think you own something, that's like walking on quicksand."[59]

What does it mean to believe? Right and wrong, true and false, have meanings; they make sense. However, this orientation, no matter how reassuring, is based on assumptions that the Bene Gesserit can bring to light. In the final analysis, the Bene Gesserit have no *fixed* ideology, philosophy, history, religion, or science. All of these are suspicious, as they are driven by discourse, foster beliefs, appear within history, and are ultimately ruled by language and speech. The Bene Gesserit are not beholden to any school of thought: "Give me the judgement of balanced minds in preference to laws every time. Codes and manuals create patterned behavior. All patterned behavior tends to go unquestioned, gathering destructive momentum."[60]

Ultimately, the Bene Gesserit's rigorous approach to thinking is both transcendental and pragmatic. Even Leto II, as he assumes control of the known universe, says, "Bene Gesserit are pragmatists in the end."[61] They seek to understand the assumptions one makes, and to know how to act accordingly. They also have a *telos*—creativity. The Bene Gesserit realize that thought, word, and deed are essentially creative; communication is essentially creative. This is why a Missionaria Protectiva can work in the first place. It creates a system of beliefs using legend and myth as a means of infusion. We are what we say, do, and believe; though, as we've seen, we need not be limited by belief. The realization that communication is essentially creative appears in Bene Gesserit thinking after the death of Lord Leto II, the God Emperor of Dune. The Golden Path now illuminates the Bene Gesserit, and in return, they illuminate it. Though, thousands of years before Leto's death, Ghanima, Paul Atreides's daughter, understood well this Bene Gesserit trajectory. She speaks this telos quietly: "The work to which we have set ourselves is the liberating of the imagination … to humankind's deepest sense of creativity."[62]

Notes

1. The Open-Ended Proof from the Panoplia Prophetica. Herbert, *Children of Dune*, 365.
2. Herbert, *Heretics of Dune,* 156.

3. Herbert, *Chapterhouse: Dune*, 46.
4. *Ibid.*, 128.
5. After all, the genetic hybrid is stronger than the purebred (a key log within the Dune series). The key log is the one log that when pulled will free a log jam. Herbert, *Heretics of Dune*, 126.
6. The Open-Ended Proof from the Panoplia Prophetica, Herbert, *Children of Dune*, 365.
7. Herbert, *Chapterhouse: Dune*, 271.
8. *Ibid.*, 271.
9. *Ibid.*, 126–27.
10. *Ibid.*
11. Herbert, *The Notebooks of Frank Herbert's Dune*, 43.
12. Herbert, *Chapterhouse: Dune*, 126–7.
13. *Ibid.*, 321.
14. *Ibid.*, 270
15. *Ibid.*, 279.
16. *Ibid.*, 280.
17. Herbert, *Dune Messiah*, 23.
18. Murbella's oath to the Bene Gesserit, in Herbert, *Chapterhouse: Dune*, 130.
19. See Herbert, *Heretics of Dune*, 157.
20. Herbert, *Chapterhouse: Dune*, 127.
21. Herbert, *Children of Dune*, 115.
22. Herbert, *Chapterhouse: Dune*, 126.
23. Hillman, *The Thought of the Heart and the Soul of the World*, 104.
24. *Ibid.*
25. Herbert, *Chapterhouse: Dune*, 126–27.
26. Foucault, *The Archaeology of Knowledge*.
27. Herbert, *Chapterhouse: Dune*, 349.
28. *Ibid.*, 162–72.
29. *Ibid.*, 165.
30. *Ibid.*, 166.
31. *Ibid.*, 167.
32. *Ibid.*
33. *Ibid.*
34. *Ibid.*
35. *Ibid.*, 168.
36. *Ibid.*
37. *Ibid.*
38. *Ibid.*, 167–69.
39. *Ibid.*, 131.
40. From "Analysis: The Arrakeen Crisis" by the Princess Irulan, Herbert, *Dune*, 76.
41. Stewart and Mickunas, *Exploring Phenomenology*, 8.
42. Gebser, *The Ever-Present Origin*.
43. Herbert, *Dune*, 151
44. Barthes, *Mythologies*; Jean Gebser, *The Ever-Present Origin*.
45. *Merriam-Webster*, "myth."
46. Campbell, *The Hero with A Thousand Faces*.
47. Roland Barthes, *Mythologies*.
48. Levi-Strauss, "The Structural Study of Myth."
49. Jean Gebser, *The Ever-Present Origin*.
50. *Ibid.*, 68.
51. Heidegger, *Being and Time*, 1962.
52. Herbert, *Children of Dune*, 279.
53. *Ibid.*, 257.
54. *Ibid.*, 307.
55. *Ibid.*, 280.

56. *Ibid.*, 257.
57. *Ibid.*, 280.
58. Herbert, *Chapterhouse: Dune*, 119.
59. *Ibid.*
60. Darwi Odrade, in *Ibid.*, 253.
61. Herbert, *Children of Dune*, 407.
62. *Ibid.*, 291.

WORKS CITED

Barthes, Roland. *Mythologies.* New York: Farrar, Straus and Giroux, 1972.
Foucault, Michel. *The Archaeology of Knowledge.* New York: Pantheon, 1972.
Gebser, Jean. *The Ever-Present Origin.* Athens: Ohio University, 1985.
Heidegger, Martin. *Being and Time.* San Francisco: Harper and Row, 1962.
Herbert, Frank. *Chapterhouse: Dune.* New York: Ace/Berkley, 1985.
Herbert, Frank, *Children of Dune.* New York: Ace/Berkley, 1976.
Herbert, Frank, *Dune.* Philadelphia, PA: Chilton, 1965.
Herbert, Frank. *Heretics of Dune.* New York: Ace/Berkley, 1984.
Herbert, Frank. *The Notebooks of Frank Herbert's Dune,* edited by Brian Herbert. New York: Perigee, 1988.
Hillman, James. *The Thought of the Heart and the Soul of the World.* Dallas: Spring Publications, 1981.
Levi-Strauss, Claude. "The Structural Study of Myth." *The Journal of American Folklore* 68, no. 270, Myth: A Symposium (October-December 1955): 428–44.
Merriam-Webster Dictionary. s.v. "myth." Accessed February 3, 2019. https://www.merriam-webster.com/dictionary/myth.
Stewart and Mickunas, *Exploring Phenomenology.* Athens, OH: Ohio University Press. 1974.

Appendix

Bibliography of Scholarship

Dominic J. Nardi *and* N. Trevor Brierly

"...and oddly enough, little literary criticism—there's not that much on Herbert to begin with—attempts to wrestle with the presentation of Realpolitik in the series, particularly in the first novel."—Senior, "Frank Herbert's Prescience," 317

While working on *Discovering* Dune: *Essays on Frank Herbert's Epic Saga,* we noticed that there was no single, updated bibliography of scholarship about Frank Herbert or his works. As readers can tell from the bibliographies attached to each essay, this is not because such scholarship does not exist. Rather, Herbert Studies never coalesced into an academic subfield that generated demand for such a bibliography. This final part of the book is our attempt to fill that gap.

We attempted to compile all publicly available scholarship about Frank Herbert's Dune saga, including academic journal articles, books, and dissertations. We also included important primary documents, including interviews and essays by Frank Herbert. This bibliography does not include news or blog articles, book reviews, videos, or podcasts, unless of special importance to the Dune scholarship or academic discussions about the novels. In the *LA Review of Books,* Haris Durrani recently provided a guide to noteworthy op-eds and blog articles about Dune.*

This bibliography built upon the work of Gregory Tidewell[†] and the Dune Academic website[‡]—both of which no longer appear to be updated regularly—and benefited from the collective efforts of all contributors to this volume, as well as the two anonymous reviewers.

We recognize that this bibliography will likely already be obsolete by the time you read this. We leave it to future scholars to update it as necessary.

---

*https://lareviewofbooks.org/article/sietchposting-a-short-guide-to-recent-work-on-dune/.

†http://fhss.solahpmo.com/.

‡https://archive.li/w8Es3.

Primary Sources

Frank Herbert's papers are stored in the California State University, Fullerton's Willis E. McNelly Science Fiction Collection.* The collection includes 93 boxes of original manuscripts, working papers, correspondence, first editions, critical studies, and ephemera pertaining to Frank Herbert's life and works between 1950 and 1986. The library's website also has a research guide for the study of Frank Herbert.†

In addition, some books from Herbert's personal holdings are part of the Frank Herbert Collection at the Siuslaw Public Library.‡ Credit to Martin Nguyen for locating this excellent resource.

Frank Herbert's Dune Novels and Short Stories

Herbert, Frank. *Chapterhouse: Dune.* New York: G.P. Putnam's Sons, 1985; Ace Books, 1987.
_____. *Children of Dune.* New York: Berkley Books, 1981.
_____. *Dune Messiah.* New York: Berkley Books, 1975.
_____. *Dune.* New York: Chilton Book Co., 1965; Berkley Books, 1977; Ace Books, 1987.
_____. *God Emperor of Dune.* New York: G.P. Putnam's Sons, 1981; Berkley Books, 1983; Ace Books, 1987.
_____. *Heretics of Dune.* New York: G.P. Putnam's Sons, 1984; Berkley Books, 1986.
_____. "The Road to Dune" In *Eye.* New York: Berkley Books: 1985.

Brian Herbert and Kevin J. Anderson's Dune Novels and Short Stories

Herbert, Brian, and Kevin J Anderson. *Dune: House Atreides.* New York: Bantam, 1999.
_____. *Dune: House Corrino.* New York: Bantam, 2001.
_____. *Dune: House Harkonnen.* New York: Bantam, 2000.
_____. *Dune: The Battle of Corrin.* New York: Tor, 2004.
_____. *Dune: The Butlerian Jihad.* New York: Tor, 2002.
_____. *Dune: The Duke of Caladan.* New York: Tor, 2020.
_____. *Dune: The Heir of Caladan.* New York: Tor, 2022.
_____. *Dune: The Lady of Caladan.* New York: Tor, 2021.
_____. *Dune: The Machine Crusade.* New York: Tor, 2003.
_____. *Hunters of Dune.* New York: Tor, 2006.
_____. *Mentats of Dune.* New York: Tor, 2014.
_____. *Navigators of Dune.* New York: Tor, 2016.
_____. *Paul of Dune.* New York: Tor, 2008.
_____. *Sands of Dune.* New York: Tor, 2022.
_____. *Sandworms of Dune.* New York: Tor, 2007.
_____. *Sisterhood of Dune.* New York: Tor, 2011.
_____. *Tales of Dune.* New York: Tor, 2011.
_____. *The Winds of Dune.* New York: Tor, 2009.

Essays, Interviews, & Archives

Frank Herbert Papers. California State University, Fullerton. University Archives and Special Collections.
Gumbel, Bryant. Interview, *Today* on NBC, 1982. YouTube (posted on July 25, 2015). www.youtube.com/watch?v=26GPaMoeiu4.
Henderson, Chris (interviewer). "Frank Herbert: From the Otherworldly Visions of *Dune* to the Terrestrial Holocaust of *The White Plague.*" *Starlog Magazine* 6, no. 66 (1983): 24–26. https://archive.org/details/starlog_magazine-066/page/n23/mode/2up.

---

*http://archives.fullerton.edu/repositories/5/resources/56.
†https://libraryguides.fullerton.edu/HerbertDune.
‡https://sprp.sirsi.net.

Herbert, Brian, and Kevin J. Anderson. *The Road to Dune*. New York: Tor, 2005.

Herbert, Frank. "Dune Genesis." *OMNI* 2, no. 10 (1980), 72–76 (available at https://archive.org/stream/OMNI197908/OMNI_1980_07#page/n39/mode/2up).

_____. "Frank Herbert." In *The Synopsis Treasury: A Landmark Collection of Actual Proposals Submitted to Publishers* (Million Dollar Writing Series Book 0). Christopher Sirmons Haviland, ed. Monument, CO: WordFire Press, 2015.

_____. "Introduction" In *Eye*. New York: Berkley Books: 1985. (Frank Herbert's commentary on the Lynch film).

_____. *The Notebooks of Frank Herbert's Dune*. Brian Herbert (ed.). Los Angeles: Perigee Trade Books, 1988.

_____. "Science Fiction and a World in Crisis." In *Science Fiction, Today and Tomorrow*. Reginald Bretnor, ed. New York: Harper & Row, 1974, 69–97.

_____. *Songs of Muad'dib*. Brian Herbert (ed.). New York: Ace Trade Books, 1992.

_____. Speech at UCLA, April 17, 1985. UCLA Campus Events Commission Archive, YouTube (posted on July 11, 2016). https://www.youtube.com/watch?v=5IfgBX1EW00.

_____. "Survival of the Cunning," *Esquire*, March 1945, 56–57.

Levack, Daniel, and Mark Willard. *Dune Master: A Frank Herbert Bibliography*. Westport, CT: Meckler Press, 1988.

McNelly, Willis E. (interviewer) "Frank & Beverly Herbert interviewed by W. McNelly" https://www.youtube.com/watch?v=1s7muoTaCpY (transcript available at http://www.sinanvural.com/seksek/inien/tvd/tvd2.htm).

O'Reilly, Timothy, ed. *Frank Herbert: The Maker of Dune: Insights of a Master of Science Fiction*. New York: Berkeley, 1987. List of contents available at https://www.worldcat.org/title/maker-of-dune-insights-of-a-master-of-science-fiction/oclc/15636296.

Stine, Jean Marie (interviewer). "Lost Interview: Futuristic Meditations from Dune's Frank Herbert Part I." *L.A. Reader* (1984). https://futurespast-editions.blogspot.com/2013/10/lost-interview-futuristic-meditations.html.

_____. "Lost Interview: Futuristic Meditations from Dune's Frank Herbert Part II." *L.A. Reader* (1984). https://futurespast-editions.blogspot.com/2013/11/lost-interview-futuristic-meditations.html.

_____. "Lost Interview: Futuristic Meditations from Dune's Frank Herbert Part III." *L.A. Reader* (1984). https://futurespast-editions.blogspot.com/2013/11/lost-interview-futuristic-meditations_25.html.

Stone, Pat (interviewer). "Frank Herbert Science Fiction's 'Yellow Journalist' Is a Homesteading 'Technopeasant.'" *Plowboy* May/June (1981): 17–23. http://libraryguides.fullerton.edu/ld.php?content_id=16184648.

Turner, Paul (interviewer). "*Vertex* Interviews Frank Herbert." *Vertex* 1.4 (1973): 34–38.

Dune Encyclopedia

McNelly, Willis E. *The Dune Encyclopedia*. New York: Berkley Books, 1984.

Academic Sources

Books and Edited Volumes

Allard, Nicolas. *Dune: Un chef-d'oeuvre de la science fiction*. France: Dunod, 2020.

Ben-Tov, Sharona. *The Artificial Paradise: Science Fiction and American Reality* (Studies in Literature and Science). Ann Arbor, MI: The University of Michigan Press, 1995.

Bogle, Bob R. *Frank Herbert: The Works*. Eugene, OR: Hotspur Publishing, 2012.

Chery, Lloyd. *Dune, le mook*. France: Coédition Atalante, 2020.

Grazier, Kevin R. (ed.). *The Science of Dune: An Unauthorized Exploration into the Real Science Behind Frank Herbert's Fictional Universe*, Science of Pop Culture. Dallas: BenBella Books, 2008.

Herbert, Brian. *Dreamer of Dune: The Biography of Frank Herbert*. New York: Tor, 2003.

Kennedy, Kara. *Women's Agency in the Dune Universe.* Cham, Switzerland: Palgrave Macmillan, 2021.

Lehoucq, Roland. (ed.). *Dune—exploration scientifique et culturelle d'une planète-univers.* Saint-Mammès, France: Le Bélial, 2020.

Lejeune, Vivien. *Les visions de Dune: Dans les creux et sillons d'Arrakis.* Toulouse, France: Third Editions, 2020.

Levack, Daniel, and Mark Willard. *Dune Master: A Frank Herbert Bibliography.* Westport, CT: Meckler Press, 1988.

McCrea, Christian. *Dune (Constellations).* New York: Auteur, 2019.

Miller, David M. *Frank Herbert* (Starmont Readers Guide No. 5). Mercer Island, WA: Starmont House, 1980.

Naha, Ed. *The Making of Dune.* New York: Berkeley, 1984.

Nicholas, Jeffery (ed.). *Dune and Philosophy: The Weirding Way of the Mentat,* Popular Culture and Philosophy Book 56. Chicago: Open Court, 2011.

O'Reilly, Timothy. *Frank Herbert* ("Recognitions" Series). New York: Frederick Ungar, 1981. (Note: also available online at https://www.oreilly.com/tim/herbert/index.html).

Pak, Chris. *Terraforming: Ecopolitical Transformations and Environmentalism in Science Fiction* (Liverpool Science Fiction Texts and Studies). Liverpool: Liverpool University Press, 2016.

Palumbo, Donald E. *A Dune Companion: Characters, Places and Terms in Frank Herbert's Original Six Novels* (Critical Explorations in Science Fiction and Fantasy). Jefferson, NC: McFarland, 2018.

_____. *Chaos Theory, Asimov's Foundations and Robots, and Herbert's Dune: The Fractal Aesthetic of Epic Science Fiction.* Contributions to the Study of Science Fiction and Fantasy, Number 100. Westport, CT: Greenwood Press, 2002.

_____. *The Monomyth in American Science Fiction Films.* Jefferson, NC: McFarland, 2014.

Roberts, Adam. *Science Fiction* (The New Critical Idiom). New York: Routledge, 2000.

Siegel, Mark R. *Gernsback, Hugo, Father of Modern Science Fiction: With Essays on Frank Herbert & Bram Stoker* (Milford Series, Popular Writers of Today). Rockville, MD: Borgo Press, 1988.

Simkins, Jennifer. *The Science Fiction Mythmakers: Religion, Science and Philosophy in Wells, Clarke, Dick and Herbert* (Critical Explorations in Science Fiction and Fantasy Book 54). Jefferson, NC: McFarland, 2016.

Stephensen-Payne, Phil. *Frank Herbert: A Voice from the Desert* (Bibliographies for the Avid Reader). West Yorkshire, UK: Galactic Central Publishing, 1991.

Touponce, William F. *Frank Herbert.* Boston: Twayne Publishers, 1988.

Van Hise, James, and Michael D. Messina. *The Secrets of Frank Herbert's Dune.* I Books, 2000.

Williams, Kevin. *Wisdom of the Sand: Philosophy and Frank Herbert's Dune* (Critical Bodies). New York: Hampton Press, 2013.

Book Chapters

Anderson, Daniel Gustav. "Critical Bioregionalist Method in *Dune*: A Position Paper." In *The Bioregional Imagination: Literature, Ecology, and Place.* Athens: University of Georgia Press, 2012. 226–242. Available at https://www.academia.edu/2156577/Critical_Bioregionalist_Method_in_Dune_A_Position_Paper.

Butkus, Matthew A. "A Universe of Bastards." In *Dune and Philosophy: The Weirding Way of the Mentat,* Popular Culture and Philosophy Book 56, edited by Jeffery Nicholas. Chicago: Open Court, 2011, 75–88.

Ciocchetti, Christopher. "Power Mongers and Worm Riders." In *Dune and Philosophy: The Weirding Way of the Mentat,* Popular Culture and Philosophy Book 56, edited by Jeffery Nicholas. Chicago: Open Court, 2011, 91–102.

Collings, Michael R. "The Epic of Dune: Epic Traditions in Modern Science Fiction." In *Aspects of Fantasy: Selected Essays from the Second International Conference on the Fantastic in Literature and Film.* Ed. William Coyle. Westport, CT: Greenwood Press, 1986, 131–39.

Csori, Csilla. "Memory (and the Tleilaxu) Makes the Man." In *The Science of Dune: An Unauthorized Exploration into the Real Science Behind Frank Herbert's Fictional Universe,* Science of Pop Culture, edited by Kevin R. Grazier. Dallas: BenBella Books: 2008, 167–76.

_____. "Prescience and Prophecy." In *The Science of Dune: An Unauthorized Exploration into the Real Science Behind Frank Herbert's Fictional Universe,* Science of Pop Culture, edited by Kevin R. Grazier. Dallas: BenBella Books, 2008, 111–26.

Elgin, Don D. "Frank Herbert." In *The Comedy of the Fantastic: Ecological Perspectives on the Fantasy Novel.* Santa Barbara, CA: Praeger, 1985, 125–52.

Ellis, R.J. "Frank Herbert's *Dune* and the Discourse of Apocalyptic Ecologism in the United States." In *Science Fiction Roots and Branches: Contemporary Critical Approaches.* Rhys Garnett and R.J. Ellis, eds. New York: St. Martin's Press, 1990, 104–24. Available at https://link.springer.com/chapter/10.1007/978-1-349-20815-9_8.

Erman, Eva, and Niklas Möller. "What's Wrong with Politics in the Duniverse?" In *Dune and Philosophy: The Weirding Way of the Mentat,* Popular Culture and Philosophy Book 56, edited by Jeffery Nicholas. Chicago: Open Court, 2011, 61–74.

Ferner, Adam. "Memories Are Made of Spice." In *Dune and Philosophy: The Weirding Way of the Mentat,* Popular Culture and Philosophy Book 56. Jeffery Nicholas, ed. Chicago: Open Court, 2011, 161–74.

Field, Sandy. "Evolution by Any Means on Dune." In *The Science of Dune: An Unauthorized Exploration into the Real Science Behind Frank Herbert's Fictional Universe,* Science of Pop Culture, edited by Kevin R. Grazier. Dallas: BenBella Books: 2008, 67–82.

Garnett, Rhys and R J Ellis. "Frank Herbert's *Dune* and the Discourse of Apocalyptic Ecologism in the United States." In *Science Fiction Roots And Branches: Contemporary Critical Approaches.* Londone: Palgrave Macmillan UK, 1990.

Gates-Scovelle, Sam. "Curse of the Golden Path." In *Dune and Philosophy: The Weirding Way of the Mentat,* Popular Culture and Philosophy Book 56, edited by Jeffery Nicholas. Chicago: Open Court, 2011, 37–50.

_____. "Son of the Curse of the Golden." In *Dune and Philosophy: The Weirding Way of the Mentat,* Popular Culture and Philosophy Book 56, edited by Jeffery Nicholas. Chicago: Open Court, 2011, 207–18.

_____, and Stephanie Semler. "A Ghola of a Chance." In *Dune and Philosophy: The Weirding Way of the Mentat,* Popular Culture and Philosophy Book 56, edited by Jeffery Nicholas. Chicago: Open Court, 2011, 131–48.

Gaylard, Gerald. "Postcolonial Science Fiction: The Desert Planet." *Science Fiction, Imperialism, and the Third World: Essays on Postcolonial Literature and Film.* Jefferson, NC: McFarland, 2010, 21–36.

Gower, Kathy. "Science Fiction and Women." *Mother Was Not a Person.* Margaret Andersen, ed. Montréal: Black Rose Books, 1974.

Grazier, Kevin R. "Cosmic Origami." In *The Science of Dune: An Unauthorized Exploration into the Real Science Behind Frank Herbert's Fictional Universe,* Science of Pop Culture, edited by Kevin R. Grazier. Dallas: BenBella Books: 2008, 177–206.

_____. "Introduction." In *The Science of Dune: An Unauthorized Exploration into the Real Science Behind Frank Herbert's Fictional Universe,* Science of Pop Culture, edited by Kevin R. Grazier. Dallas: BenBella Books: 2008, vii–ix.

_____. "The Real Stars of Dune." In *The Science of Dune: An Unauthorized Exploration into the Real Science Behind Frank Herbert's Fictional Universe,* Science of Pop Culture, edited by Kevin R. Grazier. Dallas: BenBella Books: 2008, 89–110.

Gunn, James, ed. "Inner Concerns in Outer Space." In *The Road to Science Fiction from Here to Forever, Volume 4.* Scarecrow Press: 2003.

Hart, Carol. "From Silver Fox to Kwisatz Haderach." In *The Science of Dune: An Unauthorized Exploration into the Real Science Behind Frank Herbert's Fictional Universe,* Science of Pop Culture, edited by Kevin R. Grazier. Dallas: BenBella Books: 2008, 59–66.

_____. "Melange." In *The Science of Dune: An Unauthorized Exploration into the Real Science Behind Frank Herbert's Fictional Universe,* Science of Pop Culture, edited by Kevin R. Grazier. Dallas: BenBella Books: 2008, 1–20.

_____. "The Black Hole of Pain." In *The Science of Dune: An Unauthorized Exploration into the Real Science Behind Frank Herbert's Fictional Universe*, Science of Pop Culture, edited by Kevin R. Grazier. Dallas: BenBella Books: 2008, 143–50.

Hechtel, Sibyelle. "The Biology of the Sandworm." In *The Science of Dune: An Unauthorized Exploration into the Real Science Behind Frank Herbert's Fictional Universe*, Science of Pop Culture, edited by Kevin R. Grazier. Dallas: BenBella Books: 2008, 29–48.

Herman, Peter. "The Blackness of Liet-Kynes: Reading Frank Herbert's Dune Through James Cone," Religions 9, no. 9 (2018).

Hoberek, Andrew. "*Dune*, the Middle Class and Post-1960 U.S. Foreign Policy." In *American Literature and Culture in an Age of Cold War: A Critical Reassessment*. Daniel Grausam and Steven Belletto, ed. Iowa City: Iowa University Press, 2012, 85–108.

Jackson, Roy. "Paul Atreides the Nietzschean Hero." In *Dune and Philosophy: The Weirding Way of the Mentat*, Popular Culture and Philosophy Book 56, edited by Jeffery Nicholas. Chicago: Open Court, 2011, 177–88.

Kennedy, Kara. "The Softer Side of Dune: The Impact of the Social Sciences on World-Building." In *Exploring Imaginary Worlds: Essays on Media, Structure, and Subcreation*. Mark J.P. Wolf, ed. New York: Routledge, 2020, 159–74.

Lawrence, David M.. "The Shade of Uliet." In *The Science of Dune: An Unauthorized Exploration into the Real Science Behind Frank Herbert's Fictional Universe*, Science of Pop Culture, edited by Kevin R. Grazier. Dallas: BenBella Books: 2008, 217–32.

Liddell, Elisabeth, and Michael Liddell. "*Dune*: A Tale of Two Texts." In *Cinema and Fiction: New Modes of Adapting*. John Orr and Colin Nicholson, eds. Edinburgh: Edinburgh University Press (1992).

Littmann, Greg. "Just What Do You Do with the Entire Human Race Anyway?" In *Dune and Philosophy: The Weirding Way of the Mentat*, Popular Culture and Philosophy Book 56, edited by Jeffery Nicholas. Chicago: Open Court, 2011, 103–20.

Lorenz, Ralph D. "The Dunes of Dune." In *The Science of Dune: An Unauthorized Exploration into the Real Science Behind Frank Herbert's Fictional Universe*, Science of Pop Culture, edited by Kevin R. Grazier. Dallas: BenBella Books: 2008, 49–58.

Lund, Kristian. "Wiping Finite Answers from an Infinite Universe." In *Dune and Philosophy: The Weirding Way of the Mentat*, Popular Culture and Philosophy Book 56, edited by Jeffery Nicholas. Chicago: Open Court, 2011, 149–60.

Manlove, Colin N. "Frank Herbert, *Dune*." In *Science Fiction: Ten Explorations*. London: Palgrave Macmillan UK, 1986.

McLean, Susan. "A Question of Balance: Death and Immortality in Frank Herbert's *Dune* Series." In *Death and the Serpent*. Carl Yoke, ed. Westport, CT: Greenwood Press, 1985, pp. 145–52.

Melançon, Louis. "Shifting Sand, Shifting Balance." In *Dune and Philosophy: The Weirding Way of the Mentat*, Popular Culture and Philosophy Book 56, edited by Jeffery Nicholas. Chicago: Open Court, 2011, 27–36.

Miller, Mariam Youngerman. "Women of *Dune*: Frank Herbert as Social Reactionary?" In *Women Worldwalkers: New Dimensions of Science Fiction and Fantasy* (Studies in Comparative Literature). Jane B. Weedman, ed. Lubbock, TX: Texas Tech University Press, 1985, 181–92.

Minowitz, Peter. "Prince versus Prophet: Machiavellianism in Frank Herbert's *Dune* Epic." In *Political Science Fiction*. Donald M. Hassler and Clyde Wilcox, eds. Columbia: University of South Carolina Press, 1996, 124–47.

Neely, Sharlotte. "The Anthropology of Dune." In *The Science of Dune: An Unauthorized Exploration into the Real Science Behind Frank Herbert's Fictional Universe*, Science of Pop Culture, edited by Kevin R. Grazier. Dallas: BenBella Books: 2008, 83–88.

Nicholas, Jeffery. "Facing the Gom Jabbar Test." In *Dune and Philosophy: The Weirding Way of the Mentat*, Popular Culture and Philosophy Book 56, edited by Jeffery Nicholas. Chicago: Open Court, 2011, 3–12

Palumbo, Donald E. "Dune: Herbert's Novels, Lynch's Film and the Scifi Channel's Two Miniseries " in *The Monomyth in American Science Fiction Films*. Jefferson, NC: McFarland, 2014.

Pearson, Brook W.R. "Friedrich Nietzsche Goes to Space." In *Dune and Philosophy: The Weirding Way of the Mentat,* Popular Culture and Philosophy Book 56, edited by Jeffery Nicholas. Chicago: Open Court, 2011, 189–206.

Pistoi, Sergio. "My Second Sight." In *The Science of Dune: An Unauthorized Exploration into the Real Science Behind Frank Herbert's Fictional Universe,* Science of Pop Culture, edited by Kevin R. Grazier. Dallas: BenBella Books: 2008, 21–28.

Ralston, Shane. "The American Fremen." In *Dune and Philosophy: The Weirding Way of the Mentat,* Popular Culture and Philosophy Book 56, edited by Jeffery Nicholas. Chicago: Open Court, 2011, 53–60.

Riches, Simon. "Good and Evil in David Lynch's Dune." In *Dune and Philosophy: The Weirding Way of the Mentat,* Popular Culture and Philosophy Book 56, edited by Jeffery Nicholas. Chicago: Open Court, 2011, 121–28.

Riggs, Don. "Future and 'Progress' in *Foundation* and *Dune*." In *Spectrum of the Fantastic: Selected Essays from the Sixth International Conference on the Fantastic in the Arts.* Ed. Donald Palumbo. Westport, CT: Greenwood Press, 1988, pp. 113–17.

Rogers, Brett M. "'Now Harkonnen Shall Kill Harkonnen': Aeschylus, Dynastic Violence and Twofold Tragedies in Frank Herbert's *Dune*." In *Brill's Companion to the Reception of Aeschylus* (Brill's Companions to Classical Reception Vol. 11). Rebecca Futo Kennedy, ed. Leiden: Brill, 2017, 553–81.

Ryding, Karin Christina. "The Arabic of Dune: Language and Landscape," In *Language in Place: Stylistic Perspectives on Landscape, Place and Environment.* Daniela Francesca Virdis, Elisabetta Zurru, and Ernestine Lahey, eds. Amsterdam: John Benjamins Publishing, 2021.

Schmitt-v. Muhlenfels, Astrid. "The Theme of Ecology in Frank Herbert's *Dune* Novels." In *The Role of Geography in a Post-Industrial Society.* Hans W. Windhorst, ed. Vechta Germany: Vechtaer Druckerei und Verlag GmbH, 1987.

Seger, Ges, and Kevin R. Grazier. "Suspensor of Disbelief." In *The Science of Dune: An Unauthorized Exploration into the Real Science Behind Frank Herbert's Fictional Universe,* Science of Pop Culture, edited by Kevin R. Grazier. Dallas: BenBella Books: 2008, 207–16.

Semler, Stephanie. "The Golden Path of Eugenics." In *Dune and Philosophy: The Weirding Way of the Mentat,* Popular Culture and Philosophy Book 56, edited by Jeffery Nicholas. Chicago: Open Court, 2011, 13–26.

Simkins, Jennifer. "Resisting Tradition: The Messiah Myth and Authentic Dasein in Frank Herbert's *Dune*." *The Science Fiction Mythmakers.* Jefferson, NC: McFarland, 2016.

Smith, John C. "Navigators and the Spacing Guild." In *The Science of Dune: An Unauthorized Exploration into the Real Science Behind Frank Herbert's Fictional Universe,* Science of Pop Culture, edited by Kevin R. Grazier. Dallas: BenBella Books: 2008, 151–66.

_____. "Stillsuit." In *The Science of Dune: An Unauthorized Exploration into the Real Science Behind Frank Herbert's Fictional Universe,* Science of Pop Culture, edited by Kevin R. Grazier. Dallas: BenBella Books: 2008, 127–42.

Spinrad, Norman. "Emperor of Everything." In *Science Fiction in the Real World.* Carbondale: Southern Illinois University Press, 1990.

Zaki, Hoda M. "Orientalism in Science Fiction." *Food For Our Grandmothers: Writings by Arab-American and Arab-Canadian Feminists.* Joanna Kadi, ed. Boston: South End Press, 1994, 181–87.

Journal Articles

Barbour, Douglas. "Occasional thoughts on Frank Herbert's *Dune* sequence." *The Australian Science Fiction Review* 17 (1988/1989): 10–13.

Barton-Kriese, Paul. "Exploring Divergent Realities: Using Science Fiction to Teach Introductory Political Science." *Extrapolation.* 34, no. 3 (Fall 1993): 209–15.

Cirasa, Robert. "An Epic Impression: Suspense and Prophetic Conventions in the Classical Epics and Frank Herbert's Dune." *Classical and Modern Literature* 4, no. 4 (Summer 1984): 195–213.

Day, Phyllis J. "Earthmother/Witchmother: feminism and ecology renewed." *Extrapolation* 23, no. 1 (1982): 12–21.

Dean, John. "The Uses of Wilderness in American Science Fiction." *Science Fiction Studies* 9, no. 1 (1982): 68–81.

DiTommaso, Lorenzo. "The Articulation of Imperial Decadence and Decline in Epic Science Fiction." *Extrapolation* 48, no. 2 (Summer 2007): 267–293.

_____. "History and Historical Effect in Frank Herbert's *Dune*." *Science Fiction Studies* 19, no. 3 (1992): 311–25. Available at https://www.jstor.org/stable/4240179?seq=1#page_scan_tab_contents.

Field, Gemma. "Dune Rehabilitation in Progress." *Journal of Literary Studies* 34, no. 3 (2018): 123–137.

Fjellman, Stephen M. "Prescience and Power: *God Emperor of Dune* and the Intellectuals." *Science Fiction Studies* 13, no. 1 (1986): 50–63.

Gaylard, Gerald. "Postcolonialism and the Transhistorical in *Dune*." *Foundation* 37, no. 104 (2008) 88–101.

Gough, Noel. "Speculative Fictions for Understanding Global Change Environments, Two Thought Experiments." *Managing Global Transitions* 1, no. 1 (2003): 5–27.

Grigsby, John L. "Asimov's *Foundation* Trilogy and Herbert's *Dune* Trilogy: A Vision Reversed." *Science Fiction Studies* 8, no. 24 (1981): 149–155.

_____. "Herbert's Reversal of Asimov's Vision Reassessed: *Foundation's Edge* and *God Emperor of Dune*." *Science Fiction Studies* 11, no. 33 (1984): 174–80.

Hand, Jack. "The Traditionalism of Women's Roles in Frank Herbert's *Dune*." *Extrapolation* 26, no. 1 (1985): 24–28.

Herman, Peter. "The Blackness of Liet-Kynes: Reading Frank Herbert's *Dune* Through James Cone." *Religions* 9, no. 9 (2018): 281–90. Available at https://www.mdpi.com/2077-1444/9/9/281/htm.

Higgins, David. "Psychic Decolonization in 1960s Science Fiction." *Science Fiction Studies* 40, no. 2 (2013).

Immerwahr, Daniel. "The Quileute Dune: Frank Herbert Indigeneity and Empire." *Journal of American Studies* 56, no. 2 (2022).

Kagle, Steven E. "The Societal Quest." Extrapolation 12, no. 2 (May 1971): 79–85.

Kennedy, Kara. "Epic World-Building: Names and Cultures in *Dune*." *Names* 64, no. 2 (2016): 99–108.

_____. "Spice and Ecology in Herbert's Dune: Altering the Mind and the Planet." *Science Fiction Studies* 48, no. 3 (2021): 444–61.

Kucera, Paul Q. "Listening to Ourselves: Herbert's *Dune*, 'the Voice,' and Performing the Absolute." *Extrapolation* 42, no. 3 (2001): 232–245.

List, Julia. "'Call me a protestant': Liberal Christianity, Individualism, and the Messiah in *Stranger in a Strange Land, Dune*, and *Lord of Light*." *Science Fiction Studies* 36, no. 1 (2009): 21–47.

Mack, Robert L. "Voice Lessons: The Seductive Appeal of Vocal Control in Frank Herbert's *Dune*." *Journal of the Fantastic in the Arts* 22, no. 1 (2011): 39–59.

McGregor, Gaile. "The Technomyth in Transition: Reading American Popular Culture." *Journal of American Studies* 21, no. 3 (December 1987): 387–409.

McLean, Susan. "A Psychological Approach to Fantasy in the *Dune* Series." *Extrapolation* 23, no. 2 (1982): 150–58.

McNelly, Willis E. "In Memoriam: Frank Herbert, 1920–1986." *Extrapolation* 27, no. 4 (Winter 1986): 352–55.

Mellamphy, Nandita Biswas. "*Terra-&-Terror Ecology*: Secrets from the Arrakeen Underground." *Design Ecologies* 3, no. 1 (2013): 67–91.

Meyers, Walter Earl. "Problems with Herbert." *Science Fiction Studies* 10, no. 29 (1983): 101–105.

Mohamed, Hussein Rafi. "Ecological Niche: Frank Herbert 1920–1986." *Vector* 42, no. 131 (1986): 11.

Morton, Timothy. "Imperial Measures: *Dune*, Ecology and Romantic Consumerism." *Romanticism On the Net* 21 (February 2001). Available at https://www.erudit.org/en/journals/ron/2001-n21-ron433/005966ar/.

Mulcahy, Kevin. "*The Prince* on Arrakis: Frank Herbert's dialogue with Machiavelli."

Extrapolation 37, no. 1 (1996): 22–36. Available at https://doi.org/10.3828/extr.1996.37.1.22.

Ower, John. "Idea and Imagery in Herbert's Dune." *Extrapolation* 15, no. 2 (1974): 129–139. Available at https://doi.org/10.3828/extr.1974.15.2.129.

Palumbo, Donald E. "'Plots Within Plots…Patterns Within Patterns': Chaos-Theory Concepts and Structures in Frank Herbert's Dune Novels." *Journal of the Fantastic in the Arts* 8, no. 1 (1997): 55–77. Available at https://www.jstor.org/stable/43308280?seq=1#page_scan_tab_contents.

_____. "The Monomyth and Chaos Theory: 'Perhaps We Should Believe in Magic.'" *Journal of the Fantastic in the Arts* 12, no. 1 (2001): 34–76. Available at https://www.jstor.org/stable/4240724?seq=1#page_scan_tab_contents.

_____. "The Monomyth as Fractal Pattern in Frank Herbert's *Dune* Novels." *Science-Fiction Studies* 25, no. 3 (1998): 433–58.

Parkerson, Ronny W. "Semantics, General Semantics, and Ecology in Frank Herbert's *Dune*." *ETC: A Review of General Semantics* 55, no. 3 (1998): 317–28.

_____. "Semantics, General Semantics, and Ecology in Frank Herbert's *Dune*." *ETC: A Review of General Semantics* 67, no. 4 (2010): 403–11.

Parkinson, Robert C. "Dune—An Unfinished Tetralogy." *Extrapolation* 13, no. 1 (1971): 16–24. Available at https://dx.doi.org/10.3828/extr.1971.13.1.16.

Pearson, Joshua. "Frank Herbert's *Dune* and the Financialization of Heroic Masculinity." *CR: The New Centennial Review* 19, no. 1 (Spring 2019): 155–180. Available at https://muse.jhu.edu/article/723518.

Prieto-Pablos, Juan A. "The Ambivalent Hero of Contemporary Fantasy and Science Fiction." *Extrapolation* 32, no. 1 (1991): 64–80.

Ravenwood, Emily. "Rightwise Born Kings: Feudalism and Republicanism in Science Fiction." *Extrapolation* 46, no. 4 (Winter 2005): 500–18.

Rossignol, Benoît. "Figures de l'historien dans le cycle de *Dune* de Frank Herbert." *Cycnos* 22, no. 2 (2005): 1–19.

Rudd, Amanda. "Paul's Empire: Imperialism and Assemblage Theory in Frank Herbert's Dune." *MOSF Journal of Science Fiction* 1, no. 1 (2016): 45–57.

Schwartz, Susan L. "A Teaching Review of Dune: Religion is the Spice of Life." *Implicit Religion* 17, no. 4 (2014).

Scigaj, Leonard M. "Prana and the Presbyterian Fixation: Ecology and Technology in Frank Herbert's *Dune* Tetralogy." *Extrapolation* 24, no. 4 (Winter 1983): 340–355. Available at https://dx.doi.org/10.3828/extr.1983.24.4.340.

Senior, William A. "Frank Herbert's Prescience: Dune and the Modern World." *Journal of the Fantastic in the Arts* 17, no. 4(68) (Winter 2007): 317–320. Available at https://www.questia.com/library/journal/1G1-218817916/frank-herbert-s-prescience-dune-and-the-modern-world.

Stratton, Susan. "The Messiah and the Greens: The shape of environmental action in *Dune* and *Pacific Edge*." *Extrapolation* 42, no. 4 (Winter 2001): 303–318. Available at https://dx.doi.org/10.3828/extr.2001.42.4.303.

Strick, Phillip. "Riddle of the Sands." *Sight and Sound* 11, no. 9 (2001): 20–22.

Thomason, Sue. "Living Water: Archetypal Power in 'Dune' and 'The Drowned World.'" *Vector* 37, no. 119 (1984): 33–34.

Todd, Tony. "Meanings and Authorships in Dune." *Film-Philosophy* 13, no. 1 (2009): 68–90. Available at http://www.film-philosophy.com/2009v13n1/todd.pdf.

Wendell, Carolyn. "The Alien Species: A Study of Women Characters in the Nebula Award Winners, 1965–1973." *Extrapolation* 20, no. 4 (1979): 343–354.

Williams, Kevin. "Imperialism & Globalization: Lessons from Frank Herbert's Dune," *Reconstruction: Studies in Contemporary Culture* 3, no. 3 (2003).

_____. "Politics & Power: Communicative Action in Frank Herbert's Dune," *Integrative Explorations: Journal of Culture & Consciousness* 7, no. 1 (2003): 151–72.

Zeender, Marie-Noelle. "The 'Moi-peau' of Leto II in Herbert's Atreides Saga." *Science Fiction Studies* 22, no. 2 (1995): 226–33. http://www.jstor.org/stable/4240427.

Dissertations/Theses

Allatt, Brandy Eileen. *Lies and Individuation: External and Internal Authority in the Politics and Anima of Dune* (Masters Thesis). Texas State University, San Marcos, 2015.

Ben-Tov, Sharona Eve. *Science Fiction and the Earthly Paradise: American construction of Nature* (Doctoral Dissertation). Stanford University, 1991 (UMI No. 9205600).

Brown, David Michael. *Welcome Bedfellows: Science Fiction Texts and Their Cinematic Adaptations (Frank Herbert, Philip K. Dick, David Lynch, Ridley Scott)* (Masters Thesis). Utah State University, 1998 (UMI No. 1394043).

Day, Jathan E. *Water as Power in Frank Herbert's "Dune"* (Masters Thesis). University of Alaska Anchorage, 2014 (UMI No. 1561203).

DiPasquale, Willow Wilson. *Myth-Making and Sacred Nature: J.R.R. Tolkien's and Frank Herbert's Mythopoeic Fiction* (Doctoral Dissertation). Drew University, 2018 (UMI No. 1079347 7).

Estopy, Tai. *The Fair Sex? A Look at Gender Issues in Frank Herbert's Dune Trilogy* (Masters Thesis). Fulbright College, 2004.

Evans, Carrie Lynn. *Women of the Future: Gender Technology and Cyborgs in Frank Herbert's Dune* (Masters Thesis). Université Laval, 2016.

Frisby, Elisabeth Stein. *Nietzsche's Influence on the Superman in Science Fiction Literature* (Doctoral Dissertation). Florida State University, 1979 (UMI No. 8006253).

Gass, Louise Horchler. *Leadership in Frank Herbert's Dune* (Masters Thesis).

Higgins, David M. *The Inward Urge: 1960s Science Fiction and Imperialism* (Doctoral Dissertation). Indiana University, 2010 (UMI No. 3409100).

Howard, Kenton Taylor. *Religious Violence in Frank Herbert's Dune Series* (Masters Thesis). Florida Atlantic University, 2012 (UMI No. 1520951).

Irizarry, Adella. *The Amtal Rule: Testing to Define in Frank Herbert's Dune* (Masters Thesis). Florida Atlantic University, 2013 (UMI No. 1524501).

Kněžková, Klára. *Frank Herbert's Heroines: Female Characters in Dune and Its Film Adaptations* (Masters Thesis). Masaryk University, 2007. Available at http://is.muni.cz/th/77885/prif_m/mathesis.pdf.

Luton, Lawrence S. *The Political Philosophy of Dune* (Doctoral Dissertation). Claremont Graduate University, 1979 (UMI No. 7911531).

Otto, Eric. *Science Fiction and the Ecological Conscience* (Doctoral Dissertation). University of Florida, 2002 (UMI No. 3224598).

Pearson, Joshua Danley. *Managing Power: Heroism in the Age of Speculative Capital* (Doctoral Dissertation). University of California Riverside, 2018 (UMI No. 10935410).

Racicot, Daniel. *Science-fiction et connaissance: Les discours de la science postmoderne dans "Dune" de Frank Herbert* (Masters Thesis). Universite du Quebec a Trois-Rivieres, 2006 (UMI No. MR14421).

Schreiber, John F. *The Shape of the Hero in Modern Epic Fantasy: A Comparative Analysis of the Dune Series, The Lord of the Rings & the Covenant Trilogy (Herbert, Tolkien, & Donaldson)* (Masters Thesis). Mankato State University, 1983.

Silliman, Barbara. *Conserving the Balance: Frank Herbert's Dune as Propaganda* (Doctoral Dissertation). University of Rhode Island, 1996 (UMI No. 9702075).

Singh, Sanjana. *Messiahs and Martyrs: Religion in Selected Novels of Frank Herbert's Dune Chronicles* (Masters Thesis). University of South Africa, 2012.

Sloan, Russell Terence. *Evolution, the Messianic Hero, and Ecology in Frank Herbert's Dune Sequence.* (Doctoral Dissertation). University of Ulster, 2010. https://ethos.bl.uk/OrderDetails.do?uin=uk.bl.ethos.553880.

Smith, Mary Ronella. *Dune: More than Genre Fiction* (Masters Thesis). East Carolina University, 1992.

Torres Meza, Luis Felipe. *The Bene Gesserit in Frank Herbert's Dune. An Analysis* (Masters Thesis). University of Iceland, 2011 (Kt.: 250786–3959). Available at https://skemman.is/bitstream/1946/7298/1/Bene_Gesserit_Luis_Torres.pdf.

Winzenz, Judith. *Messiah and the Bible in Frank Herbert's Dune* (Masters Thesis). University of Wisconsin, Oshkosh, 1984.

Conference Papers

Gough, Noel. "Democracy, Global Transitions, and Education: Using Speculative Fictions as Thought Experiments in Anticipatory Critical Inquiry." Annual Conference of the Australian Association for Research in Education, Brisbane. December 1–5, 2002.

Howard, Kenton. "The Shortening of the Way: Religious Violence and the Creation of Empire in Frank Herbert's *Dune*." *Empire and Dune, Part Two*. International Association for the Fantastic in the Arcs 35th International Conference, Orlando, Florida. March 19–24, 2014.

Irizarry, Adella. "The Grotesque God: The Godhead, the Colonizer, and the Colonized in *God Emperor of Dune*." *Empire and Dune, Part One*. International Association for the Fantastic in the Arcs 35th International Conference, Orlando, Florida. March 19–24, 2014.

Kennedy, Kara. "Assimilation and Exploitation: The Tension Between Colonial Rule and Indigenous Survivance in *Dune*." Science Fiction Research Association, Honolulu, Hawaii. June 21–24, 2019.

_____."Revolving Around Spice: World-Building in Dune." Mid-Atlantic Popular & American Culture Association, Online. 11 November 2021.

Lau, Maximilian. "Princess-Historians: Interpreting Irulan Corrino and Anna Komnen." Reception Histories of the Future, Uppsala University, Sweden. August 4–7, 2018.

McCullough, Aaron. "The Contingent Post-Structuralism of Frank Herbert's Dune Novels." National Conference of the Popular Culture Association, Indianapolis, IN. March 28–31, 2018.

McReynolds, Leigha High. "Eugenics and Disability in Frank Herbert's *Dune* (1965)." Mid-Atlantic Popular & American Culture Association, Online. 11 November 2021.

Nardi, Dominic J. "Political Prescience: How Game Theory Solves the Paradox of Foreknowledge in Frank Herbert's Dune." National Conference of the Popular Culture Association, Washington, D.C. April 17–20.

_____. "Bureaucrats of Dune: Frank Herbert's Deconstruction of Government." Mid-Atlantic Popular & American Culture Association, Online. 11 November 2021.

Pearson, Joshua Danley. "'Beginnings are times of such great peril': Frank Herbert's *Dune* and the Emergence of the Postindustrial Subject." *Empire and Dune, Part One*. International Association for the Fantastic in the Arts 35th International Conference, Orlando, Florida. March 19–24, 2014.

Rogers, Brett M. "(False?) Byzantinisms in *Dune*." Reception Histories of the Future, Uppsala University, Sweden. August 4–7, 2018.

Rowney, Brandy Eileen. "Empires of *Dune*." *Empire and Dune, Part Two*. International Association for the Fantastic in the Arcs 35th International Conference, Orlando, Florida. March 19–24, 2014.

Rudd, Amanda. "Paul's Imperium: Empire and Assemblage Theory in Frank Herbert's *Dune*." *Empire and Dune, Part One*. International Association for the Fantastic in the Arcs 35th International Conference, Orlando, Florida. March 19–24, 2014.

Smith, Tara. "Ecological Advocacy in Frank Herbert's *Dune* Trilogy." Science Fiction Research Association, Honolulu, Hawaii. June 21–24, 2019.

Walsh, Pam. "Power Beyond Control: Religious Mythology and Empire in Frank Herbert's *Dune*." *Empire and Dune, Part Two*. International Association for the Fantastic in the Arcs 35th International Conference, Orlando, Florida. March 19–24, 2014.

Other Notable Sources

Websites/Articles

Asher-Perrin, Emmet. "How to Handle the Baron Harkonnen in a Modern Dune Adaptation." *TOR.com*. March 6, 2019. https://www.tor.com/2019/02/05/how-to-handle-the-baron-harkonnen-in-a-modern-dune-adaptation/.

_____. "Why It's Important to Consider Whether Dune Is a White Savior Narrative." *TOR.com*. March 6, 2019. https://www.tor.com/2019/03/06/why-its-important-to-consider-whether-dune-is-a-white-savior-narrative/.

Baheyeldin, Khalid. "Arabic and Islamic Themes in Frank Herbert's Dune" (2004). Available at https://baheyeldin.com/literature/arabic-and-islamic-themes-in-frank-herberts-dune.html.

Brennan, Kristen. "Frank Herbert's *Dune*." *Star Wars Origins* (2006). Available at http://www.moongadget.com/origins/dune.html.

Carroll, Jordan S. "Race Consciousness: Fascism and Frank Herbert's Dune." *Los Angeles Review of Books* (November 19, 2020). https://lareviewofbooks.org/article/race-consciousness-fascism-and-frank-herberts-dune/.

Collins, Will. "The Secret History of Dune." *Los Angeles Review of Books* (September 16, 2017). Available at https://lareviewofbooks.org/article/the-secret-history-of-dune/.

Daniels, Joseph M. "The Stars and Planets of Frank Herbert's Dune: A Gazetteer" (1999). Available at http://www.projectrho.com/DuneGazetteer.txt.

Dodson, Steve. "CHAKOBSA." Languagehat blog (May 16, 2008). Available at http://languagehat.com/chakobsa/.

Durrani, Haris A., and Henry M. Cowles (eds.). "Sciences of 'Dune'" *Los Angeles Review of Books*. March 27, 2022. https://lareviewofbooks.org/feature/sciences-of-dune-an-introduction/.

Engleson, Mark J. "Hero and Society in Dune" (2012). Available at http://courses.oermn.org/mod/page/view.php?id=13772.

Grossman, Lev. "The Dune Abides." *TIME* (April 30, 2015). https://time.com/3841458/the-dune-abides/.

Immerwahr, Daniel. "Heresies of 'Dune.'" *Los Angeles Review of Books* (November 19, 2020). https://www.lareviewofbooks.org/article/heresies-of-dune/.

Kennedy, Kara. "Lawrence of Arabia, Paul Atreides, and the Roots of Frank Herbert's *Dune*." *TOR.com* (June 2, 2021). https://www.tor.com/2021/06/02/lawrence-of-arabia-paul-atreides-and-the-roots-of-frank-herberts-dune/.

Kunzru, Hari. "Dune, 50 Years On: How a Science Fiction Novel Changed the World." *The Guardian* (July 3, 2015). https://www.theguardian.com/books/2015/jul/03/dune-50-years-on-science-fiction-novel-world.

Leonard, Andrew. "To Save California, Read 'Dune.'" *Nautilus* (June 4, 2015). https://nautil.us/issue/25/water/to-save-california-read-dune.

Michaud, Jon. "'Dune' Endures." *The New Yorker* (July 12, 2013). https://www.newyorker.com/books/page-turner/dune-endures.

Murphy, Sean. "Building the Perfect DUNE." *Video Watchdog Magazine* Nos. 33–34 (1996). Available at http://www.figmentfly.com/published/dunearticle.html.

Salman, Sayyid. "Dune, Depolitization and Decolonizing the Future." *Constant Verlag* (May 18, 2004). Available at http://www.constantvzw.org/verlag/spip.php?article46#.

Podcasts/Videos

ComicBook Girl 19, "Dune" book club (YouTube).

Doc Sloan's Science Fiction Station. "Doc Sloan's Deep Dive into Dune" (March 31–April 24, 2021). https://www.youtube.com/playlist?list=PL_9DDewKiZhrNmsiepDRu1zQZevzPvXXT.

Fila, Jon. "Science Fiction: Dune." MN Partnership for Collaborative Curriculum (January 2012). Available at http://courses.oermn.org/mod/page/view.php?id=13686.

Ideas of Ice & Fire, "Ultimate Guide to Dune" series (YouTube).

Immerwahr, Daniel. "Empire of Dune: Indigeneity, U.S. Power and a Science Fiction Classic—A Talk by Daniel Immerwahr." Northwestern University's Center for International & Area Studies and the Evanston Public Library. (October 13, 2020). https://www.youtube.com/watch?v=AWDCgKdmly4.

Olsen, Corey. "Dune." Mythgard Academy (July 30–October 15, 2014). Available at https://mythgard.org/academy/dune/.

About the Contributors

R. **Ali** is a British writer, filmmaker and creative consultant. His student film received a Royal Television Society (RTS) award and his work was exhibited at the Visual Islamic & Traditional Arts project for HRH The Prince of Wales. He studied Arabic and Religion at The King Fahad Academy and has lectured at King Saud University in Riyadh, Saudi Arabia, for several years.

N. Trevor **Brierly** has a background in literature with an MLIS from the University of Texas at Austin and is working on a masters degree with a concentration in Tolkien studies from Signum University. His research interests focus on world-building in speculative fiction, and he has written and presented working papers about *The Lord of the Rings* and *Dune* at academic conferences.

Willow Wilson **DiPasquale** is the Visiting Assistant Professor of Writing, Rhetoric, and Literature at Jefferson University and an adjunct instructor at Arcadia University and Bryn Mawr College. She graduated from Drew University's D.Litt. program, where her dissertation analyzed representations of the environment and environmental ethics in J.R.R. Tolkien's and Frank Herbert's mythopoeic fantasy literature.

Nathaniel **Goldberg** is a professor of philosophy at Washington and Lee University in Lexington, Virginia. He is the author of *Kantian Conceptual Geography* (2015), a work in academic philosophy and, with Chris Gavaler, *Superhero Thought Experiments* (2019), a work in philosophy and popular culture.

Maximilian **Lau** has a doctorate in history from Oriel College, University of Oxford, for his research on the medieval world between the First and Second Crusades, and particularly the reign of the Byzantine Emperor John II Komnenos. He then become an assistant professor at Hitotsubashi University, Tokyo, and holds a research associateship at St. Benet's Hall, Oxford University.

Leigha High **McReynolds** received her Ph.D. in English from George Washington University, where she wrote her dissertation on science and the supernatural in nineteenth century British literature. Her research focuses on genetics and disability in contemporary science fiction, and she teaches science fiction themed classes for George Washington University The University of Maryland, College Park, and the D.C. bookstore Politics and Prose.

Dominic J. **Nardi** is a political scientist with a Ph.D. from the University of Michigan and a J.D. from Georgetown University. He has published articles about political themes in speculative fiction, including an award-winning article in *Mythlore* about J.R.R. Tolkien's views on democracy and an essay about ethnic identity in *Blade Runner 2049* and *Philosophy* (2019). He also coedited *The Transmedia Franchise of Star Wars TV* (2020).

Jeffery L. **Nicholas** is a professor of philosophy at Providence College. His current research is on love and politics. He is the author of *Love and Politics* (2021) and the editor of *Dune and Philosophy* (2011). He is the Director of Center for Aristotelian Studies in Ethics and Politics (CASEP) and a research associate of the Center for Aristotelian Studies and Critical Theory in Lithuania.

Michael **Phillips** earned his Ph.D. in English literature from the University of Ottawa where he studied the intertextuality of sample-based musical texts. His work examines how the material technology of sound recording and playback has affected conceptions of authorship and textual production and consumption.

Paul **Reef** is a Ph.D. candidate in history at Radboud University in Nijmegen, the Netherlands. His dissertation examines the transnational history of protest around the FIFA World Cup and the Olympic Games since the 1960s.

Edward John **Royston** is an assistant professor of English at Pfeiffer University in North Carolina. He earned his Ph.D. at Texas Woman's University, where he focused on rhetoric, narratology, and genre fiction. His work has been published in *The Steinbeck Review, Sci-Fi Television* and *Frontiers of Narrative*.

Caroline Anne **Womack** earned her masters in English literature from the University of Leeds. She is the recipient of the 2018 Teaching Association for Medieval Studies Teaching Prize and has published chapters on medieval literature and pop culture in edited volumes such as *For Better or Worse*. She teaches English language and literature at Frisco High School in Texas.

Curtis A. **Weyant** is a digital marketer and independent researcher whose publications focus on science fiction, fantasy literature and other media. His work has appeared in *Slayage, Joss Whedon: The Complete Companion* (2015), *PopMatters*, and *McSweeney's Internet Tendency*, among others. He co-hosts the podcast *Kat & Curt's TV Re-View*.

Kevin **Williams** received his Ph.D. in the philosophy of communication from Ohio University. He is a professor of communication at Shepherd University, West Virginia. His book *The Wisdom of the Sand* (2013) explores the philosophy of Frank Herbert's *Dune*. He has also taught an undergraduate course about the Dune saga.

Index